TEACHING FOR LEARNING

Despite a growing body of research on teaching methods, instructors lack a comprehensive resource that highlights and synthesizes proven approaches. *Teaching for Learning* fills that gap. Each chapter in this book:

- describes an approach and lists its essential features and elements;
- reviews findings from the research literature; and
- describes techniques to improve effectiveness.

Teaching for Learning provides instructors with a resource grounded in the academic knowledge base, written in an easily accessible, engaging, and practical style.

Claire Howell Major is Professor of Higher Education Administration at the University of Alabama, USA.

Michael S. Harris is Associate Professor of Higher Education and Director of the Center for Teaching Excellence at Southern Methodist University, USA.

Todd Zakrajsek is Associate Professor in the Department of Family Medicine at the University of North Carolina at Chapel Hill, USA, and President of the International Teaching Learning Cooperative, USA.

TEACHING FOR LEARNING

101 Intentionally Designed Educational Activities to Put Students on the Path to Success

Claire Howell Major
Michael S. Harris
Todd Zakrajsek

Routledge
Taylor & Francis Group
NEW YORK AND LONDON

First published 2016
by Routledge
711 Third Avenue, New York, NY 10017

and by Routledge
2 Park Square, Milton Park, Abingdon, Oxon OX14 4RN

Routledge is an imprint of the Taylor & Francis Group, an informa business

Library of Congress Cataloging-in-Publication Data
Major, Claire Howell.
  Teaching for learning : 101 intentionally designed education activities to
put students on the path to success / Claire Howell Major, Michael S. Harris,
Todd Zakrajsek.
    pages cm
  Includes bibliographical references and index.
  1. College teaching. 2. College teaching—Aids and devices. 3. Effective
teaching.   I. Harris, Michael S.   II. Zakrajsek, Todd.   III. Title.
  LB2331.M348 2016
  378.1'25—dc23
  2015011924

ISBN: 978-0-415-69935-8 (hbk)
ISBN: 978-0-415-69936-5 (pbk)
ISBN: 978-0-203-11103-1 (ebk)

Typeset in Bembo
by Apex CoVantage, LLC

Printed and bound in the United States of America by
Edwards Brothers Malloy on sustainably sourced paper

CONTENTS

FIGURES AND TABLES

Figures

Tables

PREFACE

Are we really teaching for learning in higher education? This question has come to the fore of a national conversation, spurred in part by the publication of a widely discussed book titled *Academically Adrift: Limited Learning on College Campuses*. In their work, authors Arum and Roska (2011) track 2,000 students from 24 institutions of higher education and examine their progress on the Collegiate Learning Assessment. Based on their findings, the authors suggest that students who have completed two years of college have no better broad-based knowledge and skills, such as reasoning and writing, than high school seniors. The authors lay blame squarely at the feet of colleges and college faculty. They suggest that institutions and faculty are not holding students to high standards and that instructors may well be using inappropriate teaching methods. For example, their study found that students who study together do less well than those who study alone. They use this finding to question the value of the collaborative assignments that some instructors use. The authors concede, however, that their work falls short of being able to determine the value of collaborative assignments, yet they argue that few instructors have adequate preparation for developing strong collaborative assignments (Glenn, 2011). Are the authors correct in their assumptions? Are instructors not using the best teaching methods available? Are the methods we think work as effective as we think they are?

There are many teaching and learning methods in higher education that have stood the test of time. And there is an ever-growing body of research on these teaching approaches in higher education that has demonstrated improvement in learning outcomes. Unfortunately, this information tends to be inaccessible to most instructors, as it has been published piecemeal in journals that instructors do not frequently read. As faculty frequently learn through reading and self-study

(Major & Dolly, 2003), a text that highlights effective teaching practices and presents a synthesis of evidence of the effectiveness of these approaches in higher education could provide instructors with useful, relevant, and much needed information.

That is the task that we take up in this book. In this book, we describe eight teaching approaches that have strong research support and demonstrate consistent success in higher education settings. Each chapter in this text describes a specific approach to teaching and learning, a list of its essential features and elements and an outline of its purposes as well as advantages and disadvantages. We also provide the following information:

- A synthesis of information about evidence-based teaching methods used in higher education today
- A summary of the existing data that indicates how to employ these methods to best achieve the intended learning outcomes
- A list of intentionally designed educational activities (IDEAs) that link directly to the research findings.

Thus, we align research and practice in each chapter.

By "research," we mean "empirical research" or studies that systematically gather evidence, whether through exam scores, surveys, interviews, or other data sources. Such research falls within the broader category of social science research. As such, it is focused on understanding aspects of human interactions. Some of the teaching and learning research that we found is experimental, in that it measures cause and effect through designs like randomized controlled trials. We also found quasi-experimental studies, which are like experimental designs in that the research involves manipulating an independent variable to measure its effects on a dependent variable, but they are unlike experimental designs in that participants are not randomly assigned to groups. Some of the teaching and learning research that we found is descriptive, in that it seeks to answer why or how something is happening. We also found many descriptive studies, including those that used quantitative data and others that used qualitative.

We acknowledge that social science research is not without criticism. Among such criticisms is that social science research is not scientific or is somehow less empirical and too subjective. We disagree with that position. We argue that social science researchers have adopted a rich array of research approaches, from the more objective to the more subjective, the latter of which we suggest are equally valuable and sometimes more valuable. We cite as evidence the rich array of studies that we include in our synthesis of the research. It would be misleading, however, to say that all of the evidence we found was of impeccable quality or even of equal weight and value. Many problems with the evidence were apparent in our review. The first is that much of the field's research is not grounded in theory. While some articles were particularly effective at demonstrating adoption and use of a theoretical framework, the majority were not. The second problem is that much of the quantitative literature is based upon single-institution studies with a small number of participants, which makes it more difficult to generalize. A third problem is that much of the qualitative research leaves out important contextual information, which makes it more difficult to interpret. We did not exclude those studies that might be viewed as "weaker" because we felt that even they had something to offer to our analysis and synthesis. We did exclude studies that we believed were fatally flawed in design. The result, we believe, is a useful summary of research spanning several decades that can provide information about whether a specific method is effective and how instructors may use it to its best effect.

In the book, we also describe 101 intentionally designed educational activities (IDEAs). We have named them thusly because when a faculty member chooses one of them, he or she is drawing from an evidence-based teaching method. Moreover, he or she is selecting an activity that has features directly tied to findings that indicate support for the activity. For example, if a faculty member chooses to use IDEA #1 Guided Note-Taking, he or she is drawing upon an active lecture method. Active lecturing has a research base to indicate that it is an effective method for helping students to develop foundational knowledge. Moreover, research findings indicate that providing students with partial notes that they fill in during a lecture improves learning outcomes. Thus, the technique is intentionally linked to what the instructor hopes students will learn, and it is a research-supported educational activity.

The primary audience for this book is teaching faculty members from all disciplines and from all types of institutions. The book provides those who are tasked with educating the next generation of learners with information about the best approaches to use in their own teaching, as well as evidence from social science research that documents that the teaching approaches they are using actually work. The latter is something that they can use in promotion and tenure reviews to document teaching effectiveness. Additionally, our audience includes faculty and educational development specialists and directors of teaching centers who will find this book useful in consulting with faculty members on a number of issues related to teaching and learning in the classroom. Another audience is graduate teaching assistants who are seeking to become better teachers and want to learn new strategies. Researchers with a focus on teaching and learning in higher education will also find this book helpful. It can provide scholars with the most current information available in synthesized form. This book, then, will provide instructors, faculty development professionals, students, and researchers with a resource that is not only grounded in the academic knowledge base but also tied directly to the improvement of practice.

References

Arum, R., & Roksa, J. (2011). *Academically adrift: Limited learning on college campuses.* Chicago, IL: University of Chicago Press.

Glenn, D. (2011, January 18). New book lays failure to learn on colleges' doorsteps. *Chronicle of Higher Education.*

Major, C. H., & Dolly, J. (2003). The importance of graduate program experiences to faculty self-efficacy for academic tasks. *Journal of Faculty Development, 19*(2), 89–100.

ACKNOWLEDGMENTS

We thank our families, in particularly our spouses and children, who supported us and gave us time to work during the development of this manuscript.

We also thank those who helped us as we worked on this book. Specifically, we wish to thank Molly K. Ellis for her valuable contributions to the research and development of the manuscript. In addition, we wish to thank Amanda E. Brunson for her careful reading of sections of this manuscript.

Finally, we thank our publishers at Routledge for believing in this project. In particular, we thank our editor, Alex Masulis, for not only for his encouragement but also for his patience during the development of this book.

1

THE LECTURE METHOD

Description

The word "lecture" comes from the Latin *lectare*, which means "to read aloud." Originally the lecture was an approach to transfer knowledge from experts to those who needed the information. Dating back at least to ancient Greeks and the art of rhetoric advocated by Aristotle in around the fourth century BC (Brown & Atkins, 1988), a lecture was the primary method of transmitting knowledge and information. Around the sixth century AD, scholars began to travel hundreds of miles to European monestaries to hear monks read a book aloud from a lecturn. As the monk would read, scholars would copy down the book verbatim (Exley & Dennick, 2004). This reliance on oral instruction became the foundation for teaching in the early universities. The lecture indeed was used as an instructional method in universities as early as the thirteenth and fourteen centuries. A lectern in the classroom replaced the pulpit, but the delivery method remained essentially the same as its religious origins. As colonial universities developed in America, their tutors also relied upon lecture as well as recitation for instruction (Thelin, 2011). The reliance on the lecture by university professors remained significant over time. As Garside (1996) suggests, "since the 1840s, the lecture method of instruction has been the primary method of teaching in the college classroom" (p. 212).

Although today's lectures do not typically involve reading from a text, the teaching approach still involves having an knowledgeable individual deliver oral information and ideas about a particular subject to a group of individuals who have some reason for seeking out the information. Bligh (1999) suggests a working definition of lecture as a "more or less continuous exposition by a speaker who wants the audience to learn something" (p. 4). The speaker-instructor serves as the conveyor of information to a student audience. In turn, students are expected to listen to the lecture and to learn the information being transferred. The information is typically a synthesis of the professor's own reading, research, and experience in a given content area. Listening, comprehending, and note-taking are frequent hallmarks of lectures (Biggs, 1996). Students may or may not be expected to take notes and ask questions. As Davis (2009) suggests:

> Lecturing is not simply a matter of standing in front of a class and reciting what you know. The classroom lecture is a special form of communication in which voice, gesture, movement, facial expression, and eye contact can either complement or detract from content.
>
> (p. 148)

Thus, the lecture is simply a form of direct instruction.

The lecture is used in disciplines across higher education institutions. Researchers have shown that lecturing in undergraduate liberal arts programs comprises 81% of social science classes and 89% of science and mathematics courses (Kimball, 1988). Neumann (2001) noted that lecture is most prevalent within the humanities. Dennick (2004) notes the lecture is "the cornerstone of many undergraduate courses and is believed by many academics to be the only way their subjects can be taught to an increasing number of students" (p. 1). For many, lecturing is the default method of college teaching (Biggs, 1996).

Purposes of the Lecture Method

The lecture's primary purpose is to transfer information from an expert instructor to a group of student novices, and thus "the main objective of lectures should be the acquisition of information by students" (Bligh, 1999, p. 4). Lecture is best suited for having students acquire knowledge that is factual and developing conceptual understanding (Exley & Dennick, 2004). Lectures can provide students with new information not readily available in other sources. For example, instructors may lecture on original research prior to its publication, as there is always some gap between when scholarship takes place and when it appears in a textbook (Cashin, 1985; Svinicki & McKeachie, 2013). It also gives instructors an opportunity to test their ideas in front of an audience prior to publishing them.

Lectures can help students understand the core issues and structure of a discipline or field. Lectures provide an orientation and conceptual framework for understanding a topic. Instructors can use lectures to assist students working to clarify key concepts, principles, or ideas (Svinicki & McKeachie, 2013). Lectures also can dramatize important concepts, allow instructors to share personal insights about a topic, and prove useful for highlighting similarities and differences between key concepts (Cashin, 1985).

In addition, lectures can provide a vehicle for instructors to summarize material scattered over a variety of sources. Instructors can use lectures to tailor course content to the interests and experiences of a particular group of students who come together to learn in a course (Svinicki & McKeachie, 2013). Lectures can even be used by faculty members to help organize subject matter in a way that is best suited to the course objectives. Lectures allow instructors to serve as models for their students, demonstrating the ways that members of a discipline or field think about evidence, critical analysis, and problem solving (Cashin, 1985). Lectures can also be used to demonstrate application and problem solving (Exley & Dennick, 2004). Finally, lectures provide an opportunity for instructors to convey their enthusiasm for the course content.

Types of Lecture

Several authors describe different types of lecture (Bonwell & Eison, 1991; Broadwell, 1980; Woodring, 2004). In reviewing a range of different classifications of lecture, we believe lectures may be categorized in terms of the level of student interaction, the classification of content, and the medium by which information is disseminated.

Categorized by Levels of Student Interaction:

- **Formal lecture.** The lecturer delivers a well-organized, tightly constructed, and highly polished presentation. This type of lecture works well for teaching large groups of students and has been popularized by outlets such as TED Talks (Donovan, 2013) and, more recently, massive open online courses (MOOCs), such as those offered through Coursera or EdX. In the formal lecture, students hold questions until the conclusion of the lecture.
- **Socratic lecture.** This type of lecture, which typically follows a reading assignment to give students a baseline of knowledge, is structured around a series of carefully sequenced questions. The instructor asks a single student a question sequence. The questions require the student to use logic and inference skills.
- **Semi-formal lecture.** This is the most common type of lecture. Although somewhat similar to the formal lecture, the semiformal lecture, as the name implies, is less elaborate in form and production. Occasionally, the lecturer entertains student questions during the presentation of material.
- **Lecture-discussion.** This type of lecture encourages greater student participation. The instructor presents the talk, but he or she stops frequently to ask students questions or to request that students read their prepared materials. The direction of interaction can occur in one of three ways: (1) instructor to class, (2) instructor to individual student, or (3) individual student to instructor.

- **Interactive lecture.** In this version of lecturing, the instructor uses mini-lectures of approximately 20 minutes and involves students in a range of brief content-related activities in between. Interaction may occur between instructor and students or between and among students.

Categorized by Content:

- **Expository lecture/oral essay.** The lecturer begins with a primary thesis or assertion and then proceeds to justify it, typically putting the most important information or supporting examples first and proceeding in descending order of importance.
- **Storytelling lecture.** The instructor provides content that conveys a story to illustrate a concept. The lecture proceeds in typical narrative form, with an exposition, rising action, climax, falling action, and resolution. Characters are presented and developed through the presentation of the story line. The goal is to present critical content in a way that students will remember it.
- **Point-by-point lecture.** In this type of lecture, the instructor presents information about a single concept, question, or issue. The organizational structure is typically an outline format, with a hierarchical organization of major and minor points.
- **Lecture-demonstration.** The content involves a demonstration of a process or activity. The lecture typically proceeds in chronological order, with the demonstration presented in a sequence of events that the lecturer highlights and explains.
- **Problem-solving lecture.** In this type of lecture, a problem serves as the focus. The lecturer outlines the main problem, the key known elements, and the elements that remain to be discovered. During the lecture, the instructor typically works through the problem and demonstrates a solution or various possible solutions.

Categorization by Medium:

- **Naked lecture.** The term "teaching naked" was popularized by Jose Bowen (2012) in his similarly titled book. Bowen argues that teachers have much to gain by taking technology out of their classrooms. He argues that teaching without technology, "naked," will improve student learning. Instructors who adapt this approach talk directly to students without the intervening agency of technology, or, alternately, they use technology outside of the classroom and reserve in-class time for direct communication with students.
- **Chalk and talk lecture.** This approach is so named because of early uses of lecture in a classroom with a blackboard and chalk. While some professors still use a blackboard, whiteboards and markers and smart boards are supplanting the earlier tools. Regardless of the tools used, the key characteristic of this approach is that the instructor lectures while generating notes on a medium that students can see.

- **Multimedia lecture.** A multimedia lecture, once called the slide lecture because of the slide-talk approach, is one of the most commonly used approaches today. Instructors use audio-visual software packages such as PowerPoint or Prezi to highlight key points of text. The term "death-by-PowerPoint," however, is one that teachers should keep in mind, particularly as something to avoid, when using this approach.
- **Video lecture.** This type of lecture is one in which an instructor lectures and is captured on video as a talking head. At times, the video may alternate between showing headshots of the instructor and full screen visuals of the slides. This type of lecture is often used in the service of online learning and blended learning. More recently, this approach has seen increased usage as part of the flipped classroom strategy (Ronchetti, 2010).

Lectures across different categories work together. Thus, an instructor may give a semiformal, problem-solving, chalk and talk lecture, while another may offer a lecture-discussion, point-by-point, multimedia lecture. Although different disciplines exhibit norms around a common combination, the full range of combinations appear across college and university classrooms.

Parts of a Lecture

When considering aspects of a lecture, Exley and Dennick (2004) suggest organizing the lecture into three basic parts: context, content, and closure. Context includes both the setting of the classroom environment and connecting content to other class ideas. Content describes primacy of new content, which is central to the purpose of the lecture approach. Finally, closure involves providing a summary of content and reinforcing student comprehension.

Context

The context "makes connections with other learning and provides a background from which the importance and relevance of the content to come can be supported" (Exley & Dennick, 2004, p. 46). Several elements establish the context of the lecture: setting the mood, getting students' attention, introducing the topic, outlining the structure, and stating the relevance of the lecture. We offer the following advice about setting the context of the lecture:

- Whereas other types of teaching allow for more spontaneous adjustments, a considerable amount of the work of lecturing must take place prior to the class session.
- Excellent lectures involve significant planning of the desired outcomes and the content necessary to achieve those objectives.
- Lectures should be organized in a way to clearly explain the primary points for students to retain. Organizing the lecture around these points, along with

several complementary examples, will help the students follow throughout the lecture.

- It is important not only to have an organized lecture but also to use the same structure regularly so that students recognize the format easily (Bligh, 1999).
- Slides, videos, and projectors can all enhance a presentation when integrated well within a lecture.
- Consider adding directional notes within the presentation (i.e., when to change slides) as part of organizing the lecture.
- In addition to technology, consider the physical space of the class. How large are the projection screens? Will slides show up adequately or will handouts be necessary? How are the room's acoustics? Can seats be moved easily, or are they fixed? What is the size and setup at the front of the room? Is it easy for students and the instructor to hear each other during question and answer sessions?

Content

The format and organization are important in creating an effective lecture (Bligh, 1999; Exley & Dennick, 2004). We offer the following advice about developing content:

- The tendency for lectures is to repeat much of the content presented in the textbook and readings. New instructors becoming comfortable in their own mastery of the subject matter may be particularly susceptible to this approach. Rather, the goal should be to illustrate and augment the information presented in the readings.
- Lectures can draw connections between concepts, offer real world examples, or present alternative explanations.
- Svinicki and McKeachie (2013) suggest intermittently summarizing material and checking with students to confirm understanding.

Closure

The closure of the lecture should summarize the information presented, reinforce the learning outcomes, and provide an opportunity to check for student understanding of the presented material (Exley & Dennick, 2004). An effective closure of a lecture can help to "make up for lapses in the body of the lecture" (McKeachie & Svinicki, 2006, p. 66). We offer the following suggestions for a productive closure:

- Heitzmann (2010) argues that student learning is more important than the delivery of the lecture and as such argues that the "summarization (or closure) at the end of a lecture [should] enhance learning and retention" (p. 54). In addition, asking questions at the end of the lecture or even suggesting some may appear on a future test provides an effective strategy for ending class.

- Another helpful learning technique is to include a teaser for the next lecture in the closure so that students will know what to look for when completing the reading assignment for the next class session (Heitzmann, 2010).
- In cases where it becomes apparent the class session will end before all content is delivered, resist the urge to rush through the final blocks of materials.

Advantages and Challenges of the Lecture Method for Instructors

There are many reasons why the lecture remains one of the primary teaching techniques used in higher education. First, when one becomes a faculty member and starts to teach, lecturing is the "prototype" of teaching. It is what has been seen most often and is therefore perceived as how teaching is done. Second, it is the way most classrooms are set up. Walk into just about any classroom and you will typically see many seats aimed at one spot in the room, which is where the faculty member is intended to stand and deliver content. Third, lecturing is relatively low cost both in terms of time and resources. Teachers can lecture to large numbers of students, with little added expense required for materials. The time involved in transmitting content to students is lower than many other teaching strategies such as discussion or small group work. Where many teaching strategies take time for students to figure out content, such as a class discussion or problem-based case, a lecture simply and directly presents the important concepts. This benefit also makes the preparation time less for instructors, particularly for the same lecture in subsequent courses. Finally, some students would rather have instructors lecture (Covill, 2011). In particular, students who prefer auditory learning or listening to learn often most appreciate the lecture method. Indeed, in many ways lecturing meets the expectations of a "teacher" and can also build a relationship between instructor and student.

The lecture, however, has been the subject of great criticism, particularly with the research on relative learning gains of active approaches to learning over the standard lecture (Hake, 1988). Critics decry the approach as old fashioned and out of step with new theories of learning and new educational trends. Faculty may become bored with lectures, particularly if they find they are teaching the same content over and over each semester. Yet, the primary drawback of lecturing is that the method often relies on communicating information to students who can remain relatively passive as they receive it—assuming they receive it at all. As a result, lecturers would benefit from remembering that transmitting knowledge does not guarantee student learning occurs. Moreover, it is difficult to gauge student understanding in a lecture classroom without some form of engagement on the part of the students. Students in traditional lecture classes may have limited options for interacting and feedback. The lecture may also result in students becoming easily bored; being "talked to" for long periods of time is not consistent with information processing that happens outside of academe. The large lecture hall only exacerbates this problem as students can easily feel anonymous, disengage, or decide to skip class. The physical environment of the classroom, which has

TABLE 1.1 Advantages and Disadvantages of the Lecture Method

Advantages	Disadvantages
• Provides teachers with control of information and pacing of session • Is rewarding for the teacher to be seen as expert • Provides the teacher with a chance to model desired level of thinking • Allows teacher to model enthusiasm • Provides all students with a common core of content • Provides an opportunity to enliven facts and ideas from the text • Provides teachers with ability to clarify issues • Provides an opportunity to develop ideas (that may be later used for publication) • Provides most immediate recall of information by students	• May not be as effective for higher order thinking • May not improve student long-term retention of information • Presumes students are learning at the same pace • Does not allow for personalized instruction • Can create opportunities for students to be passive • Relies on student attention span • Can be a disincentive for learning (if done poorly) • Can lead students to believe that it is a complete learning experience • Can lead to boredom on the part of professors and students

been historically been built to accommodate lectures, can present challenges for engaging students as active participants. Hundreds of fixed seats, poor acoustics, or a large stage all serve to discourage active lecturing and create barriers between instructor, students, and learning. Even other classes and students can be distracting (Chandhury, 2011). To give an effective lecture requires extensive preparation as well as involvement of the students.

In the table above, adapted from Woodring (2004), we present additional advantages and disadvantages of the lecture method.

What Research Tells Us About the General Effectiveness of the Lecture

Researchers have studied the effectiveness of the lecture, most often comparing it to other teaching methods. One of the most extensive studies involving such a comparison was conducted by Bligh (1999) who used meta-analysis of existing published studies to determine effect size of differences. He compared results of lectures against other teaching methods, including discussion, independent learning, and inquiry projects. Examining transmitting information to students, he found that "the lecture is as effective as any other method for transmitting information but not more effective" (p. 4).

More recent studies have looked at the comparisons between the lecture method and other teaching approaches, such as cooperative learning (Johnson, Johnson, & Smith, 1998), problem-based learning (Strobel & van Barneveld,

2009), case-based learning (Baeten, Dochy, & Struyven, 2012), and also more generally active learning (Deslauriers, Schelew, & Weiman, 2011; Freeman et al., 2014), to examine the influence of lecture compared to the other methods of higher-order learning. On the whole, the news is not particularly good for lecturers. In all of these other methods, in which students are more active and engaged in the learning process, students demonstrated higher gains in long-term retention of information and improving application of information, such as through critical thinking and problem solving.

What Research Tells Us About How to Improve Student Learning in Lecture Classes

Those instructors who rely on lectures need not despair, however. The studies demonstrating that lectures are not effective have relied typically on traditional, full class lectures. Recent research suggests that there are ways to make lectures more active and thus improve learning. We offer the following findings from research on lectures and suggest that they can guide teaching practice.

Finding # 1. Using Mini Lectures with Purposeful Active Learning Breakouts Can Improve Student Learning

The basis of this finding has to do with the human attention span when learning. Studies demonstrate that student attention in a lecture drops dramatically after approximately 10 minutes of lecturing (Bligh, 1999). One researcher found that students retain 70% of material from the first 10 minutes of a lecture but only 20% by the end (Svinicki & McKeachie, 2013). Penner (1984) found that students recorded items in their notes for 41% of material given in a 15-minute lecture, 25% of material given in a 30-minute lecture, and 20% of material in a 45-minute lecture. Thus, the research suggests that the students are able to give full attention and take adequate notes at the beginning of a lecture but not by the end.

Research findings demonstrate that varying instructional methods, even with a quick 1–3 minute pause every 15–20 minutes can help to reset student attention and thus improve their retention of information. In an active lecture, students must participate in an activity that directs them to be active, whether by encouraging active listening, better note-taking, self-testing, or another active approach. Eric Mazur, a physics professor at Harvard University, has conducted some of the best research to date on the effectiveness of active lecturing. A long-time lecturer who received positive course evaluations, Mazur was not convinced that his students were learning the material at a level he hoped. To test his concerns, he changed the way he taught. Rather than lecturing for the entire class period, Mazur began to integrate "Concept Tests" into his teaching, an instructional approach he calls "Peer Instruction." After about 20 minutes of lecture,

Mazur pauses and asks students to respond to a conceptual question or two. He gives them one to two minutes to think about the question(s) and formulate their answers. Students next spend two to three minutes discussing their answers in groups of three to four. The goal is for the groups to reach consensus on the correct answer. Mazur found that students made significant gains in conceptual understanding (as measured by standardized tests). He also found that they improved problem-solving skills (Mazur, 1997).

Similarly, in a study comparing students at a community college and an elite research university, Lasry, Mazur, and Watkins (2008) found that students' use of peer instruction (Mazur's method describe above) during lecture breaks increased conceptual learning and problem-solving skills. Although the effectiveness of the strategy depended on students' background knowledge, both high- and low-background-knowledge students benefited over traditional lectures.

A recent flurry of literature has formed around the use of automated response systems, or student response systems (i.e., "clickers"), in which lecturers pose questions to which students respond by selecting an appropriate option. These studies have found that the use of these clickers improves student gains in learning (Bruff, 2009; Duncan, 2005; McDermott & Redish, 1999). For example, researchers investigating student attention in a general chemistry course found that use of questions and clicker responses improved student reports of their attention (Bunce, Flens, & Neiles, 2010).

The bottom line is that research strongly supports that periodic short breaks from lectures—to include student engagement, whether to answer quiz questions, talk to their neighbors, or click an opinion—seem to be more effective than longer lectures at improving gains in learning. These strategies help students to learn the content taught during lectures. Additionally, these strategies refocus attention on student learning rather than simply instructor performance.

Finding # 2. Effective and Guided Note-Taking During Lecture Can Improve Student Learning

One option to increase the effectiveness of lectures is to teach students how to be better notetakers. Researchers have found that students who take notes in class perform better on immediate and later tests of recall and synthesis (Piolat, Olive, & Kellogg, 2005). In addition, research shows that the more students record in their notes, the more they remember and the better they perform on exams (Johnston & Su, 1994). Students benefit from having a framework for note-taking prior to hearing a lecture and demonstrate improved retention of lecture information. Indeed, providing an outline or similar structure for students to fill in has been shown to improve students' performance (Austin, Lee, & Carr, 2004; Raver & Maydosz, 2010). Findings further suggest that providing students with skeletal notes may work better than providing them with a full set of notes or transcript of the lecture (Kiewra, 2002).

Finding # 3. Focusing on the Essentials Can Improve Learning, and Helping Students to Figure Out What Is Essential Improves Student Learning

Experts easily see relationships that may be difficult for students to process. Focusing on key concepts during lectures helps students to better understand the content being delivered. When lecturing, it is easy to get caught up in interesting details to share with students, but research tells us doing so could be harmful to learning. Harp and Maslich (2005) found that when students listened to a lecture with compelling details, recall and problem solving were negatively impacted as compared to a lecture without the details. As a result, provide examples but resist the urge to include tangential details. For example, if lecturing on Thomas Jefferson's political philosophy in the Declaration of Independence, do not distract students with the fact that it was debated for two days in the Continental Congress. Alternately, instructors can help students understand what is key or not by asking questions or, as suggested above, by providing skeletal notes to guide their thinking.

Finding # 4. Frequent Quizzing and Testing Can Improve Learning

The notion of a "testing effect" has long been established. That is, students who take frequent quizzes or tests ultimately have higher outcomes. In the 1950s, Fitch, Drucker, and Norton (1951) examined the effect of frequent testing to improve student learning in a lecture course. In this study, all students were exposed to the same material during a lecture, given the same reading assignments, and given time at the end of class for open discussion. However, the experimental group was also given a ten-minute quiz each week. Students who were exposed to frequent quizzes had significantly higher achievement than students who only received monthly quizzes. As the authors state, "frequent testing of achievement in the college lecture classroom may motivate such outside endeavours as will result in superior achievement," (Fitch et al., 1951, p. 19).

Similarly, Gaynor and Millham (1976) found that students who were exposed to weekly testing performed significantly better on course examinations than those in midterm and final exam conditions. In addition, they believed they learned more than students who just received a midterm test. Finally, students who were given a weekly test reported liking their testing schedule more than students who received a midterm and final (Gaynor & Millham, 1976). These findings support the notion that frequent testing can help to ensure that students in large lecture settings are meeting the learning objectives.

In a series of studies, Roediger and Karpicke (2006) have demonstrated that practice at retrieving information facilitates the later recall of that information. What is particularly interesting in their research is that, in some cases, short-term memory is higher when more time is spent processing material, but long-term memory is higher with practice at recalling information, such as taking frequent quizzes.

Finding # 5. Style and Pace of Speech Can Improve Learning

The importance of style and pace of speech may seem obvious, but many instructors can forget their importance or struggle with issues related to these. Robinson et al. (1997) found that the rate that an instructor speaks influences both comprehension and the perceptions of the importance of the information presented. The researchers presented the same lecture at three different speeds and found that 100 words per minute outperformed 150 wpm as well as 200 wpm. The findings held true for students who only listened to the lecture as well as those who watched and listened. Many other researchers (e.g. Davis, 2009; Murray, 1997) argue for the benefits of speaking slowly and clearly, especially when delivering key concepts.

Using vocal variations, facial expressions, movement, and gesture can be difficult for the personalities of some instructors, but students will likely pay more attention to expressive and enthusiastic lecturers. Indeed, expressiveness can improve learning gains. A study examining different levels of expression (high, medium, or low) showed that students who watched highly expressive lecturers outperformed those who watched less expressive lectures on multiple-choice recall (Murray, 1997). This is not to say that lecturers should strive to be entertainers; rather, instructors should attempt to be expressive as they present important content. Students rate lectures positively based not only upon the content but also the lecturer's communication style (Hodgon, 1984). In her work, Hodgson describes the vicarious experience of relevance. This is the idea of the perception of an instructor's enthusiasm and the love of the subject matter bring the subject to life in a way that directly impacts the students' experience. Although somewhat of an elusive ideal, the ability for an instructor to use expressive cues can help students relate to the material in different ways.

Students require time to process information, and good pacing can provide that opportunity. The brain uses different processing paths for visual and oral information (Baddeley, 1998). Presenting students with too much at one time can cause cognitive overload (Mayer & Moreno, 2003). One way to cause such an overload is by requiring students to use too many sensory channels at once. For example, when a lecturer presents a PowerPoint slide full of text and then proceeds to talk about the text, students cannot read and listen at once. As a result, they have to choose which one to do. Presenting a simple image or just a few words to highlight the point and providing a verbal explanation offers a better solution. Instruction that effectively uses dual-channel processing of verbal and visual information improves students' learning (Mayer, 2001).

Students prefer "performance" lectures to "presentation" (traditional) lectures (Short & Martin, 2011). Performance lectures can include humor, personal anecdotes, questions to the class, and student activities. Student learning has been shown to be improved in "performance" lectures when compared to "presentation" lectures.

We also refer back to finding #1. That is, we assert that presenting mini-lectures and pausing between segments can improve the pacing of a given lecture. It provides students with an opportunity to collect their thoughts and reflect upon their learning, typically with guidance from the instructor.

Using IDEAs to Improve Learning in Lectures

In the following section of this chapter, we provide detailed descriptions of 11 intentionally designed educational activities that correlate with the research findings we presented above. We suggest that these eleven activities correlate with these key research findings, which we illustrate in the following table:

TABLE 1.2 Lecture IDEAs and Research Findings

Lecture IDEAs	Description	Links to Research Findings
Guided Note-Taking	This is a scaffolding activity in which the instructor provides students with a structure for note-taking during a lecture.	Guided Note-Taking (Research finding #2)
Pause Procedure	The Pause Procedure is an interactive instructional approach that proceeds much as its name suggests: Mini-lectures are interspersed with pauses. These strategic pauses provide an opportunity for students to review and clarify course material. Overall, the Pause Procedure presents a low-risk and high-reward opportunity to improve student learning through lectures.	Mini-lectures with breakouts (Research finding #1); Pacing (Research finding #5)
Punctuated Lecture	A Punctuated Lecture is an active learning technique in which students answer questions about what they are doing at a given moment during a class.	Mini-lectures with breakouts (Research finding #1); Pacing (Research finding #5)
Wake-Up Call	Students must stay in a state of readiness, as they could be called on at any given time. While lecturing, the instructor stops periodically and randomly chooses a student to respond in a predetermined way.	Mini-lectures with breakouts (Research finding #1); Quizzing and frequent testing (Research finding #4)
Interpreted Lecture	During a brief pause in a mini-lecture, the instructor randomly selects a student to "translate" what the instructor has just said into plain English for the rest of the class.	Mini-lectures with breakouts (Research finding #1)

(Continued)

TABLE 1.2 Continued

Lecture IDEAs	Description	Links to Research Findings
Responsive Lecture	The instructor asks students to develop a list of questions from content covered in an out-of-class reading or video assignments for the instructor to answer in a lecture format.	Mini-lectures with breakouts (Research finding #1)
Socratic Seminar	The instructor systematically asks questions that require students to examine issues and principles related to a particular unit of content. The IDEA is to prompt deeper understanding of that text. This activity is named for Socrates, who believed in questions, inquiry, and discussion and is known to have developed the Socratic Method.	Mini-lectures with breakouts (Research finding #1); Quizzing and testing (Research finding #4)
Take a Guess	Before a lecture, learners pair up. Partners create a list of three to six important facts about the topic that they believe the instructor will discuss in the lecture. As the lecture proceeds and students hear a fact they though the instructor might mention, they circle the corresponding item. This activates background knowledge and therefore prepares them for what they are about to learn.	Guided Note-Taking (Research finding #2); Focusing on essentials (Research finding #3)
Lecture Bingo	The instructor makes out bingo cards comprising terms from the upcoming lecture. Students listen for the terms and then cross them off when they hear them in class.	Frequent testing (Research finding #4)
Find the Flaw	Instructors plant misinformation in their lectures, which students have to identify and record.	Guided Note-Taking (Research finding #2); Focusing on essentials (Research finding #3)
Field Lecture	The Field Lecture IDEA centers on the notion of holding lecture in a location that is relevant to the course content being taught.	Mini-lectures with breakouts (Research finding #1)

The research basis behind these IDEAs means faculty can go into a lecture classroom with confidence that they have a good and intentional design for improving student learning and putting students on the path to success. Following are detailed descriptions for how to go about implementing these techniques in the classroom.

IDEA #1: Guided Note-Taking

Overview

Guided Note-Taking is an IDEA that uses the concept of scaffolding to provide students with a structure for taking notes during a lecture. Scaffolding is a fundamental aspect of learning. It is the process by which individuals learn new information by building on what is known. This process serves as a guide for helping students to focus on important concepts and to write down specific information. Instructors also can provide background information and cues that prompt students to write in key facts, concepts, or relationships (Heward, 2001).

Guided Note-Taking provides students with a format for active listening, and research suggests that being active can improve learning (Deslauriers et al., 2011). Students have specific questions to answer or blanks to fill in, and this IDEA can improve their willingness and ability to pay attention. The IDEA prompts students to be more cognitively engaged during the lecture. Through scaffolding, students identify the most important concepts introduced and begin to make distinctions between these concepts and less important ones. Heward (2001) has shown that this activity also helps students to improve the accuracy and efficiency of their note-taking.

Guiding Principles

This approach may seem backward to students, as typically the most important information is missing from the skeletal that you provide prior to the session. However, as the information missing from the note-taking structure is only provided during lecture, Guided Note-Taking shows students which information is most valuable and gives them an incentive to come to class and pay attention. Essentially, this IDEA means "holding out" on the information they most need in order to be successful on the test. Thus, this IDEA can also have a positive effect on class attendance (which typically improves performance).

The human brain looks for patterns and makes decisions based on importance of material (Doyle & Zakrajsek, 2013). The way in which students organize knowledge influences how they learn and how well they apply what they learn. When students make connections between information, when the connections are accurately and meaningfully organized, they are better able to learn. Guided Note-Taking allows students to learn not only the content but also how to organize information by providing a skeletal structure around which they can include important information. This process of scaffolding knowledge for students provides support in the early stages and teaches them the process of learning as they progress.

Preparation

For this IDEA, develop your notes as if you were going to provide a summary of your "take" on the material. Then, create a note-taking structure that students can "fill in" during a lecture. If you post notes prior to class, simply leave out critical information. If you use PowerPoint or Prezi, remove key words and phrases and insert blanks in their place. Of course, this technique is greatly enhanced if you remove concepts and insert conceptual questions. Simply removing individual words alone tends not to prompt the desired level of thinking. Explain to students that you are using this technique to enhance learning and that your hope is that they will come to class in order to "fill in" the information that is missing from the outline.

Process

- Provide students with the note-taking structure, whether ahead of time by email or Web or in class as a handout.
- Present your lecture on course content using the same note-taking structure.
- As information is presented during the lecture, ensure the students are filling in missing content to complete the guided notes. You may do so by asking key questions or even asking specifically, "Based on what you have learned, what do you think goes in this space?"

Sample IDEA Pairings

Pause Procedure (IDEA #2). To check for understanding and accuracy of the material being supplied by the students, stop periodically and encourage students to ask questions. Doing so can provide them with a chance to ask you to repeat information they missed or to clarify any points upon which they might be confused while completing their notes.

Pairs Check (IDEA #26). Pause periodically and ask students to confer with peers to compare what has been written and correct their own notes.

Concept Map (IDEA #79). Have students use an existing structure as a starting point to organize their thoughts of the material to be presented.

Pro-tips

Students will regularly ask you for the information that they are being asked to provide. Resist the urge to give them the information, as this activity is most effective when the students in the context of the surrounding material fill in the missing information. The goal here is to get them to think about the material in a more meaningful way. If the information is in the text or easily available online, they will be less likely to value the content of the lecture, fail to learn the process of differentiating important material, and typically learn material at a more "surface" level.

The note-taking structure should be specific but fairly skeletal. Fuller notes require less work on the part of the students, which means less effort is required and less learning is likely occurring. Completely unstructured tasks, however, leave students to their own devices, and they are often less skilled at note-taking than we might imagine. As you use this IDEA, you will learn the best amount of material to exclude and what type of information to require students to produce. Of course, students will need more assistance at the beginning of the course and then less and less as the course progresses.

Finally, it is important to verify that students are completing the note-taking structure. One option is to do a visual spot check of student effort and progress. You may also monitor the effectiveness of this IDEA by pausing and asking students questions (either individually or following a quick peer comparison of notes) pertaining to what they are adding in the provided spaces. Of course, for smaller classes, you might periodically collect notes and review them for accuracy.

IDEA #2: Pause Procedure

Overview

The Pause Procedure IDEA is an instructional approach that proceeds much as its name suggests: mini-lectures are interspersed with intentional pauses of 30 seconds to 2 minutes. These pauses are designed specifically for the purpose of allowing students time to reflect on the newly learned material, to think about questions that might be asked, and to clarify concepts not firmly understood. During the pause, the instructor takes questions from the students, generally to allow students to clarify information from the lecture.

One major limitation of the traditional lecture is that neither the instructor nor the students may understand the extent to which the learners understand the material being presented. Through the use of the Pause Procedure, instructors can alleviate this major failing by requiring students to stop, reflect, think, and act. Overall, the Pause Procedure presents a low-risk and high-reward opportunity to improve student learning through lectures. Indeed, researchers have documented an increase in student learning outcomes when the Pause Procedure is used in addition to a traditional lecture (Ruhl, Huges, & Schloss, 1987).

Guiding Principles

Advocates of the Pause Procedure suggest that during traditional lectures, mental lapses can occur at a rate that exceeds students' ability to organize and store information (Rowe, 1980). That is, students typically only listen actively for a short time and then begin to drop in and out of attention. If those drops are frequent enough, they miss too much information to be able to put the pieces together and thus cannot store the information in their long-term memories.

Pausing also allows students to deal with the physiological and psychological responses that keep them from listening effectively for longer periods. When they have a "break" from active listening, they can use the time to consolidate the smaller block of information that they have received. Because they are tasked with asking questions, this approach requires them to take an active stance toward the information presented in the lecture. It allows them to return to listening, refreshed after a change in activities.

Preparation

Determine ahead of time when to allow students to ask whatever questions they might have and when to provide some structure to their questions (e.g., students will ask about points they need to clarify in their notes). This decision should rest on the level of knowledge and understanding of students; the newer the students, the more structure they will need. If questions are to be provided, it is advisable to have a few questions at hand that require the students to really think about the material or how to apply what was just learned. Avoid simple recall or recognition types of questions.

Process

- Give a mini-lecture lasting approximately 10–15 minutes.
- Following the mini-lecture, pause for 30 seconds to 2 minutes. During this pause, students are given the chance to assimilate, clarify, and record the information presented during the prior mini-lecture. If you plan to ask a question, provide the question and let the students know they are to pause for the amount of time you designate BEFORE they are to answer.
- Resume class, alternating mini-lectures and pauses as time permits.

Sample IDEA Pairings

Guided Note-Taking (IDEA #1). During the pause, ask students questions about their notes. This variation provides them with a framework or prompt for asking questions, which is particularly useful for new students.

Note-Taking Pairs (IDEA #25). Simply have individuals work for a few minutes to reconstruct notes and identify what they have questions about, then work with their group members attempting to answer as many questions as possible. They next ask you any questions still unresolved by peers.

Concept Maps (IDEA #79). During the pause, ask students to draw a Concept Map of ideas presented during the prior mini-lecture. This pause presents an opportunity to demonstrate an understanding of new ideas.

Pro-tips

The effectiveness of the Pause Procedure rests with what students do during the pause. Advanced students may be able to manage their time effectively on their own, using the time in the way that can best benefit them. New students, however, may not have the skill needed to make effective use of the time. Some scaffolding suggestions can be of use. For more introductory-level students, you may wish to suggest that students check their notes for gaps and ask questions about those gaps. Another alternate is to have short prompts for student thinking. For example, "What point is clearest to you? What is the least clear point from the lecture?"

The pause provides students with an opportunity to ask questions to clarify any points upon which they might be confused. This opportunity can allow students to ask for information they might have missed, clarify anything confusing, and catch up in their note-taking. All of these activities in turn can prevent students from internalizing misinformation.

IDEA #3: Punctuated Lecture

Overview

In a Punctuated Lecture, students answer questions about what they are doing at a given moment during class. This IDEA promotes active listening and self-reflection with respect to learning. If the students' attention has wandered, this technique will help them to refocus. Punctuated Lectures are also designed to give students time to reflect upon their engagement in their own learning.

Helping students to become more aware of their attention strategies, their meaning-making strategies, or their note-taking strategies will help them with independent learning in the future as it promotes students' metacognition (or a learner's ability to think about their own thinking) (Bransford, Donovan, & Pellegrino, 1999). This IDEA is also a useful approach to gathering information about students' learning approaches. As Angelo and Cross (1993) suggest, Punctuated Lectures help instructors to encourage and gauge students' ability to monitor their own learning.

Guiding Principles

Mere repetition does not improve one's effectiveness at the task. In order to get better at any complex task, it is imperative to work at that task in a systematic way. The same is true about being an effective learner. Students benefit from continuously working on their ability to learn. Included in such processes are assessing the task, evaluating one's own strengths and weaknesses, planning learning approaches, using and monitoring appropriate learning strategies, and monitoring the effectiveness of the learning process.

Punctuated Lectures deliberately require students to engage in such tasks. This IDEA helps them not only use such processes in this one instance but also hopefully to be able to take the strategy and apply it in future situations. These actions could potentially help students develop the intellectual habits to improve their learning in the future (Ambrose, Bridges, DiPietro, Lovett, & Norman, 2010). Students are not typically naturally good at metacognition. As a result, explicit training in metacognition is necessary to becoming a more effective learner (Azevedo & Cromley, 2004).

Preparation

Before deciding to use this IDEA, develop a format for students to show what they are doing at the time the lecture stops. This format might include a few questions to answer with a Likert-type close-ended scale (e.g., rate the level of attention you were paying to the lecture, from 5 being extremely high levels of attention to 1 being extremely low levels of attention) or provide an open-ended question (e.g., "write for one minute on what you were just doing"). Alternatively, you could ask any number of questions designed to assess the effectiveness of the learning process:

- Were you fully concentrating on the lecture when we paused?
- What were you doing to record the information from the lecture?
- What were you doing to make connections between this new information and what we have already discussed?
- Did you get distracted at any point? If so, what distracted you?
- Were you able to bring your attention back into focus?
- What was the most recent point covered in the lecture? What do you expect to come next in the lecture and why?

In addition, determine how students will respond to your question(s), whether a paper and pencil response or automated response system (clickers). Finally, decide whether and when you will collect responses and whether you will score contributions or have them completed simply as an expectation of the course.

Process

- Develop and deliver mini-lectures of about 15 to 20 minutes.
- Stop at a predesigned place in the material.
- Ask students to reflect on what they were doing physically or mentally.
- After about two minutes, ask some specific questions for students to answer (see the preparation section above).

- Have the students hand in their responses at this point if you noted that you would be collecting responses.
- Resume the lecture, repeating the activity if time allows (thus allowing you to determine whether attention has improved).

Sample IDEA Pairings

Think-Pair-Share (IDEA #15). Conclude this "punctuated" portion of the activity by having students share their responses with a classmate and asking for volunteers to share what they have written.

Journaling (IDEA #68). Students may compile their entries over time and make a more comprehensive assessment of the efforts.

The 140-Character Memoir (IDEA #94). Ask students to tweet or briefly respond to your prompts as part of Punctuated Lecture.

Pro-tips

This activity is particularly useful to students new to college, such as those who are in first- and second-year courses. It is also useful when conducted regularly over time. Simply repeat the activity each week for two or three weeks, stopping after progressively longer lecture segments.

If you plan to use these activities frequently, ask students to save their written reflections. After several exercises, students can examine their responses by looking for patterns and changes over time.

As part of an effort to explicitly discuss the learning process, students can benefit from you also directly appealing for them to develop more active listening habits as they participate in this IDEA.

IDEA #4: Wake-Up Call

Overview

In the Wake-Up Call IDEA, students stay in a state of readiness, as they may be called on at any time during a given class. While lecturing, the instructor stops periodically and randomly chooses a student to respond to a question or prompt. Calling on students without warning helps students to monitor and regulate their own attention.

Guiding Principles

Student attention spans are often diverted away from a lecture during class. As a result, students may miss critical pieces of information without even realizing the gaps in their understanding of the material (Staley, 2003). This IDEA gives them added incentive to pay attention as they know they may be called upon to respond.

This IDEA also establishes the expectations that the students will be an integral part of the class. One added benefit of this technique is that the random selection of the student, for example by pulling a number from a "hat," will be perceived to be fairer. That is, the instructor does not appear to be singling out any one student or simply trying to call out anyone not paying attention. Instead of a tone of "gotcha," when done correctly, the IDEA breaks up a lecture by getting the perspective of a random student.

Preparation

In order to use the Wake-Up Call IDEA, prepare a lecture with identifiable chunks of information. Structure the chunks into 10–15 minute segments. The size of your class will impact how you might carry out this technique. The difficulty in larger classes is tied to determining how to randomly call on students. For smaller classes, students' names may be placed in a box and randomly drawn for response. In larger classes, it may be necessary to devise a scheme for identifying a single student in a class of perhaps hundreds of students. Regardless, the most important preparation is to determine a system to select the number of the student who will reply. Prepare students by telling them about the activity before the class period so they can come to class prepared. Also, remind them at the beginning of class that you will randomly call on students. Inform students how they should respond when called on. For example, you might suggest that they could respond in one of three ways: (1) Ask a question, (2) make a comment on the material, or (3) make a connection to a real life experience.

Process

- Announce the activity prior to the class to give time for preparation and then again at the beginning of your lecture.
- Present your lecture for approximately 15 minutes, and then pause.
- Randomly identify a student who will respond.
- Continue the lecture, pausing every 10–15 minutes to call on a different student.

Sample IDEA Pairings

Guided Note-Taking (IDEA #1). Give groups a few minutes to reconstruct their notes, and then call on one student to respond as you have determined. This few minutes of thought can help students produce better answers.

Interpreted Lecture (IDEA #5). When you call on the student, simply have him or her (or alternately small groups) summarize the last few minutes of the lecture.

Freewriting (IDEA #63). Give students a few minutes to write prior to calling on one of them. This activity will likely help to improve their responses, and it will help alleviate anxiety.

Pro-tips

This IDEA can make students feel anxious, as they never know when they will be called on to answer. Some students can struggle with feelings of anxiety. You may wish to use it sparingly to set the stage for paying attention. You may also want to make certain that it is appropriate for the intended student audience; advanced students may be more comfortable with it than novice students, for example.

Consider letting a student select another student in the class if he or she needs help. This "phone a friend" approach can help relieve some anxiety.

IDEA #5: Interpreted Lecture

Overview

The Interpreted Lecture IDEA has students restate what has just been learned. During a brief pause in a lecture, the instructor selects a student to "translate" what the instructor has just said into plain English for the rest of the class. Having the student state what was just learned is helpful as the selected student will be closer to the knowledge of those who are currently learning the material. In addition to having an original way to express the information, which assists other learners in the class, this activity is beneficial to the person being asked to provide the interpretation. Expressing newly learned information into one's own words is a powerful way to both check understanding and to enhance later recall of the information. Fundamentally, the Interpreted Lecture IDEA engages students in the learning process.

This IDEA also provides instructors with real-time feedback on the level of understanding of students. By asking students to translate what was just said, instructors get immediate information about whether students understand the content. Getting feedback on learning is one of the principles of good practice in teaching and learning (Chickering & Gamson, 1987) because it allows instructors to change course if necessary or alternately continue to move forward if students seem to comprehend the content.

Guiding Principles

Research has consistently shown that learning is facilitated when students are actively involved in the process (Hake, 1988). When sitting in lectures, however, students often lapse in and out of attention, becoming passive rather than active in their pursuit of information and knowledge. Requiring them to take action during a lecture, particularly action that reinforces the key concepts from the lecture, can enhance their ability to pay attention.

Interpreted Lecture is a form of peer tutoring. The selected student translates information into their own words to share it with others. Others in the class listen to the information translated into a language that is more compatible with their own level of expertise, which can help them better understand and thus internalize the information (Ambrose et al., 2010).

Preparation

To use this IDEA, prepare a lecture that breaks into relatively brief segments of approximately 10–15 minutes each. The information in the lecture should be logically chunked so that students can remember and repeat it. Warn students ahead of time that you will be selecting people to interpret what you have said in a lecture. You can mention that many students will be called on during the activity and that you are not trying to single out any one student. In addition, you may note also that after you call on the first student, others will be invited to augment the interpretation of the lecture. Letting students know ahead of time they will be assisting one another with this task will reduce the pressure felt by any one student, particularly if care has been taken to build community within the group. The concept here is to augment learning, NOT to catch a student who appears to be daydreaming or texting on their phone.

Process

- Present a lecture and pause at about 10–15 minutes. It may be helpful to set a timer.
- Randomly select a student.
- Pause for 30 seconds to one minute, during which a student can organize his or her thoughts.
- Ask the student to "translate" the lecture segment into plain English, using just a few sentences.
- If necessary, ask others to clarify or add missing information.
- Repeat the process every 10 to 15 minutes or so, as time allows.

Sample IDEA Pairings

Guided Note-Taking (IDEA #1). Give students time to write and compare their notes with others prior to interpreting the lecture. This approach allows them the opportunity to collect their thoughts and try them out on others first. Also, if they have written responses, they likely will have less stage fright and can read their responses if necessary.

Think-Pair-Share (IDEA #15). When you pause, ask students to think about the lecture segment for one minute. Ask them to turn to their partners and compare responses. Then, select a pair to share their interpretations with the group. This variation will reduce student anxiety about being called on and will allow them time to rehearse their responses in a low-threat environment before having to speak in front of an entire class.

Freewriting (IDEA #63). During the pause, students complete a Freewriting activity about the recently completed lecture. They will then be better able to share their interpretations based on their writing.

Pro-tips

Keep in mind that student understanding of the material and their sophistication for being able to interpret new information will move from relatively simple at the beginning of the course to relatively complex thinking later in the course. The point here is to not expect too much of them early but expect quite a bit of them later. Also, as the students in the class practice with interpretation of information, they should become better and better at the process simply through modeling and practice.

This lecture IDEA is particularly useful with complex topics because it has a built-in layer of repetition. Instead of hearing the information just once, students hear it repeated at least twice, by two different individuals who have different ways of articulating the information, and it is presented at two different levels. Repetition reinforces the information, helping students to both transfer it from short-term to long-term memory and to practice retrieval of the information.

Interpreted Lectures may also be used in groups and in writing classes. Each participant prepares a summary of the main points at the end of a presentation. Teams of participants switch their summaries and select the best summary from each set. This approach eliminates the stress of having to stand and deliver.

IDEA #6: Responsive Lecture

Overview

There are many benefits to having students work together to pool their knowledge and develop questions from a unit of content that they would like for the instructor to answer. The Responsive Lecture IDEA is designed to have the students ask the question and then have the instructor "respond" to the inquiry during the lecture, giving students a timely response.

Students often come to lecture with minimal preparation. Students often fail to consider what they know and what they do not about a topic. This IDEA allows for students to engage in class time in a purposeful way by having them come to class with peer-developed and peer-reviewed questions. The activity also allows students to clarify many issues among themselves that might otherwise be "easier" questions, leaving the final questions to be deeper and more difficult. Moreover, it allows instructors to focus on bigger issues and tougher concepts during class, when instructional time is at a premium.

Guiding Principles

By developing questions ahead of time, students create their own motivation for learning. They have questions that they need answered, and learning often happens best in the context of a question (Ewell, 1998). Moreover, this IDEA provides a tool for improved student attention and self-regulation. Students need to pay attention to the content of the lecture in order to be able to ask good questions. In addition, motivation is increased to hear the response to a well-developed question. This is a tool then that can serve students well beyond the limits of a single class.

This technique establishes a community of learners whereby the instructor demonstrates a genuine desire for student contribution. By taking their questions, the instructor is responding to their ideas, opinions, and learning needs. Instructors are also ensuring that they are teaching ideas and concepts that students find difficult.

Preparation

Before using the IDEA, develop content or an activity to be completed outside of class that helps the students in your course to develop content knowledge. This may be a reading assignment, video assignment, research assignment, or some other presentation of new information. Next, determine how students will let you know their questions. They may, for example, drop off a question in a box on the way out of class, or a leader from each group may email you with responses from the group discussion. The most important aspect of this IDEA is that you address the questions you are asked. If you choose to lecture and ignore the questions, students will quickly disregard future assignments from you.

Process

- Assign the out-of-class activity.
- In class, inform students that they should develop and rank open-ended questions related to the out-of-class activity. The list should include at least one question from each student, but it should also represent the collective thinking of the group.
- Provide 5 to 15 minutes for groups to work on their list of questions (depending on the difficulty of the material and the level of sophistication

of the question desired), and monitor student progress, assigning additional questions to groups that finish quickly.

- At the end of the class session, ask students to submit their responses to you but to also retain a copy of the questions for their own records.
- Out of class, review the students' questions. Organize them in a way that you can respond to them throughout your next lecture.
- When you return to class, as you start the class session, remind students to take careful notes pertaining to their questions.
- Provide time at the end of the session to have students summarize the answers to their questions and to ask for clarification for any unanswered questions.

Sample IDEA Pairings

Crossword Puzzles (IDEA #36). You can use student questions as a basis for crossword questions and have students listen in class for the answers to the clues.

Text Coding (IDEA #56). Students can use Text Coding on the out-of-class activity and use their notes as a starting place for question development with the group.

Today I Learned (IDEA #90). Students may respond to the Responsive Lecture with a Today I Learned minute paper to summarize the response to their question(s).

Pro-tips

A primary challenge for students will be writing questions at the appropriate level. For the first few class sessions using this activity, select examples of good questions and post the questions for the class along with a quick description of why it is a good question. Another challenge of this activity is addressing random student questions in a coherent and organized fashion. It can make lecture preparation more challenging, but the upsides of having student investment in the information and piquing their interests can outweigh the extra organizational challenges.

Having questions ahead of time can help with planning lectures. Patterns and gaps in student knowledge will become apparent, allowing for the opportunity to plan content and information in a way that best fills those gaps.

Be sure to provide sufficient closure after the activity, particularly by ensuring that all students felt that their questions were fully answered. Doing so may mean moving to a more traditional question and answer session at the end of the lecture.

IDEA #7: Socratic Seminar

Overview

The Socratic Seminar IDEA involves dialogue between the instructor and the students that is centered on open-ended questions about a text. In a Socratic Seminar, the instructor systematically asks questions that require students to examine issues and principles related to a particular unit of content. The IDEA is to prompt deeper understanding of that text and to model critical thinking about a concept. This activity is named for Socrates, who believed in questions, inquiry, and discussion. He developed what was later called the Socratic Method.

Guiding Principles

Students learn best when they are engaged in a task with an appropriate level of challenge and in which they receive feedback about their performance (Ambrose et al., 2010). A Socratic Seminar provides a scaffolded approach to discussion in which the professor leads students through increasingly complex levels of thought. The questions become more challenging as the conversation proceeds, and thus all students hear questions and answers that are directed to their level of understanding.

Students receive feedback in the form of prompting from the instructor and from agreements and disagreements on the part of their peers. Through this process, students develop a deeper understanding of the concept being discussed (Knezic, Wubbels, Elbers, & Hajer, 2010).

Preparation

Choose a few pages of text that are directly relevant to the material on which you will give a lecture. This IDEA will work best with authentic text, such as a case, short story, conflicting documents, article, or speech. It is helpful to have a text that is controversial, as this will help to motivate students and stimulate conversation. Consider numbering the paragraphs for easy reference during the activity. Prepare three to five questions for the discussion, depending on the length of time devoted to this activity. Keep in mind a single question might easily prompt 15–20 minutes of discussion. These questions, or statements, should be thought provoking, inviting exploration and inquiry, and not basic content with "right" or "wrong" answers. Ideally, the questions should proceed in logical order, leading students to higher and higher levels of thinking. You will want to ask questions about the text specifically (e.g., What is the main idea the writing is attempting to convey to you as the reader?) as well as questions that involve moving the conversation forward (e.g., Who has a different perspective to share?). Prepare the students for what you have in mind. Students should know that they will participate in a Socratic Seminar and your reason for doing so. Explain to students that it is important they read the text carefully ahead of time and be prepared to be called on and put "on the spot."

Process

- Ask the first question, tell the students to think about the question for about 30 seconds, and then either call on someone or ask for a volunteer.

- Ask student to note where the response is located in the readings. It is typically helpful to give the students an example response to get the conversation going, particularly the first time you use this technique.
- Ask another question that probes students to deeper thinking. You can continue with the same student, as others listen in, or you may move to a different student.
- Facilitate the conversation to make sure that everyone has a chance to participate.
- Take notes during the discussion that you can use to provide closure to the discussion.
- Give yourself time at the end of the class period to offer a short lecture summarizing the major points of what was learned during the class session.

Sample IDEA Pairings

Guided Note-Taking (IDEA #1). Have students prepare notes prior to the IDEA, perhaps collecting the notes at the beginning of the class so you can skim quickly.

Journals (IDEA #68). To bring additional value to the activity, ask students to think about what they have learned. They may want to consider how much text-centered time they spent in the activity. It is also valuable to have students reflect upon their own participation.

Self-Assessment (IDEA #95). Students consider their participation in the Socratic Seminar and evaluate their learning during the class session.

Pro-tips

There are many ways to adapt this approach. You can use it as a high-stakes approach, in which a student is called on and put in the "hot seat" for several rounds of questioning. This adaptation can lead to anxiety from students, but it has the advantage of making it more important for students to adequately prepare. In short, not wanting to be embarrassed in front of their peers can be motivating. This approach works best for advanced students.

Whenever the intention is to have engaged conversations, establish ground rules prior to using the IDEA. Establishing some norms for the seminar can be useful. For example, suggest that students not raise their hands but wait for an opening, address each other respectfully, stick to the text when making assertions, and so forth. In addition, seek to involve students in developing the rules, as doing so will improve buy-in.

You can use this IDEA as a low-stakes instructional activity, in which students can volunteer and conversation proceeds from student to student as someone wishes to contribute. Indeed, you can make this activity a much more student-centered one, in which students themselves develop the questions and run the IDEA. This variation has the advantage of making it a low-threat activity and providing students with some control over their own learning.

IDEA #8: Take a Guess

Overview

In the Take a Guess IDEA, students consider what "clusters" or "categories" of information should be expected in class as they prepare for the class session. As class progresses, student match their expectations against the information the instructor delivers. If students are correct, they have a good sense of what is happening in the class. If students are drastically incorrect, it will indicate difficulty in understanding the learning expected to take place.

Guiding Principles

Thinking of specific schemata activates background knowledge and therefore prepares students for what they are about to learn. This activation allows students to make connections to their prior knowledge, which is critical for their learning (Anderson, 1984). When new learning is planned, this IDEA makes the prior information accessible, allowing students to graft new ideas more easily onto existing ideas. And when the instructor covers the expected points, it reinforces the information. Learners can make a connection between what they have already learned and what they will be learning, which can have both a legitimizing effect on the information and be a way to better organize new information into one's existing knowledge.

Like many other of the lecture IDEAs, Take a Guess requires students to take an active stance in a lecture. They have to assume roles of active listeners in order to match information from the lecture with the information they expected. They also have to listen for new information. In this way, this IDEA requires students to stay engaged during the lecture.

Preparation

Aside from preparing the content for the class session, little preparation is necessary for this activity. Simply set aside a few minutes of Brainstorming (IDEA #62) time prior to presentation of a lecture to remind students they are to identify when relevant schemata have been noted. Also, plan to allow time at the end for reflection and closure activities.

Process

- Before a lecture, ask students to create a list of three to six important concepts about the topic that they think you will discuss in your lecture.

- At the beginning of the class session, remind students to circle any concepts covered that corresponds to items on their list.
- At the end of the lecture, ask students to reflect as follows:
  - Ask them to note where their expectations were met.
  - Ask them to list any information that you covered that they did not anticipate.
  - Ask them to report on any facts they thought you would mention but did not.
- Spend time in a class discussion, clarifying any important points or misunderstandings that become apparent.

Sample IDEA Pairings

Note-Taking Pairs (IDEA #25). Ask students to work together to take notes as collaborators. Their lists tend to be more complete when they work together rather than alone, and they can discuss the process and their results after the lecture.

Speak-Write Pairs (IDEA #64). Following the Take a Guess lecture, student pairs discuss what they learned from the activity. This information forms the basis of a writing assignment related to the lecture content.

Today I Learned (IDEA #90). Students respond with a Today I Learned paper about what *new* knowledge they developed through lecture participation. This step requires them to retrieve the information one more time, which helps move it to long-term memory.

Pro-tips

One of the most important aspects of this approach is to note the extent to which students understood the important concepts within a block of material before it was discussed. Building the ability to make predictions about learning elements is an important skill. Expect students at lower levels and early in the semester to struggle with this activity. As the course progresses, students should get better at making correct predictions and become more sophisticated in their ability to tease out the nuance of the material.

This activity also has the advantage of improving students' ability to self-monitor and self-regulate. As such, this IDEA has potential benefit to their long-term prospects as learners.

Overall, the potential rewards of thinking ahead and staying active and engaged during a lecture makes this a helpful activity. This IDEA can be used as an ongoing class activity, which can improve student thinking and attention over time.

IDEA #9: Lecture Bingo

Overview

Attention is a critical aspect of the learning process. For this IDEA, the instructor creates a bingo card with terms that will be discussed in a lecture. During the lecture, students listen for the terms and mark them accordingly on their bingo cards when the terms are used in the lecture.

At times, students may find the rate of information being presented during a lecture to be overwhelming. In those cases, a task that helps them to listen and take notes for important bits of information can be helpful. This IDEA is particularly useful when the content is factual, conceptual, or early in a block of material when students have little foundational knowledge of the information.

Guiding Principles

Using an activity such as Lecture Bingo allows for intermittent "wins" (Silberman, 1995). That is, instead of having a lost feeling due to the presentation of a lot of complex information, students feel a positive effect when identifying various words, keeping them interested in maintaining attention (Silberman, 1996). Also, with multiple distractions, such as cell phones and laptops, an activity that helps focus attention on course material proves beneficial.

Lecture Bingo also promotes active listening, which is a process that requires the listener to go beyond surface-level listening for information. Instead, this type of listening typically requires an additional action on the part of the receiver of information to indicate that he or she has heard. Lecture Bingo gives students a specific task: to listen for specific concepts and to make a physical motion when they have heard them. This task not only helps them focus their attention but also to actively interact with content.

Preparation

When using Lecture Bingo, you will first need to create a bingo card, with five cells across and five cells down. Mark the center with "free space." Populate the rest of the card with terms you will use in your lecture. (Note: There are many free Internet-based, bingo-card-generating programs.) See the example in Table 1.3. on the next page.

Create one Bingo Card for each student. Vary the arrangement of the terms on each card you create to ensure that each student receives a unique card (or that only a few of the students have the same card if you have a large lecture class). Next, decide how students should mark their responses. You can copy the cards so that students mark off the appropriate space as they hear the term. If you plan to reuse the cards, however, consider using tokens (such as poker chips) that students can use to cover the spaces but not permanently change the cards. You can also laminate the cards and have them use colored stickers to mark their responses.

TABLE 1.3 Lecture Bingo Example

Mitosis Lecture Bingo				
Replicate	Interphase	G1	S Phase	Diffusion
Chromosome	Chromatid	G2	Centromere	Cell Cycle
Prophase	Centriole	Free Space	Spindle	Metaphase
Anaphase	Telophase	Cytokinesis	DNA	Nucleus
Membrane	Cytoplasm	Daughter cells	Eukaryote	Cell division

Process

- Announce the activity and distribute the bingo cards to the students.
- Inform students that they should mark the corresponding space when they hear the term mentioned in the lecture. Tell them how they should mark their responses.
- As participants collect five vertical, horizontal, or diagonal dots in a row, they yell "Bingo!"
- Conclude the game as one person wins or, alternately, continue the lecture, allowing as many students as possible to yell "Bingo."

Sample IDEA Pairings

Pairs Check (IDEA #26). After the lecture game concludes, form pairs and ask students to compare the concepts they have marked on their cards.

Crossword Puzzles (IDEA #36). Have students use the concepts on the Lecture Bingo Cards to answer Crossword Puzzles at the end of the lecture. This pairing has the advantage of expecting students to move beyond simple recognition of terms to understanding them and being able to answer questions about them.

Main Idea-Detail Chart (IDEA #80). Following Lecture Bingo, students use the card concepts to create a Main Idea-Detail Chart with the concepts as main ideas and the details created from the content gained during the lecture.

Pro-tips

Preparing bingo cards can be a task unto itself, particularly creating unique ones for each student. Modify this technique to have students fill in their own squares with concepts they learned from the previous day's lecture or from the reading assignment. Simply pass out a blank bingo card at the start of class. Give students a few minutes to fill in concepts they expect to be covered. If possible, circulate around the room to ensure that they are filling in the cards completely. Students can mark through each concept with an X as they hear it. The game ends as someone calls "Bingo!" and turns in the winning card (consider giving a small prize, or a small amount of extra credit, for winning).

Lecture Bingo may also be done in teams. Simply assign students to small groups and give each group a card. As with individuals playing the game, the winning team is the first to earn five marks in a row, whether vertically, horizontally, or diagonally.

If you do not typically lecture, you can allow students to mark off terms heard during a class discussion. In this case, allow each person to contribute only one time and remind students that for them to discuss a term they wish to check off their card, they must tie that concept into the current discussion. In this way, the activity is also an effective method to generate discussion in the class.

IDEA #10: Find the Flaw

Overview

In Find the Flaw, lecturers deliberately include misinformation in their lectures and ask students to identify these flaws. Having students actively looking for misinformation presented during a lecture enhances critical listening and thinking skills. Students often construct their own misinformation while learning (e.g., taking a multiple-choice test may internalize one of the incorrect responses; misconstrued essay questions generated when students do not have sufficient understanding can prompt them to try to construct a response that seems reasonable to them) (McTighe & O'Connor, 2005), and this IDEA can make students more aware of the problem.

The Find a Flaw IDEA is designed to encourage active listening and critical thinking by engaging students in a game of "being the first to find an error." This is an effective activity to keep those who feel knowledgeable about a topic engaged in the presentation of information.

Guiding Principles

On the surface, this activity seems counterintuitive. Why give students misinformation and risk the possibility that they will internalize it? This is a good question, indeed. The answer is, however, that having misinformation embedded with accurate information is a closer approximation to the types of information processing students will do upon graduation. It is becoming more and more common to find misinformation in everyday life as information is placed into digital space without the benefit of peer review and editing. The IDEA teaches the students to look for confirming and disconfirming evidence in a presentation of a new concept, a skill that is important for lifelong learning.

Students need to be aware that it is important for them to analyze everything they read, hear, and see. Essentially, the message to our learners is to have their critical-thinking filters engaged all the time. Indeed, being effective evaluators of information is one of the top skills individuals living in an Internet age need to have (Rheingold, 2012). The Find a Flaw IDEA teaches students that, for educated individuals, there is no such thing as a passive recipient of new information.

Preparation

There are many variations of this IDEA. Therefore, preparation will depend on how you use this concept. One method is to tell students that periodically you will insert a flaw and the first person to raise her hand and state the flaw and correction will receive a prize (e.g., small trinket). Another method is to have students respond on a card what was flawed and then pass the card in at a designated time. Notecards can be particularly useful for collecting the information quickly and making it easy for you to keep responses together cleanly, but notebook paper will work well. In addition, identify how you will respond to student responses. Ideally, you will address the information quickly so that no student leaves the lecture without either the correct information or a clear idea of the purposely inserted misinformation. Address the misinformation immediately or, alternately, let students know what the misinformation is before class is over and have everyone look up the correct response.

Process

- If you intend to have the students note the flaw and turn in their responses, pass out index cards or ask students to have a piece of notebook paper ready to record their responses. The point here is that students should not need to look for paper at the time the flaw is noted.
- If you intend to reward the first person to raise his hand, note the flaw, and give the correct information, this first step is not required.
- As you begin the class session, announce that you will intentionally insert a piece of misinformation.
- Inform them that when they hear it, they should make a note of it on their index cards or raise their hand.
- When note cards and paper responses are used, ask students to present the flaws at the end of the class period.
- Provide feedback before the class session ends. Be careful to watch the clock and correct the error prior to the end of class. If students are staring to pack up because the class period has officially ended, they will not listen to, or process, the corrected information. Always be certain to let students know the real information. One alternative is to clearly state the flaw and ask them to find the correct answers for themselves.

Sample IDEA Pairings

Speed Interviews (IDEA #35). During a pause, ask students to put their heads together in a quick discussion prior to submitting their responses.

Main Idea-Detail Chart (IDEA #80). Students can track the lecture by writing out the main ideas. You can inform them that the misinformation will be one of the details. They can indicate which detail is misinformation by circling it.

Today I Learned (IDEA #90). After correcting the misinformation, ask students to write a brief Today I Learned statement that highlights what they learned from participating in the Find the Flaw IDEA.

Pro-tips

For most classes, and particularly entry-level courses, it will be helpful to assist students in finding a flaw. For example, tell them at the beginning of the class that flaws will always occur when you are in one part of the room. The idea here is not that there will be flaw every time you stand in certain area, but that flaws will occur only when you are in that area. This variation will help the students to focus particularly well when you move to that area. Gradually increase that area until there are no bounded areas. Another option is to pause the lecture and show them a slide that contains one piece of misinformation. Students can search for it during the pause, and you can clarify before moving ahead.

Be aware that many students have engrained the concept that the faculty member is THE authority and is not to be questioned. Unfortunately, some faculty perpetuate this concept. As such, it may be difficult for some students (particularly from cultures that emphasize power and respect of elders and those in authority positions) to point out flaws.

A key challenge of this technique is that if students do not recognize the misinformation, it can reinforce student misunderstanding. Be careful to provide the corrected information in a way that ensures the proper information has been attended to and processed.

IDEA #11: Field Lecture

Overview

Changing where a class meets and a lecture occurs holds the potential to have a positive impact on a student's experience and learning. The Field Lecture IDEA means holding mini-lecture in a location that is relevant to the course content being taught. It means capitalizing on the moment during a field trip to be able to provide pertinent information to students on a need-to-know basis. For example, if an instructor is teaching a course on criminal courts and judicial processes, having class at the local courthouse presents an opportunity to observe what is going on and provide a brief lecture to solidify content being presented to students. In this way, the lecture occurs in a real-world and course-relevant context.

The Field Lecture IDEA allows for students to get on-the-spot information and likely see firsthand how the knowledge they are gaining is, or can be, applied in the real world. Additionally, the change of venue from a typical classroom setting can help promote a more informal learning environment that can increase student interactions with each other and the instructor.

Guiding Principles

The environment surrounding a class has a dramatic impact on student learning (Weinstein, 1979). Students, like everyone else, actively and selectively process elements of their surroundings using existing knowledge to make sense of the new information being learned (Graetz, 2006). Field Lecture taps into this notion by providing students with information and knowledge complimenting the environment where instruction takes place. During the activity, the class will benefit from the instructor lecturing to ensure that students realize the relevant aspects of the environment around them.

Additionally, Field Lectures tie lecturing to what is sometimes considered an oppositional idea of experiential learning. That is, Field Lectures provide the opportunity to offer students information in a relevant context. It has long been held that showing how abstract concepts work in the real world is helpful to learning (James, 1907). When taking place amid an unfamiliar environment, experiential learning provides a chance for student growth and increased self-awareness (McClellan & Hyle, 2012). Furthermore, the creation of an experience that allows students to draw connections between lecture content and the immediately present environment aids in students' abilities to see the relevant links between the knowledge shared and the application for that knowledge (Furman & Sibthorp, 2013).

Preparation

Before deciding to engage in the Field Lecture activity, first assess what information students will need to know. Next determine whether going to a different location will improve their learning of that information. If a relevant location is available, possible, and potentially desirable, determine whether it worth the energy involved. If you will be leaving campus, research campus policies regarding taking a class off campus as well as transportation options.

Determine what facilities are available to hold class once you arrive at the location. Consideration should be made regarding both the technology and space needed to conduct an effective class. Also, take into account that a new environment may be noisy or busy and therefore distracting for students.

Give consideration to transportation in getting to the location. It is advisable to speak with someone on your campus that understands the risks and liabilities of taking your class off campus. Depending on your campus policy, it may not be possible for you to drive students to an off-campus location or to have them ride with each other to get to a class-sponsored event. That said, it may also be inexpensive to use a campus van to transport a small class.

Finally, consider what options exist for those who are not able to make the trip due to scheduling conflicts. Often, a paper or other reasonable exercise is possible. It may also be possible to record the experience for those who were not able to attend and make it available online.

Process

- Well in advance of the activity, share with the class all of the important logistical details as well as background about the location and any individuals the class may be meeting during the Field Lecture.
- Meet at the location if on campus; if off campus, identify where you will meet for transportation, if necessary.
- Take a tour of the facility or point out defining features of why you are at the physical location. Doing so will not only help orient students but also provide concrete examples to be used during lecture.
- Offer a mini-lecture at the appropriate time to highlight important information and ideas and to help students understand what they are seeing.
- During the lecture, help students make connections between course content and the on-site location. If possible, include speakers or visitors from the location to help enrich the student learning experience of a Field Lecture.

Sample IDEA Pairings

Socratic Seminar (IDEA #7). Ask students a series of questions to help encourage deeper learning and consideration of the on-site location and content in the Field Lecture.

Seeded Discussion (IDEA #20). Provide students with questions ahead of time that help to tie the location of the class with the content being discussed during the lecture.

Visual Lists (IDEA #82). Have students create a comparison list of the course material and information from the lecture and location including the people, culture, and other relevant environmental factors.

Pro-tips

Lecturing "on the run" is more difficult than it seems at first blush. You need to prepare well in advance, considering the concepts you will likely need to cover. You also have to expect the unexpected. While a well-rehearsed lecture can be an advantage in the field, you will need to be flexible enough to change directions depending on what the situation requires.

It is crucial to make a connection with someone at the location you plan to hold class. In addition to having a facilitator to help with all of the relevant logistical details, a local contact can serve as a resource for lecturing to the class or identifying relevant experts to visit with the class and enhance the student experience.

Although not always possible, taking a tour of the facility prior to class has many added benefits. First, the tour may raise questions or ideas to be used as part of lecture. Second, meeting in a different location can be initially distracting from the normal course routine. Participating in a tour can help students work through the dynamics of the new location and prepare students to engage in class.

Today's students have many competing obligations in addition to class. As a result, it is essential that advance notice for the Field Lecture be given to students to allow them plenty of time to plan accordingly and make accommodations as needed to be able to meet at the location.

References

Ambrose, S.A., Bridges, M.W., DiPietro, M., Lovett, M.C., & Norman, M.K. (2010). *How learning works: Seven research-based principles for smart teaching.* San Francisco: Jossey-Bass.

Anderson, R.C. (1984). Role of the reader's schema in comprehension, learning, and memory. In R.C. Anderson, J. Osborn, & R.J. Tierney (Eds.), *Learning to read in American schools: Basal readers and contact text* (pp. 243–257). Hillsdale, NJ: Lawrence Erlbaum.

Angelo, T.A., & Cross, K.P. (1993). *Classroom assessment techniques: A handbook for college faculty.* San Francisco: Jossey-Bass.

Austin, J.L., Lee, M., & Carr, J.P. (2004). The effects of guided notes on undergraduate students' recording of lecture content. *Journal of Instructional Psychology, 31,* 314–320.

Azevedo, R., & Cromley, J.G. (2004). Does training on self-regulated learning facilitate students' learning with hypermedia. *Journal of Educational Psychology, 96,* 523–535.

Baddeley, A. (1998). *Human memory.* Boston: Allyn & Bacon.

Baeten, M., Dochy, F., & Struyven, K. (2012). Using students' motivational and learning profiles in investigating their perceptions and achievement in case-based and lecture-based learning environments. *Educational Studies, 38*(5), 491–506.

Biggs, J. (1996). Enhancing teaching through constructive alignment. *Higher Education, 32,* 347–364.

Bligh, D.A. (1999). *What's the use of lectures?* London: Jossey-Bass.

Bonwell, C.C., & Eison, J.A. (1991). *Active learning: Creating excitement in the classroom.* Washington, DC: George Washington University.

Bowen, J.A. (2012). *Teaching naked: How moving technology out of your college classroom will improve student learning.* San Francisco, CA: Jossey-Bass.

Bransford, J., Donovan, M., & Pellegrino, J. (1999). *How people learn: Bridging research and practice.* Washington, DC: National Academy Press.

Broadwell, M.M. (1980). *The lecture method of instruction.* Englewood Cliffs, NJ: Educational Technology.

Brown, G., & Atkins, M. (1988). *Effective teaching in higher education.* London: Methuen.

Bruff, D. (2009). *Teaching with classroom response systems: Creating active learning environments.* San Francisco, CA: Jossey-Bass.

Bunce, D.M., Flens, E.A., & Neiles, K.Y. (2010). How long can students pay attention in class? A study of student attention decline using clickers. *Journal of Chemical Education, 87*(12), 1438–1443.

Cashin, W. (1985). Improving lectures. *Idea Paper, 14.*

Chandhury, S.R. (2011). The lecture. *New Directions for Teaching and Learning, 128,* 13–20.

Chickering, A.W., & Gamson, Z.F. (1987). Seven principles for good practice in undergraduate education. *American Association of Higher Education Bulletin, 39*(7), 3–7.

Covill, A.E. (2011). College students' perceptions of the traditional lecture method. *College Student Journal, 45*(1), 92–101.

Davis, B.G. (2009). *Tools for teaching.* San Francisco, CA: Jossey-Bass.

Dennick, R. (2004). Justifications for learning outcomes: More appropriate educational theories. *Medical Education, 38*(11), 1205.

Deslauriers, L., Schelew, E., & Weiman, C. (2011). Improved learning in a large enrollment physics class. *Science, 332*(6031), 862–864.

Donovan, J. (2013). *How to deliver a TED talk: Secrets of the world's most inspiring presentations.* New York: McGraw-Hill.

Doyle, T., & Zakrajsek, T. (2013). *The new science of learning: How to learn in harmony with your brain.* Sterling, VA: Stylus.

Duncan, D. (2005). *Clickers in the classroom—How to enhance science teaching using classroom response systems.* San Francisco, CA: Addison Wesley, Pearson Education.

Ewell, P.T. (1998). National trends in assessing student learning. *Journal of Engineering Education, 87*, 107–113.

Exley, K., & Dennick, R. (2004). *Small group teaching: Tutorials, seminars, and beyond.* London: Routledge.

Fitch, M.L., Drucker, A.J., & Norton, J.A. (1951). Frequent testing as a motivating factor in large lecture classes. *Journal of Educational Psychology, 42*(1), 1–20.

Freeman, S., Eddy, S.L., McDonough, M., Smith, M.K., Okoroafor, N., Jordt, H., & Wenderoth, M.P. (2014). Active learning increases student performance in science, engineering, and mathematics. *Proceedings of the National Academy of Sciences, 111*(23), 8410–8415.

Furman, N., & Sibthorp, J. (2013). Leveraging experiential learning techniques for transfer. *New Directions for Adult and Continuing Education, 137*, 17–26.

Garside, C. (1996). Look who's talking: A comparison of lecture and group discussion teaching strategies in developing critical thinking skills. *Communication Education, 45*(3), 212–227.

Gaynor, J., & Millham, J. (1976). Student performance and evaluation under variant teaching and testing methods. *Journal of Educational Psychology, 68*(3), 312–317.

Graetz, K.A. (2006). The psychology of learning environments. *EDUCAUSE Review, 41*(6), 60.

Hake, R.R. (1988). Interactive-engagement versus traditional methods: A six-thousand student survey of mechanics test data for introductory physics courses. *American Journal of Physics, 66*(1), 64–74.

Harp, S., & Maslich, A.A. (2005). The consequences of including seductive details during lecture. *Teaching of Psychology, 32*(2), 100–103.

Heitzmann, R. (2010). 10 suggestions for enhancing lecturing. *Education Digest, 75*(9), 50–54.

Heward, W.H. (2001). Guided notes improving the effectiveness of your lectures: The Ohio State University Partnership Grant, Improving the Quality of Education for Students with Disabilities. Retrieved June 2, 2015, from http://ada.osu.edu/resources/fastfacts/Guided-Notes-Fact-Sheet.pdf

Hodgon, V. (1984). *Lectures and the experience of relevance: Implications for teaching and studying in higher education.* Edinburgh: University of Edinburgh.

James, W. (1907). *Pragmatism: A new name for some old ways of thinking.* Cambridge, MA: Harvard University Press.

Johnson, D.W., Johnson, R.T., & Smith, K. (1998). Cooperative learning returns to college: What evidence is there that it works? *Change, 30*(4), 27–35.

Johnston, A., & Su, W.Y. (1994). Lectures—A learning experience? *Education in Chemistry, 31*(1), 75–76.

Kiewra, K.A. (2002). How classroom teachers can help students learn and teach them how to learn. *Theory into Practice, 41*(2), 71–80.

Kimball, B. (1988). The historical and cultural dimensions of the recent reports on under-graduate education. *American Journal of Education, 96*, 293–322.

Knezic, D., Wubbels, T., Elbers, E., & Hajer, M. (2010). The Socratic dialogue and teacher education. *Teaching and Teacher Education, 26*(4), 1104–1111.

Lasry, N., Mazur, E., & Watkins, J. (2008). Peer instruction: From Harvard to community colleges. *American Journal of Physics, 76*, 1066–1069.

Mayer, R.E. (2001). *Multimedia learning.* New York: Cambridge University Press.

Mayer, R.E., & Moreno, R. (2003). Nine ways to reduce cognitive load in multipedia learning. *Educational Psychologist, 38*(1), 43–52.

Mazur, E. (1997). *Peer instruction: A user's manual.* Upper Saddle River, NJ: Prentice Hall.

McClellan, R., & Hyle, A.E. (2012). Experiential learning: Dissolving classroom and research borders. *Journal of Experiential Education, 35*(1), 238–252.

McDermott, L.C., & Redish, E.F. (1999). Resource letter PER-1: Physics education research. *American Journal of Physics, 67*, 755–767.

McKeachie, W. J., & Svinicki, M. (2006). *MeKeachie's teaching tips: Strategies, research, and theory for college and university teachers* (12th ed.). Boston, MA: Houghton Mifflin.

McTighe, J., & O'Connor, K. (2005). Seven practices for effective learning. *Educational Leadership, 63*, 10–17.

Murray, H.G. (1997). Effective teaching behavior in the college classroom. In R.P. Perry & J.C. Smart (Eds.), *The scholarship of teaching and learning in higher education: An evidence-based perspective* (pp. 171–204). New York: Agathon Press.

Neumann, R. (2001). Disciplinary differences and university teaching. *Studies in Higher Education, 26*(2), 135–146.

Penner, J.G. (1984). *Why many college teachers cannot lecture: How to avoid communication break-down in the classroom.* Springfield, IL: CC Thomas.

Piolat, A., Olive, T., & Kellogg, R.T. (2005). Cognitive effect during note-taking. *Applied Cognitive Psychology, 19*(3), 291–312.

Raver, S.A., & Maydosz, A.S. (2010). Impact of the provision and timing of instructor-provided notes on university students' learning. *Active Learning in Higher Education, 11*(3), 189–200.

Rheingold, H. (2012). *Netsmart: How to thrive online.* Cambridge, MA: MIT Press.

Robinson, S.L., Sterling, H.E., Skinner, C.H., & Robinson, D.H. (1997). Effects of lecture rate on students' comprehension and ratings of topic importance. *Contemporary Educational Psychology, 22*(2), 260–267.

Roediger, H.L., & Karpicke, J.D. (2006). The power of testing memory: Basic research and implications for educational practice. *Perspectives on Psychological Science, 1*(3), 181–210.

Ronchetti, M. (2010). Using video lectures to make teaching more interactive. *International Journal of Emerging Technologies in Learning, 5*(2).

Rowe, M.B. (1980). Pausing principles and their effects on reasoning in science. *New Directions in Community College, 31*, 27–34.

Ruhl, K., Huges, C., & Schloss, P. (1987). Using the pause procedure to enhance lecture recall. *Teacher Education and Special Education, 10*, 14–18.

Short, F., & Martin, J. (2011). Presentation vs. performance: Effects of lecturing style in higher education on student preference and student learning. *Psychology Teaching Review, 17*(2), 71–82.

Silberman, M. (1995). *101 ways to make training active.* San Diego, CA: Pfeiffer.

Silberman, M. (1996). *Active learning: 101 strategies to teach any subject*. Boston, MA: Allyn & Bacon.

Staley, C. (2003). *50 ways to leave your lectern: Active learning strategies to engage first year students*. Belmont, CA: Wadsworth/Thomson Learning.

Strobel, J., & van Barneveld, A. (2009). When is PBL more effective? A meta-synthesis of meta-analyses comparing PBL to conventional classrooms. *Interdisciplinary Journal of Problem-Based Learning, 3*(1), 44–58.

Svinicki, M., & McKeachie, W.J. (2013). *McKeachie's teaching tips: Strategies, research, and theory for college and university teachers* (14th ed.). Belmont, CA: Cengage Learning.

Thelin, J. (2011). *A history of American higher education* (2nd ed.). Baltimore, MD: Johns Hopkins University Press.

Weinstein, C.S. (1979). The physical environment of the school: A review of the research. *Review of Educational Research, 49*(4), 577–610.

Woodring, B.C. (2004). Lecture is not a four letter word! In A.J. Lowenstein & M.J. Bradshaw (Eds.), *Fuzzard's innovative teaching strategies in nursing* (pp. 124–125). Burlington, MA: Jones & Bartlett Learning.

2

THE DISCUSSION METHOD

Description

Discussion via student questioning has origins that date back centuries; this method indeed has been traced to classic teachers such as Socrates (469–399 BC). Socrates purportedly did not believe that the lecture was an effective method of teaching and instead relied upon probing questions for the purpose of stimulating critical thinking and deeper levels of understanding. While this form of questioning has its supporters, it also has its critics, who see it as a veiled form of the banking method of education where the teacher deposits the information into the empty vaults of student minds (Freire, 1970). Therefore, although Socrates is credited as being one of the first to use a discussion-oriented teaching strategy, the way he applied questions led us to include his method in our chapter on lecture techniques.

When referring to the contemporary discussion method of teaching, the term "discussion" typically means instructional strategies that emphasize participation, dialogue, and two-way communication. Nilson (2010) defines discussion broadly "as a productive exchange of viewpoints, a collective exploration of issues" (p. 127). Many educators have further argued for a more democratic perspective on the classroom discussion (Brookfield & Preskill, 2005). Discussions such as the kind these educators advocate require an open-ended and collaborative exchange of ideas and information between a teacher and students or among students (Lowman, 1995). Morrison et al. (2009) similarly define discussion teaching as "the most common form of face to face teaching where ideas, opinions, and facts are exchanged" (p. 231).

Many discussion-teaching strategists believe that students have to engage in a procedure that involves a real conversational setting and immediate audience (McCann, Johannessen, Kahn, & Flanagan, 2006). In this setting, student responses are not filtered through the instructor, but are offered to the group in its raw form. Students then filter the raw information using critical thinking to evaluate and respond. On the other hand, Nilson (2010) argues that "to bear fruit and not degenerate into a free-association, free-for-all bull session, you as the instructor must chart its course and steer it in the right direction. It is your responsibility to plan and control the content and conduct, to keep hot air from blowing it off course" (p. 127). Finding the balance between the two extremes is vital for effective discussion.

Purposes of Discussion

The fundamental purpose of discussion is to have students engage with course content and concepts, applying them in thoughtful discussion in an effort to lead to higher-order thinking. This form of discussion typically is done for the purpose of deepening students' thinking and learning (Lowman, 1995; Morrison et al., 2009). Discussion teaching is considered to be a critical-thinking exercise performed in a group setting (McCann et al., 2006). Unlike critical-thinking exercises such as solving puzzles, quizzes, and brainteasers, discussion teaching requires the learner to evaluate the problem while working with a group. In this way, discussion encourages deep learning (Hedley, 1994; Kember & Gow, 1994). Unlike lecture in which the purpose is to convey information, the purpose in discussion is to apply and integrate information.

Brookfield and Preskill (2005, pp. 21–22) offer the following list of outcomes that discussion can offer the college classroom:

1. It helps students explore a diversity of perspectives.
2. It increases students' awareness of and tolerance for ambiguity or complexity.
3. It helps students recognize and investigate their assumptions.
4. It encourages attentive, respectful listening.
5. It develops new appreciation for continuing differences.
6. It increases intellectual agility.
7. It helps students become connected to a topic.
8. It shows respect for students' voices and experiences.
9. It helps students learn the processes and habits of democratic discourse.
10. It affirms students as cocreators of knowledge.
11. It develops the capacity for the clear communication of idea and meaning.
12. It develops habits of collaborative learning.
13. It increases breadth and makes students more empathetic.
14. It helps students develop skills of synthesis and integration.
15. It leads to transformation.

Through discussion, then, students can develop a range of skills. In addition to the ones listed above, students may also improve their abilities to articulate and defend their positions on important topics and issues, evaluate evidence, and formulate and execute responses (Brookfield & Preskill, 2005; McGonigal, 2005). Discussion teaching has the added benefit of helping students to pay attention and think more actively (Svinicki & McKeachie, 2013).

Discussion also can enhances students' motivation to learn (Brookfield & Preskill, 2005). Discussion may, for example, contribute to students' affective development by increasing interest in a range of subjects and issues, helping students to clarify their beliefs and values, and aiding them in recognizing and potentially changing some of their attitudes (Cashin, 2011). When students have the opportunity to engage with course material and consider it in relation to their own lives and experiences, they are more likely to retain and remember the content (Eble, 1976; Goldsmid & Wilson, 1980; Hollander, 2002). As Frederick (1994) explains, "the fundamental value of discussions is that through them students develop a sense of ownership and responsibility for their own learning" (p. 100).

Types of Discussion

The literature offers a variety of different "types" of discussion, which we organize in the following categories of size, function, level of structure, and environment.

By Size

One way discussion may be "typed" is based upon the grouping patterns of the students. We see the following forms:

- **Whole class**—In this form of discussion, the teacher leads the discussion and asks questions to the full class. This form is often used in smaller classes, which allows for the instructor to better facilitate the involvement of most of the students in the course. This form also allows all students in the class to hear all comments from peers.
- **Small group**—In this form of discussion, students work together in small groups of four to six students to discuss a topic. Small groups may be used in classes of any size. Although having a classroom with tables facilitates small group discussion, tables are not necessary, and many faculty successfully use small groups in fixed-seat auditoriums.
- **Dyads**—In this form of discussion, students pair off to discuss the topic. This may precede a discussion within a small group or at a full-class level. Dyads are the most engaged of the discussion groupings; at any given moment 50% of the students in the class are speaking. Contrast this to the whole class form in which only one student in the class is speaking at a time.

By Function

Discussions may also be "typed" based upon the function or purposes of the discussion. Kurfiss (1988, p. 67) suggested the following types of discussion:

- **Informational**—the teacher encourages students to share information and assist one another in understanding course material. For this approach, the instructor's role is to defer controversy and create a community of learners where ideas may be challenged but not attacked.
- **Problematical**—In a problem-posing query, the participants consider the information or values needed to address a presented issue intelligently.
- **Dialectical**—The teacher makes a request for participants to state opponents' views accurately and sympathetically (i.e., take a "devil's advocate" view). This encourages students to "synthesize diverse opinions into a new formulation of the issue or to agree to disagree but with a better understanding of the nature of their differences."
- **Reflexive**—Participants discuss what was learned in their own discussion groups in order to learn from the process.

By Level of Structure

- **Spontaneous discussion**—This kind of discussion begins with the posing of a question about a current event. It is typically unstructured, with one point leading to another.
- **Planned discussion**—This form of discussion typically involves the teacher's development of a list of unified questions that can help structure the discussion. It is a fairly structured form of discussion and may proceed from one student to the next, until all students have had the opportunity to participate.

By Environment

- **Face-to-face (F2F) discussions**—These discussions take place in a conventional classroom, with the instructor and students in the same place at the same time.
- **Online discussions**—These discussions take place online, most often (currently) in a discussion forum, threaded discussion area, or chat room. The discussions may be asynchronous (in which students post thoughts and comments at different times) or synchronous (in which students work together simultaneously, typically in a chat area).

Types of Discussion Questions

Good discussion questions or prompts are typically open-ended and designed to be thought provoking and require students to use topic understanding. Davis (2009, pp. 119–120) offers the following suggestions for question types:

- **Exploratory questions** probe facts and basic knowledge: "What research evidence supports the theory of a cancer-prone personality?"

- **Challenge questions** examine assumptions, conclusions, and interpretations: "How else might we account for the findings of this experiment?"
- **Relational questions** ask for comparisons or themes, ideas, or issues: "What premises of *Plessy v. Ferguson* did the Supreme Court throw out in deciding *Brown v. Board of Education*?"
- **Diagnostic questions** probe motives or causes: "Why did Jo assume a new identity?"
- **Action questions** call for a conclusion or action: "In response to a sit-in at California Hall, what should the chancellor do?"
- **Cause and effect questions** ask for causal relationships between ideas, actions, or events: "If the government stopped farm subsidies for wheat, what would happen to the price of bread?"
- **Extension questions** expand the discussion: "How does this comment relate to what we have previously said?"
- **Hypothetical questions** pose a change in the facts or issues: "Suppose Greg had been rich instead of poor; would the outcome have been the same?"
- **Priority questions** seek to identify the most important issue: "From all that we have talked about, what is the most important cause of the decline of American competitiveness?"
- **Summary questions** elicit syntheses: "What themes or lessons have emerged from today's class?"

Principles of Learning That Support Use of the Discussion Method

Based on traditional learning theories and the framework of humans being social animals, the new field of social neuroscience is helping to uncover the foundations of human social interaction (Cacioppo, Berntson, & Decety, 2010). Discussion is a form of teaching that takes advantage of the natural need of humans to communicate, share ideas, and tell stories. The discussion teaching method is a valuable form of information delivery and can fall under many different learning theories depending on the particular observer's preference (Gagne, 1984). For example, Gibbons (2006) believes that language is the basis for all learning. Interactions between students and teachers and among students therefore help students to construct understanding. Many learning theorists believe, for example, that humans learn through interaction with each other and through the formation of communities of learners (Lave & Wenger, 1991; Vygotsky, 1978).

Organization and Sequence of the Discussion Method

The Initiate-Response-Evaluate (IRE) model of questioning is most common sequencing of the discussion method.

In the initiation phase, the instructor opens the topic for discussion with a lead-off question that prompts the students to participate. Many authors suggest that instructors open a discussion session with a question that does not have a single correct answer. By beginning with the response to a question, students are able to immediately engage with peers, the instructor, and the course content (Kloss, 1996; Lowman, 1995; Svinicki & McKeachie, 2013).

In the response phase, students bring in their ideas, opinions, and personal experiences about the topic. Each student listens to the other participants in the discussion and formulates ideas on the topic by combining the knowledge learned in the discussion with their own understanding (Gagne, 1984). A discussion builds upon a foundation of civic dialogue that must be the foundation for students to freely form and share ideas (Brookfield & Preskill, 2005). Students need the freedom to form ideas and connect them with the discussion topic (Gagne, 1984). One of the roles of the instructor is to be attentive and responsive to what students say to help facilitate student learning (Christensen, 1991). This focus on what students say can help discussions from escalating into heated arguments, which should be avoided (Johnson & Johnson, 1997). It is the instructor's function to direct the discussion and keep the discussion focused on the concepts and issues raised and away from personal attacks.

In the evaluation phase, the instructor provides an acknowledgement and critique of the student response. One of the roles of the instructor is to help clarify misunderstandings that may arise from students or discussions. Unlike a lecture where an instructor directly shares the facts and concepts, discussions can bring out misunderstanding or confusion that an instructor must dispel (Lowman, 1995). Wrapping up a discussion and bringing closure can help provide additional answers to students' questions as well as solidify course content (Clarke, 1988).

While IRE is an overly simplified account of what happens in a discussion, it does provide a general sense of the kinds of activities that take place. Moreover, the success of any discussion is necessarily dependent upon the appropriate level of discussion for the quality of each of these phases. For example, if the question asked is too simplistic, the discussion will be rote and unproductive. If the question is too complex, students will not know how to respond, and there will be little, if any, participation. If students do not work hard in the response phase, and instead give superficial answers, the quality of the discussion will not be as high. Finally, if the instructor does not effectively encourage or critique, the quality of the discussion will be lower. That said, if too much critique is given, the focus of the discussion will shift from the student to the instructor.

Advantages and Challenges of the Discussion Method for Instructors

Discussion can help instructors ensure students are meeting course goals. As Lowman (1995) states, "(I)n addition to clarifying content, teaching rational thinking, and highlighting affective judgments, discussion is particularly effective at increasing student involvement and active learning in classes" (p. 164).

Discussion provides instructors with feedback on how well students are understanding content (Frederick, 1994; Smith, 1977). The constant exchange between peers and instructor also presents opportunities to ask probing questions to improve understanding (Cashin, 2011). Discussion also helps to elaborate on existing information. As the discussion proceeds, students incorporate ideas and information heard from others into existing knowledge. This solidification of knowledge is important in the long-term retention of newly learned information.

Discussions require significant preparation time (Cashin, 2011). Murphy, Wilkinson, Soter, Hennessey, and Alexander (2009) suggest that "simply putting students into groups and encouraging them to talk is not enough to enhance comprehension and learning; it is but a step in the process" (p. 761). As an instructor, you typically plan a large number of interrelated questions, and this takes time and effort.

Discussions are time consuming and not a particularly effective way to cover a large amount of material (Cashin, 2011). They will be most effective when students have some knowledge and are applying that knowledge in a discussion centered around higher-order thinking skills.

Discussions can be challenging for some teaching styles and preferences. Some instructors enjoy the role of "sage on the stage" and may not be comfortable relinquishing authority and control. Such instructors may find more structured approaches to discussion more satisfying and consistent with their teaching preferences. In addition, some instructors do not feel confident enough with the material to let the conversation go in whatever direction it is taken. Giving a lecture requires much less mastery of material than does a group discussion. Moreover, discussions require a certain level of spontaneity and quick thinking. Students' questions and interests often take the group in directions that are not consistent with the initial plan (Cashin, 2011). By asking carefully planned questions, however, the instructor can—with some reliability—anticipate student responses and keep the discussion moving toward preset learning goals (Brookfield & Preskill, 2005).

It can also be difficult to encourage student participation in a discussion, particularly when some students do not have the knowledge or skills to participate (Cashin, 2011). One of the concerns of many instructors, which may even lead them to avoid discussions, is what to do about silence. What happens when a question is asked and no one responds? In other classes, the problem is too much or unequal participation. Overparticipation from a select number of students permits other students to stay quiet and generally unengaged (Karp & Yoels, 1976). Students do not always come to discussions with well-developed speaking or listening skills, which can influence the quality of their participation. For this reason, students may need some scaffolding or training in order to be effective participants. The literature suggests several different options for instructors to handle silence, including waiting it out (Bean & Peterson, 1988; Kendall, 1994), calling on students to respond (Gurung, 2002), or starting small group discussions to work on the question asked (Svinicki & McKeachie, 2013).

One challenge to discussions is that they can be difficult to assess and grade. Zaremba and Dunn (2004) suggest self-evaluation of participation to help assess students; others recommend peer-to-peer evaluation of class participation (Dancer & Kamvounias, 2005). Melvin (1988) argues for clear grading schemes for peer and professor evaluations of participation. Whether an instructor decides to grade participation or not, considering various types of evaluation may prove useful for instructors.

Sometimes students do not immediately see the benefits of discussion to their learning. Instructors, however, can save a few minutes at the end of a discussion for students to assess how the session went and provide reflection (Hollander, 2002). Doing so can help both the students and instructor assess the overall effectiveness of the discussion. Davis (1976) recommends video recording a discussion to analyze after class. This reflection provides an opportunity to gauge aspects of discussion teaching that are often difficult to do in the moment, such as the instructor's role and decisions as well as student engagement and participation.

A topic may be controversial or elicit excessive emotional reactions (Brookfield & Preskill, 2005). Such topics can create levels of discomfort by those experiencing them as well as those witnessing them. Particularly new students may need to start off with more informational discussion approaches.

What Research Tells Us About the General Effectiveness of the Discussion Method

In one of the earliest empirical investigations of discussion in a college classroom, Axelrod, Bloom, Ginsburg, O'Meara, and Williams (1949) investigated differences in learning between students in classes that were dominated by instructor presentations and students who were in classes that featured discussions. They found that students in the discussion-based classes learned more and were generally more satisfied with their classes than those in the presentation-based classes. More recent studies have upheld these early findings. Garside (1996), for example, compared the effectiveness of lecture to group discussion in improving students' critical-thinking skills. Participants included 118 students enrolled in introductory interpersonal communication courses. Although both methods improved critical thinking between the pretest and post-test, group discussion produced significantly more learning on higher-level items.

What Research Tells Us About How to Improve Student Learning in Discussion-Based Classes

From our review and synthesis of the research on discussion-based teaching, we offer the following findings.

Finding #1. Active Preparation for Discussion Improves Learning

The research points to the need for having students prepare sufficiently for participation in a discussion. In a graduate accounting course, for example, researchers examined the relationships between preparation for discussion, participation in discussion, comfort with discussion, confidence about future participation, and effect of participation on learning. The researchers found that active preparation for discussion is linked to students' reports of their oral and written communication skill development (Dallimore, Hertenstein, & Platt, 2008).

In a formally structured discussion approach called Interteaching, the instructor uses a preparation guide to help students through an assigned reading. Students have several days to complete the guide prior to class. In class, students work in pairs to discuss the guide. Teachers ask questions and help students stay focused. Students then complete a record sheet on how their discussions went and which guide questions were difficult. The instructor uses these to clarify points of confusion at the next class. Students then regroup to continue discussing the prep guide. This approach has been shown to improve student-learning outcomes, particularly when compared to students in more traditional teaching environments (Saville, Lambert, & Robertson, 2011).

Finding #2. Small Group Discussion (as Opposed to Whole Class) Can Increase Participation and Student Perceptions of Learning

The research points to the notion that smaller groups for discussion may lead to greater outcomes in student learning when compared to students who participate in whole-class discussion. In a study comparing the benefits of small- versus large-class discussion in an upper-level political science course, researchers found that participation is higher in small-group discussion. Moreover, student perceptions of their own learning outcomes are also higher when they participate in small groups rather than full-class discussion. Finally, there is increased participation by students with different ethnic backgrounds when small-group discussion is employed (Pollock, Hamann, & Wilson, 2011).

Finding #3. Grading Participation Improves Participation in Discussion

One question instructors often have is whether to grade or score class discussions. The idea is that it could potentially have a stifling effect on the discussion. On the other hand, not grading participation could lead to a lack of investment in the activity. The research seems to point to the latter. In one research study, for example, researchers found that courses with graded class participation encouraged students to participate more actively in class discussions and engage in their own learning (Dallimore, Hertenstein, & Platt, 2006).

Enticements can also be used to encourage student participation. The use of tokens has been shown to have an impact on students' joining in the conversation. In one research study, researchers examined the effectiveness of using tokens on student participation (Boniecki & Moore, 2003). Students earned tokens for participation and exchanged them for extra credit. Researchers found that directed and nondirected participation increased with the use of tokens. Students also responded faster to questions while the token system was in place and continued once the system ended.

Finding #4. Comfort with Discussion and Class Community Improves the Level of Student Learning

Research suggests that to fully engage in a discussion, students have to be comfortable with the format. Research also suggests that how much students prepare for and how much they participate in discussion is related to students' level of comfort with participating. In a study of 323 sophomore business students enrolled in accounting courses, for example, researchers examined completed pre- and postcourse surveys of student perceptions about class discussion along with students' grades. Path model results indicated that preparation was positively related to frequency of participation, which, in turn, was positively related to students' comfort participating in class discussion. Moreover, students' comfort level for participation in a class discussion was positively related to their learning (Dallimore, Hertenstein, & Platt, 2010).

Comfort develops from knowing one another and being in a classroom where a sense of community has been established. It also facilitates engagement among students. Community building can be done in a number of ways. Junco, Heiberger, and Loken (2011) used Twitter (i.e., microblogging) to stimulate various academic and cocurricular discussions. Engagement was measured by a scale developed based on the National Survey of Student Engagement. Results indicated that in the Twitter group, both faculty and students were engaged in the learning process. This study demonstrated the positive effect of building community on student engagement.

Finding #5. Cold Calling on Students Can Increase Voluntary Participation, Comfort with Discussion, and Learning

One question that instructors have about discussions is whether they should allow students to participate voluntarily or whether they should call on them. The research points to a relationship between these two extremes. For example, in one study, researchers examined the relationship between cold calling as well as student voluntary participation in class discussions and students' level of comfort with participating in discussions. Cold calling is when the instructor chooses someone who has not volunteered to provide a response. The researchers found that a significantly higher number of students answer questions voluntarily in classes that also have a high level of cold calling. Moreover, they found that the number of students who voluntarily answer questions in high cold-calling classes increases over time, as compared to courses with low rates of cold calling. Finally, in classes that had high levels of cold calling, students' comfort participating in class discussions increases while students' comfort participating does not change in classes with low cold calling (Dallimore, Hertenstein, & Platt, 2013).

Using IDEAs to Improve Learning with the Discussion Method

The IDEAs we share in this chapter are designed around some of the key findings from the research. We suggest that they correlate with key research findings as indicated in the following table:

TABLE 2.1 Discussion IDEAs and Research Findings

Discussion IDEAs	Description	Links to Research Findings
Snowball	Students participate in increasingly larger groups before discussing a topic in the full class.	Preparation (Research Finding #1); Comfort and Community (Research Finding #4);
What If	This IDEA calls for asking students to examine an actual event, whether recent or from the distant past, and to write about how the outcome that surrounds it might differ if one crucial condition were changed. This IDEA moves students from summary and even critical analysis toward creative thinking about course-related content.	Small Groups (Research Finding #2)
Scored Discussion	Students form two circles. The inside circle discusses a topic, while the outside circle listens and scores inside circle. Then circles reverse rolls.	Graded Discussion (Research Finding #3)
Think-Pair-Share	The instructor poses a question of some substance, asks students to think for a moment, and then has each person share with one person next to him or her. The instructor then asks for responses from a few pairs.	Preparation (Research Finding #1); Comfort and Community (Research Finding #4)

(Continued)

TABLE 2.1 Continued

Discussion IDEAs	Description	Links to Research Findings
In the News	Students bring in news articles related to the day's session as a springboard for discussion.	Preparation (Research Finding #1); Cold Calling (Research Finding #5)
Formal Argument	In teams, students adopt opposite sides of an issue and engage in structured argument.	Small Groups (Research Finding #2)
Circle of Voices	The instructor chooses an interesting topic, problem, or case related to the topic. Students can weigh in on an issue by raising their hands. Once one student speaks, he or she chooses another student to participate.	Small Groups (Research Finding #2)
Can We Have Class Outside?	The instructor holds class outside so that student discussion unfolds in a different environment.	Comfort and Community (Research Finding #4),
Seeded Discussion	The professor uses primer questions to promote student discussions, providing questions to students ahead of time.	Preparation (Research Finding #1)
Observation Team Discussion	Students observe an environment that is pertinent to class before describing and discussing what they observed within a small group.	Small Groups (Research Finding #2)
Campus and Community Events	Students attend campus and community events relevant to course content. The instructor ties course content to activities.	Preparation (Research Finding #1)
Journal Club	The Journal Club activity provides an opportunity for students to read scholarship related to the course content, critically analyze research, and apply findings to a specific context or practice.	Preparation (Research Finding #1)
Case Study	Students are provided a case to work and talk through. Students are encouraged to apply concepts as a framework to other contexts.	Preparation (Research Finding #1); Small Groups (Research Finding #2)

These direct links to research findings suggest that faculty can go into a discussion-based classroom with confidence that they have a good and intentional design for improving student learning and putting students on the path to success. Use the following IDEAs to ensure discussions are intentionally designed and grounded in the research that suggests good educational practices.

IDEA #12: Snowball

Overview

The Snowball IDEA (also at times designated in the literature as Pyramids) involves progressively adding students to groups at each iteration of the discussion cycle. Students begin by working alone, then in pairs, then in groups of four, then in groups of eight, and so on. The instructor provides questions or tasks of increasing complexity that require progressively larger groups to complete the assignment.

This activity is ideal for providing a safe environment for students to speak who may be shy or have apprehension about speaking in class. Students are able to build confidence by developing arguments alone and in small groups before having to share in a larger group or entire class setting. It also helps students get to know each other and therefore can help to build classroom community.

Guiding Principles

Collaborative learning, which serves as the foundation for the Snowball strategy, is based on the notion that students learn from each other (Gerlach, 1994). For the Snowball IDEA, students work in groups to examine and apply course materials. By learning together, students talk with one another, and much of both the teaching and the learning takes place through this communication (Golub, 1988). By assigning students to work and talk together, students engage course content in active ways that fosters critical thinking and problem-solving skills. Snowball discussions encourage student communication and value the interaction between students to encourage learning (Esfandiari & Knight, 2013). Allowing students to engage with each other encourages critical thinking and improving communication skills.

Preparation

After deciding to use the Snowball IDEA, identify a topic, problem, or set of questions that can be broken into smaller parts. Determine which part of the topic will be handled by which group size and how long each round will last. Finally, outline how you will describe both the structure and purpose of the Snowball activity.

Depending on the number of iterations desired, a Snowball discussion can take a significant amount of class time and may engage students for an entire class period. It is helpful to consider carefully the amount of time appropriate for the topic(s) to be discussed. Spending too much class time on lower-level discussions is not a good use of class time, which may well be noted by students. The activity should be structured so that students need to move fairly quickly to work through the assigned topic.

Process

- Explain the structure and purpose of the Snowball IDEA, including the estimated amount of time to be devoted to each step.
- Provide a question or task for students to complete individually.
- Pair students up with an assignment. Students may self-select pairs, or assign them by asking students to work with their neighbors or alternately having students count off. After allowing time to complete this new or complementary assignment, pairs are then combined into groups of four. This pattern of combining groups can continue as long as you desire, but you may prefer stopping at groups of four.
- The time can vary between each round, but typically 5–10 minutes should be sufficient. The assignment for individuals should be shorter (around 3 minutes) while the assignment for the larger groups (8+) may require 10–15 minutes to complete.
- As an entire class, ask a representative from each group to report on their discussions and results.

Sample IDEA Pairings

Scored Discussion (IDEA #14). This pairing reduces the number of groups and pairings needed. An inside group can go through the Snowball exercise while the outer group observes and scores the discussions or activity undertaken.

Anonymous Cards (IDEA #29). Ask students to write down a problem or question. Distribute the cards and have students come up with answers using the Snowball format.

Matrix (IDEA #84). Using the Snowball format, students work to complete a Matrix, adding to cells through the various rounds of the Snowball.

Pro-tips

Students risk getting bored if the tasks do not change or are not challenging enough as the groups combine and grow larger.

Depending on the time allocated for each round of pairings, students may feel rushed or not have time to complete the assignment. This potential challenge can be mitigated by carefully considering the time needed to complete the assignments given to each group and the succession of assignments to the progressively larger groups. Assignments that build upon one another will enable students to take the ideas from previous rounds and apply them to the current group assignment.

Monitor the conversations and activities occurring in the groups. These observations will help keep groups on tasks and identify points where groups struggle.

Depending on the time available, you may wish adjust the time for each round (shorter or longer) depending on the groups' progress.

One option is to introduce information between rounds. For example, after dyads are formed, provide each dyad with a short newspaper article pertaining to the discussion topic. When the dyads then form groups of four, this new information may be considered.

IDEA #13: What If

Overview

In this IDEA, students examine an actual event, whether recent or from the distant past, and discuss how the outcome that surrounded the event might differ if one crucial condition were changed. For this IDEA, students move away from summary and even critical analysis toward creative thinking and discussion about course-related content.

The What If IDEA has applicability in a range of disciplines and fields. Students in political science, for example, might analyze an election and consider what might have happened if a different candidate had won. A business student could consider what would happen if the government had not supported the banks during the recession of 2008. Students in art might consider what would have happened in the art world if a selected artist (e.g., Michelangelo) had never been discovered.

Guiding Principles

Imaginative inquiry is an approach to teaching and learning that harnesses students' power of imagination to create meaningful and challenging learning experiences (Egan, 2005). The notion for this IDEA is that with the rise of industrialism, our curriculum and teaching methods have become too objective based, too rote, and too standardized. Rather than teaching and testing for memory of objective facts, higher education should instead be teaching students to think creatively, to learn to do and to "make." Beyond foundational knowledge, colleges should also help students develop skills and demonstrable outcomes in creative thinking (Fink, 2013).

Preparation

In advance of using the What If IDEA, you will need to select a suitable course-related event. Next, identify one variable to change or have students discuss which variable to change themselves. Finally, determine the level of formality of the discussion and how long students will have to think about the event prior to engaging in the discussion.

Process

- Announce the activity and tell students the parameters of the discussion.
- Provide students with time to prepare.
- Have students form small groups to discuss the implications of the changed variable on the event and aftermath.
- Debrief as a class and consider other potential impactful variables.

Sample IDEA Pairings

Case Study (IDEA #24). Simply present the event in a case and have the What If discussion analyze a key variable from the Case Study.

Jigsaw (IDEA #31). Ask students to take different parts of the same topic in expert groups and then discuss with Jigsaw groups how the outcomes might have been different. The Writing Across the Curriculum (WAC) Clearinghouse (2014) Jigsaw example, presented in Table 2.2 below, shows how a topic might be split into several areas.

Brainstorming (IDEA #62). Prior to the What If discussion, provide time for students to conduct Brainstorm writing about the possible consequences of the variable changed. This writing can provide fodder for the subsequent discussion.

Pro-tips

This IDEA can be challenging for some students, particularly those who are most comfortable with learning the "facts" and proving that they have learned them by way of performance on objective tests. Other students will relish the opportunity to engage in learning in a different way. If a class has more of the former group, consider making the discussion less formal. If a class has the latter, you may want to ensure that some structures are in place to ensure that the discussion includes analysis rather than shifting too far out into speculation.

Consider how variables will be changed and then in what ways students might share with one another. For example, in a class of 30 students, you may have three different scenarios, each changed in one or two different ways. When used in this

TABLE 2.2 Writing Across the Curriculum Clearinghouse Jigsaw Example

What if Dolly, the famous cloned sheep, had been successfully produced on the *first* try? Students in science disciplines can speculate about scientific elements of this event; students in agriculture courses can focus on the immediate impacts in food production; students in ethics courses could examine the balance of world-wide patterns of food production v. individual identity; students in political science could focus on government funding issues; and so on (WAC, 2014).

fashion, five students might be assigned each of the scenario/variable combinations. This approach allows for several topics to be discussed in class and also allow for some overlap to demonstrate to students that, even with the same scenario/variable combinations, responses will differ.

IDEA #14: Scored Discussion

Overview

In a Scored Discussion, the inner circle discusses the topic while the outer group scores the discussion by assigning "points" for persuasive arguments or ideas drawn from the readings. This IDEA is somewhat similar to the Fishbowl or Inside Outside Circles technique, in which an outer group watches the inner/fishbowl group. Scored Discussion has the benefits of Fishbowl in that students effectively model or watch group processes in action (Hensley, 2002; Young, 2007). The activity adds a scoring component, which ups the ante of the activity. The scores identified by the outer circle are identified by themes, patterns, and arguments. Research has shown that having a moderate amount of anxiety can benefit performance (Broadhurst, 1957), which the scoring aspect can add. The Scored Discussion IDEA then increases the "stress level," along with student engagement in it, but it is still at heart a collaborative activity. It also provides a built-in way for instructors to "grade" discussion, which at times can be daunting.

Scored Discussions encourage students to engage with course content through dialogue. The activity can support free-flowing and richer discussions on course material. Students in the inner circle feel a greater sense of responsibility for contributing, which can encourage better preparation, reflection, and participation. If desired, the circles can switch places halfway through the activity to give students the opportunity (and responsibility) to occupy both roles.

Guiding Principles

Scored Discussions are based upon the benefits of collaborative learning and provide a bit of extra incentive as individuals in the inner circle know those in the outer circle are scoring their discussion. Students talk with each other and observe conversations between students, which leads to improved student learning (Golub, 1988). The engagement between students encourages their critical thinking and communication development. By allowing students to discuss with one another in a free-flowing environment, the Scored Discussion activity fosters collaborative learning.

Preparation

First, identify a set of questions or topics for the inner circle to discuss. Construct a brief scorecard for use by the outer circle. This card may include a few notes as to what "scores" points during the discussion. Prepare a list of talking points for the conclusion of the exercise. This preparation will be helpful for ensuring that major issues not raised during the Scored Discussion activity are at least addressed.

A traditional classroom arrangement in rows hinders participation in discussion. The attention in the room is focused on the front of the room and the instructor, as that is where the chairs are all oriented. Students have a difficult time engaging with one another as a result of the classroom setting. Arranging seats into circles with students facing each other leads to improved participation (Steinzor, 1950).

Process

- Outline briefly the expectations of the activity, including the amount of time to be spent on the discussion and also what students in both roles should do. Moreover, provide instructions related to how students should submit scores when the exercise concludes.
- Pose a topic or set of questions for students in the inner circle to address. Encourage students to support their ideas and not interrupt others.
- Give students in the outer discussion the role as observers and scorekeepers. This role includes tallying strong points from each side and evaluating how the discussion went.
- Ask the inner group to begin the discussion, and let it run without moderation.
- Wait the predetermined amount of time and then have groups switch roles or end the activity.

Sample IDEA Pairings

Formal Argument (IDEA #17). One group of students participates in the Formal Argument while others observe the activity, making notes and scoring the discussion.

Role Play (IDEA #44). The inner group conducts the Role Play with the outer circle observing and scoring.

Journaling (IDEA #68). Both inside and outside groups can reflect and write about their experiences related to the topic discussed during the Scored Discussion IDEA.

Pro-tips

This activity is most effective when students remain engaged. Variations can allow for students to change roles. Some instructors use set times to alternate roles; others prefer to let outer circle students tap inner circle students on the shoulder to switch places.

Students in the outer ring can become bored if their task and role is not sufficiently challenging. In addition to switching roles to maintain engagement, ensure that the outer group has defined tasks and roles to follow. This might include not only giving points but also looking for themes and content as well as examining the inner group dynamic. Monitor the outer group too.

One additional adaptation is for you to serve as the "bull's eye" for the activity. You sit in the very center of the circles and engage the inner circle in a dialogue while the outer circle scores the questions and responses of those in the inner circle.

Scored Discussion works best with sufficient space and moveable seating. Arranging chairs into concentric circles with sufficient space will help the dynamic and allow easier movement between the two circles.

IDEA #15: Think-Pair-Share

Overview

This IDEA is one of the easiest methods for having student pairs talk with one another about a class topic and then share their talking points during a full-class discussion. As the name suggests, the Think-Pair-Share IDEA provides students with a brief opportunity to think about an issue, discuss with a paired partner, and then share thoughts with the class. The activity is designed to encourage class participation and interaction with classmates. In addition, the IDEA can be useful for gauging student comprehension of class concepts.

Think-Pair-Share requires students to develop an understanding of course content, draw conclusions, and critically consider the views of others. The activity can be used for a variety of purposes, including review of key concepts and ideas, brainstorming new conclusions, peer teaching, or exam preparation. One of the biggest draws of the Think-Pair-Share is that it encourages engagement in classes of essentially any size and can accomplish this task quickly. The activity can be done in a small or large class in only a few minutes.

Guiding Principles

Think-Pair-Share takes advantage of the benefits of cooperative learning to improve student outcomes through direct peer engagement. Peer learning emphasizes students working together to achieve shared learning goals (Cortright, Collins, & DiCarlo, 2005; Lyman, 1992). By having students work together, they are able to help each other, thus maximizing the learning for both the individual and the pair (Dutt, 1997).

In discussions, students can often respond impulsively without considering their thoughts. Additionally, students process information in different ways that can result in unequal levels of participation. Think-Pair-Share requires students to wait, which can lead to better and more thoughtful responses (Rowe, 1986). By ensuring that students pause and think, the instructor can better manage students' reflection and encourage better responses to questions.

Preparation

Before beginning the Think-Pair-Share activity, consider the primary purpose of the activity. You may want students to work on key concepts from class that day or tackle a challenging part of the textbook. Identifying this goal will enable you to develop a question to guide each Think-Pair-Share session. Guiding questions should ideally encourage students to synthesize course content as well as their own opinions.

Process

- Pose a question for the students to consider. Have the students pause for one to two minutes (depending on the complexity of the questions asked or prompt provided) to consider their answers individually.
- Ask students to pair up (or if the number of students is uneven, form groups of three) and discuss their ideas and opinions (three minutes).
- As an entire class, ask some or all of the groups (depending on the size of the class) to share their discussion insights (three minutes).

Sample IDEA Pairings

Pause Procedure (IDEA #2). Use the Think-Pair-Share IDEA as an activity during the structured pauses.

Note-Taking Pairs (IDEA #25). Allow students to use their notes as part of their Think-Pair-Share discussions.

Venn Diagrams (IDEA #78). The Think portion of the exercise can be extended to allow time for the students to prepare a Venn Diagram. Students then can pair up and share their graphics with each other while discussing their conclusions. Pairs can then share with the class as usual.

Pro-tips

This activity is most effective when students can explain their ideas and opinions to their partners. Discussion questions that elicit a range of opinions and views provide more material for pair discussions than questions with clear, black-and-white answers.

During the activity, monitor and encourage student conversations by walking around the classroom. Listen to make sure students are engaging with the material and for key ideas emerging across multiple groups. These commons ideas can provide useful information during the debriefing of the activity.

When starting the full-class discussion as the third phase of this IDEA, consider asking for one or two volunteer groups and then call on other groups. This approach allows the more self-confident groups to contribute first and give cues to less confident groups of the types of responses you expect.

IDEA #16: In the News

Overview

It has long been known that students are more likely to learn and to retain information for which they see practical use and relevance (Dewey, 1938). The In the News IDEA can be used in a variety of different formats and course subjects to illustrate to students that concepts learned in class are directly relevant to societal issues. Students may bring in news stories of their choice to discuss, or the instructor may select a "hot topic" for the class. The core concept is to cold-call on students to describe their news story or share thoughts about a current event to encourage class discussion and application of course content to contemporary contexts. In the News is particularly engaging when controversial situations are brought to class that provide fodder for discussion.

Discussion of current events fosters critical thinking and analytic skills. Students enter class with a variety of social, political, and religious perspectives. Encouraging productive discussion on contemporary events can help students consider their own opinions as well as differing views held by their classmates (Borg & Borg, 2001).

Guiding Principles

As part of their college education, students undergo intellectual development that helps them think critically and develop their own perspectives of the world (Belenky, Clinchy, Goldberger, & Tarule, 1986; Perry, 1970). In order to encourage students to develop more complex thinking, instructors should appropriately challenge students. Students may not initially be ready to engage in thinking that questions their initial assumptions. However, In the News can be used as a vehicle to create a class structure and environment that challenges and supports students through the intellectual growth process.

In today's information- and media-rich environment, students receive news and information from a variety of sources. Many of these sources include a range of editorial comment and direction. Conrad and Dunek (2012) suggest that students need the ability to challenge these sources and trust their own analytic ability to achieve success in such an environment. In their view, the goal of higher education is to create inquiry-driven learners who cultivate the learning process rather than gaining a specific body of knowledge. In the News provides a way to guide students in this process by helping to identify bias, evaluate claims, and draw conclusions for themselves.

Preparation

Prior to using In the News, consider the potential controversy of the topic to be discussed. Determining a set of ground rules is helpful to maintaining an appropriate classroom environment for any discussion-based activity. It is also helpful to come up with a plan for leading the discussion. When students have brought in a relevant news story, you can cold-call on individual students to describe their stories. Also consider plans for how to encourage reticent students to participate and identify questions that emphasize a particular view rather than an individual. Using phrases such as "critics suggest" or "proponents argue" can reduce comments directed toward individuals. It is also helpful to decide before class if your own personal opinions will be shared or withheld during or following the discussion. Depending on the course or topic to be discussed and your overall goals of the activity, determine ahead of time whether students will bring in news stories of their own choosing or you will select the topic.

Process

- Prepare readings on a current event prior to class or have students bring in news stories.
- If the topic is controversial, discuss ground rules for establishing a supportive environment for discussion prior to the discussion commencing.
- Cold-call on students to discuss their news stories or the day's current event. You may facilitate the discussion or allow students to engage directly with each other.
- To conclude the discussion, summarize the relevant viewpoints and encourage students to consider the views of the news source.

Sample IDEA Pairings

Snowball (IDEA #12). Students gather in progressively larger groups, discussing the major ideas and implications of their respective news stories.

Timeline (IDEA #81). Students create a Timeline that illustrates the major events, people, and themes related to their news story. This activity ensures preparation in advance of the class discussion.

Post Hoc Analysis (IDEA #100). After the In the News discussion, students reflect on their news stories by looking for larger patterns and trends that may not have been evident prior to the class discussion.

Pro-tips

When discussing current events, some students may be eager to share their views and process the issues quickly. Other students may prefer not to participate. To encourage equal participation, set up ground rules or a structure that helps enable everyone to engage in the discussion.

Through verbal and physical cues, you can help keep a discussion of a controversial current event from getting out of hand. By moving around the class or providing supportive comments, you can facilitate the discussion and maintain a positive classroom climate.

Particularly if a significant majority of the class feel similarly about an issue, you may wish to play the role of devil's advocate. By supporting the weaker side or even the weaker argument, you illustrate how to support an argument and expose weaknesses in the other side (Payne & Gainey, 2000).

IDEA #17: Formal Argument

Overview

Arguing from a logical position in order to learn dates back to Protagoras in Athens over 2,000 years ago. The Formal Argument activity has students hear various views prior to coming to a judgment. This IDEA can vary from two individuals to multiple groups formally arguing about an issue. Students benefit from participation in Formal Arguments by developing critical thinking and oral communication skills (Kennedy, 2007). This activity also helps students consider various views related to course content and can be used in a variety of classroom settings. Finally, it helps teach a student that disagreement and discussion related to an issue can lead to positive outcomes.

Formal Arguments require students to understand their own views as well as those of others. This activity can help challenge preconceived notions and encourage students to engage dynamically with course content. Formal Arguments also can be helpful for demonstrating comprehension and opinions related to key course concepts and ideas.

Guiding Principles

Formal Argument is a useful activity for encouraging active learning (Bonwell & Eison, 1991). The activity requires students to analyze, discuss, and apply course content in meaningful and active ways. Active learning encompasses a variety of strategies that all have the goal of encouraging students to do something and think about what they are doing. In-class formal argument utilizes active learning by making students responsible for engaging and understanding course content (Snider & Schnurer, 2002).

As with many forms of discussion, Formal Argument requires the development of oral communication skills. Students not only must figure out what they want to say but also think about how they want to effectively communicate their ideas. Students often cite the improvement of oral communication as one of the biggest benefits of the use of Formal Arguments (Kennedy, 2007).

Preparation

Prior to the use of a Formal Argument, it is helpful to give consideration about the issue to be addressed. Often arguments present only two views (e.g., pro and con), but many complex issues have multiple sides that can be explored.

Formal Arguments can vary dramatically in length and structure depending on the time available, the physical space in the classroom, and the complexity of issue to be explored. For example, consider whether students will speak from behind a podium or argue their position in the center of the room.

Finally, consider ahead of time how you will evaluate the students' performance. Some faculty use a pass/fail grading scale to decrease the anxiety of students. Others prefer to use a rubric to evaluate aspects of the Formal Arguments performance from delivery to analysis. If you are uncertain about how to grade such an activity, it might be helpful to seek out assistance from a colleague who uses this approach regularly (e.g., philosophy, law, business ethics).

Process

- Tell students the format of the formal argument (e.g. conversation pairs or quads or formal debate groups).
- Announce the time frame and the prompt; ask students to discuss their opinions until the time ends.
- Following the activity, discuss the major points of the arguments as well as their respective strengths and weaknesses. It is also helpful to review the value of using this approach with respect to the learning process, particularly for critical thinking and oral communication.

Sample IDEA Pairings

Scored Discussion (IDEA #14). Two small groups of students debate each other while remaining students watch and score the positive points raised by each debate team.

Role Play (IDEA #44). Students argue as different personas. For example, students can assume the role of historical figures and debate major issues in history.

Yesterday's News (IDEA #73). Students write a memo to a real or fictional student who missed the Formal Argument. The memo highlights and evaluates the arguments presented.

Pro-tips

This activity is most effective when everyone participates. Develop an approach that encourages everyone to speak and does not let any one person dominate the debate. For example, consider argument rules that indicate that a student can only speak a second time after everyone has spoken. Some faculty prefer a strategy where students receive three cards and a student has to turn one in every time they speak. Only once all cards are used can those without cards speak again. The key is to not let some students dominate and provide an environment where soft-spoken students or those who take longer to process can still participate.

Budesheim and Lundquist (2000) found that students who are forced to argue for a position opposite their own are more likely to change their position. Consider having students argue the opposite viewpoint to their own. Some faculty do not announce which position a group is taking until just before the argument and may flip a coin to determine positions.

Another possible adaptation is to have a point in the argument where students (or groups) are told to take a short break and then come back and argue the opposite side. This approach allows students to recognize positions made by the opposing team and then argue the position from a different point of view, all within the same debate.

IDEA #18: Circle of Voices

Overview

The Circle of Voices IDEA encourages students to participate and engage with one another as they work in groups of four to six to address a given challenge. In this activity, pose a question with multiple answers or interpretations. Within each group, students share their answers or insight into the question. Circle of Voices encourages equal participation and allows every student to express an idea. It has a built-in aspect of elaboration of ideas, which can provide a powerful learning experience that involves building on something that is known by investigating an idea or concept from multiple perspectives.

Circle of Voices discussions are useful for encouraging students to brainstorm collaboratively around a course concept or process (Brown & Paulus, 2002). Generating ideas for additional consideration and discussion at a later time is difficult as individuals often begin to critique options as soon as they are recorded. This instance is problematic because many potential ideas are never considered. The

Circle of Voices IDEA encourages groups to identify multiple perspectives prior to discussion. The activity is designed to elicit as many answers or ideas as possible. In addition to fostering participation, this activity encourages students to refer to course materials to generate additional answers.

Guiding Principles

The Circle of Voices IDEA provides a structure for cooperative learning and provides a vehicle for all students to participate and interact with one another (Kagan, 1994). By providing structure to the interactions, the IDEA facilitates the opportunity for students to join in course discussions and actively participate in the class in a meaningful way.

One of the principles of a democratic society is the process of discussion. Circle of Voices is a significant tradition within Native American and Aboriginal cultures because each person's views are important and should be considered in conversations and dialogue (Brookfield & Preskill, 2005). One of the strengths of this IDEA is that it encourages equity of participation. By allowing each person a turn to share their ideas, the activity helps ensure that both talkative and quiet students engage equally.

Preparation

Begin preparation by identifying a question or set of questions to seed the group discussions. Next, consider the benefits and challenges of assigning readings around the discussion topic prior to class. These readings may be comprised of required textbook chapters, journal articles secured for this activity, or even popular press information identified by the students. Having prior readings provides perspectives that help provide useful material for group discussions.

Process

- Explain the amount of time to be devoted to the Circle of Voices idea generation, specify how the group will record responses, and note whether you will collect Circle of Voices responses or only a summary of the final group considerations.
- Have the students form groups of ideally four to six people.
- Pose the concept or question for the groups to consider.
- Going around the circle, each member of the group provides their answer to the question.
- Students can go around the circle multiple times considering the original question, or you can pose an addition prompt after a set time period.
- At the conclusion, have a spokesperson from the group report on the answers generated by the group.

Sample IDEA Pairings

Scored Discussion (IDEA #14). An inner circle participates in the Circle of Voices discussion while an outer group observes and scores the points raised.

Role Play (IDEA #44). Students respond to the instructor's question based on assigned roles. The use of readings before class can provide background for students to respond in role as part of the Circle of Voices discussion.

Cause & Effect Chain (IDEA #85). The Circle of Voices groups develop ideas, relationships, and effects to cooperatively generate the Cause & Effect Chain organizer.

Pro-tips

start with enough questions for each person in the group to have one

A Variation of Circle of Voices is the Round Table. This variation works similarly to Circle of Voices except that students write down their answer, which is then passed around to the other students.

One of the challenges of using the Circle of Voices approach is to make certain that all students participate. You may decide to allow a student one "pass" in a round, but encourage students that what some consider to be the "wrong" answer is simply another way to look at the issue.

Another variation of this strategy is the Town Hall. The purpose of a Town Hall is to offer the opportunity for students to express different perspectives. Rather than simply working in groups, town halls may include the entire class as students take turns sharing their ideas and views. A structure that encourages equal participation should be put into place to avoid having a few students dominate the discussion.

IDEA #19: Can We Have Class Outside?

Overview

When the weather is nice and there is a good place to gather as a class, holding class outside periodically can be beneficial to learning. The change in the environment can modify the class environment, encourage more interaction between the class and instructor, and make it easier for students to remember the discussion from that class session.

This activity requires little to no additional preparation as standard discussion strategies can happen in the same format, simply in a different place. For example, checking the forecast may allow a few days to prepare a discussion in a philosophy class whereby the instructor walks slowly through the campus discussing critical ideas or an instructor might sit outside with physics students and have students present examples of the processes being discussed. In addition to using outside experiences to augment course discussions, the Can We Have Class Outside? IDEA can help change the class dynamics with benefits that extend after the outside class session. Moreover, having class outside can be fun for both the students and instructor.

Guiding Principles

The Can We Have Class Outside? IDEA presents an excellent opportunity to build a stronger student cohort and class learning community. Students who feel supported by an instructor's responsiveness and concern for their preferences develop better relationships and demonstrate better outcomes (Seed, 2008). Fundamentally, the fun and change of pace of Can We Have Class Outside? assists in developing relationships and a learning community among students.

Having class outside spurs learning by creating a more informal learning environment. Simply moving the students outside of the classroom environment can reach students in different ways (Melber & Abraham, 1999). By leaving the confines of the classroom, the barriers to engaging in discussions are lowered between the instructor and the students. In addition, being outdoors and participating in a more informal class provides an opportunity for students to learn without the high levels of stress that college students often feel.

Finally, being outside allows for different information to be learned as context influences which memories are recalled. When we are in a novel context, we tend to draw on existing memories frequently and are more likely to create new episodic memories (Hupbach, Hardt, Gomez, & Nadel, 2008). Essentially, being in a new environment, outside the classroom, can have an impact on how one thinks and remembers what is discussed.

Preparation

Prior to taking your class outside, there are a couple of factors to consider. First, give some prior thought to the location. Depending on the temperature, you may want to find a spot in the sun to stay warm or in the shade of a tree to stay cool. Also, you will want to think about where the students will sit, particularly after a rain if the area is muddy. You may select a spot near a bench so a few students do not have to sit on the ground. Pay specific attention to sitting if any of the students have physical limitations, including recent injuries that affect mobility. Finally, consider what you have planned for class and if it can be suitably completed outdoors. For example, a class session with heavy technology requirements may be less ideal than a session focused on discussing assigned readings.

The most important preparation is to visit the space in which you intend to take your class. Ideally, go to the area at a similar time of day as when your class will meet to see if the area is loud or distracting. Finally, determine how you will "reserve" the space or ensure that when your class arrives it is available. It will be disruptive if you arrive only to find a group of students sitting in the area having discussions or even another class in "your" spot.

Process

- Just prior to class, have two students go to the area where you intend to hold class. One can "hold" the spot while the other returns to confirm it is available. The point is to ensure the space is available before proceeding with your entire class.

* Walk to the spot and hold the class session.

Sample IDEA Pairings

Socratic Seminar (IDEA #7). Present material, have students respond to the information presented, and then proceed to discuss material in a way that prompts deeper thinking.

What Counts as Fact? (IDEA #54). Ask students to write or discuss the different facts from two or more articles. The informal outdoor setting can relax students and allow successful analysis of the competing types of evidence.

Journaling (IDEA #68). The Journaling IDEA provides a helpful structure for students to use for writing and reflecting about their own experiences and class material while appreciating nature.

Pro-tips

Although nearly any teaching approach can work outside, you want to consider noise factor from passersby, the wind, or traffic. Group discussions work particularly well as it is easier to converse in a small group than as a whole class.

In addition to noise, remember that students lose focus in class after a few minutes, and they may have even greater difficulty paying attention outside. This added distraction can be particularly challenging for students with attention disabilities. If you have students registered with your Office of Disability Services, you will want to check with them to ensure that the activity is appropriate. Even for students who have normal levels of attention, the additional distractions of being outside can be challenging. Consider switching up the number and type of activities that you use in class. In addition to our suggested pairings above, any peer teaching or small group discussion IDEAs can be useful.

Students typically like going outside. Allow them to have an asynchronous chat or leave five minutes at the end of a class for students to create a solid rationale for why the class should be held outside. They may well come up with good reasons that you had not considered.

IDEA #20: Seeded Discussion

Overview

Seeded Discussion is an activity that provides students a structured format for discussion. The activity is centered on the provision of a set of questions students answer as a guide to a class discussion. Formal questions allow for an organized dialogue that ensures key topics are covered during conversations. Additionally, this activity allows for easy assessment of student progress toward course learning outcomes.

Fundamentally, this activity serves to prime students for discussing a class topic. It is helpful in aiding student discussions centered on complex readings or difficult theoretical content covered in lectures, as well as comparing and contrasting topics across the course material and throughout the curriculum.

Guiding Principles

Rooted in answering relevant questions regarding course content, Seeded Discussion is an effective activity to gauge student learning (Nilson, 2010). When questions are designed around learning outcomes, students are provided the opportunity to demonstrate attainment of the learning outcome, thus instructors are able to quickly measure student competency of a class concept.

As with many forms of discussion, Seeded Discussion requires students to actively engage with each other and course content. The active engagement of students during discussion with peers leads to an increased understanding of course material and thus results in improved performance (Smith et al., 2009). During a Seeded Discussion, students, particularly those who may be less secure in their knowledge of a course concept, are provided the opportunity to systematically learn the material through engagement with their peers as they discuss answers to the questions.

Preparation

Prior to the use of a Seeded Discussion, you need to give consideration to the goals and learning outcomes of the activity and develop questions accordingly. If the discussion will be centered around a class reading, you may want to provide the questions to students at the time of assigning the reading as an aid for identifying relevant material for the discussion. In this case, the questions would need to be prepared in advance. If a Seeded Discussion is going to be used as an opportunity to review and assess student knowledge from throughout the course or from a lecture or activity that day, you can develop the questions just prior to the start of the activity and thus reserve the right to adjust the focus of the discussion as needed in order to ensure the most effective learning opportunity for students.

Process

- The instructor develops a set of two or three questions to serve as seeds or prompts for class discussion and shares the questions with the students prior to class or alternately prior the start of the discussion.

- In small groups or as a whole class, students methodically discuss each question provided.
- At the conclusion of the activity, the instructor sums up the main points that surfaced during the dialogue and fills in possible pertinent information that was missed.

Sample IDEA Pairings

Think-Pair-Share (IDEA #15). This pairing helps ensure that all students participate. Students take a moment to formulate their answers to the questions by themselves then discuss their initial answers with a partner prior to joining in a whole-class discussion.

Anticipation Guide (IDEA #50). By having students attempt to answer the questions presented about a reading prior to actually tackling the reading, the students are able to engage in a Seeded Discussion using the same questions after they gain the knowledge from the class reading.

Brainstorming (IDEA #62). Have students write down their initial thoughts about the questions in a short amount of time prior to starting the activity.

Pro-tips

As with most discussions, this activity is most effective when all students participate. It is important to not let certain students dominate the conversation and provide an environment where quieter students or those that need longer to process can still participate.

Certain questions may not perpetuate as much discussion as anticipated. You may want to consider having one or two back-up questions prepared in the event that the initially provided questions fail to spur effective student conversation.

Student discussion should stay focused on the initial goal of the activity. Listen closely to the exchange among students and be prepared to steer the conversation should it go off in a possibly irrelevant direction.

IDEA #21: Observation Team Discussion

Overview

Observation Team Discussion allows students to leave the classroom and observe an environment relevant to key course concepts before returning to discuss what they learned. The activity allows individual students to conduct a structured field observation where students gather primary research within a specific environment and then meet in small groups to discuss, much in the way of a research team meeting. This IDEA emphasizes discussions of social interactions and dynamics (Marshall & Rossman, 2010). Specifically, students discuss what they saw while observing people, events, or locations.

This IDEA helps students learn research skills that can benefit them throughout their educational experiences. In addition, discussions of the collected data and the research process assists students in learning how to work with and talk about research. It can prepare them for being a part of a research team. Observation Team Discussions are used in a variety of fields as a primary research method including the social sciences, natural sciences, and education. As a result, this activity may be considered for use across a wide spectrum of disciplines and classes. Students from those in their first semester to advanced doctoral students may complete the activity.

Guiding Principles

The growing body of literature supporting involving undergraduate students in research supports the use of Observation Team Discussion. Conducting research brings multiple benefits to students, including research skill enhancement, improved retention, and graduate school preparation (Craney et al., 2011). Observations allow students to work through the steps of the research process and provides valuable experience in conducting data collection.

In addition to observing others, the Observation Team Discussion activity allows for one to be a participant (Jorgensen, 1989) in which human interactions are viewed from the perspective of people who are part of a situation or environment. For example, students observing interactions in the campus recreation center are participants as students but also observers looking for meaning. The ability to analyze one's own situation and environment using an analytic perspective can help students critically examine their own lives and see how course material relates to everyday life. The ability to discuss their observations with others provides students with a mechanism for engaging in the social construction of knowledge.

Preparation

Prior to assigning Observation Team Discussion, identify the type of environment and interactions that the students will be observing. Determine whether the Observation Team Discussion is a participant or nonparticipant observation. When deciding what will be observed, it is possible to have the students observe based on class material already covered or in anticipation of a new topic.

In addition, you may want to create a template, set of questions, or coding rubric to help frame the activity for the students. Providing students with a few

TABLE 2.3 Observation Template

Name:
Topic of observation
Date of observation:
Location of observation:
Time of observation:

Action observed:	Comments:

points to make sure they observe can help serve as a useful guide to make sure students are identifying the most significant aspects to bring back to the subsequent class discussion. Involving students in this phase of preparation can increase student buy-in to the activity. Even a simple template such as the one in Table 2.3 above can be useful:

Process

- Describe the activity observation and the parameters for the activity (i.e., location, time frame, length of activity, notes to be taken).
- Ask students to meet in their teams to discuss the observation methods and to make plans for their observations.
- Outside of the classroom (either during regularly scheduled class period or in between sessions), students conduct their observations, mostly likely with individuals conducting their own observations for later group comparison; this aspect can be negotiated with student teams, however.
- After the observations, students return to class to summarize and discuss their findings in their groups. Through the discussion, students are able to relate common themes and draw connections across their results. One approach is to ask the students to discuss what surprised them about their observation. Surprises are often where we see the most thinking.

Sample IDEA Pairings

What If (IDEA #13). In addition to discussing their observed findings, students discuss the environment that they observed and what might change if a crucial condition were different.

Freewriting (IDEA #63). Following the observation, but prior to the discussion, students engage in Freewriting about what they saw, which can provide ideas to be raised in the discussion.

Post Hoc Analysis (IDEA #100). After completion of the observation and follow-up discussion, students reflect back about the experience of looking for patterns that were not apparent prior to observing.

Pro-tips

This IDEA presents an excellent venue to discuss the ethics of research. The activity of observing humans without their knowledge brings about questions about research choices, the use of data, and questions of consent may be addressed. Establishing sound ethical norms can prepare students to engage in appropriate research methods in the future.

Although you may wish to assign a specific location for the activity, students often benefit from having to make a choice about where to conduct their Observation Team Discussion. You can also ask students to evaluate and discuss the benefits of their location as an analytic point after the conclusion of the observation stage of the IDEA.

If you intend to provide students with a guide or rubric for conducting their Observation Team Discussion, or to ask them to create one, the format should be specific with respect to the types of points to be observed. However, the overall structure should be fairly loose, allowing students to raise interesting additional points they identify during the activity. By providing a few specific points, the students, who may have limited experience conducting observations, will be able to complete the activity, but they will still be required to think through additional elements that arise throughout the experience.

IDEA #22: Campus and Community Events

Overview

The primary purpose of the Campus and Community Events IDEA is to encourage students to attend events related to course content that can serve as material for classroom discussion. Learning is facilitated by making connections and application during the discussion of an attended event. The instructor's role is to tie together the course material and the activity, helping students draw connections between the two. This activity provides an easy avenue for students to engage in events, thereby providing context to classroom learning.

Campus and Community Events require students to engage outside the classroom by participating in events. For example, students in an interior design course might attend a gallery opening, or students in a humanities class might attend a lecture hosted by the library. The activity can be used to provide students with opportunities for real-world application, new experiences in which they may never have participated otherwise, and avenues to engage with other students through discussion of Campus and Community Events.

Guiding Principles

College campuses and the surrounding communities offer numerous opportunities for students to engage in meaningful extracurricular activities. This IDEA takes advantage of the resources available on and off campus to improve students' learning (Dardig, 2004). The use of this activity provides students with experiences that can then complement classroom discussions by leveraging community resources.

Numerous studies cite the benefits of student engagement through purposeful educational activities (Kuh, Cruce, Shoup, Kinzie, & Gonyea, 2008). Improved grades, retention, and persistence all are positively impacted by getting students more involved on campus. Not only does this IDEA provide useful information for class discussions, but it also offers these broader benefits to students.

Preparation

Before assigning students to participate in Campus and Community Events, consider the purpose of the activity and how it will tie into subsequent course discussions and objectives. It is unwise to simply give credit for students to engage in such activities. Also, you will want to think about transportation issues and offer alternatives where needed. For example, students may not all have automobiles or a safe way to get to a given venue. For such situations, it may be acceptable to research a topic and write a short paper as an alternative. Determine whether all students will attend the same events, select from a list of possible events, or be able to identify their own to attend. It is also a good idea for you to attend as many events as possible so you know what students have experienced and ways the events fit with course discussions.

Process

- Inform the class of the expectations for the activity, logistics, and purpose of the activity, and pose a question for the students to consider.
- Provide students with as much information about the event and transportation to the event as possible.
- Students attend events and may compile a brief written assignment by a set date.
- After the deadline, lead a discussion or other class activity that allows students to share their experience at the events and relate back to course content.

Sample IDEA Pairings

Seeded Discussion (IDEA #20). Primer questions based on Campus and Community Events are shared with the students ahead of time and discussed as part of class.

Yesterday's News (IDEA #73). Students write a memo describing the event they attended to another student (real or fictional) that missed the activity.

140-Character Memoir (IDEA #94). With this variation, students can live tweet or otherwise provide reactions, reflection, and learning during the Campus and Community Event.

Pro-tips

Check with the venue for which you decide to make a learning opportunity available for students to see if you can secure discounts on admission. Small venues, particularly those right on campus, may well be excited enough to have students to let them attend for free.

Depending on the nature and types of events that students will be attending, you may want to spend a few minutes in class or provide brief written advice to the students prior to the event. For example, if certain attire or etiquette is required, do not assume that everyone in class understands this expectation. In addition, if certain types of behavior are expected or prohibited, share this information as well. Ensuring students understand these norms will help set them up to successfully attend the event and maximize their learning.

It may be worthwhile to have small groups of students elect to attend given events and then facilitate the class discussion regarding their experience and how it augmented their learning of course content.

Finally, consider the possibility that some students will not be able to attend the event, particularly if it does not occur during class hours. Students may have unavoidable work, childcare, or other responsibilities that would prevent them from participating. If that is likely, consider whether the event is worth it. If it is, consider whether it might be recorded so that students who cannot attend will be able to access it.

IDEA #23: Journal Club

Overview

The Journal Club IDEA provides an opportunity for students to read scholarship related to the course content, critically analyze research, and apply findings to a specific context or practice through a discussion of the research. Frequently used in health-related disciplines of medicine and nursing, the Journal Club IDEA can be used in a variety of classroom settings and content areas.

A Journal Club can help students improve their knowledge and reading habits (Deenadayain, Grimmer-Somers, Prior, & Kumar, 2008). Within and outside of health disciplines, Journal Clubs offer students a chance to read, respond, and discuss current research. All students read an article or set of articles, one student is assigned to facilitate the discussion, and students critically discuss the research.

Guiding Principles

A Journal Club helps students learn to critically evaluate research. By reading research and discussing during class, students learn to analyze scholarship. The class conversation helps students learn to work through questions that arise while reading and to consider the perspectives of other students about the article under consideration.

Discussions of research allow students to engage in team learning (Cooper, Prescott, Cock, & Smith, 1990). Students dialogue with each other and think through the article and research problem together. With this approach, students increase their involvement with the course content and assist each other in developing an analysis of the research article.

Preparation

To prepare for the Journal Club activity, you need to determine how much influence students should have into the article(s) selected. You may want to identify specific articles or a general area or allow students to choose. Additionally, students will benefit by hearing from you prior to the start of the Journal Club about its purpose and how it will help develop their understanding and ability to apply research.

Process

- The instructor assigns a student to moderate the Journal Club discussion prior to class. The student or instructor identify an article or set of articles for students to read.
- Prior to class, the student moderator comes up with three to five questions about the article.
- The student moderator provides brief comments on his or her impressions of the research and facilitates a discussion among class. Alternatively, the instructor can play the role of moderator.

Sample IDEA Pairings

Microteaching (IDEA #32). Rather than simply facilitating the conversation, the assigned student develops and delivers content based on the article or articles.

Select a Sentence (IDEA #61). Prior to the Journal Club discussion, each student identifies a sentence that contains a significant concept to bring up for discussion.

Reader Response Paper (IDEA #67). Students write a Reader Response Paper on the article under discussion to provide information that can be used as part of the discussion.

Pro-tips

This IDEA works particularly well in professional fields and graduate education where students have a special responsibility to learn the scholarship of a field and apply this knowledge to a specific context.

While a Journal Club typically focus on research articles, depending on the course or students' ability, a Book Club can be completed in a similar fashion. Students read all or a portion of a book. The rest of the activity can be the same as with journals, although more time for discussion may be needed depending on the text selected.

Student moderators should understand that they do not have to have all of the answers. The moderator's role is to ask some initial questions and facilitate a discussion among the class. Students may benefit from a brief set of instructions to clarify their role in the Journal Club discussion.

IDEA #24: Case Study

Overview

Popularized by the Harvard Business School, the Case Study method may be taught using a variety of approaches but primarily relies upon real-life examples to teach students. Case Study teaching may simply be described as sharing stories that have an educational message at their heart (Herreid, 2007). For this IDEA, the instructor presents the case using discussion as an entire class or with small groups as the most common approach (Herreid, 2011).

Instructors using Case Study report that students develop better critical-thinking ability, the ability to apply knowledge, and an overall enriching of the teaching experience for students and instructors (Healy & McCutcheon, 2010; Yadav et al., 2007). One of the most valuable aspects of the Case Study activity is that students are encouraged to apply concepts as a framework to other contexts. As a result of this application, students must analyze the case example and then make a comparison to other circumstances while taking into account facts, context, and variables that might result in a similar or different experience.

Guiding Principles

The Case Study IDEA utilizes the value of experiential learning most notably articulated by Kolb (1984). Kolb's experiential learning model suggests that the use of concrete experience, reflective observation, abstract conceptualization, and active experimentation fosters student learning. Students engaging in these four areas generate knowledge. A Case Study provides an opportunity for students to use these aspects by using an example to allow students to solve problems, engage content, and critically analyze information (Kreber, 2001).

Through a Case Study, students can bridge the gap between theoretical concepts and real-world practices. In particular, students can use abstract models of how concepts should work and compare them to how problems exist in practice. A Case Study also allows an instructor to bring together various types of data to present to students. As students work through the details of the case, they are better able to sift through large amounts of information to apply the concepts learned in class.

Preparation

Prior to the use of the Case Study, decide what course concepts a case should address. After this decision, a case or cases should be identified. You may choose to write your own case, or you may seek out a case from books or other repositories of case studies. Each discipline will vary, but almost all have sources for case studies easily discoverable with a quick online search.

You next write discussion questions. Discussion questions/topics should focus on an analysis of the problem presented in the case. Additional questions should consider contextual factors such as key facts, major actors, and relevant course theories and concepts.

Process

- Distribute the case for students to read prior to class or allow time in class for students to read through the case.
- Present small groups with a set of questions, and ask them to work through them.
- Hold a full-class discussion in which you ask groups to report out their thoughts; probe them to deeper levels of thinking by asking questions about their responses.
- In the final part of the discussion, focus on generating alternative solutions. Encourage creativity and imagination in the design of solutions, as doing so motivates students to analyze and apply knowledge gained during the Case Study.

Sample IDEA Pairings

Panel Presentation (IDEA #33). Using the Case Study as a basis, students conduct Panel Presentations to describe the major aspects of the case to their classmates.

Role Play (IDEA #44). Students can be assigned roles that correspond to the major actors in the Case Study. Role Play requires students to analyze and make decisions as the actors, which in turn encourages students to analyze the case.

Timeline (IDEA #81). Students use a Timeline to describe the major events and actors in the Case Study. The combination encourages students to carefully consider the major elements within the case.

Pro-tips

Case Studies are most effective when students must weigh evidence and consider incomplete information. As a result, cases may include irrelevant or even missing data. As in the real world, decisions use the information available, and the messiness of context helps students operate in such an environment.

The structure and length of Case Studies may vary a great deal. Some may be a single paragraph; others may be 20 pages long with many appendices. Consider the goal for the case when deciding which to use. A small case will help students quickly discuss a decision point, but a longer, more involved case will allow students to make use of data. There is no one-size-fits-all approach for a Case Study, so consider your instructional aims when deciding what kind of case to use.

In addition to providing cases for students, consider having students, individually or in groups, write or discuss their own Case Studies. This version of the activity allows students to research and use their own creativity to design a case for discussion.

Finally, this activity may be cast as a Writing-to-Learn IDEA. That is, instead of serving as the basis of discussion, students can analyze the case individually and write their responses.

References

Axelrod, J., Bloom, B.S., Ginsburg, B.E., O'Meara, W., & Williams, J.C. (1949). *Teaching by discussion in the college program.* Chicago, IL: College of the University of Chicago.

Bean, J.C., & Peterson, D. (1988). Grading classroom participation. *New Directions for Teaching and Learning, 74,* 33–40.

Belenky, M.F., Clinchy, B.M., Goldberger, N.R., & Tarule, J.M. (1986). *Women's ways of knowing: The development of self, voice, and mind.* New York: Basic Books.

Boniecki, K.A., & Moore, S. (2003). Breaking the Silence: Using a token economy to reinforce classroom participation. *Teaching of Psychology, 30*(3), 224–227.

Bonwell, C.C., & Eison, J.A. (1991). *Active learning: Creating excitement in the classroom.* Washington, DC: George Washington University.

Borg, J.R., & Borg, M.O. (2001). Critical thinking in interdisciplinary economics courses. *College Teaching, 49*(1), 20–27.

Broadhurst, P.L. (1957). Emotionality and the Yerkes-Dodson Law. *Journal of Experimental Psychology, 54,* 345–352.

Brookfield, S.D., & Preskill, S. (2005). *Discussion as a way of teaching: Tools and techniques for democratic classrooms.* San Francisco, CA: Jossey-Bass.

Brown, V.R., & Paulus, P.B. (2002). Making group brainstorming more effective: Recommendations from an associative memory perspective. *Current Directions in Psychological Science, 11*(6), 208–212.

Budesheim, T.L., & Lundquist, A.R. (2000). Consider the opposite: Opening minds through in class debates on course-related controversies. In M.R. Hebl, C.L. Brewer, & L.T. Benjamin (Eds.), *Handbook for teaching introductory psychology. Vol. 2: Discussion exercises and group activities* (pp. 78–89). Mahwah, NJ: Lawrence Erlbaum Associates.

Cacioppo, J.T., Berntson, G.G., & Decety, J. (2010). Social neuroscience and its relationship to social psychology. *Social Cognition, 28*(6), 675–685.

Cashin, W. (2011). *Effective classroom discussions IDEA paper #49*. Manhattan: Kansas State University, Center for Faculty Evaluation and Development.

Christensen, R.C. (1991). The discussion teacher in action: Questioning, listening, and Response. In C.C. Roland, D.A. Garvin, & A. Sweet (Eds.), *Education for judgment* (pp. 15–34). Boston, MA: Harvard Business School.

Clarke, J.H. (1988). Designing discussions as group inquiry. *College Teaching, 36*(4), 140–143.

Conrad, C., & Dunek, L. (2012). *Cultivating inquiry-driven learners: A college education for the twenty-first century*. Baltimore, MD: Johns Hopkins University Press.

Cooper, J., Prescott, S., Cock, L., & Smith, L. (1990). *Cooperative learning and college instruction: Effective use of learning teams*. Dominguez Hills: California State University.

Cortright, R.N., Collins, H.L., & DiCarlo, S.E. (2005). Peer instruction enhanced meaningful learning: Ability to solve novel problems. *Advances in Physiology Education, 29*(2), 107–111.

Craney, C., McKay, T., Mazzeo, A., Morris, J., Prigodich, C., & de Groot, R. (2011). Cross-discipline perceptions of the undergraduate research experience. *Journal of Higher Education, 82*(1), 92–113.

Dallimore, E.J., Hertenstein, J.H., & Platt, M.B. (2006). Nonvoluntary class participation in graduate discussion courses: Effects of grading and cold calling. *Journal of Management Education, 30*(2), 354–377.

Dallimore, E.J., Hertenstein, J.H., & Platt, M.B. (2008). Using discussion pedagogy to enhance oral and written communication skills. *College Teaching, 56*(3), 163–172.

Dallimore, E.J., Hertenstein, J.H., & Platt, M.B. (2010). Class participation in accounting courses: Factors that affect student comfort and learning. *Issues in Accounting Education, 25*(4), 613–629.

Dallimore, E.J., Hertenstein, J.H., & Platt, M.B. (2013). Impact of cold-calling on student voluntary participation. *Journal of Management Education, 37*(3), 305–341.

Dancer, D., & Kamvounias, P. (2005). Student involvement in assessment: A project designed to assess class participation fairly and reliably. *Assessment & Evaluation in Higher Education, 30*, 445–454.

Dardig, J.C. (2004). Urban connections: A course linking college students to the community. *College Teaching, 52*(1), 25–30.

Davis, B.G. (2009). *Tools for teaching*. San Francisco, CA: Jossey-Bass.

Davis, J.R. (1976). *Teaching strategies for the college classroom*. Boulder, CO: Westview Press.

Deenadayain, Y., Grimmer-Somers, K., Prior, M., & Kumar, S. (2008). How to run an effective journal club. *Journal of Evaluation in Clinical Practice, 14*(5), 898–911.

Dewey, J. (1938). *Experience and education*. Toronto: Collier-MacMillan Canada.

Dutt, K.M. (1997). The quick fix: The fishbowl motivates students to participate. *College Teaching, 45*(4), 143.

Eble, K.E. (1976). *The craft of teaching*. San Francisco, CA: Jossey-Bass.

Egan, K. (2005). *An imaginative approach to teaching*. San Francisco, CA: Jossey-Bass.

Esfandiari, M., & Knight, P. (2013). Using pyramid discussions in the task-based classroom to extend student talking time. *World Journal of English Language, 3*(3), 20–26.

Fink, D. (2013). *Creating significant learning experiences: An integrated approach to designing courses*. San Francisco, CA: Jossey-Bass.

Frederick, P. (1994). Classroom discussion. In K.W. Prichard & R.M. Sawyer (Eds.), *Handbook of college teaching*. Westport, CT: Greenwood.

Freire, P. (1970). *Pedagogy of the oppressed*. New York: Seabury.

Gagne, R.M. (1984). Learning outcomes and their effects: Useful categories of human performance. *American Psychologist, 39*(4), 377–385.

Garside, C. (1996). Look who's talking: A comparison of lecture and group discussion teaching strategies in developing critical thinking skills. *Communication Education, 45*(3), 212–227.

Gerlach, J.M. (1994). Is this collaboration? In K. Bosworth & S.J. Hamilton (Eds.), *Collaborative learning: Underlying processes and effective techniques* (pp. 12–19). San Francisco, CA: Jossey-Bass.

Gibbons, P. (2006). *Bridging discourses in the ESL classroom: Students, teachers, and researchers.* London: Continuum.

Goldsmid, C., & Wilson, E.K. (1980). *Passing on sociology: The teaching of a discipline.* Belmont, CA: Wadsworth.

Golub, J. (Ed.). (1988). *Focus on collaborative learning.* Urbana, IL: National Council of Teachers of English.

Gurung, R. (2002). Sleeping students don't talk (or Learning: Enhancing active learning via class participation). In P. Price (Ed.), *Active learning in the classroom: Overview and methods.* New Orleans, LA: Symposium conducted at the 14th annual meeting of the American Psychology Society.

Healy, M., & McCutcheon, M. (2010). Teaching with case studies: An empirical investigation of accounting lecturers' experiences. *Accounting Education: An International Journal, 19*(6), 555–567.

Hedley, A.R. (1994). Interpersonal and interactional aspects of teaching. *Teaching Sociology, 18*(1), 32–38.

Hensley, L.G. (2002). Teaching group process and leadership: The two-way fishbowl model. *Journal for Specialists in Group Work, 27*(3), 273–286.

Herreid, C. (2007). *Start with a story: The case study method of teaching college science.* Arlington, VA: NSTA Press.

Herreid, C. (2011). Case study teaching. *New Directions for Teaching and Learning, 128*, 31–40.

Hollander, J. (2002). Learning to discuss: Strategies for improving the quality of class discussion. *Teaching Sociology, 30*(3), 317–327.

Hupbach, A., Hardt, O., Gomez, R., & Nadel, L. (2008). The dynamics of memory: Context-dependent updating. *Learning and Memory, 15*, 574–579.

Johnson, D.W., & Johnson, R.T. (1997). Academic controversy: Increase intellectual conflict and increase the quality of learning. In W.E. Campbell & K.A. Smith (Eds.), *New paradigms for college teaching.* Edina, MN: Interaction Book.

Jorgensen, D.L. (1989). *Participant observation: A methodology for human studies.* Newbury Park, CA: Sage.

Junco, R., Heiberger, G., & Loken, E. (2011). The effect of Twitter on college student engagement and grades. *Journal of Computer Assisted Learning, 27*(2), 119–132.

Kagan, S. (1994). *Cooperative learning.* San Juan Capistrano, CA: Kagan Cooperative Learning.

Karp, D.A., & Yoels, W.C. (1976). The college classroom: Some observations on the meanings of student participation. *Sociology and Social Research, 60*(4), 421–439.

Kember, D., & Gow, L. (1994). Orientations to teaching and their effect on the quality of student learning. *Journal of Higher Education, 65*(1), 58–74.

Kendall, B. (1994). Moment of silence. In E. Bender, M. Dunn, B. Kendall, C. Larson, & P. Wilkes (Eds.), *Quick hits: Successful strategies by award winning teachers.* Bloomington: Indiana University Press.

Kennedy, R. (2007). In-class debates: Fertile ground for active learning and the cultivation of critical thinking and oral communication skills. *International Journal of Teaching and Learning in Higher Education, 19*(2), 183–190.

Kloss, R.J. (1996). Writing things down vs. writing things up: Are research papers valid? *College Teaching, 44*(1), 3–7.

Kolb, D.A. (1984). *Experiential learning.* Englewood Cliffs, NJ: Prentice Hall.

Kreber, C. (2001). Learning experientially through case studies? A conceptual analysis. *Teaching in Higher Education, 6*(2), 217–228.

Kuh, G.D., Cruce, T.M., Shoup, R., Kinzie, J., & Gonyea, R.M. (2008). Unmasking the effects of student engagement on first-year college grades and persistence. *Journal of Higher Education, 79*(5), 540–563.

Kurfiss, J.G. (1988). Critical thinking: Theory, research, practice and possibilities. *ASHE-ERIC Higher Education Report* (Vol. 2). Washington, DC.

Lave, J., & Wenger, E. (1991). *Situated learning legitimate peripheral participation.* Cambridge: Cambridge University Press.

Lowman, J. (1995). *Mastering the techniques of teaching* (3rd ed.). San Francisco, CA: Jossey-Bass.

Lyman, F.T. (1992). Think-pair-share, Thinktrix, Thinklinks, and weird facts: An interactive system for cooperative learning. In N. Davidson & T. Worsham (Eds.), *Enhancing thinking through cooperative learning* (pp. 169–181). New York: Teachers College Press.

Marshall, C., & Rossman, G.B. (2010). *Designing qualitative research* (3rd ed.). Thousand Oaks, CA: Sage.

McCann, T.M., Johannessen, L.R., Kahn, E., & Flanagan, J.M. (2006). *Talking in class: Using discussion to enhance teaching and learning.* Urbana, IL: National Council of Teachers of English.

McGonigal, K. (2005). Teaching for transformation: From learning theory to teaching strategies. *Speaking of Teaching, 14*(2), 1–3.

Melber, L., & Abraham, L. (1999). Beyond the classroom: Linking with informal education. *Science Activities, 36*(1), 3–4.

Melvin, K.B. (1988). Rating class participation: The prof/peer method. *Teaching of Psychology, 15*, 137–139.

Morrison, G.R., Ross, S.M., Kemp, J. E., & Kalman, H. (2009). *Designing effective instruction* (6th ed.). Hoboken, NJ: Wiley.

Murphy, K.P., Wilkinson, I.A.G., Soter, A.O., Hennessey, M. N., & Alexander, J.F. (2009). Examining the effects of classroom discussion on students' comprehension of text: A meta-analysis. *Journal of Educational Psychology, 101*(3), 740–764.

Nilson, L.B. (2010). *Teaching at its best: A research-based resource for college instructors.* San Francisco, CA: Jossey-Bass.

Payne, B.K., & Gainey, R.R. (2000). Understanding and developing controversial issues in college courses. *Journal of Criminal Justice Education, 11*, 2.

Perry, W.G. (1970). *Intellectual and ethical development in the college years.* New York: Holt, Rinehart & Winston.

Pollock, P.H., Hamann, K., & Wilson, B.M. (2011). Learning through discussions: Comparing benefits of small-group and large class setting. *Journal of Political Science Education, 7*(1), 48–64.

Rowe, M.B. (1986). Wait time: Slowing down may be a way of speeding up! *Journal of Teacher Education, 31*(1), 43–50.

Saville, B.K., Lambert, T., & Robertson, S. (2011). Interteaching: Bringing behavioral education into the 21st century. *Psychological Record, 61*, 153–166.

Seed, A.H. (2008). Cohort building through experiential learning. *Journal of Experiential Learning, 31*(2), 209–224.

Smith, D.G. (1977). College classroom interactions and critical thinking. *Journal of Educational Psychology, 69*, 180–190.

Smith, M.K., Wood, W.B., Adams, W.K., Wieman, C., Knight, J.K., Guild, N., & Su, T.T. (2009). Why peer discussion improves student performance on in-class concept questions. *Science, 323*(1), 122–124.

Snider, A., & Schnurer, M. (2002). *Many sides: Debate across the curriculum.* New York: International Debate Education Association.

Steinzor, B. (1950). The spatial factor in face to face discussion groups. *Journal of Abnormal and Social Psychology, 45*(3), 552–555.

Svinicki, M., & McKeachie, W.J. (2013). *McKeachie's teaching tips: Strategies, research, and theory for college and university teachers* (14th ed.). Belmont, CA: Cengage Learning.

Vygotsky, L.S. (1978). *Mind in society: The development of higher psychological processes.* Cambridge, MA: Harvard University Press.

Writing Across the Curriculum Clearinghouse (WAC). (2014). Event analysis. Retrieved November 14, 2014, from http://wac.colostate.edu/intro/pop5q.cfm

Yadav, A., Lundeberg, M., DeSchryver, M., Dirkin, K., Schiller, N.A., Maier, K., & Herreid, C. (2007). Teaching science with case studies: A national survey of faculty perceptions of the benefits and challenges of using cases. *Journal of College Science Teaching, 37*(1), 34–38.

Young, J. (2007). Small group scored discussion: Beyond the fishbowl, or, everybody reads, everybody talks, everybody learns. *History Teacher, 40*(2), 177–181.

Zaremba, S.B., & Dunn, D.S. (2004). Assessing class participation through self-evaluation: Method and measure. *Teaching of Psychology, 31*, 191–193.

3

RECIPROCAL PEER TEACHING

Description

The term "peer teaching" is used numerous ways; for this reason, it is not particularly easy to define. For example, some scholars refer to peer teaching as an exchange between an expert tutor and a novice learner, often accompanying a paid or at least formalized position. They refer to "peer teaching," "peer tutoring," and "peer mentoring" in similar ways. Others describe a variation "peer learning" as learning that takes place amongst peers in a more reciprocal and democratic process without the differences in authority and control (Boud, 2001).

The term "peer learning" is another term that is relatively difficult to define. Researchers often describe "peer learning" as an overarching concept that covers cooperative learning and a host of other approaches such as "peer tutoring" and "peer editing" (Olsen, 2011). Other authors describe peer learning as a specific form of cooperative learning (Christudason, 2003; Topping, 2005). However, peer learning need not be necessarily as structured as cooperative learning, which requires that all students participate interdependently upon performing a shared task; instead, peer learning can be more akin to collaborative learning (Brazil, 2011).

In consideration of the various definitions of "peer learning" and "peer teaching" found in various publications, we have opted for the term "reciprocal peer teaching" for the approach that we describe in this chapter. We believe that this term best fits the variety of activities included in this section. Specifically, we use the term "reciprocal peer teaching" to indicate an approach in which one student teaches others, who then reciprocate in kind. The primary consideration is that students are intentionally teaching each other.

Thus, when participating in reciprocal peer teaching, students alternate between the roles of teachers and students. Reciprocal teaching does not require a specific group size or a single specific activity. The defining characteristic of this approach is that students learn from and with each other in fairly intentional ways. That said, there are several characteristics essential to our conception of reciprocal peer teaching:

- Reciprocal peer teaching requires peer interaction for the learning to occur (Rae & Baillie, 2005). That is, the communication must be among the learners rather than one-way communication from the instructor or a peer.
- Reciprocal peer teaching should be as beneficial for the teacher/tutor as it is for the learner in both phases of the process (Rae & Baillie, 2005). The teacher should learn both while teaching and while learning. The learner should learn both while being taught and in turn while doing the teaching. The process should involve interdependent or mutual learning (Boud, 2001).
- Peers are students who share a similar level of authority with each other. They do not have a formalized role as teacher or expert practitioner which means that students should share status as fellow learners and view each other as such. Peers should not hold any power over each other; they should be on equal footing as far as their positions and responsibilities relative to the class (Boud, 2002).
- Reciprocal peer teaching occurs within a given class or cohort (Boud, 2002). It requires students to learn and contribute to others' learning simultaneously or nearly so. It may occur in exchanges within small groups, through asynchronous online chats, or with students taking turns teaching the whole class.
- The process of learning is as important as the product itself. Roles may shift during the activities, and students support each other in different ways. Part of the activity is learning how to work with and learn from others, which is valuable to the students' future capacity to learn (Barkley, Major, & Cross, 2014).

Purposes of Reciprocal Peer Teaching

The main purpose of reciprocal peer teaching is to improve student learning. Many instructors know that one of the best ways to learn is to formulate our ideas with the intent to communicate them to others. In short, teachers often learn best through the process of teaching. The same holds true for students. Students learn more deeply through assimilating new information, organizing the new information in context with previously learning information, defining aspects to teach the information to others, planning activities for learners, and reflecting upon the process. By assuming shared responsibility for teaching the class, students deepen their understanding of course content. They have to learn the material particularly well in order to teach it to another; they typically recognize any errors in their knowledge, or learners point it out to them. In addition, students may improve a host of dispositions, such as confidence, respect, and empathy, and skills, such as leadership, communication, and teamwork. Reciprocal peer teaching also requires students to learn to think quickly and respond to questions from their peers. Finally, peer teaching helps students to understand the process and energy faculty must put into the teaching process on a daily basis.

Students also can learn a great deal from their peers when the latter are serving as the teachers. When a peer formulates information that students need and puts it into a language compatible to their own, they can understand it better. Given both the "teacher" and the "learner" in peer reciprocal teaching are at similar levels, it is often easier for them to better understand the level of content provided. As they are at a similar age, references and examples are also often better understood. In addition, as students interact on an equal level with each other, they may feel more comfortable and confident in their shared communication. The learner is not subordinate, and thus the interactions may create a more relaxed environment, which can improve learning (Falchikov, 2001). Keep in mind that although peer reciprocal teaching has many benefits, it is intended to be a supplement to the teaching done by faculty members, not a substitute (Boud, 2002).

Types of Reciprocal Peer Teaching

Several researchers have identified different types of peer teaching and peer learning (Goldschmid & Goldschmid, 1976; Griffiths, Houston, & Lazenbatt, 1995). We find the following types of peer instruction as the most compatible to what we mean by "reciprocal peer teaching."

- **Partner checks.** This type of reciprocal peer teaching is similar to a learning "buddy system." Partners, whether pairs or small groups, are responsible for helping each other on a range of tasks, including homework checks, filling in gaps in notes from class, and being in touch when one student is absent supply details of what happened in class.
- **Learning cells.** Learning cells involve students in the same course partnering to tutor each other. The tutoring is accomplished through activities such as developing practice questions and quizzing each other in order to study for a test. Students typically work in dyads, asking and answering questions in alternating order.
- **Work groups.** Students in work groups may engage cooperatively or collaboratively in order to complete an assignment or project. A work group might form for the purpose of proposing a new hypothetical business for a business course, writing a paper for a history course, or designing a Web site for a course in social work.

- **Class-wide teaching**—In this type of reciprocal peer teaching, students take turns teaching the entire class a topic or unit. One or two students serve in the role of "teacher" for a specified unit of content, and the remaining students serve as learners. The students exchange roles, with each student taking a turn as the teacher and all students serving as learners at one point or another.
- **Peer assessment and peer editing**—In this form of reciprocal peer teaching, students evaluate each other's performance, whether as members of the group or in their performance as individuals. Thus, they participate in the "evaluation" component of the teaching role. Common forms of this type includes peer editing papers before the paper is turned in to the instructor or assigning a grade to peers in a group project based on extent of contribution.

An important note is that scholars often classify "discussion groups" as a form of reciprocal peer teaching. We placed "discussion groups" in Chapter 2, in large part because we believe that the teaching and learning roles in such groups are not as clearly defined as in other forms of reciprocal peer teaching.

Organization of Reciprocal Peer Teaching

This method may be carried out in many different ways, and there is no one specific process. The primary objective is to make sure that students take on both the role of teacher and of learner at some point in the process.

Prepare: This phase requires specified content or an identified skill of some kind. The student prepares by considering the requisite information or procedural skill and determining what he or she knows, needs to know, and needs to do. Preparation also involves spending time determining the level at which the new information or skill will be taught and how to communicate knowledge to peers.

Share: The share phase requires the student to communicate his or her understanding to the other students. This sharing may be formal or informal; it may happen in a linear fashion with students taking turns, or it may happen in a simultaneous sharing session. Students must occupy the role of sharing prepared information with peers.

Synthesize: This phase requires students to listen to peer learners, to acknowledge correct responses, to correct any errors, and to add the information they bring to their knowledge bases. The phase may also provide an opportunity for processing information and newly acquitted skills.

Reciprocate: The reciprocate phase requires students who have been teachers to become the learners and vice versa. As a result, each student participates in the activity in reciprocal fashion, both teaching and learning.

Reflect: Upon completion of the learning episode for both teaching and learning, students reflect on both the learning gains made and the process employed. Ideally, students will not only learn but also learn about the learning process.

Advantages and Challenges of Reciprocal Peer Teaching for Instructors

The advantage to the instructor of this method is that there are times when the size of the class makes it impossible to interact with students in small groups or individuals directly, although we know that doing so can improve student learning. This problem is what has been referred to as Bloom's 2 sigma problem. Bloom reported that the average student tutored one-to-one using a mastery learning approach outperformed students who learned in a conventional approach by two standard deviations (Bloom, 1984). He found that "the average tutored student was above 98% of the students in the control class" (p. 4). Bloom challenged teachers and researchers to find methods of replicating this tutoring effect, which is too expensive to carry out extensively in higher education.

Reciprocal peer teaching provides instructors with a way to attempt to bridge the gaps. Rather than direct contact, the instructor creates situations in which others occupy the teaching role by proxy. Typically, peers can provide each other with more interaction than they might get from an individual instructor, and thus the ratio of teachers to students can decrease (i.e., instead of the teacher communicating information to 100 students, 20 peers can communicate information to 5 learners each). The idea is that the instructor can reach students more efficiently and effectively.

Another advantage is one of resolving disconnect with students. Often, due to both age and knowledge-level differences, it can be difficult to know at what level to teach the material or the examples to use when teaching. This allows instructors the check the level of their own teaching and to amass examples that might be used in other classes.

The primary challenge of this approach is that doing it well requires a great amount of preparation on the front end. The instructor must spend considerable time selecting the activity *and* introducing the concept of reciprocal peer tutoring and its purpose to the students. The approach cannot be introduced in an ad hoc way. If it is, students may be confused about what they are supposed to do and how they are expected to learn (Boud, 2002).

Another challenge is that students range in their knowledge as well as in their capacity for teaching. Put simply, some students are simply more able instructors than others. But, as we discuss in the next section, both the teacher and the learners benefit from the activity. The challenge is helping the more advanced or better-prepared students learn as much as they can.

The final challenge is that students can get frustrated with the concept of their peers teaching them when they expect to be "taught" by a faculty member.

Explaining to students the value of teaching a topic as a mechanism for learning is challenging but important.

What Research Tells Us About the General Effectiveness of Reciprocal Peer Teaching

Research on small-group learning, particularly cooperative learning (of which we consider reciprocal peer teaching a part) (Barkley et al., 2014), has been going on for decades, and the findings are overwhelmingly positive. Cooperative learning demonstrates student gains in key areas of learning, from knowledge development to higher-order thinking skills, such as critical thinking and problem solving, to affective skills, such as team skills and self-confidence. In a recent meta-analysis, founders of the cooperative learning method, Johnson, Johnson, and Smith (2014), examined over 305 studies on the effectiveness of cooperative learning. The researchers found that cooperative learning improved academic success, especially when compared to individualist and competitive learning. They also found that the quality of relationships improved; cooperative learning promoted greater liking amongst classmates. Cooperative learning promoted psychological adjustment; specifically, self-esteem was improved in cooperative classrooms. Finally, they found that cooperative learning improved positive attitudes toward their university experiences.

Reciprocal peer teaching as a specific form of cooperative learning has been investigated as well. For example, Youdas et al. (2007) conducted a study of physical therapy students that showed that students who participated in reciprocal peer tutoring rated the method highly with respect to improving their learning, and they also had significantly increased student grades on anatomy examinations when compared to students who did not experience the peer tutoring activities. There are several studies that indicate that a specific reciprocal teaching activity, the Jigsaw (IDEA #31), improves student learning as well. These learning gains have been documented in electrochemistry (Doymis, Karacop, & Simsek, 2010; Karacop & Doymus, 2013) and language teaching (Maden, 2010).

Research on student opinions of the approach have also documented the benefits of reciprocal peer teaching to their learning. Several studies have investigated the use of reciprocal peer teaching in science courses, particularly those with a laboratory component. In an anatomy course, for example, Krych et al. (2005) assessed student attitudes after the course using a debriefing questionnaire. Students believed that reciprocal peer teaching increased their understanding when they held the learner role as much as it did when they held the teaching role. Similarly, Waghmare et al. (2010) found from a debriefing questionnaire that students believed that the reciprocal peer teaching improved their learning, both in understanding of information and retention of information. Students also agreed that the activities improved their communication skills. Bentley and Hill (2009) found no significant difference between objective performance and laboratory performance. However, they did find that students perceived that the reciprocal peer teaching improved their learning. In a study examining 66 first-year medical students who participated in reciprocal peer teaching, researchers found that students believed that they acquired greater knowledge of topics they personally taught and as much knowledge when taught by peers, as compared to being taught by professors. They felt their own teaching and their peers' teaching was as good as or better than that of the professors. Students also felt that they would be better able to communicate with patients because of the reciprocal peer teaching experience (Hendelman & Boss, 1986). In an electrotechnical laboratory course, researchers found that students (N=181) believed that reciprocal peer teaching improved their learning in a laboratory setting (Munoz-Garcia, Moreda, Hernandez-Sanchez, & Valino, 2013).

Researchers in other fields have also found positive results with reciprocal peer teaching. For example, learners in an introductory Chinese language class took turns teaching the whole class. Researchers who investigated the outcomes of this instructional intervention found that the activity helped students improve their individual responsibility and motivation for learning. The activity also improved solidarity among class members (Liu & Devitt, 2015). Research from other fields have shown similar positive responses from students. A study that took place in an engineering course, for example, also demonstrated that attitudes were good; in particular, they improved with increased exposure to the method (Maceiras, Cancela, Urrejola, & Sanchez, 2011).

What Research Tells Us About How to Improve Student Learning in Reciprocal Peer Teaching Activities and Classes

There is abundant research suggesting that students believe that reciprocal peer teaching improves learning and some evidence that it actually does improve learning. There is also evidence about what specific aspects of the approach improve student learning.

Finding #1. Appropriate Preparation for the "Teaching Phase" Improves Learning

One question about this approach is whether it can be done in the moment. The short answer is that it can. However, adequate preparation time is even more beneficial. Research documents that having sufficient time to both learn the material and then determine a way to teach it to others improves both interest in the activity and the ultimate performance of the group. For example, Benware and Deci (1984) compared a group who studied a topic to teach it to others to a group who studied only in preparation for an exam. The authors discovered that students who studied for the purpose of teaching peers had higher conceptual learning scores.

They were also more intrinsically motivated, and they perceived themselves to be more actively engaged in the course than students who studied for the purpose of recall information for an examination. In addition, students found the experience to be more interesting.

In an early but fairly extensive study, Fantuzzo, Dimeff, and Fox (1989) assessed reciprocal peer teaching in a human development class. The researchers measured cognitive gains and also social and evaluation anxiety and depression. Moreover, they examined satisfaction with the course. The authors found several things that improved learning; among them was adequate preparation for the teaching task.

Finding #2. Structured Tasks for Teachers and Learners Improve Learning

Some researchers have questioned whether a structured or unstructured task is most beneficial with respect to learning content. Although structure is clearly a useful thing, the idea is that students might enjoy some relaxed formats and freedom for their own expression. This may well be the case. The researchers in the study described above (Fantuzzo et al., 1989) compared results within groups examining independent and dyadic/pair work using both structured and unstructured approaches. Based upon data from 100 students who were randomly assigned to groups, the researchers hypothesized that the most active components of the reciprocal peer teaching strategy were the structured-learning format and the mutual exchange of information process that occurs during dyadic peer tutoring. Their study supported these hypotheses. Students in the structured reciprocal peer teaching group showed greater improvements in cognitive abilities, lower levels of perceived distress, and higher levels of course satisfaction than students who worked independently. Thus, for this particular group of students, the structure was an important component of the process.

Finding #3. Individual and Group Accountability for the Results of the Process Improves Learning

One of the key characteristics of cooperative learning is individual accountability (Davidson, Major, & Michaelsen, 2014). Researchers have found accountability to be an important component of reciprocal peer teaching. Sarfo and Elen (2011), for example, investigated both interdependence and individual accountability on learning and the potential relationship between the two. Using a two-by-two post-test experimental design, the researchers found students should each be responsible for studying all, rather than part, of the information before group discussion. They also demonstrated that if students know that a student will be randomly called upon to respond for the group and that the students' score will be the score for the full group, learning will be strengthened.

Finding #4. Groups Typically Outperform Individuals in Answering Questions Accurately

We have all heard the expression that "two heads are better than one," and research on reciprocal peer teaching seems to fully support this concept. In a specialized form of peer teaching that Michaelsen, Davidson, and Major (2014) calls Team-Based Learning, students study and take a test individually. Next, they join their permanent groups, and there they take the same test again as a team. The group must come to consensus on the answers (which is the peer teaching aspect of the activity). Students receive scores from the team test immediately. They have the opportunity to write appeals, in which they make valid arguments about why they see their answer to questions as correct. Michaelsen has collected information from students for several years and has found that the teams always outscore the individuals (Michaelsen et al., 2014). The lesson here for reciprocal peer teaching is that it can be useful to harness the knowledge of the group in the teaching activity instead of individuals alone.

Using IDEAs to Improve Learning with Reciprocal Peer Teaching

The IDEAs we share in this chapter are designed around some of the key findings from the research. The activities are linked to one or more research findings that suggest their potential efficacy. We suggest that they correlate with key research findings as indicated in the following table:

TABLE 3.1 Peer Teaching IDEAs and Research Findings

Peer Teaching IDEAs	Description	Links to Research Findings
Note-Taking Pairs	In pairs, students review and compare their notes, looking for similar themes and identifying possible misunderstandings.	Structured Tasks (Research Finding #2)
Pairs Check	Pairs listen to each other's work while providing each other with coaching and feedback. It is a useful exercise for giving and accepting constructive criticism as well as praise.	Structured Tasks (Research Finding #2)
Milling	Students answer a set of questions about a given unit of content and poll each other for information about questions that they cannot answer.	Groups Outperform Individuals (Research Finding #4)

(*Continued*)

TABLE 3.1 Continued

Peer Teaching IDEAs	Description	Links to Research Findings
Gallery Walk	The instructor develops several questions or prompts and places them at different locations around the room. Small groups of students move from question to question, writing responses to each question. At the end of the activity, each group summarizes and reports on their last question.	Groups Outperform Individuals (Research Finding #4)
Anonymous Cards	Students write questions that are redistributed to peers; in turn, students then research and answer the questions that they have received. In the last phase of the activity, students share the questions they received and the answers they developed with the rest of the class as they teach the class what they have learned.	Groups Outperform Individuals (Research Finding #4)
Each One, Teach One	The IDEA is that instead of listening to a lecture for information transfer, students transfer content to each other. Students are responsible for and share a single fact with the rest of their classmates through this information exchange activity.	Preparing to Teach (Research Finding #1); Individual Accountability (Research Finding #3).
Jigsaw	Students develop expertise in one of many components of a problem by first participating in a group solely focused on a single component. In the second stage of the exercise, groups are reformed with	Structured Tasks (Research Finding #2); Individual Accountability (Research Finding #3)

Peer Teaching IDEAs	Description	Links to Research Findings
	a representative from each expert group who together now have sufficient expertise to tackle the whole problem	
Microteaching	Students develop and deliver a lesson on a content module.	Individual Accountability (Research Finding #3)
Panel Presentation	A "panel" of students develops expertise on a topic, which they share with a peer audience.	Structured Tasks (Research Finding #2)
Clustering	This IDEA involves having students transfer factual or conceptual information to each other while looking for connections and links between concepts and ideas.	Groups Outperform Individuals (Research Finding #4)
Speed Interviews	Each student has a question and individually asks each student in the class for an answer. The student then develops a consensus answer to the question using the information gained from classmates.	Groups Outperform Individuals (Research Finding #4)

Faculty can take up Reciprocal Peer Teaching with confidence. The research supports that it is a solid way to help students deepen their learning and develop higher-order skills. These IDEAs provide faculty a good and intentional design for helping students to improve their learning and ensuring that they are on the path to success.

IDEA #25: Note-Taking Pairs

Overview

In Note-Taking Pairs, students work individually and then together in pairs to develop useful notes during a lecture. This IDEA involves having students work independently to select and write down relevant information. The instructor pauses periodically and asks students to work with one another to help reconstruct information from the lecture by filling in gaps, adding information, correcting mistakes, and so forth.

Note-taking helps students remember important information by requiring them to take an active stance during a lecture. It also provides the class with a study resource; when studying for a test, they can go back to their notes as a review mechanism. Students, however, may not be good notetakers. They may not be able to maintain sufficient attention to record information accurately, and, as novices, they may not have the mental structures necessary to organize information. For this reason, it is important to help students develop a better set of notes.

The Note-Taking Pair IDEA is useful because taking good notes is a skill any learner can improve, and comparing notes provides them an opportunity to learn from another student. Also, when learning, if a specific concept is particularly challenging, even if for a short period of time, taking useful notes can be hindered. Comparing notes provides students with an opportunity to fill in gaps of information they might have missed. During this activity, students work to understand the big picture and key concepts while they reconstruct ideas and information presented by the lecturer.

Guiding Principles

Providing students with time to fill in their notes is a form of scaffolding, particularly if time is allocated for students to ask questions. It provides students with support in the form of time to complete a specified task (developing notes), and it offers some cognitive support, as the instructor supplies the class with objectives. Actively trying to use their memories to reconstruct notes while discussing concepts with peers helps students to move information from short-term to long-term memory (Smith, Wood, Krauter, & Knight, 2011). Moreover, the Note-Taking Pairs IDEA gives instructors an opportunity for coaching on the finer points of taking good notes.

Preparation

In advance of using Note-Taking Pairs, prepare a lecture with three to four identifiable chunks of information. The lecture should be structured into 10–15 minute segments, each focused on a different chunk of information. Finally, gather any supplies you anticipate needing. You may want to have paper and pencils at the ready, for example, in case students are not prepared to take notes.

Process

- Provide students with a list of objectives.
- Tell students to listen so they can recall as much information as possible.
- Ask students to listen to the lecture without writing anything down.
- Have the students write individually for approximately five minutes, trying to write down everything from the lecture segment that they can recall.

- Ask students to work in pairs for five minutes to teach each other significant ideas, concepts, and facts, reconstructing a better set of notes in the process.
- Allow time for students to ask questions for approximately five minutes to fill in or expand on missing information.

Sample IDEA Pairings

Guided Note-Taking (IDEA #1). Provide students with a structured but partially empty set of notes for a lecture. Ask them to work alone and then in pairs to complete the notes.

Speed Interviews (IDEA #35). Students briefly pair up and ask questions about the lecture. The interview answers can be used to complete the lecture notes.

Hypothesis Proof Organizer (IDEA #77). Taking advantage of the Note-Taking Pairs framework, dyads complete a Hypothesis Proof Chart with information learned during a lecture.

Pro-tips

This activity can lead to problems when students develop and pool together faulty information. Doing so can reinforce misunderstandings on the part of students. You will want to reemphasize key points, and you may also choose to review and assess students' notes for accuracy.

Some students are better notetakers than others, and those who are good notetakers may feel that they are doing more than their fair share of work in this activity. This may be particularly the case if they find themselves working in a group of other students who are not good notetakers. Consider changing group membership frequently and rewarding students for good note-taking, such as offering bonus points to a group's best notetaker. Alternately, find another way to illustrate that everyone is benefitting from the activity, for example, by sharing the benefits of teaching others to your own learning.

Many students today choose to take notes with laptops rather than paper and pencil. Providing them with the option of using their laptops can be useful (many students type faster than they write). When allowing students to use technology, agree beforehand that the technology will be used only for course-related work.

IDEA #26: Pairs Check

Overview

Pairs Check is a Reciprocal Peer Teaching activity that is particularly useful when students are working on mastery-oriented problems. For the IDEA, pairs of students listen to each other's work and provide their partner with coaching and feedback. It is a useful exercise for checking understanding, giving and accepting constructive criticism, praising what is done well, and adjusting incorrect information. Trying out ideas by explaining concepts and hearing perspectives of others both assist the learning process.

In this IDEA, everyone benefits from the peer work. Those who are having difficulty learn from those who have a better grasp of the material or are more proficient at the skill. Those who are more advanced are more likely to retain the information better due to the repetition and practice of teaching it to someone else. One important step in this process is for students giving assistance not to provide their partners with the correct answers before the students recognize answers for themselves. The concept is to provide assistance with actions that guide toward the correct answer, not to provide the answer itself.

Guiding Principles

The principle that guides this IDEA is that students receive immediate feedback during the learning process. That is, feedback is given while they are working on a problem. A partner can help a colearner know whether he or she is taking the correct steps and can help the individual self-correct as soon as he or she begins going in the wrong direction. This feedback on performance is beneficial when completing a task (Pahler, Cepeda, Wixted, & Rohrer, 2005).

Preparation

First, you will need to develop a set of problems for student pairs to solve. The problems should be mastery oriented, and the process will likely be more effective with problems that have both a clearly correct and a clearly incorrect answer. Practice the problem set yourself to determine how long it will take to solve the problems. Depending on your skill level, it may well take students three to five times longer than it takes you to solve the problem independently. Having a "solutions manual" ready for reference can be helpful. Problems that are worked out in sequential steps will be a handy reference for you to have and save valuable time if asked about a specific step on a problem.

Process

- Form pairs of students. This can be done by asking for volunteers or assigning pairs.
- Provide each pair with a problem set.
- The first student in each pair completes the first problem with the second student watching.
- The pair partner serves as a coach while the first student is working, giving feedback as well as offering praise.
- When the pair agrees on a solution, they move to the next problem.

- In the second problem, partners change roles, and student two becomes the problem solver while student one serves as a coach.
- The pair joins another pair to check responses and work toward agreement.
- The students repeat the process until they have solved all of the problems.

Sample IDEA Pairings

Icebreakers (IDEA #46). Particularly if students do not know each other well, a brief Icebreaker can serve to introduce students, which will help them work on their Pair Check.

K-W-L Chart (IDEA #86). Prior to the Pairs Check, students write down what they know and want to learn from the activity. After, they write down what they learned. This preparation helps set the stage for a successful Pairs Check activity.

Today I Learned (IDEA #90). After completing the Pairs Check, students reflect on what they learned from their partners during the activity.

Pro-tips

Pairs Check can be a challenge if students are not familiar with a topic. Students who are new to a topic may not have a good idea about when a student is working accurately or not. This IDEA works better when students have a fairly good grasp on the kinds of skills that they need to use in solving the problem. Novices leading novices can create some problems and, unfortunately, solidify misinformation.

It may be helpful to develop a sheet defining the responsibilities of each partner when first using this strategy with students. The sheet can provide examples of good coaching and praising skills, as well as the difference between coaching and providing the answer.

One variation of Pairs Check is to have the students take turns within the given problem. The first person in the pair does step one with the second serving as a coach, and they then reverse roles for the second step, and so on. This approach is particularly effective if there are multiple complex steps in a process.

IDEA #27: Milling

Overview

The Milling IDEA prompts students to respond to a set of questions about a given unit of content for items they know and to poll each other for information about questions that they cannot answer. Helping students to develop the skills to answer when they know and seek answers from others when they need assistance is a valuable approach in lifelong learning. The basis for the IDEA is that students have both individual accountability (the charge to do their best at responding to the questions) and cooperative interaction (the charge to both give and seek assistance). These are two components that can help collaborative learning be successful.

Guiding Principles

Students are at different levels of academic development, even with closely related content, and sometimes the one-size-fits-all approach does not bring about the best learning. Milling provides students with the opportunity to demonstrate competence at different levels at different times. Indeed, some educators have proposed a zone of proximal development (ZPD) (Vygotsky, 1978). That is, students learn best when they work at their own level, completing tasks that challenge them but are not too easy or too difficult. The notion is that when the questions are too easy students get bored. When the content, or presentation of the content, is too difficult, the proposition is that students become frustrated and tune out.

This IDEA has students attempt to answer a range of questions, from easy to difficult, and to seek out help when they need it. High-achieving students are challenged by the difficult questions and by the opportunity to explain easier questions to students who need assistance. Low-achieving students get to demonstrate some mastery when they answer the easier questions, and they are able to seek out peer tutors for those questions that are more challenging and thus are less likely to become frustrated.

Preparation

In anticipation of using this IDEA, select an assignment for students to complete as homework, such as a reading or video lecture. Next, create a list of related questions that students should be able to answer after having completed the assignment. The list should contain a mixture of easy, moderately difficult, and difficult questions. It may include definitions, multiple-choice questions, incomplete sentences, or short essays. Practice responding to the questions yourself to get a sense of the time frame students will need to complete the Milling IDEA (they will need longer than you do to answer the questions).

Process

- Announce the activity and the time frame that students will have to complete it.
- Provide students with the question list.
- Ask students to complete the list by filling in the answers to the questions as well as they can.
- Ask students to mill around the room, finding other students who could answer the questions they could not. Encourage students to help each other.

- Reconvene as a full class, and discuss the answers.
- Supply any answers that any students do not yet have.

Sample IDEA Pairings

Responsive Lecture (IDEA #6). Use the unanswered questions as the starting place for your next lecture.

Trivia (IDEA #40). Structure the questions in a way that they will work in a Trivia game environment. After implementing Milling, as a follow up in the next session, use Trivia with questions based on those completed through the Milling IDEA.

Today I Learned (IDEA #90). After Milling around the room, ask students to reflect and share something they learned that is new information for them.

Pro-tips

This activity is an IDEA that can be used in any sized class but will work best in a medium-sized class. Very large classes may become a bit chaotic as students need space to move around, and very small classes may not have enough heterogeneity inability to answer a range of questions and a limited number of peers from whom to seek advice.

One variation is to stop periodically and ask what students are finding particularly challenging. You could then provide a quick tip or suggestion to get many of the students on the right track. Although using this variation too often would be disruptive, stopping once or twice might mitigate feelings of frustration.

IDEA #28: Gallery Walk

Overview

For the Gallery Walk IDEA, the instructor develops several questions or prompts and places them at different locations around the room. Students are placed into small groups, which move from station to station, writing responses to each question, both adding to what previous groups have contributed and clarifying any misconceptions that have been written. At the end of the activity, each group summarizes and reports on its last question.

Using approaches to learning that include getting students to move around a physical space can be beneficial. This movement, if planned well, can also facilitate both learning and retention of new information. The Gallery Walk IDEA gets students physically moving around the room. Physical activity has been shown to improve attention to learning and interrupt lethargy, particularly when it interrupts long periods (Jensen, 2005).

Guiding Principles

This IDEA requires students to think beyond simple recall of information, as they must evaluate information that other students have shared. This prompts and reinforces higher-order thinking skills. In the final report out, students evaluate and synthesize important concepts. These activities compel students to use deep learning approaches, which can help them develop as learners (Marton & Säljö, 1976a, 1976b).

Gallery Walk has the additional advantage of promoting cooperation, listening skills, and team building. Cooperative learning activities have been shown to improve student learning of higher-order thinking skills (Millis & Cottell, 1998). By asking students to build on others' contributions, this IDEA encourages cooperation among the class.

Preparation

In order to use the Gallery Walk IDEA, first develop a series of prompts and write one prompt each on large pieces of papers that will be put on the walls during the class period. This activity works best with open-ended questions or problems that may be answered from several different perspectives. Short texts, such as quotations, or images can also work well as prompts. Next, decide how long the activity will take and how much time groups will have at each station. Make decisions about how to display the prompts, such as using flip chart paper taped to walls of the classroom (gallery style), or you might use file folders with a sheet of paper and prompt inside, which are placed on desks or tables through the class. Create as many "stations" as you will have groups. Finally, secure the supplies you will need. In addition to the pads of paper to list the prompts, you will need tape and a variety of dry erase markers, which are less likely to bleed through the paper.

Process

- Post the prompts at several stations just prior to class. Students can assist with this task.
- Form teams and assign each group with a station.
- Inform students how they should proceed through the different stations (e.g., clockwise).
- Ask teams to read the question they have and to provide a bullet response to the question. Ask them to identify their work in some way, such as through initialing their response.
- Ask teams to rotate to the next question when the time ends. Students read and discuss the previous group's response and add content of their own.
- Repeat until all groups have visited each station.

- At the end of the activity, the group at the last station reports out on the responses to the prompt by synthesizing them into a new response.
- Provide teams with sufficient time to revisit each station to see the additions others have made. They will be particularly interested in the earliest stations they visited.

Sample IDEA Pairings

Each One, Teach One (IDEA #30). Students are responsible for transferring information from their Gallery Walk station to the rest of the class using the Each One, Teach One activity to share content.

Graffiti Board (IDEA #65). During or immediately following the Gallery Walk, the class writes responses to a question by creating graffiti with content from the class.

Concept Maps (IDEA #79). Ask students to diagram the concepts on the different stations, showing interrelations between ideas.

Pro-tips

Variations in this IDEA include giving each person in the group a task as they move from prompt to prompt. For example, you might have students form groups of four and then number off. After they have numbered assign each number to a role (e.g., 1 = recorder for the group; 2 = make sure everyone in the group contributes something to the prompt; 3 = points out what looks to be the best contribution to that point and why; and 4 = timekeeper during the walk).

The Gallery Walk IDEA has great flexibility, as it can be a 15-minute activity or a week-long project that involves graded oral and written reports. Student time at each station could range from 1–5 minutes to work to 20–30 minutes or longer.

Overall, this activity is a fun change of pace to a traditional lecture and discussion classroom. However, if used too often, it can begin to have a rote feel to it as well. Vary instructional approaches to keep it fresh, using Gallery Walk only a few times during a term and in different ways, such as to spark interest in a lesson you are about to start or to wrap up a unit of content.

IDEA #29: Anonymous Cards

Overview

Anonymous Cards is an activity in which students write questions that are redistributed to peers, who then research and answer the questions that they have received. When students pose questions and answers to one another, it centers the learning at the appropriate level for the students in the course by default. This

IDEA also allows students to ask questions that most concern them and use each other as resources to find answers. In the last phase of the activity, students share the questions they received and the answers they developed with the rest of the class as they teach the class what they have learned.

Students, particularly ones who are new to the topic, may be too embarrassed to ask a question during class. This activity allows all students to ask questions and promotes the ideas that one should have questions while learning. Although it is beneficial for students to be able to ask what they really want to know without being embarrassed, it can also be challenging for a peer to answer, which can push them to learn more.

Guiding Principles

Sometimes students are reticent to ask questions in class for fear of making mistakes or "looking stupid." Having learners write questions and sharing them anonymously with others empowers them to ask the questions they might not otherwise ask. This IDEA creates a climate in which students can openly share their questions and get the answers they need. It can also help them realize others often have similar questions; a process that demonstrates learning is a struggle for others as well. Thus, this IDEA helps to create a positive climate for learning and motivates students to engage in the course, as Svinicki (2004) suggests is important.

This activity also means that students are made more aware of other students, who in turn are responsive to their questions. As Chickering and Gamson (1987) suggest in their seven principles of effective teaching: "Sharing one's own ideas and responding to others' reactions sharpens thinking and deepens understanding." In this IDEA, students get to do both.

Preparation

This IDEA requires little preparation. You simply need to determine how students will record their questions and how their responses will be distributed such that students do not know which question belongs to which student. The most basic option is to have students take out a piece of paper and write a question. Another option is to hand out index cards and have students use those, as they are easy to retrieve, shuffle, and redistribute. The only other preparation is to think through how to distribute responses. Students could pass all questions forward, and you could put them in a box, bowl, or other container; shake them; and pass them out. You might also have students write questions on papers, ball them up, and then throw them into the air on your signal. Students then pick up the paper that landed nearest to them. Again, there are many options; the key is that the system result in students not knowing who wrote which question.

Process

- Ask students to write down a question they have about the learning material (whether reading assignment, lecture, or other).
- Collect questions, shuffle, and distribute one question to each student.
- Provide time for students to research the question they have received and prepare a short answer.
- Provide students with a short time (e.g., three minutes) to state and answer the question for the rest of the class.

Sample IDEA Pairings

Think-Pair-Share (IDEA #15). Students receive a question, think about it for a minute, and talk about it with a peer prior to sharing with the full class. Just as with Speed Interviews, the collaborative aspect of this pairing can help students develop better responses.

Speed Interviews (IDEA #35). Allow students to convene briefly with a partner in order to conduct a Speed Interview to develop responses to the questions. Many times, the collaborative nature of this combination will allow students to create better answers than when working alone.

Freewriting (IDEA #63). Simply take up questions and ask the students to answer them with a few minutes of Freewriting prior to presenting them to the class.

Pro-tips

While students are working on the responses, it is valuable for you to circulate to facilitate the process. Reinforce to the students that it is their responsibility to answer the questions but that you may serve as a resource to assist them by giving hints or pointing them in the correct direction if needed. It will be extremely important that you do not spend much time with any one individual or group in providing assistance. Not only would dallying make you less available to others, but it would also reinforce students asking you to answer the questions they are supposed to be answering. Consider assigning the research phase of the IDEA as homework and be prepared to take questions from students who may need assistance interpreting the question and finding the best way to answer it.

Just as some may be embarrassed to ask a question, some students will be nervous about providing their "answer" in front of their peers. The Think-Pair-Share and Speed Interviews sample IDEA pairings can help with this issue, as they provide opportunities for students to rehearse. Moreover, writing a response that they can read can help students cope with their anxieties.

All engaged learning has the risk of students getting frustrated because as the instructor you should be "providing information," not having them answer each other's questions. Consider explaining to the students that you are using this IDEA because answering questions is one of the best ways to learn material.

IDEA #30: Each One, Teach One

Overview

When students have specific areas of content for which they are responsible for teaching their peers, the motivation to come prepared increases dramatically. In addition, as an expert, it is difficult to know at what level to present information. The Each One, Teach One IDEA addresses both of these areas in that students are responsible for teaching a small amount of course material and are presented the information from the level of the learner. Also, instead of listening to a lecture for information transfer, students are directly involved in both class preparation and delivery of content.

Guiding Principles

This IDEA is directly opposite of what most students perceive should happen in a class. Instead of a single expert explaining content to a group of learners, the learners are working with each other to learn the course material. In his book on engaging students in the learning process, Doyle (2011) argues, "he who does the work does the learning." Learning is not a spectator sport, and students do not learn as much by sitting in class and listening to lectures as they do when they relate material to be learned to their past experiences and daily lives. This activity provides an opportunity for that to happen.

Each One, Teach One provides an opportunity for students to learn together. Learning becomes a team effort, as all of the students have something to contribute to the knowledge of others. It is not a competition, but rather it is an opportunity for students to share their information with others and to respond to their information as well. This approach is one of the core principles of effective practices of undergraduate education (Chickering & Gamson, 1987).

Preparation

To prepare for Each One, Teach One, place a list of facts or concepts related to a single topic to be learned in a given class period on separate index cards. If there are more students in the class than concepts, it works well to have multiple cards with the same concept. Determine whether you will have all students comparing information with each other or if you will need to break students into smaller groups. The former works well in small classes, whereas the latter works well with larger classes in which time will not permit each student to connect directly with every other student. Finally, you need to decide how much time to allocate to the activity. The amount of time it will take to complete this activity depends upon the complexity of the facts and concepts that you include.

Process

- Distribute a card to each student, announcing that each student is responsible for teaching one fact or statistic to the rest of the class.
- Ask students to move around the room and talk to other students to share their fact with the other students.
- Students should be encouraged to elaborate and give examples.
- At the close of the activity, conduct a short quiz to see which questions the students can correctly answer.

Sample IDEA Pairings

Guided Note-Taking (IDEA #1). Give the student a set of notes with gaps for the information that will appear on the index cards. Students must listen for answers to complete the notes.

Note-Taking Pairs (IDEA #25). At the end of the activity, simply allow students to form pairs so that they can build their notes from the activity by putting their heads together. They likely will recall more information together than they could alone.

Main Idea-Detail Chart (IDEA #80). Students take the information shared during Each One, Teach One to develop a Main Idea-Detail Chart visually depicting the day's content.

Pro-tips

Sufficient space is necessary for this activity to work well. Students need to be able to move around in the room so that they have contact with other students. Alternately, choose a fewer number of facts to share, arrange students into smaller groups, and direct that the sharing be done among members of the group.

Let students "teach" the fact or concept they are assigned to teach. If you step in too much, or restate their work too often, students will stop putting in the work as they come to expect you to "reteach" everything. It is fine to correct errors and misconceptions but keep in mind that a different way of explaining something is not an incorrect way, and it may well not be necessary to explain it your way if the students have learned from the student presenters' perspectives.

This IDEA is a great way to get students talking to teach other and exchanging information. It can have a chaotic feel to it, however, which can be exciting but can also be overwhelming for students. Having so many different perspectives and levels of understanding presenting information can feel disorienting. It can also cause students anxiety if they are worried that they will not get the answers they need to do well in the class. Debriefing to help them see the way the information fits together can be useful. A debriefing in which you provide them key ideas and issues can help to alleviate some of this anxiety.

IDEA #31: Jigsaw

Overview

For students to learn a challenging new concept, particularly one that is multifaceted, it is helpful to divide the work into meaningful chunks and have students discuss and learn among one another. The Jigsaw IDEA structures student learning in two sets of groups to allow the students to discuss as part of a second group to learn content and then return to their primary group to discuss and teach it to others. This approach allows each person to be an "expert" in a given area and talk with and learn from colleagues in other areas.

Guiding Principles

This IDEA gives each student an important role in the learning of the class, which promotes positive interdependence (Davidson et al., 2014; Johnson et al., 2014). That is, students must discuss with each other because they need the content that each has to share. The fact that students need information from classmates encourages participation and discussion of the course content.

Moreover, each student has to translate content into his or her own language in order to communicate it to others. This act deepens student understanding. Students need to fully comprehend the information in order to discuss with classmates. As a result, the need to discuss content increases student motivation to ensure understanding (Johnson et al., 2014).

Preparation

Before implementing Jigsaw, develop a unit of content that can be broken into four discrete parts. Determine whether you will create resources and guides for students to use during the independent study phase of this activity or whether you will have them do research on their own. Additionally, decide whether you will leave it up to groups to determine how to teach their content or whether you will provide some parameters. There is some value to letting students be creative, but it can also be overwhelming, particularly for students who have not used the Jigsaw IDEA previously. Finally, identify how students will share their final product: quick report out, poster, online presentation, or some other method.

Process

- Assign students to Jigsaw groups of four to five students.
- Ask students to number off within their groups.
- Assign study topics to a student with a corresponding number (e.g., all number 1s study topic a, all number 2s study topic b, all number 3s study topic c, and all number 4s study topic d).
- Ask students to study their respective topics independently (may also be work done in preparation for the class session).
- Form new "expert" teams by having students with the same topic work together (all number 1s are a team, all number 2s are a team, and so forth).
- Ask expert groups to discuss what they know collectively about the topic and what they still need to know. Ask them to learn what is needed and decide how they will teach their topics to their home/Jigsaw teams.
- Ask the expert group members to return to their home groups and discuss and teach each of the four content areas.
- Involve the class in a whole-group review.
- Assess students on what they have learned.

Sample IDEA Pairings

Houston, We Have a Problem (IDEA #42). In order to play the game, each student develops an expertise in one area that can help solve the problem faced in gameplay.

Journalists' Questions (IDEA #66). Students use the framework of Journalists' Questions to write up the information about their area that can be used as notes when completing the Jigsaw activity.

Visual Lists (IDEA #82). Each expert groups creates a Visual List of significant information to use as a visual when they discuss their areas with their home groups.

Pro-tips

The Jigsaw IDEA is a well-researched (Johnson, Johnson, & Stanne, 2000) and often used activity that has been tried throughout the world (Kilic, 2008). Experiment with Jigsaw groups of different sizes from three to six. As the group size increases, timing is more challenging, but complexity also increases.

The Jigsaw can be a useful tool for managing challenging classroom dynamics. For example, when one student tends to dominate class discussions, Jigsaw takes away the person's leverage for doing that because the individual in question will not hold all of the information that needs to be shared. Likewise, if one student is not participating or if several are not participating as fully as they might, the Jigsaw creates a space for them to have a specific job to do, and thus it gives them a way to participate and an opportunity for doing so; it makes social loafing much more difficult.

IDEA #32: Microteaching

Overview

Organizing information and placing that material in a context with other material is a critical skill in learning. Microteaching is an approach in which students take turns developing short teaching modules and then teaching that material to the class. The Microteaching IDEA allows for every student to take a turn, and every student must learn something from the person who is teaching. In the final phase of the activity, students complete a self-evaluation of what they have learned and a peer evaluation of other students' teaching sessions.

Guiding Principles

Peer teaching has a range of benefits for students. Those who are doing the teaching benefit by having to learn, organize, and communicate information to others. Those who learn have the advantage of having peers translate information into a language and level that they can understand. Moreover, providing them the opportunity to teach suggests to students that you value their skills and abilities and have confidence that they will be able to get the job done.

For this activity, the student teachers must take ownership for their own learning as well as the learning of other students in the class. Taking active responsibility helps deepen the learning process (Davis & Murrell, 1993). Taking responsibility for their own learning pushes students to higher-order thinking skills, and it helps students engage in deep learning.

This activity also asks students to participate in reflection on their own work, which allows them processing time. It has long been suggested (Dewey, 1933) that reflective thinking requires active, persistent, and careful consideration. Such thought processes help to deepen student learning.

Preparation

Organize the content into short, teachable chunks of information. Identify a sufficient number of short topics related to the content area that each student in your class may be assigned one. For example, if you have 30 students, you will need 30 short topics. These topics may be based on concepts and content such as key definitions, famous people, and short problems.

Determine how long each student may have to teach the rest of the class. These segments may be short, such as three to five minutes, or the segments may be as long as an entire class period for a relatively small and more experienced class.

Determine whether you will give students any guidelines; for example, they have to include a visual aid, or they have to be creative in their teaching approaches. Also consider providing them with an evaluation rubric so that they will know how they will be assessed.

Process

- Announce the activity at the start of a unit to be taught by the students. Explain at this time the value of the process and that you will still ensure essential content is taught well.
- Assign topic areas.
- Give students time to prepare their presentations.
- Provide students with time to teach their topics, informing those who are being taught that they need to be able to take one thing away from the teaching.
- Consider having a full-class discussion about the experience.

Sample IDEA Pairings

Concept Maps (IDEA #79). When students complete their teaching assignments, ask students to create Word Webs to map out the concepts presented and the relationships between them.

Self-Assessment (IDEA #95). Devise forms for self or peer evaluation. Self-evaluation forms might include the following: describe the processes you undertook preparing, describe what you did well and what you could improve in your presentation, and describe what you might do differently next time. Peer evaluation might include the following: What did you hope to learn from the presentation, what did you actually learn from the presentation, was the material taught in a way that helped you to understand the content, and what do you still need to know. Samples of more extensive self and peer review forms are available online and are easy to find through search engines with the terms "self-evaluation form" and "peer evaluation form."

Pro-tips

Although in most situations, students will be given time to prepare their material, advanced students may be well pleased to have impromptu presentations. Such spur of the moment teaching modules can add an air of excitement to the classroom.

You can also have students work together in small groups to teach the class, which will take fewer topics. On the other hand, group presentations (in which one student talks as the remaining shuffle their feet) can be a difficult process to manage. If you decide to use groups, be specific that all students must be involved in the presentation and that their teaching approaches should not be straight lecture, one student at a time, but rather should be more creative.

While the Microteaching IDEA is effective with new students in brief segments, it is particularly effective for more advanced students who may eventually want to teach themselves. Indeed, it is often used in teacher training as well as in formal professional development of graduate students.

IDEA #33: Panel Presentation

Overview

Panels of experts are often used at conferences and symposia to convey specific information from multiple perspectives. The Panel Presentation IDEA uses this same conference "expert panel" concept to develop expertise for a complicated topic within a course by allowing students to break up the work into manageable chunks. It also teaches students how to better work together as a collective.

Panel Presentations also work well for discussions related to sensitive topics (Silberman, 1995). This IDEA allows for diffusion of responsibility on an otherwise difficult dialogue (Finkel & Bollin, 1994). The activity can improve student research skills, organizational skills, and presentation skills. It also demonstrates to students the value of collaborations of individuals working on individual, yet related aspects of an intellectual challenge.

Guiding Principles

The primary goal of the Panel Presentation IDEA is to provide students with a chance to practice communicating with an audience in a low-threat situation, as they have their peers with them and they are also presenting to their peers. It also gives students practice framing a large issue or concept in a way that allows for breaking the work into related, yet independent chunks and then presenting that information as an integrated entity. When done well, students also learn to formulate questions about important topics or issues in the field. Finally, it allows students to get the "feel" of being an "expert" in a specific area. It is a form of active learning (Faust & Paulson, 1998).

Preparation

The first step in preparing for Panel Presentation is to select topics (or alternatively have students select their own topics). Next, prepare an outline of expectations for working and presenting as a collaborative including who will moderate the presentations (you or the students). You may provide them with a list of suggestions for their research, and you may wish to instruct them what to bring with them to class (for example, index cards with notes for their own presentations as well as a handout for the audience with a brief summary of their topic area with selected readings). It is also possible to assign panelists specific roles, such as for a particular position and against it, which can help to stimulate conversation. Roles may include setting timelines, peer review of material, and identifying in advance what will happen if a member of the panel does not delivery on promised material. Finally, decide how many groups you will have (four to six per group works best) and how long each will have (recommend a minimum of 10–15 minutes).

Process

- During a class session, explain what a Panel Presentation is and how one works. In this same class period, discuss why you are using Panel Presentations, including specifically the value in learning material and practicing working as a collaborative to address a large issue.
- Assign students to panel groups. You may allow them to choose the topic that interests them most, or you may wish to stratify group selection based upon student achievement level.
- Ask students to complete fairly extensive individual research on their own topics as homework. Ask them to complete some research on the other students' topic, sufficient research to come to class with a list of questions.
- In class, arrange five chairs at the front of the room and ask panelists from the first group to take their positions.
- Ask the moderator to introduce the panelists and, following a brief presentation of two to three minutes per person to state their major findings, to take questions.

Sample IDEA Pairings

Journaling (IDEA #68). After each Panel Presentation, ask students to journal about what they have learned from the discussion.

Concept Maps (IDEA # 79). Ask students to keep a running list of the concepts the panelists are discussing. Then ask them to map out the concepts, showing connections between them.

Today I Learned (IDEA #90). After the Panel Presentation sessions, ask students to reflect on what they learn from the class session. This reflection reinforces the importance of the activity, and it provides an important time in which students can consolidate their ideas, thus strengthening their learning.

Pro-tips

If students are new to higher education or to the field, you will likely want to be the moderator yourself so that you can help steer the conversation and avoid any problems. If they are more advanced students, student moderators can work well.

Panel Presentations work best when you allocate sufficient time to them. Under 10 minutes can feel like they are rushed, and it may not be sufficient time for conversations to occur. On the other hand, if they run too long, they can feel forced and like they are dragging out. Allow sufficient time, but keep the activity moving.

You may also want to prepare the audience by giving students specific roles. You may assign a critic, an encourager, a summarizer, and an extender, for example, or alternately roles of specific stakeholders with interests in the topic (if the panel is on higher education for example, you might assign students, faculty, administrators, policy makers, and so forth). This approach can help students understand the kinds of questions they can ask.

IDEA #34: Clustering

Overview

Identifying connections among concepts and teaching someone newly learned information is helpful for both understanding and later recall. Clustering IDEA involves having students transfer factual or conceptual information to each other while looking for connections and links between concepts and ideas. The IDEA is something similar to a physical model of a concept map, with individuals holding a single concept and then grouping that concept together with similar or related concepts.

Guiding Principles

This IDEA has three important guiding principles. The first is that ideas that are similar to or dependent on one another are more easily learned and later recalled when they are connected in time and space (Mayer, 2001). With Clustering IDEA, students move physically together and away from each other, grouping like ideas together and creating space between disparate ideas.

The second principle is that grounding learning in a perceptual motor experience can improve learning (Glenberg & Kaschak, 2002). Once learners have participated in this activity, they will have additional cues for later recalling the information based on the various groups and the connections developed among the concepts. Students also have a shared understanding, as the whole class shares the same image and experience.

The third principle is that students are physically networking and connecting with each other. This interaction helps them get to know each other better and can help to create a stronger classroom community of learners. When learners are more comfortable with each other and are sharing information, they are learning from and with each other. Collaboration has shown to be a powerful tool for learning (Barkley et al., 2014).

Preparation

Develop a list of factual bits of information or conceptual statements around a single topic that can be grouped into different subcategories. Put each concept or statement on a separate index card. Shuffle the deck of cards so that linked ideas are not all grouped together.

Process

- Give one card to each student. Have students draw a card from a container.
- Give students two to three minutes to look up information about their concept or statement if needed to ensure everyone understands the card they are holding.
- Ask students to move around the room, comparing their cards with other students' cards and explaining their card to others as needed.
- When students find links between their statements, they form a cluster.
- Students continue moving around the room, adding individuals to their clusters as appropriate.
- When each student has found a cluster, students determine whether they need to be broken into subclusters.
- Students give their clusters a name and a description.
- Students introduce the cluster to the rest of the class, explaining why they have formed a cluster.
- Students record their clusters, either on the board or a flip chart. They may then explain any relations they see between clusters.

Sample IDEA Pairings

Responsive Lecture (IDEA #6). After clusters have formed and discussed their statements, ask them to compile a list of questions, and base your lecture around answering them.

Snowball discussion (IDEA #12). Ask clusters to talk with each other about their statements and then ask them to join another cluster to learn. Clusters may re-form once more.

Pro-tips

This activity requires a generous amount of open space for students to engage in it fully. Do not use this IDEA if it will result in students tripping over fixed seating or if there are other physical limitations. It is a good approach to use in a smaller class that has moveable tables and chairs. If desks are not movable, students can work around a central table or a few desks and can consolidate their cards on the desk. If the weather is nice and there is space outside, this is an ideal activity to take outside the classroom.

Debriefing on the activity and talking about the different clusters can help students solidify their understanding and can also help them see the value of the activity to their learning. This activity could also be done in rounds. After the first round, have the students repeat the activity, with the restriction that clusters formed in the second round have to be completed with the rule that no individual may be in a group with more than one person from round one. This approach will force students to form different clusters and look for similarities in those clusters.

IDEA #35: Speed Interviews

Overview

Increasing participation of students, particularly in larger classes, is challenging. The Speed Interviews IDEA engages students in short, information discussions around a specific question or topic. Students quickly form pairs and conduct short interviews. Similar to speed dating, students spend approximately three to five minutes interviewing each other before changing partners. After a few rounds, the instructor calls on students to report on their conclusions from the interviews. As students present the conclusions, write the main points on the board to include in subsequent lectures or discussions.

Student participation is beneficial to student learning (Svinicki & McKeachie, 2013), and this approach can help to achieve it. The approach is helpful in activating prior knowledge, solving problems, and getting feedback from peers during a discussion. This activity is also effective at prompting student brainstorming around newly introduced ideas or topics.

Guiding Principles

Active learning is a process where students learn new material and relate this new information into their prior knowledge. This approach encourages learning-centric activities rather than teaching-centric ones (Barr & Tagg, 1995). A substantial amount of empirical data suggests that active learning improves student mastery, long-term retention of skills, and problem-solving abilities and increases the likelihood of completing a degree program (Braxton, Jones, Hirschy, & Hartley, 2008; Hake, 1988). The use of Speed Interviews helps students engage actively with course material rather than passively listening.

Preparation

Identify key concepts or points in class where Speed Interviews will be used and plan to set aside approximately 10–15 minutes of time in class for each round of interviews. Identify the goal of the discussion, and then create a question or prompt for the group that will facilitate that goal. The goal will determine the prompt given and the amount of time allocated for the activity. Prepare a few follow-up questions to ask the groups when they report out to the entire class. Note: Keep in mind that not all groups must report out. For very large classes, it may be possible to call on only a few groups.

Process

- Provide a question or prompt for students to focus the interviews.
- Students gather in pairs with others seated near them.
- The time allowed can vary tremendously from as little as one minute to as many as 10 minutes, depending on the question or prompt. Most Speed Interview discussion rounds last about five minutes.
- Ask students to report on the conclusions from their interviews. To accomplish this, you may ask for volunteers to report out or cold-call on students. One option is to have a few students volunteer and then call on one or two additional ones. When volunteers are used all of the time, some students will fail to do the work, as the fear of being called on decreases.

Sample IDEA Pairings

Pause Procedure (IDEA #2). The Pause Procedure may be used immediately after the Speed Interview discussions and before reporting out to the entire class. This variation will give groups an opportunity to collect their thoughts prior to reporting out.

Journalists' Questions (IDEA #66). Students use the Journalists' Questions during the interviews and write out the responses they receive.

Concept Maps (IDEA #79). Students create Concept Maps to display the main themes from their interviews.

Pro-tips

In large classes, there is often insufficient time to have every student report on their discussions. In addition, the overlap in interview findings can lead to students simply reporting their conclusions were the same as those already stated. To avoid this potential problem, call on a student to report and then ask for individuals to raise their hands if their Speed Interviews had similar conclusions.

One of the challenges in using this IDEA is how to regain the attention of the class, particularly in large classes. You may choose simply turn off and on the lights or you may use an alarm on the classroom computer. Think through your approach before class in order to avoid having to yell over the groups to get their attention.

It is often helpful to capture the information discussion, although it may be possible to call on only a few students. One option is to have the students post a tweet of their root discussion. If these Tweets are posted, students could look for similarity to what other groups posted, and the discussion could be based on reactions of students to the tweets, which are summaries of the discussions.

References

Barkley, E.F., Major, C.H., & Cross, K.P. (2014). *Collaborative learning techniques: A handbook for college faculty*. San Francisco, CA: Jossey-Bass.

Barr, R.B., & Tagg, J. (1995). From teaching to learning: A new paradigm for undergraduate education. *Change, 27*(6), 12–25.

Bentley, B.S., & Hill, R.V. (2009). Objective and subjective assessment of reciprocal peer teaching in medical gross anatomy laboratory. *Anatomical Sciences Education, 2*(4), 143–149.

Benware, C., & Deci, E.L. (1984). Quality of learning with an active versus passive motivational set. *American Educational Research Journal, 21*, 755–765.

Bloom, B. (1984). The 2 sigma problem: The search for methods of group instruction as effective as one-to-one tutoring. *Educational Researcher, 13*(6), 4–16.

Boud, D. (2001). Moving towards autonomy. In D. Boud (Ed.), *Developing student autonomy in learning*. London: Kogan Page.

Boud, D. (2002). Introduction: Making the move to peer learning. In D. Boud, R. Cohen, & J. Sampson (Eds.), *Peer learning in higher education: Learning from & with each other*. Stering, VA: Stylus.

Braxton, J.M., Jones, W.A., Hirschy, A.S., & Hartley, H.V. (2008). The role of active learning in college persistence. *New Directions for Teaching and Learning, 115*, 71–83.

Brazil, J. (2011). P2PU: Learning for everyone, by everyone, about almost anything. Retrieved from dmlcentral website: http://dmlcentral.net/blog/jeff-brazil/p2pu-learning-everyone-everyone-about-almost-anything

Chickering, A.W., & Gamson, Z.F. (1987). Seven principles for good practice in undergraduate education. *American Association of Higher Education Bulletin, 39*(7), 3–7.

Christudason, A. (2003). Peer learning #37. *Centre for the development of teaching and learning*. Retrieved from http://www.cdtl.nus.edu.sg

Davidson, N., Major, C.H., & Michaelsen, L.K. (2014). Small-group learning in higher education-cooperative, collaborative, problem-based, and team-based learning: An introduction by the guest editors. *Journal on Excellence in College Teaching, 25*(3–4), 1–6.

Davis, T.M., & Murrell, P.H. (1993). *Turning teaching into learning: The role of student responsibility in the collegiate experience*. Washington, DC: George Washington University.

Dewey, J. (1933). *How we think: A restatement of the relation of reflective thinking to the educative process*. Boston, MA: Heath.

Doyle, T. (2011). *Learner-centered teaching: Putting the research on learning into practice*. Sterling, VA: Stylus.

Doymis, K., Karacop, A., & Simsek, U. (2010). Effects of jigsaw and animation techniques on students' understanding of concepts and subjects in electrochemistry. *Educational Technology Research and Development, 58*(6), 671–691.

Falchikov, N. (2001). *Learning together: Peer tutoring in higher education.* London: Routledge Falmer.

Fantuzzo, J.W., Dimeff, L.A., & Fox, S.L. (1989). Reciprocal peer tutoring: A multimodal assessment of effectiveness with college students. *Teaching of Psychology, 16*(3), 133–135.

Faust, J.L., & Paulson, D.R. (1998). Active learning in the college classroom. *Journal on Excellence in College Teaching, 9*(2), 3–24.

Finkel, J., & Bollin, G.G. (1994). Integrating race, class & gender. *Teaching Education, 6*(2), 113–119.

Glenberg, A. M., & Kaschak, M. (2002). Grounding language in action. *Psychonomic Bulletin and Review, 9*(3), 558–565.

Goldschmid, B., & Goldschmid, M.L. (1976). Peer teaching in higher education: A review. *Higher Education, 5,* 9–33.

Griffiths, S., Houston, K., & Lazenbatt, A. (1995). *Enhancing student learning through peer tutoring in higher education.* Coleraine: Educational Development Unit, University of Ulster.

Hake, R.R. (1988). Interactive-engagement versus traditional methods: A six-thousand student survey of mechanics test data for introductory physics courses. *American Journal of Physics, 66*(1), 64–74.

Hendelman, W.J., & Boss, M. (1986). Reciprocal peer teaching by medical students in the gross anatomy laboratory. *Journal of Medical Education, 61*(8), 674–680.

Jensen, E. (2005). *Teaching with the brain in mind* (2nd ed.). Alexandria, VA: Association for Supervision and Curriculum Development.

Johnson, D., Johnson, R.T., & Smith, K.A. (2014). Cooperative learning: Improving university instruction by basing practice on validated theory. *Journal on Excellence in College Teaching, 25*(3/4), 85.

Johnson, D.W., Johnson, R.T., & Stanne, M.B. (2000). Cooperative learning methods: A meta-analysis. Retrieved from http://www.ccsstl.com/sites/default/files/Cooperative LearningResearch.pdf

Karacop, A., & Doymus, K. (2013). Effects of jigsaw cooperative learning and animation techniques on students' understanding of chemical bonding and their conceptions of the particulate nature of matter. *Journal of Science Education and Technology, 22*(2), 186–203.

Kilic, D. (2008). The effect of the jigsaw technique on learning the concepts of the principles and methods of teaching. *World Applied Sciences Journal, 4*(1), 109–114.

Krych, A.J., March, C.N., Bryan, R.E., Peake, B.H., Pawlina, W., & Carmichael, S.W. (2005). Reciprocal peer teaching: students teaching students in the gross anatomy laboratory. *Clinical Anatomy, 18*(4), 296–301.

Liu, W., & Devitt, A. (2015). Using reciprocal peer teaching to develop learner autonomy: An action research project with a beginners' Chinese class. *Language Learning in Higher Education, 4*(2), 489–505.

Maceiras, R., Cancela, A., Urrejola, S., & Sanchez, A. (2011). Experience of cooperative learning in enginnering. *European Journal of Engineering Education, 36*(1), 13–19.

Maden, S. (2010). The effect of jigsaw IV on the achievement of course of language teaching methods and techniques. *Educational Research and Reviews, 5*(12), 770–776.

Marton, F., & Säljö, R. (1976a). On qualitative differences in learning—1: Outcome and process. *British Journal of Educational Psychology, 46,* 4–11.

Marton, F., & Säljö, R. (1976b). On qualitative differences in learning—2: Outcome as a function of the learner's conception of the task. *British Journal of Educational Psychology, 46,* 115–127.

Mayer, R.E. (2001). *Multimedia learning.* New York: Cambridge University Press.

Michaelsen, L.K., Davidson, N., & Major, C.H. (2014). Team based learning practices and principles in comparison with cooperative learning and problem based learning. *Small-Group Learning in Higher Education: Cooperative, Collaborative, Problem-Based, and Team-Based Learning, 25*(4), 1–6.

Millis, B., & Cottell, P. (1998). *Cooperative learning for higher education faculty.* Cincinnati, OH: Oryx Press.

Munoz-Garcia, M.A., Moreda, G.P., Hernandez-Sanchez, N., & Valino, V. (2013). Student reciprocal peer teaching as a method for active learning: An experience in an electro-technical laboratory. *Journal of Science Education and Technology, 22*(5), 729–734.

Olsen, T. (2011). Using peer learning in the classroom. *Tennessee Teaching and Learning Center.*

Pahler, H., Cepeda, J.T., Wixted, J.T., & Rohrer, D. (2005). When does feedback facilitate the learning of words. *Journal of Experimental Psychology: Learning, Memory, & Cognition, 31*, 3–8.

Rae, J., & Baillie, A. (2005). Peer tutoring and the study of psychology: Tutoring experience as a learning method. *Psychology Teaching Review, 11*(1), 53–63.

Sarfo, F.K., & Elen, J. (2011). Investigating the impact of positive resource interdependence and individual accountability on students' academic performance in cooperative learning. *Electronic Journal of Research in Educational Psychology, 9*(1), 73–94.

Silberman, M. (1995). *101 ways to make training active.* San Diego, CA: Pfeiffer.

Smith, M.K., Wood, W.B., Krauter, K., & Knight, J.K. (2011). Combining peer discussion with instructor explanation increases student learning from in-class concept questions. *CBE-Life Sciences Education, 10*(1), 55–63.

Svinicki, M. (2004). *Learning and motivation in the post-secondary classroom.* Bolton, MA: Anker.

Svinicki, M., & McKeachie, W.J. (2013). *McKeachie's teaching tips: Strategies, research, and theory for college and university teachers* (14th ed.). Belmont, CA: Cengage Learning.

Topping, K.J. (2005). Trends in peer learning. *Educational Psychology, 25*(6), 631–645.

Vygotsky, L.S. (1978). *Mind in society: The development of higher psychological processes.* Cambridge, MA: Harvard University Press.

Waghmare, J.E., Sontakke, B.R., Tarnekar, A.M., Bokariya, P., Wankhede, V., & Shende, M.R. (2010). Reciprocal peer teaching: An innovative method to learn gross anatomy. *Journal of Mahatma Gandhi Institute of Medical Sciences, 15*(2), 40–43.

Youdas, J.W., Krouse, D.A., Hellyer, N.J., Hollman, J.H., & Rindflesh, A.B. (2007). Perceived usefulness or reciprocal peer teaching amond doctor of physical theray students in the gross anatomy laboratory. *Journal of Physical Therapy Education, 21*, 30–38.

4

ACADEMIC GAMES

Description

Games date back centuries; some scholars suggest that they date back to the Stone Age (Perla, 1990). Many of these early games were just what the name suggests: games. Yet, some also were "serious games" or games designed for purposes other than sheer entertainment. For example, many early games were designed with educational or training ends in mind. In particular, many of the earliest educational games were developed for military and warfare purposes, such as to teach strategy and tactics. This historical background is evidenced in the legacy of war games in the gaming market today (Perla, 1990). The research literature formally defines games as an "artificially constructed, competitive activity with a specific goal, a set of rules and constraints that is located in a specific context" (Hays, 2005, p. 15).

More recently, games have been used in higher education environments, and the earliest ones also drew upon warfare for their design. Spacewar, for example, was one of the first digital computer games introduced into an academic learning environment during the 1960s (Herz, 2001). Other early games in collegiate environments include the McClintic Theater Mode at the Army War College and Naval War Gaming System at the Naval War College (Allen, 1987).

Over time, educators became more interested in gaming technology, and in the mid-1980s, they began to seek a more engaging student-learning environment (Jonassen & Land, 2000). One of the first intentionally educational games was created around this time: Math Blaster, which was developed by Davidson & Associates, an educational software company. Other serious games soon were developed along the lines of the first, including Reader Rabbit, Oregon Trail, Microsoft Flight Stimulator, America's Army, and the New Manager Roadmap Challenge. Educators have maintained their interest in games, which has arguably increased with the advent of the Internet as a tool to discover new and creative ways to learn (Pivec, 2007).

In academic games, students compete as they seek to achieve a goal. They also require learning. Games can make instruction more enjoyable for the learner (Garris, Ahlers, & Driskell, 2002). Whether in class games or online games, the level of interest in games seems to be on the rise, and for good reason, because they have the potential to serve many purposes for the college classroom.

Purposes of Academic Games

Academic games are a form of experiential learning (Svinicki & McKeachie, 2013), and as such, they have a particular potential benefit to higher education. That is, they provide the opportunity for learners to use course content and skills in a contextualized environment. In this way, gaming provides an authentic learning experience for students. While playing games, students are engaged in the learning process; when games are designed well, students build strong connections to course content that aid later retrieval.

Educational games have the potential to help students reach important educational goals such as acquiring important foundational knowledge (Hertel & Millis, 2002). As learners move through game levels, they may be expected to process more and more information as they complete goals and tasks. Typically, games provide students with stimulation and reinforcement for learning basic content. When games are at the appropriate level of challenge, students are required to exert sufficient mental effort to complete them, which improves learning.

Games also have the potential to help students to develop higher-order thinking skills (Hertel & Millis, 2002). Games often require the learner to move from simple to more complex environments during gameplay, analyze rules using thinking skills, and develop strategies for success using creating thinking skills. Games also often provide a method through which students have the opportunity to solve problems. Finally, students build communication skills as they develop complex strategies for communicating with team members (Nilson, 2010).

Some games help students develop affective skills and appropriate dispositions. As entertainment and challenge are primary characteristics of instructional games, students can be motivated for learning when engaged in well-designed gaming experiences (Huang, Johnson, & Han, 2013; Plass et al., 2013). Games also have the advantage of competition, which is also helpful in engaging some students. Indeed, games promote holistic learning by encouraging students to engage different modalities, such as cognitive, affective, and kinesthetic learning (Barkley, Major, & Cross, 2014).

Games may be used to improve memory of terms and facts, reinforce materials and improve mentor transfer (Barkley et al., 2014; Sugar, 1998), review of relevant course concepts, or deeper exploration of issues and ideas (Kaupins, 2005; Moy, Rodenbaugh, Collins, & DiCarlo, 2000).

Hays (2005, p. 17) identifies several potential uses for academic games:

- Assess entry level performance
- Measure criterion performance
- Aid in formative and summative evaluations of instructional approaches and programs
- Provide instructional information on specific knowledge and skills
- Help change attitudes
- Serve as advance organizers prior to other forms of instruction
- Replace alternate forms of instruction to transmit facts, teach skills, and provide insights
- Serve as a means for drill and practice
- Help integrate and maintain skills
- Illustrate the dynamics or abstract principles of a task

Types of Academic Games

There are many different types of games used in college and university classrooms. We have grouped games into seven categories, based on the underlying learning framework employed. Most games may be done either face to face or online. Indeed, some of the latter categories of games are particularly effective when enacted online and even in virtual worlds.

- **Puzzles** are normally designed such that missing information must be identified and used in a strategic way in order to solve some overarching goal or concept. Clues are typically given for puzzles, with the level and type of clues given having a heavy influence on the difficulty of the puzzle. These clues may be obvious and involve direct recall of basic information or ill-defined and complex in determining the relationship of the clue to the puzzle strategy or solution. Our IDEA Crossword Puzzles is an example of this category of game.
- **Guessing games** typically have a single answer or concept the player must identify. These games are often heavily dependent on verbal communication. This category of game typically offers a set of questions or clues that students must use to deduce the answer to a prompt. For instance, Taboo is an example of a game in this category.
- **Trivia games** require the student to answer specific content questions. With respect to use in the classroom, these games are typically adaptations of games from television, where participants have to compete to accumulate points in order to win. Our IDEA Trivia is an example in this category.
- **Role plays** are games in which students assume identities that are different from their own and engage with each other in a predetermined way. This category of game relies on students recalling information relative to their role and then engaging that information in a way that is consistent with the

scenario given. The Role Play IDEA is an obvious example of a game in this category.

- **Simulations** involve setting up alternate worlds or situations in which students may practice their skills and knowledge in a safe environment. They often require more extensive preparation time than some of the other categories of games. Simulations have been used in health professions for a long time; with ready availability and reduced cost of technology, they have been increasingly used as an online learning tool (e.g., Everquest or Sims). Increasingly, due to advancements in technology making programming easier for those without specific training, instructors are designing their own simulation games according to their specific and particular educational objectives (Hertel & Millis, 2002).

Organization of Academic Games

Given the wide variety of games, there is no one pattern of organization or one way to sequence the activities. There are, however, several key elements that we believe must be present for it to be an academic game (Barkley et al., 2014; Sugar, 1998):

- **Goals.** Academic games begin with the instructor establishing well-defined learning goals and objectives. Learning objectives and goals primarily address what the educator wants the student to learn through engaging in the gaming process. They also likely tie to a particular module of content.
- **Student preparation.** An important aspect of using educational games is to consider the students, their needs, and their level of readiness when selecting or creating a game. As with all games, to achieve the expected outcomes, it is beneficial to prepare students for appropriate play by providing rules and gaining acceptance of the rules.
- **Tools.** This element includes any necessary elements to play the game. Gathering or creating the tools necessary for the user's behavioral actions to receive desirable feedback results in increased engagement levels and better learning outcomes. With respect to educational games, tools include handouts, materials, and equipment required for the game.
- **Activity.** This phase involves the ways in which the players come to understand the meaning of the activity itself, how the play is initiated, and the way in which the activity unfolds.
- **Monitoring.** While students play the game, it is helpful to observe students' performance and intervene when necessary to ensure that students are playing the game in the desired manner. The type of intervention will vary depending on the extent to which the structure and play is well defined. For ill-defined games that emphasize creativity and problem solving, it is helpful to let students know intervention will be kept to a minimum.

- **Assessments.** While playing instructional games, students' performance directly reflects their mastery of target knowledge and skills. As a result, it is possible to assess students in real time and to give constructive feedback immediately. Having guidelines for how the students' learning outcomes will be measured will assist students in being successful at the gaming experience. Many games have a built-in method of assessment through the scoring system (Barkley et al., 2014).
- **Closure.** Debriefing and system feedback play a significant role during the gaming process. Three different forms of assessment typically used include postgame assessment, postgame debriefing or evaluation, or in-game assessment (van Staalduinen & de Freitas, 2011). The postgame assessment includes administering an oral or written examination, exclusive of the gaming experience. The postgame debriefing or evaluation consists of an evaluation session between the instructor and user in which they discuss possible postgame learning outcomes (Peters & Vissers, 2004; Peters, Vissers, & Heijne, 1998). The in-game feedback measures the learning outcome of the user by calculating scores obtained within the game (Juul, 2005; Salen & Zimmerman, 2004; Wilson et al., 2009).

Beyond the basic structures, five game characteristics that play a prominent role in improving learning are as follows (Malone, 1981; Nilson, 2010; van Staalduinen & de Freitas, 2011):

- **Challenge**—the level of difficulty needed to keep the learner's interest at a high level. If the level is too low, the activity will be boring; if too high, it will be frustrating.
- **Control**—the student's freedom to make choices that may have desirable rewards or detrimental consequences. Allowing control will increase creativity and problem solving. However, having too many choices may well lead to disagreement as to how the game "should" be played.
- **Curiosity**—the learner's interest in new information or rules for reaching goals associated with the game.
- **Fantasy**—the set up or imaginary world that holds the student's attention for more effective learning.
- **Collaboration and competition**—games are often thought of as presenting opportunities for competition, but with academic games, collaboration is often present because most games are run as team games. That is, teams compete with each other; individuals on teams collaborate with each other. Educational games allow for collaborative learning because they bring students together to work as a team and increase students' interaction with their peers. Learners interact with others during gameplay in which they acquire new knowledge from each other. This concept is not limited to one individual, but learners are able to develop skills from social interaction. As Barkley et al. (2014) note, instructional games offer "strong networking and bonding opportunities among team members" (p. 331).

Advantages and Challenges of Academic Games for Instructors

One of the chief advantages for faculty who use games is that they make teaching and learning fun. Thus, they can be highly rewarding professionally and break up the routine of teaching the same classes each semester. Games also provide an opportunity for instructors to examine course content in new and interesting ways. When creating an academic game, instructors have to think through content, how to use it in a game, and how students will learn through gameplay. This exercise presents a valuable way for instructors to evaluate their instructional approach and strategies.

Of course, there are challenges to games as well. It can be difficult at times for instructors to match games with instructional goals, and a poor fit will hamper learning. Games tend to be time consuming and often require a great amount of time to create and implement, which places high demands on design and instructional time. Academic games can require special materials, which can be costly, or can require special facilities to which faculty may not have ready access. If they are not done well, educational games can be decidedly unfun, which can make gaming outside of class less fun and learning in class less effective. While some students thrive on competition, it can be off putting, or even traumatizing, for others. Finally, games can have a trivializing effect on instruction, making the teaching and learning process seem less important.

What Research Tells Us About the General Effectiveness of Academic Games

Approximately a decade ago, Hays (2005) conducted a review of early studies and found mixed results with respect to the effectiveness of academic games:

- Most studies showed no significant difference between traditional instruction and games (Fraas, 1982; Fritzsche, 1981; Klein & Frietad, 1991; Rowland & Gardner, 1973; Shrestha, 1990; Szafran & Mandolink, 1980; Williams, 1980).
- A few studies showed that games increased effectiveness (Barak, Engle, Katzir, & Fisher, 1988; Bredemeir, Bernstein, & Oxman, 1982; Gremmen & Potters, 1995; Westbrook & Braithwaite, 2001; Wood & Stewart, 1987).
- One showed that games decreased effectiveness (Rieber & Noah, 1997).

More recent studies reveal more positive findings. One of the most extensive meta-analyses to date found overall positive results from games (Clark, Tanner-Smith, Killingsword, & Bellamy, 2013). This study focused on digital games in particular and examined results from studies investigating K-12 and postsecondary education. The authors began with a sample of 61,887 studies and screened them for focus and quality. Eighty articles ultimately comprised their study, with 77 distinct study populations. Studies ranged in publication date from 2000–2012. The largest body of literature the authors found compared games to other instructional intervention. The authors concluded that:

> The findings from this meta-analysis indicate that compared with non-game instruction, digital games can enhance student learning as measured by cognitive competencies and some intrapersonal competencies. Furthermore, there was no evidence in any of the analyses that digital games were associated with statistically significant adverse outcomes (i.e., worse learning outcomes).
>
> (p. 10)

The findings from this study are supplemented by several studies that indicate that students simply like games and they find them effective for their learning. Students seem willing to spend significant amounts of time playing academic games. In one study examining the effects of the game called Nuclear Mayhem, Pløhn (2014) found that students played the game even outside of required lab times and that it became a pervasive part of students' lives. Moreover, interviews with students suggested that they found the game to be exciting and fun. Brinker et al. (2014) used the Game of Late Life and found that it helped students improve their attitudes about aging. Students found the game to be interesting and engaging. Similarly, Grimley et al. (2012) found that students believe that games are more challenging than the lecture method. Increased liking of games can lead to increased motivation and increased time studying, which in turn can have positive influences on learning.

What Research Tells Us About How to Improve Student Learning in Courses That Use Games

From the research that compares different courses using games, we can draw several important conclusions for how to improve games.

Research Finding #1. Instructional Support and Scaffolding Can Improve Student Performance in Games

Very few research studies examine games used in lieu of traditional instruction. Most focus on games used in tandem with direct instruction, such as readings or lectures. Some of these studies have done comparisons between traditional instruction supplemented with games, and recent studies tend to show that they are a good supplement. For example, Arena and Schwartz (2014) used games in a statistics course. Their theory was that students would have preconceived ideas that were contradicted by normative theories, which would make the concepts more difficult to learn. The researchers hypothesized that games would provide students with an alternate set of experiences. They used a game called Stats Invaders!, which is a variant of the videogame Space Invaders. In Stats Invaders!, the locations of descending alien invaders follow probability distributions, and players need to infer the shape of the distributions to play well. The researchers examined whether the game helped participant intuitions about the structure of random events, thereby preparing them for future learning from a subsequent written passage on probability distributions. Community college students who played the game and then read the passage learned more than students who only read the passage.

Other studies have examined how students do within game environments and found that scaffolding is helpful there as well. In a study of the effectiveness of online modules on information technology for undergraduate psychology students, Castaneda (2008) compared simulation condition of a self-guided game to other guided simulations. Students in either type of environment demonstrated knowledge gains if they were exposed to the game after expository instruction.

The meta-analysis by Clark et al. (2013) that we described in the general effectiveness section of this research review also compared different features of games in their study. The researchers found that games that included scaffolding (specifically supports for the player within the game or alternately features of the game that can adapt to the needs or actions of the player) showed beneficial effects on cognitive processes and strategies as well as on knowledge-related outcomes. These gains were higher than the increases to knowledge or skills that were due to enhancements to the game's interface or to player configuration, meaning changes in the social arrangements between players, specifically whether the game required completely individual play or varying combinations of collaboration and competition.

Studies using supports provided by the instructor such as pictorial representations (Mayer, Mautone, & Prothero, 2002) or 3D images (Hilbelink, 2009) support the idea that additional instructional support and scaffolding can enhance learning in games.

Research Finding #2. Collaboration Improves the Student Experience

Whether students play games individually or collaboratively is up to the instructor and the goals of the activity. However, research suggests that collaboration can have a positive effect on student perceptions. Lavega et al. (2014) examined different social structures and their influences on the emotional experiences of 556 students studying in Spanish universities. Using a Games and Emotions Questionnaire, researchers found significant differences in student responses. The intensity of the positive emotions that students felt appeared to be higher in cooperative games and lower in individual games.

Older studies support the idea that cooperation matters. For example, Fisher (1976) found that different sized groups influenced student performance. Similarly, Wellington and Faria (1996), who used a simulation game in a marketing course with 108 students and teams of 3–4, found that student teams that were more cohesive at the start outperformed teams that were less cohesive. The group cohesiveness remained constant through the gaming activity.

Research Finding #3. Noncompetitive Games Mean There Are No Losers

Lavega et al. (2014), who conducted the research at the Spanish universities that we described above, found that winning games gave students the highest intensity ratings for positive ambiguous emotions. On the other hand, losing produced the highest intensity ratings for negative emotions. In noncompetitive games, students are not defeated by another team or individual; as might be expected, the researchers found that intensity ratings for negative emotions were lower in noncompetitive games than in games that presented contests in which some players lost. Thus, instructors who use competitive games need to consider the potential consequences of doing so.

Research Finding #4. Feedback Is Critical in Game Activities

Feedback is the single most commonly mentioned success factor among studies on simulation and games on improving student learning. In a systematic review of simulations used in medical education, Issenberg, McGaghie, Petrusa, Gordon, and Scalese (2005) found that feedback was one of the most critical factors of success. This feedback could be built into the game or provided by the instructor after gameplay.

Using IDEAs to Improve Learning in Academic Games

In the following section of this chapter, we provide detailed descriptions of 14 intentionally designed educational activities (IDEAs) that correlate with the research findings we presented above. We suggest that these 14 activities correlate with these key research findings as we indicate in the following table:

TABLE 4.1 Game IDEAs and Research Findings

Game IDEAs	Description	Links to Research Findings
Crossword Puzzles	The instructor creates a crossword puzzle using key facts, definitions, and terminology.	Instructional Support (Research Finding #1); Noncompetitive game (Research Finding #3); Built-In Feedback (Research Finding #4)

(*Continued*)

TABLE 4.1 Continued

Game IDEAs	Description	Links to Research Findings
Scavenger Hunt	Students participate in a scavenger hunt game that requires them to answer questions relating to course content.	Instructional Support (Research Finding #1); Collaboration (Research Finding #2)
Who Am I?	The game provides students the opportunity to use their content knowledge to figure out a significant person or idea. The activity often involves a famous or significant person, place, or an object related to course content. Students have to ask questions to try to solve the answer in a manner similar to the Twenty Questions game.	Instructional Support (Research Finding #1); Built-In Feedback (Research Finding #4)
Pictionary	Similar to those versions of the game, a student selects a card with a course idea, fact, or person on it. The student draws pictures to illustrate the idea while teammates try to guess the word on the card.	Collaboration (Research Finding #2)
Trivia	This activity works particularly well in reviewing recent lessons or in preparing for exams. The game provides students an opportunity to recall course ideas along with the provision of immediate feedback of whether an answer is right or wrong.	Instructional Support (Research Finding #1); Collaboration (Research Finding #2); Built-In Feedback (Research Finding #4)
Hollywood Squares	The game follows the model of the classic TV show, where students play X's and O's answering course-related questions.	Instructional Support (Research Finding #1); Built-In Feedback (Research Finding #4)
Houston, We Have a Problem	The instructor provides a problem and a set of items to students. Students have to come up with a solution using the items provided, like the NASA engineers in Apollo 13.	Collaboration (Research Finding #2); Noncompetitive (Research Finding #3)

Game IDEAs	Description	Links to Research Findings
Monopoly	This game is an adaptation of the classic board game. It can be used for reviewing concepts, exam preparation, or applying class material to different contexts. Specifically, Monopoly can help make material more accessible for students by providing a vehicle for application through gameplay.	Instructional Support (Research Finding #1); Built-In Feedback (Research Finding #4)
Role Play	Students assume different personas and act out troublesome solutions in class.	Collaboration (Research Finding #2); Noncompetitive Game (Research Finding #3)
Taboo	In this game, a player receives a card and has to provide clues to partners without using the word itself or up to five additional words listed on the card. The players' partners have to guess the word.	Collaboration (Research Finding #2); Built-In Feedback (Research Finding #4)
Icebreakers	The goal is to "break the ice" by playing a game to provide an avenue for students to interact, meet each other, and build community.	Collaboration (Research Finding #2)
Top 10	The Top 10 technique asks students to generate a list of ten items related to course content. The structure allows students to consider either their prior knowledge or what they gained through the course to create a Top 10 list.	Instructional Support (Research Finding #1); Collaboration (Research Finding #2); Noncompetitive Game (Research Finding #3)
Pic of the Day	Students capture key aspects of the course in pictures and present them to the class.	Instructional Support (Research Finding #1)
Webquest	Students follow a series of clues and prompts from the instructor to help find information online. This game helps students develop research skills and better understand resources (library, etc.).	Instructional Support (Research Finding #1); Collaboration (Research Finding #2)

Following are detailed descriptions for how to implement these techniques in the classroom.

IDEA #36: Crossword Puzzles

Overview

When challenged at the appropriate level and given quick feedback, a person is motivated to complete a task. That is a primary draw of the daily crossword puzzle. The Crossword Puzzles IDEA serves as a teaching technique that allows students to demonstrate an understanding and recall of key concepts, terminology, and definitions. It also provides quick feedback and, if done at the correct level, challenges students. The strategy involves the instructor creating a puzzle to reinforce key course material. Crossword Puzzles have been shown to lead to positive results, particularly when used in class as a method for review (Weisskirch, 2006).

In addition to improving students' motivation to learn and an increased retention of content, students report enjoying the activity (Crossman & Crossman, 1983). A significant advantage of Crossword Puzzles is that the activity receives consistently high marks from students in a variety of empirical studies (Franklin, Peat, & Lewis, 2003). The game also allows students to test their knowledge.

Guiding Principles

Crossword Puzzles allow students to actively engage with course concepts and work to better understand course material. The use of games helps students practice recalling course information, solve problems, and receive prompt feedback. This combination builds upon and helps establish relevance and application through the completion of the puzzle.

In order to improve students' learning of important vocabulary and terminology, the learner needs practice at retrieval (Karpicke & Roediger, 2008). The active engagement of Crossword Puzzles helps provide another approach to retrieve and produce course-related vocabulary. The use of games and puzzles serves as an additional vehicle to not only improve mastery but also the speed with which students gain this understanding (Jaramillo, Losada, & Fekula, 2012).

Preparation

Most of the work for this technique involves developing the vocabulary list and the corresponding clues. Although faculty members using Crossword Puzzles in the past necessarily spent significant time creating the layout of the puzzle, software has made that task easy. A quick web search for free crossword puzzle makers will provide you with several options. When possible, it is helpful for you or a colleague or teaching assistant or even a former student to test the puzzle before using it with class. These testers can ensure the cues are easy to understand and at the correct level of difficulty, and they can help to identify any potential problems with the layout of the puzzle or specific clues. Finally, decide ahead of time whether this will be a task to be used independently as a review, an in-class activity to be done in groups, and open versus closed book/notes.

Process

- Simply pass out the puzzle or share the web address if the activity will be completed online.
- Inform the students of any rules for the activity. Will they complete it individually or in a small group? Will the task be graded? Are they to identify the theme of the puzzle?
- As you deem appropriate, serve as a resource for students with questions or the need for additional clarification on a topic included in the puzzle. One technique when using the Crossword Puzzle as a group activity in class is to allow each group to ask you for one hint.

Sample IDEA Pairings

Guided Note-Taking (IDEA #1). Use the Crossword Puzzle as the guide for the note-taking by providing a specific clue and having students fill in the puzzle for that clue and augment notes as appropriate.

Pause Procedure (IDEA #2). While lecturing, pause periodically and encourage students to fill in the two or three items that pertain directly to the material just covered.

Directed Reading and Thinking (IDEA #52). Rather than providing a list of concepts, provide the puzzle that students complete with information gathered from readings.

Pro-tips

There are many free online sources for creating crossword puzzles. Some of these sites let you create online or print versions. Sites have advantages and disadvantages, so experiment with a few different ones before determining which one best suits your needs.

Vocabulary words are often listed at the end of the chapter or in course support software. A variation of long and short words are helpful. Long words have plenty of letter options to use when arranging the puzzle, while short words are effective for connecting longer words together. You may also want to use some noncourse-specific terms to provide additional word options and to show how the course material is related to other areas. Additionally, it is fun to periodically use campus landmarks or traditions to offer more words for the program to use when creating the puzzle and to demonstrate that you created the puzzle for them.

An alternative is to have the students make adjustments to a puzzle you create that they feel would benefit the puzzle. These "corrections" can be used to make future Crossword Puzzles.

A final option is to have the students create a Crossword Puzzle. Divide the class into groups and give each group a vocabulary list of a given number of words. Have the students create the cues. This variation helps students to better learn the content by creating the clues. Asking questions to generate a given response is a powerful learning technique in itself.

IDEA #37: Scavenger Hunt

Overview

In this IDEA, the teacher prepares a list of clues related to items or tasks for students to find or complete. The information may be located within course materials, around campus, in the community, or on the Web. Scavenger Hunts have been used effectively for decades to generate excitement and deeper thinking about course content (Dodge, 1991; Gaskill, McNulty, & Brooks, 2006). Depending on the intended outcomes for the activity, students may be asked to work individually or in teams. The items on the list can be given a point value (based on difficulty to complete), or students can try to complete as many as possible within a set time limit.

The goal of this activity is to facilitate student learning through the completion of the items as part of the Scavenger Hunt. The game is intended to enhance and develop cooperation, creativity, and engagement. In addition, the Scavenger Hunt IDEA can get students to engage with course concepts outside of the four walls of the classroom.

Guiding Principles

An underlying principle of Scavenger Hunts is the notion of inquiry-based learning. The goal of this type of learning is to involve students in the learning process by forcing them to seek answers to questions and develop new knowledge (Brickman, Gormally, Armstrong, & Hallar, 2009). In order to complete the list, students have to complete tasks and solve questions, often creatively. This process engages students in the learning process through a specific set of instructor-designed tasks (the clue or task list).

Scavenger Hunts also have students engage in experiential learning, where students gain knowledge from direct experiences (Kolb, 1984). The game allows students to experience information rather than passively listening. For example, students in a botany class may have to search around campus for specific plants and identify aspects of the plant. Similarly, students in a sociology class may search the campus for areas in which individuals cluster. The Scavenger Hunt requires students to actively experience course content as they solve clues to find the next item.

Preparation

Scavenger Hunts require some initial setup work. First, identify a list of tasks for students to complete or items for them to gather. Give consideration to the amount of time allotted to this activity (even if done outside of the regular class period) and whether a point structure will be used. Also develop any rules for the hunt. Scavenger Hunts encourage competitiveness, and clear rules can help use this to your advantage. Well-defined rules will focus the activity on locating specific items or concepts, whereas ill-defined rules will focus the activity on creativity and problem solving. Finally, decide whether you will give a specific list or clues for items.

Process

- Pass out the Scavenger Hunt task list and break students into groups (or tell students to work individually).
- Go over the rules, ask for questions, and provide clarification where needed.
- Have the students work on the Scavenger Hunt list until completed or the set time elapses.
- Depending upon the goal of the hunt, you may want to debrief regarding items that students struggled with or observations made during the game.

Sample IDEA Pairings

Can We Have Class Outside? (IDEA #19). A Scavenger Hunt is a great out-of-class activity. Give students their lists, let them hunt, and then announce winners and discuss what they learned.

Pic of the Day (IDEA #48). Ask students to compile photos from tasks on the Scavenger Hunt list and then use the items to demonstrate their knowledge of a particular topic.

Annotations (IDEA #72). Ask students to write Annotations for each item on the Scavenger Hunt list.

Pro-tips

Many students will engage with this activity competitively. This excitement will improve participation. You may foster excitement by providing a small reward. You can offer extra credit points or simply some candy for the winning group. Not all students will be comfortable with high levels of competition, however. If your class tends to have students who do not like team competition, structure the activity for individual achievement of the tasks, and keep the results private.

This activity can be effective when students work with a partner or small group. Working together, they will share their ideas and opinions with their partner. Scavenger Hunts also provide an opportunity for students to get to know each other more informally, which can improve interactions within class.

Scavenger Hunts can be an innovative way to make effective use of technology in the classroom. One option is to have students work in small groups and have each group create a single Scavenger Hunt item. At a given time, all groups share their items, and other groups are challenged to find as many of the collegially developed items as possible in a given amount of time.

One of the most common uses of this IDEA is the library Scavenger Hunt. In this version of the game, students receive a Scavenger Hunt list that requires them to locate and use a range of library resources (Glasberg, Harwood, Hawkes, & Martinsek, 1990; Marcus & Beck, 2003). Often, students have to write down how they found a resource, which can serve as a reminder when using the library later for assignments.

IDEA #38: Who Am I?

Overview

The Who Am I? IDEA is a game that provides students the opportunity to use their content knowledge to identify a significant person or idea. The activity often involves a famous or significant person, place, or object related to course content. Students have to ask questions to try to solve the answer in a manner similar to the Twenty Questions game (Siegler, 1977).

This activity requires students to develop an understanding of course content and think through key concepts by asking questions. Specifically, Who Am I? encourages students to consider foundational elements of material in order to ask questions to uncover the mystery. This practice in asking questions and thinking about elements of course material can help students' comprehension.

Guiding Principles

The use of Who Am I? is supported by the benefits of the generation effect. Student learning improves when they have to generate answers versus simply recognizing the correct answer (Butler & Roediger, 2007). By forcing students to ask questions to come up with the answer, Who Am I? improves student learning and recall of course material.

Related to the benefits of generating an answer, student learning is enhanced by organizing information. Students use additional effort when acquisition and recall promote the development of multiple retrieval paths (Bereiter & Scardamalia,

1985; Bjork, 1988). Although this process slows initial learning, it has been shown repeatedly to aid long-term recall. Who Am I? allows students to organize and recall information through the course of the game, which can aid student learning and retention.

Preparation

Prior to using Who Am I?, identify a list of people, places, or objects from course content. It is helpful to include information or items used in prior material to help students to integrate information. Write down the names or objects on index cards that students can draw. It is also helpful to think through why you are using this activity and share that information with students. Learning is generally better facilitated when learners understand the rationale behind the strategies being used.

Process

- Select a student (or group of students) to draw a card with a name, place, or object on it.
- Allow a couple of minutes for selected students to reference readings or other materials to prepare to answer questions.
- Students in class ask questions to the selected student in order to determine who or what was on the card selected. The questions must be phrased to allow for only a "yes or no" response.
- After each question, the student or group of students asking the question may guess or pass.

Sample IDEA Pairings

Pause-Procedure (IDEA #2). Use Who Am I? as an activity during the pauses to reinforce particular ideas from the lecture.

Role Play (IDEA #44). Role Play has built-in characters that can be used in the Who Am I? IDEA.

Interviews (IDEA #70). Students develop a set of questions that get asked using the framework of the Who Am I? IDEA. This pairing works well when a common set of questions is used to ask each pair in order to determine the person, place, or object. (Note: both people need the same category of card. For example, both have a person or both have a place).

Pro-tips

A useful variation of this activity is to have several games happening simultaneously. For example, you might select three students who will be three famous playwrights or scientists. Students can ask questions to any of the three until reaching a set number or until they guess the person. Using this variation can facilitate comparisons between people, places, or ideas.

If enthusiasm is lagging for the activity, you may want to add competitive elements. You can divide students into teams, and each gets to ask a question until one team solves the answer. Also, you might add a point system where a team gets 19 points if they guess the answer after one question, 18 points after two questions, and so on.

Rather than selecting students to respond to questions, you may decide to play this role. You know the material and may be in a better position to answer questions. If using the technique on material that students may not fully comprehend yet, when you answer the questions, it opens up additional possibilities for the game's use (e.g., as a warm-up activity before discussing a topic).

IDEA #39: Pictionary

Overview

The Pictionary technique is based on the guessing game popularized by the game of the same name as well as the television game show *Win, Lose, or Draw*. Similar to those versions of the game, a student selects a card with a course idea, fact, or person on it. The student draws pictures to illustrate the idea while teammates try to guess the word or phrase on the card.

This technique is easy to implement using the materials found in virtually any classroom. Students can draw on the board or on an easel pad. The activity encourages students to participate and use their understanding of material in playing the game. Pictionary requires students to think about how to draw a course concept, which encourages application and synthesis of material.

As with other games and competitions in the classroom, winning results in a release of the neurotransmitter dopamine, which increases motivation and has a positive impact on learning (Wise, 2004).

Guiding Principles

Pictionary encourages creativity, which in turn can help develop evidence-based reasoning and problem-solving skills (DeHaan, 2009). By fostering creativity, instructors help students make connections, better understand relationships, and apply new knowledge. The ability to transfer knowledge benefits students and helps them use information in new and different contexts (Mestre, 2005). The process of figuring out what to draw, how to draw it, and responding to teammates' guesses in Pictionary can stimulate this learning process for students.

One of the primary purposes of Pictionary is to use what some researchers call stealth learning (Sharp, 2012). This idea suggests using clever and nontraditional approaches to learning that engage students in fun. As a result, students have fun, better motivation, and better learning outcomes. Pictionary allows students to have fun with course content, which keeps them engaged and reinforces new knowledge.

Preparation

Prior to the use of Pictionary, create a list of concepts, people, objects, and terms significant to the course or lesson for the day. Ideally, this list will include some questions of varying difficulty. You may also want to categorize the cards as a hint to players depending on the difficulty of the terms to be drawn.

Process

- Explain the rules and have a stack of cards with course content words and phrases from which students will select.
- Divide students into teams.
- Taking turns, have each team send a person to draw the word(s) on the card. A team has between 30–60 seconds to guess the answer.
- If the team is not able to guess the answer, allow another team the chance to guess the answer and gain a point.

Sample IDEA Pairings

Text Coding (IDEA #56). Instead of the instructor creating the cards, students write down a concept identified during their Text Coding. The game is then played using these student-generated cards.

Freewriting (IDEA #63). After a round of Pictionary, students Freewrite about the concepts from the cards.

Main Idea-Detail Chart (IDEA #80). Students chart the concepts from the cards, identifying which are the main ideas and which are the details.

Pro-tips

Creating the items to go on the cards that students will draw is critical for this activity to work well. Key terms from lectures and textbooks are great for drawing ideas. Additionally, terms that have varying degrees of difficulty can keep enthusiasm high by providing different challenges and encouraging teams to steal points away.

Near the end of the activity, you may want to institute a lightning round. Each team has two minutes, and a series of students take turns, each drawing one card. Within the allotted time, whichever team gets more cards correct wins.

Until you learn how long it takes teams to go through a series of cards, you may want to make sure you have plenty of extra cards for gameplay. Additionally, you may want to create some particularly easy or difficult cards to substitute into the card stack as needed.

Another option is to have students create the cards across several class periods. You then sort the cards and find those that would work best for the game. This approach will make the task easier for you and also help the students to better learn the concepts.

IDEA #40: Trivia

Overview

The Trivia technique is a game that increases the students' ability to recall course content. Most frequently, this activity is designed for testing specific course ideas, concepts, and facts. The technique is easy to use and requires little setup or design. Many versions of Trivia exist, and the game can be made more elaborate through the use of teams, points, and timers.

Similar to the game show *Jeopardy* or the board game Trivial Pursuit, Trivia asks students a short question that they answer individually or in teams. This activity works particularly well in reviewing recent lessons or in preparing for exams. The game provides students an opportunity to recall course ideas along with the provision of immediate feedback of whether an answer is right or wrong.

Guiding Principles

Practice at retrieval of information is a powerful way to increase the long-term retention of information (Karpicke & Roediger, 2008). Retrieving information helps to create pathways to the selected information that makes it easier to recall at a later time. A second foundational element of the use of Trivia is in the use of classroom assessments, more specifically formative assessments (Angelo & Cross, 1993). The primary purpose of formative assessment is the improvement of students' understanding and learning rather than grading or evaluating students. Through the use of Trivia questions, instructors are better able to consider how well students comprehend important class content. As a result, Trivia focuses on student learning rather than the instructional process.

Answering Trivia questions as a learning tool is powerful as it gives immediate feedback for students. In order to provide effective feedback, instructors have to help students improve their comprehension, and students have to be open to hearing the response. Feedback that is specific, timely, clear, focused, and expressed in an appropriate way helps students advance their work (Brown, Bull, & Pendlebury, 1997).

Preparation

The primary requirement for the Trivia technique is to generate good questions related to course content. If exams and quizzes have been given back to students in prior semesters, then questions from those assessments are an ideal place to draw your Trivia questions. Questions from the textbook or other textbooks in the course content area are other places from which you may generate Trivia items. One option is to spontaneously ask questions and seek student answers throughout the class period. However, you may benefit from compiling a list of questions prior to class that address key class objectives for the day and having students work in groups at the beginning of the class period to identify answers as quickly as possible. If you wish to have a more involved game, you can come up with additional rules, rewards, and structure. The goal of the Trivia questions in most cases is to entice students to recall significant course content quickly and accurately.

Process

- Pose a question to a student or groups of students. After an answer is given, explain if the answer is correct. In some cases, it will be helpful to explain why the question was chosen and why the answer is important.
- If desired, award points for correct answers, have students play or pass the question to another group, or incorporate other aspects of gameplay.
- For incorrect answers, it is helpful to give hints to the class to prompt the correct response. It is also beneficial to create a culture in the classroom where incorrect responses are seen as learning opportunities and as a class work through why an incorrect response may have been given and what it reveals about the way one thinks about the content.

Sample IDEA Pairings

Pause Procedure (IDEA #2). Ask Trivia questions during the lecture and pause to recap ideas articulated during the lecture session immediately prior. Questions could also be used to recall earlier course concepts relevant for the next lecture to be delivered.

Journaling (IDEA #68). Students write about what they learned in their journals.

Concept Maps (IDEA #79). Students create Concept Maps from the Trivia questions, grouping similar ideas together.

Pro-tips

Adding a timing element or other competitive aspects may get students more into the activity, increase energy level of the class, and provide extra incentive for faster recall.

Small rewards may increase student interest. These rewards could be as simple as a piece of candy. Depending on the students, the reward could also be a sticker. This depends upon your comfort level with rewards and the culture developed in the classroom. At times, university students will work hard to earn a sticker. Anything that adds an element of fun can help improve student participation in the activity.

Students can benefit from playing Trivia in pairs or small groups. The brief discussions that occur in determining an answer can result in peer teaching, content synthesis, and better student interaction. The act of coming up with a shared team answer can prove as useful to student learning as the recall of the answer itself.

One option is to create groups of students and have the groups develop Trivia questions to be answered by other groups. A combination prize can be given for the most questions answered by a given group and the least number of questions other groups are able to answer from a group's questions. This helps to encourage groups to write challenging questions.

IDEA #41: Hollywood Squares

Overview

The Hollywood Squares IDEA utilizes the format of a well-known television game show that ran for 36 seasons from 1966 to 2004. Although the show has been "off the air" for over 10 years, it is based on the timeless game of tic-tac-toe and provides a format for a classroom activity. In this show, a host asked celebrities sitting in the nine tic-tac-toe boxes questions. The celebrities answered the questions, and then the contestants either agreed that the answer was correct or disagreed, indicating they did not feel the answer was correct. As with using any television game show format, you can adapt: modify with class content, rules, and number of participants (Yaman & Covington, 2006).

One of the primary benefits of Hollywood Squares is that it involves multiple students. Similar to the TV game, nine students serve as the roles played by celebrities in the television show, with two students (or teams of students) as the contestants. You serve as the host of the show and ask the questions. Often without students even realizing it, the use of Hollywood Squares allows students to demonstrate their mastery of course content and ideas. The activity can be used for a variety of purposes but works particularly well in reviewing key course concepts, preparing for exams, and applying key ideas. Hollywood Squares is an easy method for encouraging student participation as it provides a low-stakes avenue for students to join in the class.

Guiding Principles

Hollywood Squares builds upon active learning that engages students as participants in their own learning. The activity helps students analyze and synthesize course material through the course of gameplay (Sarason & Banbury, 2004). By using the popularity of television game shows, instructors are easily able to include active learning in class. In addition, this game works for classes with a variety of levels as the "contestants" simply have to agree or disagree with the response provided by the person in the square. It is important to emphasize to the person in the square that it is not necessary to know the answers to all questions, but the people providing the response should always act as if they know the answer. Squares are won not by the accuracy of the response but by the ability of the contestant (or contestant groups) to correctly agree or disagree as to the correctness of the response. A person on team X "wins" a square by either agreeing or disagreeing accurately or having the Team O incorrectly responding when it is their turn.

An underlying principle of the Hollywood Squares technique is offering students feedback. Within the low-stakes environment of the game, students or teams answer questions related to course content. Students receive immediate feedback through the game show format, which can help students fix their errors, improve recall, and enhance test performance (Butler & Roediger, 2007).

Preparation

Hollywood Squares requires some setup prior to use in class. You will need to identify questions to ask the celebrity students. Depending on how many rounds of the game you play, you'll need six to nine questions per round. You can simply draw a tic-tac-toe board on the board and mark X's and O's as needed, create a game board, or have the celebrity students sit in seats that are arranged three rows across and three rows deep. Each student should have a paper with an "X" on one side and an "O" on the other side to note who won the square.

Process

- Explain the game to the class. Select nine students and assign each as the celebrity for a corresponding square on the 3x3 board.
- Have two students as contestants. One will be assigned X and another O.
- Taking turns, the contestants will select a square. You (as host) will ask a course content question to the celebrity who will answer (again it is important that the celebrity always look as if he or she is giving the correct answer). The student contestant will agree or disagree with the student celebrity's answer. If the contestant is correct, he or she gets the square. If incorrect, the opponent gets the square.
- Two potential variations to consider. First, the student has to get the correct answer to get three in a row and win the game, rather than the opponent missing an answer. Second, to avoid draws, the student with five squares wins.

Sample IDEA Pairings

Scored Discussion (IDEA #14). One group of students plays the game while the rest form an outer group of students. The outer group makes notes of key ideas in the game. These notes can be shared with the class to form a study guide.

Role Play (IDEA #44). Students playing the celebrity role in the game are assigned to roles. They play this character while answering questions as part of Hollywood Squares.

Pro-tips

This activity can provide students with a gauge of what material students comprehend and where they are struggling. As Simkin (2013) found, the indirect feedback of game shows demonstrated that students had more difficulty with what he considered easy questions while they understood the more difficult concepts. This information can prove useful for helping students improve deficiencies in their understanding.

Many instructors may feel the need to have elaborate props or other materials to play the game. While prompts can be fun for both instructor and student, they are unnecessary. For the purposes of the technique, drawing X's and O's on the board or having students sit in a 3x3 grid and hold up paper X's and O's are as useful as electronic versions of a Hollywood Squares board.

Typically, it is best for you to serve as game show host. This role helps both logistically in terms of playing the game and allows you to interject quick facts or remind students of course material during the course of gameplay. Student learning occurs primarily through playing the game, but these short insertions can help immediately clarify points for students.

IDEA #42: Houston, We Have a Problem

Overview

In the popular movie *Apollo 13*, the astronauts are trapped with their oxygen running out. In a classic scene, all of the NASA engineers gather in a room with all of the stuff in the spacecraft and have to figure out how to make a square air filter fit a hole made for a round filter. Literally, the engineers had to make a square peg fit in a round hole. In the Houston, We Have a Problem IDEA, students are given a collection of items or information that they must use to solve a problem presented by the instructor.

The game is designed to encourage class participation, creativity, and problem solving. The structure allows the opportunity for students to work together to think of innovative ways to use a set collection of items to solve a problem. Students may understand basic concepts related to class but have a difficult time integrating and applying material. Houston, We Have a Problem can be a fun activity that forces students to think through various issues, hypothesize solutions, and use knowledge gained from class.

Guiding Principles

Research from cognitive theory suggests that skills and knowledge are not learned separately and abstractly. Rather, instructional environments that organize learning and skills practice within the context of application of knowledge improve motivation and learning (Resnick, 1989). Houston, We Have a Problem provides a useful structure and construct to apply and create knowledge within the classroom environment.

This IDEA also builds upon the benefits of cooperative learning to teach problem-solving abilities. Using cooperative learning proves an effective method of helping students learn complex skills while effectively managing the demands on instructors (Heller, Keith, & Anderson, 1992). During the Houston, We Have a Problem activity, students can learn from each other about how to approach problems, use course content, and develop solutions.

Preparation

The first step to prepare for Houston, We Have a Problem is to identify the problem for students to solve. The problem should be related to an application of course content and preferably (although not necessarily) one with multiple paths to a solution. Next, you will need to collect items or information for students to use to solve the problem. You might literally put the items on a table or provide a list. The items might be objects (e.g., lab equipment) or information (e.g., equation or formula) that can be used to figure out a solution. It is also useful to provide red herring items that likely will not be useful but will require students to think about their possible use.

Process

- Divide the students into groups and present the problem to be solved. The problem should be presented clearly but avoid any suggestion of possible solutions. Provide the groups with the items available for use in solving the problem.
- Have the students work on creating a problem. Answer questions from the groups seeking clarification about the problem but do not provide examples of how to use the items or ways to come up with a solution.
- After each group is finished, ask each to briefly report on their solution. Time permitting, you can also ask each group to explain the process they used.

Sample IDEA Pairings

Gallery Walk (IDEA #28). After students complete their solution for Houston, We Have a Problem, they walk around looking at the solutions and summarize trends that they noted from other groups.

Today I Learned (IDEA #90). Students reflect upon what they learned through the exercise of playing the game.

Post Hoc Analysis (IDEA #100). Students complete Houston, We Have a Problem and then reflect back on the activity though writing about the important patterns and issues related to the problem.

Pro-tips

Particularly at the beginning of the game, groups may struggle with how to get started or approach the problem. They may ask for help or seek direction, but you should avoid the temptation to assist. The best learning during Houston, We Have a Problem is when students are forced to figure out an approach. Mental challenge may be difficult and uncomfortable for some groups, but it is a necessary part of learning how to problem solve.

While the students are completing the activity, wander around from group to group. Your presence will lead to questions but, again, only answer those about the problem. As you move between groups, listen for how students are working through the process of problem solving so you can ask process-related questions at the conclusion of the activity.

Although the problems identified can be many different types, the best problems present details that the students can use when using the items to create solutions. In addition, the students do not necessarily need to build something from the items to complete this activity. The students may have to identify the lab equipment and the order of how to use it in order to complete an experiment. Alternatively, students might have to use various class concepts and formulas to determine an answer to the problem. The goal is to have students solve a problem by selecting what and how to use the items available.

IDEA #43: Monopoly

Overview

This technique uses the well-known board game Monopoly or elements of the game to serve as the framework for classroom engagement. Monopoly, as originally designed, focuses on economics, math, negotiation, and probabilities. However, the structure of the game works well in a variety of different formats. The benefit of this technique is in encouraging students to engage with course concepts and peers. This technique can be used for reviewing concepts, exam preparation, or applying class material to different contexts. Specifically, Monopoly can help make material more accessible for students by providing a vehicle for application through gameplay.

Guiding Principles

At the foundational level, Monopoly is useful because the game provides students with a fun and engaging way to apply course material. Moreover, the game can teach both course content as well as other skills such as communication, teamwork, negotiation, and cooperation. For example, in a classroom version of Monopoly, students might learn about economics or math in one part of gameplay while also learning negotiation skills when trading properties. The ability to teach content and skills make Monopoly and board games in general a particularly useful activity (Mummalaneni & Sivakumar, 2008).

Versions of Monopoly, as with nearly all games, can fall into three categories: collaborative, cooperative, or competitive (Zagal, Rick, & His, 2006). Collaborative games force students to develop win-win scenarios; competitive games require strategies that oppose other players. Cooperative games fall into the middle of the spectrum. Monopoly can include any of these, which allows the game to be versatile in classroom use. The strategy behind the game not only provides a context for learning and interaction but also can drive the engagement of students playing the game. Students can play the game in the typical fashion where one tries to win and bankrupt the other players. Alternatively, the use of Chance or Community Chest type cards can be added to many activities including having students work together.

Preparation

One option is to play the game as designed and look to concepts pertaining to your course. For example, you might use the abbreviated version of the game (see game instructions) and then focus on negotiation and teamwork as the principles to be learned. Alternatives are based on any number of possible variations on the actual game. If adapting the game, you will need to devise the game as well as rules. You will find it helpful to think through course content you want students to use through playing Monopoly (Salter, 2013). If you are new to using a board game in class, you may find it helpful to look at the goals of Monopoly and see which aspects might match up best with your course content. You may not want to have students play the entire game but simply use an aspect of the game for an activity. For example, the properties around the board escalate in value. You could have students arrange key course terms similarly using a monetary or other value basis.

Process

- Explain the game and rules to the students.
- Have the students form groups of an appropriate size for the game. If playing the full game, groups of no more than five are preferred. If only using certain aspects of the game (such as Monopoly money), you can use almost any size group.
- Distribute the needed game pieces/equipment and have students play the game.
- If appropriate, when stopping the game, discuss the key aspects of the game as related to the course ideas.

Sample IDEA Pairings

Circle of Voices (IDEA #18). At the conclusion of the game, the group of students discuss the main ideas from the game. If the game has a winner, this person's prize can be moderating the postgame discussion.

Role Play (IDEA #44). Students assume a role or philosophy (such as a buyer or saver) as a part of the game, which can add an additional wrinkle to gameplay.

Cause & Effect Chains (IDEA #85). Students can describe the events and actions that led to the conclusion of the game. This approach can work well with content that closely aligns with the board game. By describing the game, students are also describing the flow of course ideas.

Pro-tips

This technique requires fairly extensive preparation, particularly to develop an effective variation of the original board game. You may find it less time intensive to just use a single element of the game. For example, you might use Monopoly money to illustrate finite resources and the cost of certain courses of action. Even this small element of a game can help students better grapple with key course concepts.

Be careful not to assume that students know how to play a given board game, even a "classic" such as Monopoly. This is particularly true of international students. At the beginning, you may need to visit the groups playing the game and help clarify any questions regarding gameplay. Most students will pick up how to play the game quickly, but providing prompt feedback can help students engage with the activity.

In addition to instructor-designed board games, you may find the students enjoy creating and even playing their own games. This activity can work well as a class or group project. Students have to design a Monopoly-style game (or any other kind of board game) that illustrates key ideas from class that they determine or you can assign. In the course of designing the game, students have to develop a mastery of the material in order to apply it to a game scenario.

IDEA #44: Role Play

Overview

In Role Play, students act out a scenario or persona. This IDEA allows students to gain more context for new information. Role playing can include historical, contemporary, or artificial perspectives to encourage students to consider alternative views and opinions. This technique is often relatively unstructured; however, efforts to provide more real-life experiences can include more structure.

An advantage of Role Play is allowing students to experience, react, and reflect on course-related people and ideas (Bonwell & Eison, 1991). Role Play encourages students to actively participate in class and use course information relevant to their assumed persona. The technique can provide a fun activity for students to engage with each other, apply course knowledge, and practice communication skills (Nestel & Tierney, 2007). The Role Play technique has been used across a wide range of disciplines from social sciences such as political science and economics to math and science fields (Jackson, 2000).

Guiding Principles

This technique uses many of the aspects of cooperative learning into group tasks, positive interdependence, and encouraging interpersonal skill development (Johnson, Johnson, & Holubec, 1994). The activity provides a structure for interaction and group processing to facilitate learning. The instructor's role is to facilitate and intervene only when necessary. As a result, students together are responsible for their own learning.

Role Play allows students to assume a persona and consider the world through the perspective of someone who experienced or even developed the concepts being discussed. This process helps students develop empathy for people or their circumstances in addition to considering their position. By "walking in the shoes" of a person or idea, students are able to more fully consider the view and relate their own opinions to those expressed in the Role Play.

Preparation

Prior to the Role Play, determine the goal and format of the activity. Assign or determine how you want the roles or scenario to play out. Prepare background information on the character or position each student will play. Finally, determine what material students will read to prepare for their roles.

Process

- Give students background information on their roles by providing specific details about the characters or the setting. Such information can be shared just with the individual or the entire class.
- Have the students engage in the Role Play based on the predetermined format or setting.
- After the conclusion of the Role Play, facilitate a discussion of the activity, evaluate various characters positions, and relate the information back to course content.

Sample IDEA Pairings

Scored Discussion (IDEA #14). Students in the inner group participate in the Role Play while students in the outer circle makes notes and observe the activity.

Case Study (IDEA #24). The case provides the setting, context, and characters for students to assume in the Role Play. Through the Case Study, students are able to apply course concepts to a real-life example and practice the skills necessary for success outside of higher education.

Interviews (IDEA #70). Interviewer or interviewee may assume a Role Play character and interact with each other. The interview format provides a structure to the Role Play and defines the students' participation with each other.

Pro-tips

Role Playing works best when students are required to use course information as part of the activity. The characters and settings should encourage students to make use of this knowledge to participate in the role play. As a result, students synthesize and apply content directly, which facilitates learning.

One of the most difficult aspects of the Role Play IDEA is ensuring everyone participates fully in the activity. As the instructor, it may be helpful for you to move around and provide subtle hints and clues that help stimulate the activity. For example, you may want to give a tip to a group about an idea they had not considered or suggest a course of action to spark a group that is struggling to get going. The key is to provide encouragement to get the students going but allow them to work through the Role Play and relevant material for themselves.

Particularly creative students will often make up details and ideas about their characters. Within reason, this behavior is evidence that students are making sense of course material. However, be sure these assumptions are reasonable within the confines of the Role Play. The students will often look to you to serve as referee in these cases, so consider how much leeway you are willing to offer.

IDEA #45: Taboo

Overview

This activity is modeled after the popular word guessing party game. To play Taboo, a student tries to have another student or group of students guess a word or concept on a card without using the word in question or a list of additional "taboo" words typically associated with the word. The structure of the activity helps students review course content as well as increase class participation. Taboo encourages students to think outside the box about key concepts and thus allows the instructor to gauge students' level of understanding.

Taboo requires students have a thorough grasp of course content. Additionally, the activity asks students to think both critical and creatively while playing. An instructor can use this lighthearted activity for many different purposes, including reviewing key concepts and ideas prior to exams or demonstrating comprehension of new terminology.

Guiding Principles

Taboo facilitates students' developing critical-thinking and problem-solving skills. Instruction geared toward critical thinking builds on how students think about an idea by changing their "default" understanding of a key concept (Halpern, 1999). By asking students to describe a course concept without using the terms or details of which they are most familiar, Taboo forces students to draw connections with other ideas from within and outside of class.

This IDEA builds upon word associations, which form the basis for many aspects of recall and recognition (De Deyne, Navarro, & Storms, 2012). The relationship between words and building networks of connecting words form the basis of human knowledge and language. By building on the advantages of word associations, Taboo encourages students to think about the connections between key course concepts as well as prior knowledge. Moreover, by creating "taboo" words that students are not allowed to use during the game, the activity forces students to build additional networks and associations that can help deepen their understanding.

Preparation

Before playing Taboo in class, decide on the core purpose of the activity. If the goal is to review course concepts, you may want to involve the students in the development of the cards for play. To do so, you may want to provide the students with a list of words or short phrases relating to course content and have them come up with details that relate to that topic to be considered "unmentionable" words during gameplay. These cards will need to be prepared ahead of time or earlier in class prior to play.

Process

- Provide students with a set of cards for the activity. Each card has a keyword as well as a list of "unmentionable" words or short phrases on it.
- The students are divided into two teams, and a representative from each team takes turns drawing a card and trying to get his teammates to guess the keyword on the card without using any of the other listed forbidden words.
- Play continues until each student has played a card, the cards run out, or a set score or time limit is reached.

Sample IDEA Pairings

Each One, Teach One (IDEA #30). Students might be asked to share an additional facts about the keyword presented on their card with the class. Be sure to provide students a little time to prepare to share their information after the game.

Speed Interviews (IDEA #35). Use the Taboo framework for each Speed Interview pair to discuss these keywords. Students take turns trying to get their partner to guess the keyword before trading partners.

Main Idea–Detail Chart (IDEA #80). Ask students to first develop a main idea to serve as the main word for gameplay, and then ask them to develop details to serve as the "taboo" or forbidden words or phrases.

Pro-tips

Taboo requires students to have a fairly thorough knowledge of the course material in order to play the game. As a result, the IDEA often works best later in a class so students have had the opportunity to grasp many course concepts that they may use to successfully play the game.

When asking students to develop their own cards, be sure that the concepts are clear and distinct from one another to ensure a breadth of review while both developing and playing the game. You can have students seek your approval of their keywords before preparing their cards. This safeguard also helps prevent duplication of keywords.

During the activity, encourage all students to participate in guessing. Watch to see if certain questions or concepts are tripping students up (e.g., they are unable to adequately describe the word presented, or teammates are unable to guess the word in play). These types of struggles may be an indicator that additional review of that topic is necessary.

IDEA #46: Icebreakers

Overview

Icebreakers are used in a variety of formal and informal instructional settings to build community and to illustrate expectations of participation. The goal is to "break the ice" by providing an activity to provide an avenue for students to interact, meet each other, and build community. Most frequently, Icebreakers are used at the beginning of the semester or at the start of an individual class session to get students to talk to one another and to get to know something about each other. The goal is to help students build a comfort level and community in the class that can improve discussions and other class activities.

There are literally hundreds of examples of Icebreaker activities designed for use in class, meetings, workshops, or trainings (West, 1999). This technique is one of the shortest and easiest ways to help students get to know one another. Students are also acquainted with Icebreakers, as they are used frequently in higher education.

Guiding Principles

Icebreakers help to foster a classroom that encourages students to work together. More specifically, developing a classroom community helps students learn more thoroughly and efficiently (Bruffee, 1998), build connections to each other, and develop relationships with peers. The resulting community of learners is then able to collaborate and encourage one another during later class discussions and activities (Zhao & Kuh, 2004).

Another value of Icebreakers is that they help prepare students to engage in the university community as well as the class. While particularly true for first-year students, Icebreakers can engage students in a fun activity that helps establish initial knowledge of the course content. Icebreaker activities can introduce students into the learning environment both with personal community engagement and content-specific interaction (Kavanagh, Clark-Murphy, & Wood, 2011).

Preparation

Before looking at the wide variety of icebreakers listed on the Internet, consider your goal. Take into account class setting, content, and desire for community when deciding which specific activity to use. For example, your first goal may be to help students on the first day of class to learn the names of classmates. Thus you might use a name association icebreaker, such an adjective that starts with the first letter of your first name that describes your personality, such as Active Anna, Brave Bonita, or Creative Carlos. Alternatively, your goal in using an Icebreaker may be to get students to start thinking of applications of the content to be learned in the course. The one general rule is to be certain the Icebreaker will accomplish something. Thus you might ask students to share what experiences they have related to course content. A fairly general consensus is that class time is limited for every course, and most people dislike Icebreakers that have no apparent purpose (Henslee, Burgess, & Buskist, 2006).

Process

- A quick Google search will elicit many different types of Icebreakers that can be used. Based on the goals for the technique, pick an option that best suits your needs.
- Tell the class that the Icebreaker will take five to seven minutes of class time.
- Briefly explain how the Icebreaker works, and have students complete the activity. If appropriate, explain why you selected the specific Icebreaker you selected and the overall outcome that you noticed.
- Ask students to respond, round table fashion, to the Icebreaker questions.

Sample IDEA Pairings

Take a Guess (IDEA #8). Students make guesses about the lecture content either through the course of the Icebreaker or in groups formed as a result of the activity.

In the News (IDEA #16). Ideas or topics from the news stories collected by the students can be used as fodder in an Icebreaker.

Pairs Check (IDEA #26). Students complete an Icebreaker that has them form a pair. These pairs then complete the homework check process.

Pro-tips

The primary advantage of this technique is that it builds up students' comfort level in class and quickly begins to build a class community. As a result, discussion-based classes or courses dealing with difficult (or controversial) topics may especially benefit from the use of Icebreakers.

Although Icebreakers are typically used at the beginning of the semester or the start of a class meeting, you can use them effectively at many different points. Consider using an Icebreaker when transitioning between topics or when the energy in class is dwindling. Also consider keeping a few good Icebreakers ready to use at any time needed during the semester.

Remember that Icebreakers should be brief. Most types of Icebreakers are only designed to be used for a few minutes and can cause disinterest among students if continued for too long. If you are looking for a more involved activity, another game IDEA would likely better suit your needs.

Finally, be careful to ensure that Icebreakers will not cause discomfort or bring about disharmony in the classroom. For example, early in the semester is not a good time to share personal information with others.

IDEA #47: Top 10

Overview

Top 10 is a game that is deceptive in that it appears easy to generate a list, but based on the topic or content, it may be very challenging to find 10 good items. When used in an educational environment, the Top 10 activity asks students to generate a list of ten items related to course content. The structure may allow students to consider a combination of their prior knowledge and what they gained through the course to create the list. This IDEA helps students synthesize and recall important information. These lists can be factual or speculative. For example, in a political science class, students might list the 10 states with the most votes in the Electoral College, the top policy priorities of the AARP, or even the 10 most controversial public policy challenges in 2025.

The goal of Top 10 is to have students identify the most significant or relevant items according to a set of criteria (Sugar, 1998). This activity encourages students to recall material, synthesize knowledge, and demonstrate a mastery of content. When students are asked to work in teams to complete the list, the activity also encourages discussion and peer learning.

Guiding Principles

Providing students with a problem to solve can serve as an effective teaching method. Instructors can motivate and encourage the use of a variety of knowledge bases through the use of problems (Barkley et al., 2014). Cognitive theory suggests the generation of a Top 10 list builds up knowledge by synthesis and application of previously learned concepts. The result of this learning process is increased recall, application of knowledge, and practice problem solving (Svinicki & McKeachie, 2013).

Learning increases when students are forced to create answers, which forms a significant foundation of the use of Top 10. To create the list, students must use a variety of information from the course as well as other sources to generate answers. The act of generating list items improves learning over the process of identifying the correct answer (e.g., multiple-choice exam) (Butler & Roediger, 2007).

Preparation

In order to use the Top 10 IDEA, gather sample list items to use in the activity as examples. You may self-generate these or gather them from reading materials such as trade publications, journal articles, textbooks, or the Internet. Also, decide if you are going to use a scoring system. Finally, decide whether students will play multiple rounds or simply have them generate one list.

Process

- Provide the topic or category of the list for students to create. Also give any instructions and the time limit for creation of their list. At this point, it may be helpful to give one or two sample items.
- Have the students form groups of three to five and generate their list.
- As an entire class, ask each group, in turn, to provide one item from its list and the rationale for the items included. If you have a very large class, sample from different groups. The point here is to NOT have an individual group read through their entire list before moving to the next group. Doing so decreases the participation level of different groups.
- If you have a specific target list, reveal the correct answers and award points (if applicable). If there is no target list, points may be allotted for unique responses or the most number of items on a list.

Sample IDEA Pairings

Take a Guess (IDEA #8). Students create a Top 10 of facts or ideas they think will be discussed in the lecture. As you lecture, they check off items you discuss.

Snowball (IDEA #12). Students form increasingly larger groups and work on developing their Top 10 list.

Case Study (IDEA #24). After distributing a complex case, the class works in groups to identify a list of the main problems, complicating factors, or possible solutions to the case.

Pro-tips

Creating a point system can encourage students to consider the rank order of the list. If students correctly guess the #1 item, they receive 10 points. If they guess #2, they get 9 points, and so on.

Rather than having students generate the list items, provide a list and have students identify the significance of the list. Depending on the nature of the list, you may provide a list in ranked or random order to increase the difficulty. Also, you can create of list of your own views on the subject and ask students to guess your Top 10.

During the activity, students may struggle to generate ideas and may ask for hints. They may also seek to use research materials to help come up with ideas. A benefit of the Top 10 technique is forcing students to think through creating their list. The first four or five items may come easily, but the last few will be more difficult. Some of the best learning can come from this challenge, so resist providing too much help and support. You want to provide encouragement without providing the answer quickly. Finally, a discussion of why the later items were difficult is a powerful learning opportunity. Many individuals can generate a few items in response to a prompt; experts are able to dig deeper.

IDEA #48: Pic of the Day

Overview

Pic of the Day asks students to capture key concepts or ideas from class in photographs, newspaper clippings, or screen captures and then share these images with class. The widespread availability of digital photography has increased the quality and quantity of pictures. The Pic of the Day IDEA builds on this trend by using photographs to illustrate course concepts.

Although any graphic image can be used, the ideal submission will be a photograph that the student has taken. This activity encourages students to look for aspects of a course in their daily lives. In addition, Pic of the Day provides an outlet for students to use their creativity and share their own perspectives regarding class content. The activity provides an opportunity to gauge student comprehension of course concepts, particularly as the photographs demonstrate nuanced understanding of topics. Examples of Pic of the Day include displays used in department stores to discuss diversity and inclusion, street signs to illustrate communication, or images of the campus to illustrate to what extent physical objects on campus enhance a feeling of community among students.

Guiding Principles

Photographs provide a rich opportunity to share how someone views something as they are taken from a particular perspective and point of view (Bogdan & Biklen, 1998). Although photos that are selected are not as personal as those taken from the person's point of view, the selection of specific photos from the mass quantity of images individuals are bombarded by every day still holds information regarding the one identifying why a photo was chosen. The use of images offers a window into how students view topics that they may even have a hard time articulating for themselves (Taylor, 2002). Pic of the Day builds on these principles by eliciting images from students to demonstrate key components of class.

Although this IDEA may be used for all students, it is particularly beneficial in reaching reluctant or unmotivated students (Crozier, 2009). Traditional teaching approaches and certain types of content may not connect directly with students. In those cases, alternative approaches such as Pic of the Day provide a different way to reach students and engage them with the content. It also provides creative students with an expressive outlet.

Preparation

Before assigning Pic of the Day, decide what aspects of class or content the activity will cover. The parameters can be as broad or defined as you see fit. You may want to allow room for a great deal of creativity and perspective, or you may want students to seek out specific things to photograph. In addition, the photographs might be limited to content to be covered in the next class session or used as more of a review near the end of a course. Finally, determine how the pictures will be presented. Will the images be used as part of the class? Will students need to do some type of writing to accompany the images?

Process

- Provide a few short examples of the types of images students may secure.
- Assign the activity and provide the framework for Pic of the Day including due dates, guidelines for what to photograph, how many images, and in what final form they will be presented.
- Students complete the activity outside of class.
- When the students complete the activity, facilitate an opportunity for students to share their work. This information share could be completed as a class or with students working in small groups.

Sample IDEA Pairings

Gallery Walk (IDEA #28). The students' pictures are displayed around the room, and students move around and write responses to the photographs.

Scavenger Hunt (IDEA #37). Students participate in a Scavenger Hunt and take pictures of their answers to course-related questions and clues.

Reader Response Paper (IDEA #67). Instead of responding to a reading, students draft a response to one of their photographs or that of a classmate focusing on the meaning of the image.

Pro-tips

This activity works best when students are able to express their ideas and perspective through the photographs. As a result, complex, personal, and even controversial topics provide great prompts for completing Pic of the Day. Additionally, students respond well to taking pictures of their daily events and relating these experiences to course content.

To add a competitive element to the activity, you could hold a contest with winners for the best picture or other relevant criteria. Students can serve as judges, which encourages them to critically review images from classmates.

Taking photographs related to course content allows students to more directly connect with the material presented. For example, Bagno, Eylon, and Levy (2007) found that physics students who took pictures of physics concepts responded more positively than through traditional teaching approaches. This activity can help make difficult concepts more accessible to students by allowing them to apply and interact with significant course objectives.

Remember that not all students will have access to cameras. Try to secure on-campus support for the activity, such as through a media center.

IDEA #49: Webquest

Overview

The Webquest is an activity in which a portion if not all the information students work with comes from Internet or digital-based resources (March, 2004). Webquest builds on this foundation and incorporates the notion of gameplay.

This activity requires students to search the Internet for answers to clues or find specifically defined information and compete with one another in the process. Participating in Webquest helps students develop critical thinking skills as well as grow more informationally literate.

Guiding Principles

The use of Webquest allows students to develop their critical-thinking skills. During the activity, students are tasked with a varying degree of challenging problems designed to require students to apply, analyze, synthesize, and evaluate information online, all of which require higher-level or critical-thinking skills to solve (Bissell & Lemons, 2006).

Additionally, Webquest aids in students' information literacy, specifically digital information literacy. An information-literate person as able to recognize when specific information is needed and have the ability to locate, evaluate the value, and effectively use the new information (Brown, Murphy, & Nanny, 2003). Information-literate students are able to navigate the "data smog" produced by the massive amount of information readily available (Shenk, 1997). Webquest supports this notion through the use of guiding questions.

Preparation

Prior to using Webquest, decide on a scenario or a basic list of questions to guide the activity. The context of the game needs to be related to both course content and student learning outcomes, as well as vary in difficulty. Additionally, any questions should vary in purpose between asking for direct answers and asking for the process of finding the information. A direct answer question is one where one specific answer exists, for example, "What are Newton's three laws of motion?" A process question may have multiple possible approaches to the answer, for instance, "Find and cite a journal article that discusses Newton's three laws of motion." Finally, decide on the point value of each phase of the question or each question relative to each other and the level of difficulty. The number of questions will be dependent on the desired length of the activity as well the difficulty of questions.

Process

- Provide students with a list of questions they must complete for the Webquest.
- In pairs, students work through the provided questions.
- At the conclusion of class, students receive points for each correctly answered question, and the pair with the most points is declared the winner.

Sample IDEA Pairings

Case Study (IDEA #24). Use the premise and goals of the case to guide the questions used for the Webquest.

Pairs Check (IDEA #26). After the Webquest is complete, have pairs combine together and share among each other their answer and processes for approaching each question.

Pro-tips

Ensure that each question serves a learning purpose for the student. If you want to develop multiple online research skills, develop multiple questions for each to reinforce the concept.

Students will complete the activity at different paces. Plan on the possibility that certain students may finish before the anticipated completion time. You may plan to have a few spare extra-credit questions available in the event this happens.

Decide whether the students will be required to answer the questions in a specific order or if they are able to just answer as many as possible. This decision will most likely influence students' approaches toward completing the activity. If students are allowed to choose which questions and what order to answer them in, you may want to prescribe certain specific parameters that ensure each question type is reviewed during the students' completion of the activity.

References

Allen, T.B. (1987). *War games*. New York: Berkeley Books.

Angelo, T.A., & Cross, K.P. (1993). *Classroom assessment techniques: A handbook for college faculty*. San Francisco, CA: Jossey-Bass.

Arena, D.A., & Schwartz, D.L. (2014). Experience and explanation: Using videogames to prepare students for formal instruction in statistics. *Journal of Science Education and Technology, 23*(4), 538–548.

Bagno, E., Eylon, B., & Levy, S. (2007). Photography as a means of narrowing the gap between physics and students. *Physics Education, 42*(1), 45–49.

Barak, A., Engle, C., Katzir, L., & Fisher, W.A. (1988). Increasing the level of empathic understanding by means of a game. *Simulation & Games, 18*(4), 458–470.

Barkley, E.F., Barkley, E.F., Major, C.H., & Cross, K.P. (2014). *Collaborative learning techniques: A handbook for college faculty*. San Francisco, CA: Jossey-Bass.

Bereiter, C., & Scardamalia, M. (1985). Cognitive coping strategies and the problem of "inert knowledge." In S.F. Chipman, J.W. Segal, & R. Glaser (Eds.), *Thinking and learning skills. Vol. 2: Current research and open questions* (pp. 65–80). Hillsdale, NJ: Erlbaum.

Bissell, A.N., & Lemons, P.P. (2006). A new method for assessing critical thinking in the classroom. *BioScience, 56*(1), 66–72.

Bjork, R.A. (1988). Retrieval practice and maintenance of knowledge. In M.M. Gruneburg, P.E. Morris, & R.N. Sykes (Eds.), *Practical aspects of memory: Current research and issues* (pp. 396–401). New York: Wiley.

Bogdan, R.C., & Biklen, S.K. (1998). *Qualitative research in education*. Boston, MA: Allyn and Bacon.

Bonwell, C.C., & Eison, J.A. (1991). *Active learning: Creating excitement in the classroom*. Washington, DC: George Washington University.

Bredemeir, M.E., Bernstein, G., & Oxman, W. (1982). BA FA BA FA and dogmatism/ethnocentrism: A study of attitude change through simulation-gaming. *Simulation & Games, 13*(4), 413–436.

Brickman, P., Gormally, C., Armstrong, N., & Hallar, B. (2009). Effects of inquiry-based learning on students' science literacy skills and confidence. *International Journal for the Scholarship of Teaching and Learning, 3*(2), 1–22.

Brinker, J.K., Roberts, P., & Radnidge, B. (2014). The game of late life: A novel education activity for the psychology of ageing. *Educational Gerontology, 40*(2), 91–101.

Brown, C., Murphy, T.J., & Nanny, M. (2003). Turning techno-savvy into info-savvy: Authentically integrating information literacy into the college curriculum. *Journal of Academic Librarianship, 29*(6), 386–398.

Brown, G., Bull, J., & Pendlebury, M. (1997). *Assessing student learning in higher education.* Oxford: Routledge.

Bruffee, K.A. (1998). *Collaborative learning: Higher education, interdependence, and the authority of knowledge.* Baltimore, MD: Johns Hopkins University Press.

Butler, A.C., & Roediger, H.L. (2007). Testing improves long-term retention in a simulated classroom setting. *European Journal of Cognitive Psychology, 19*(4/5), 514–527.

Castaneda, R. (2008). *The impact of computer-based simulation within an instructional sequence on learner performance in a Web-based environment* (PhD dissertation). Arizona State University, Tempe.

Clark, D., Tanner-Smith, E., Killingsword, S., & Bellamy, S. (2013). Digital games for learning: A systematic review and meta-analysis (executive summary). Menlo Park, CA: SRI International.

Crossman, E.K., & Crossman, S.M. (1983). The crossword puzzle as a teaching tool. *Teaching of Psychology, 10*(2), 98–99.

Crozier, K. (2009). *Engaging reluctant learners.* Orlando, FL: ASCD, Learning Beyond Boundaries.

De Deyne, S., Navarro, D.J., & Storms, G. (2012). Better explanations of lexical and semantic cognition using networks derived from continued rather than single-word associations. *Behavior Research Methods, 45*(2), 480–498.

DeHaan, R.L. (2009). Teaching creativity and inventive problem solving in science. *CBE-Life Sciences Education, 8*(3), 172–181.

Dodge, B.J. (1991). Computers and creativity: Tools, tasks, and possibilities. *CAG Communicator, 21*(1), 5–8.

Fisher, J.E. (1976). Competition and gaming: An experimental study. *Simulation & Games, 7*(3), 321–328.

Fraas, J.W. (1982). The influence of student characteristics on the effectiveness of simulations in the principles course. *Journal of Economic Education, 13*(1), 56–61.

Franklin, S., Peat, M., & Lewis, A. (2003). Non-traditional interventions to stimulate discussion: The use of games and puzzles. *Journal of Biological Education, 37*(2), 79–84.

Fritzsche, D.J. (1981). The role of simulation games: Supplement or central delivery vehicle? *Journal of Experiential Learning and Simulation, 2*, 205–211.

Garris, R., Ahlers, R., & Driskell, J.E. (2002). Games, motivation and learning: A research and practice model. *Simulation & Gaming, 33*(3), 441–467.

Gaskill, M., McNulty, A., & Brooks, D.W. (2006). Learning from webquests. *Journal of Science Education and Technology, 15*(2), 133–136.

Glasberg, D.S., Harwood, J., Hawkes, R., & Martinsek, C. (1990). The library scavenger hunt: Teaching library skills in introductory sociology courses. *Teaching Sociology, 18*(2), 231–234.

Gremmen, H., & Potters, H. (1995). Assessing the efficacy of gaming in economics education. *Journal of Economic Education, 28*(4), 291–303.

Grimley, M., Green, R., Nilsen, T., & Thompson, D. (2012). Comparing computer games and traditional lecture using experience ratings from high and low achieving students. *Australasian Journal of Educational Technology, 28*(4), 619–638.

Halpern, D.F. (1999). Teaching for critical thinking: Helping college students develop the skills and dispositions of a critical thinker. *New Directions for Teaching and Learning, 80*, 69–74.

Hays, R. (2005). *The effectiveness of instructional games: A literature review and discussion.* Orlando, FL: Naval Air Warfare Center Training Systems Division.

Heller, P., Keith, R., & Anderson, S. (1992). Teaching problem solving through cooperative grouping. Part 1: Group versus individual problem solving. *American Journal of Physics, 60*(7), 627–636.

Henslee, A., Burgess, D., & Buskist, W. (2006). Student preferences for first day class activities. *Teaching of Psychology, 33*(Summer), 189–191.

Hertel, J.P., & Millis, B.J. (2002). *Using simulations to promote learning in higher education: An introduction.* Sterling, VA: Stylus.

Herz, J.C. (2001). *Joystick nation.* London: Abacus.

Hilbelink, A.J. (2009). A measure of the effectiveness of incorporating 3D human anatomoy into an online undergraduate laboratory. *British Journal of Educational Psychology, 40*(4), 664–672.

Huang, W.H., Johnson, T., & Han, S. (2013). Impact of online instructional game features on college students' perceived motivational support and cognitive investment: A structural equation modeling study. *Internet and Higher Education, 17*, 58–68.

Issenberg, S.B., McGaghie, W.C., Petrusa, E.R., Gordon, L., & Scalese, R.J. (2005). Features and uses of high-fidelity medical simulations that lead to effective learning: A BEME systematic review. *Medical Teaching, 27*(1), 10–28.

Jackson, P.T. (2000). Role-playing in analytical chemistry: The alumni speak. *Journal of Chemical Education, 77*(8), 1019–1025.

Jaramillo, C.M.Z., Losada, B.M., & Fekula, M.J. (2012). Designing and solving crossword puzzles: Examing efficacy in a classroom exercise. *Developments in Business Simulation and Experiential Learning, 39*, 213–222.

Johnson, D.W., Johnson, R.T., & Holubec, E.J. (1994). *Cooperative learning in the classroom.* Alexandria, VA: Association for Supervision and Curriculum Development.

Jonassen, D.H., & Land, S.M. (2000). *Theoretical foundations of learning environments.* Mahwah, NJ: Erlbaum.

Juul, J. (2005). *Half-real: Video games between real rules and fictional worlds.* Cambridge, MA: MIT Press.

Karpicke, J.D., & Roediger, H.L. (2008). The critical importance of retrieval for learning. *Science, 319*(5865), 966–968.

Kaupins, G. (2005). Using popular game and reality show formats to review for exams. *Teaching Professor, 19*(1), 5–6.

Kavanagh, M., Clark-Murphy, M., & Wood, L. (2011). The first class: Using icebreakers to facilitate transition in a tertiary environment. *Asian Social Science, 7*(4), 84–92.

Klein, J.D., & Frietad, E. (1991). Effects of using an instructional game on motivation and performance. *Journal of Educational Research, 84*(5), 303–308.

Kolb, D.A. (1984). *Experiential learning.* Englewood Cliffs, NJ: Prentice Hall.

Lavega, P., Alonso, J.I., Etxebeste, J., Lagardera, F., & March, J. (2014). Relationship between traditional games and the intensity of emotions experienced by participants. *Research Quarterly for Exercise and Sport, 85*(4), 457–467.

Malone, T.W. (1981). Toward a theory of intrinsically motivating instruction. *Cognitive Science, 4*, 333–369.

March, T. (2004). The learning power of WebQuests. *Educational Leadership, 61*(4), 42–47.

Marcus, S., & Beck, S. (2003). A library adventure: Comparing a treasure hunt with a traditional freshman orientation tour. *College & Research Libraries, 64*(1), 23–44.

Mayer, R.E., Mautone, P., & Prothero, W. (2002). Pictorial aids for learning by doing in a multimedia geology simulation game. *Journal of Educational Psychology, 94*(1), 171–185.

Mestre, J.P. (Ed.). (2005). *Transfer of learning: From a modern multidisciplinary perspective*. Greenwich, CT: Information Age.

Moy, J.R., Rodenbaugh, D.W., Collins, H.L., & DiCarlo, S.E. (2000). Who wants to be a physician? An educational tool for reviewing pulmonary physiology. *Advanced Physiology Education, 24*, 30–37.

Mummalaneni, V., & Sivakumar, S. (2008). Effectiveness of a board game in fostering a customer relationship orientation among business students. *Journal of Relationship Marketing, 7*(3), 257–273.

Nestel, D., & Tierney, T. (2007). Role-play for medical students learning about communication: Guidelines for maximising benefits. *BMC Medical Education, 7*(3), 1–9.

Nilson, L.B. (2010). *Teaching at its best: A research-based resource for college instructors*. San Francisco, CA: Jossey-Bass.

Perla, P. (1990). *The art of wargaming*. Annapolis, MD: Naval Institute Press.

Peters, V., & Vissers, G. (2004). A simple classification model for debriefing simulations games. *Simulation & Games, 35*(1), 70–84.

Peters, V., Vissers, G., & Heijne, G. (1998). The validity of games. *Simulation & Gaming, 29*(1), 20–30.

Pivec, M. (2007). Play and learn: Potentials of game-based learning. *British Journal of Educational Technology, 38*(3), 387–393.

Plass, J.L., O'Keefe, P.A., Homer, B.D., Case, J., Hayward, E.O., Stein, M., & Perlin, K. (2013). The impact of individual, competitive, and collaborative mathematics game play on learning, performance, and motivation. *Journal of Educational Psychology*.

Pløhn, T. (2014). Pervasive learning—Using games to tear down the classroom walls. *Electric Journal of e-Learning, 12*(3), 299–311.

Resnick, L. (Ed.). (1989). *Knowing, learning, and instruction: Essays in honor of Robert Glaser*. Hillsdale, NJ: Erlbaum.

Rieber, L.P., & Noah, D. (1997). *Effect of gaming and visual metaphors on reflective cognition within computer-based simulations*. Paper presented at the AERA Conference, Chicago, IL. Retrieved from http://lrieber.coe.uga.edu/gaming-simulation/Rieber-gaming-simulation.pdf

Rowland, K.M., & Gardner, D.M. (1973). The use of business gaming in education and laboratory research. *Decision Sciences, 4*, 268–283.

Salen, K., & Zimmerman, E. (2004). *Rules of play: Game design fundamentals*. Cambridge, MA: MIT Press.

Salter, A. (2013). Making board games in the classroom. Retrieved January 31, 2015, from http://chronicle.com/blogs/profhacker/making-board-games-in-the-classroom/48983

Sarason, Y., & Banbury, C. (2004). Active learning facilitated by using a game show format, or who doesn't want to be a millionaire? *Journal of Management Education, 28*(4), 509–518.

Sharp, L.A. (2012). Stealth learning: Unexpected learning opportunities through games. *Journal of Instructional Research, 1*(2), 42–48.

Shenk, D. (1997). Data smog: Surviving the info glut. *Technology Review, 100*(4), 18–26.

Shrestha, L.B. (1990). *Computer based training: The effects of game characteristics on motivation and learning*. Orlando: University of Central Florida.

Siegler, R.S. (1977). The twenty questions game as a form of problem solving. *Child Development, 48*(2), 395–403.

Simkin, M.G. (2013). Playing Jeopardy in the classroom: An empirical study. *Journal of Information Systems Education, 24*(3), 203–210.

Sugar, S. (1998). *Games that teach: Experiential activities for reinforcing training.* San Francisco, CA: Jossey-Bass/Pfeiffer.

Svinicki, M., & McKeachie, W.J. (2013). *McKeachie's teaching tips: Strategies, research, and theory for college and university teachers* (14th ed.). Belmont, CA: Cengage Learning.

Szafran, R.F., & Mandolink, A.F. (1980). Test performance and concept recognition: The effect of a simulation game on two types of cognitive knowledge. *Simulation & Games, 11*(3), 326–335.

Taylor, E.W. (2002). Using still photography in making meaning of adult educators' teaching beliefs. *Studies in the Education of Adults, 34*(2), 123–139.

van Staalduinen, J.P., & de Freitas, S. (2011). A game-based learning framework: Linking game design and learning. In M.S. Khine (Ed.), *Learning to play: Exploring the future of eudcation with video games.* New York: Peter Lang.

Weisskirch, R.S. (2006). An analysis of instructor-created crossword puzzles for student review. *College Teaching, 54*(1), 198–201.

Wellington, W.J., & Faria, A.J. (1996). Team cohesion, player attitude, and performace expectations in simulation. *Simulation & Games, 27*(1), 23–40.

West, E. (1999). *The big book of icebreakers: Quick, fun activities for energizing meeings and workshops.* New York: McGraw-Hill.

Westbrook, J.I., & Braithwaite, J. (2001). The health care game: An evaluation of a heuristic, web-based simulation. *Journal of Interactive Learning Research, 12*(1), 89–104.

Williams, R.H. (1980). Attitude change and simulation games: The ability of a simulation game to change attitude when structured in accordance with either the cognitive dissonance or incentive models of attitude change. *Simulation & Games, 11*(2), 177–196.

Wilson, K., Bedwell, W., Lazzara, E., Salas, E., Burker, S.C., Estock, J.L., . . . Conkey, C. (2009). Relationships between game attributes and learning outcomes. *Simulation & Gaming, 40*(2), 217–266.

Wise, R.A. (2004). Dopamine, learning, and motivation. *Nature Reviews Neuroscience, 5*, 483.

Wood, L.E., & Stewart, P.W. (1987). Improvement of practical reasoning skills with a computer game. *Journal of Computer-Based Instruction, 14*(2), 49–53.

Yaman, D., & Covington, M. (2006). *I'll take learning for 500: Using game shows to engage, motivate, and train.* San Francisco, CA: Pfeiffer.

Zagal, J.P., Rick, J., & His, I. (2006). Collaborative games: Lessons learned from board games. *Simulation & Gaming, 37*(1), 24–40.

Zhao, C.M., & Kuh, G.D. (2004). Adding value: Learning communities and student engagement. *Research in Higher Education, 45*(2), 115–138.

5
READING STRATEGIES

Description

Reading is a complex and interactive process during which readers construct meaning from symbols that taken together form a text. In 1917, Thorndike explained the act of reading in this way:

> Understanding a paragraph is like solving a problem in mathematics. It consists of selecting the right elements of the situation and putting them together in the right relations, and also with the right amount of weight or influence or force for each. The mind is assailed as it were by every word in the paragraph. It must select, repress, soften, emphasize, correlate and organize, all under the influence of the right mental set or purpose or demand.
>
> (p. 329)

Readers strive to comprehend meaning based upon cues from the text and based upon their prior understandings (Rayner, Foorman, Perfetti, Pesetsky, & Seidenberg, 2001). Reading itself is an act of communication of information from the author to the reader. Reading then enables the reader to receive a message. Thus, reading is a key way in which we gain knowledge and develop understanding. The reading process is a learned skill that can open doors to opportunities and progress (National Institute of Literacy, 2009).

The skills and strategies that readers use as they attempt to construct meaning from a text vary in complexity (Pressley, Ghatala, Woloshyn, & Pirie, 1990). They initially have to recognize words and understand their meaning or deduce meaning from surrounding text. They then have to comprehend sentences, which are connections of words that make an idea. Next, readers use analytical skills as they seek to understand various parts of a text. They also need evaluation skills to weigh the worth and quality of what they are reading as well as the author's claims and credibility. Reading proficiency develops over a lifetime, and it requires time, attention, practice, and effort (Houck & Ross, 2012).

At the college level, students need to be fluent readers, but not just for the sake of reading. The ability to read impacts student learning and success, regardless of the course, discipline, or field. In short, we learn to read at a young age; as adults in college, we must read to learn. There are indeed few courses in which students are not required to complete some form of reading assignment to help them learn about the subject at hand. To be able to do this task well, students need to recognize, understand, and comprehend a written text automatically. In college, they are expected to be ready readers who have a range of reading skills that they can employ for the purpose of learning (ACT, 2012).

Yet, college students vary in their reading ability. Some students come to the task of reading to learn with a preexisting set of skills and strategies. These students in particular may read with an eye toward gauging relevance of readings to their own needs. When they read actively, they stay focused on the material, are more efficient, and are likely to remember what they have read afterward. Many college students, however, are unprepared to read at the college level. According to ACT's most recent report, as of 2012, only 52% of all students who took the test met the benchmark for college readiness in reading. Many students do not know how to approach the task of reading; as a result, they do not have the skills and strategies they need to be successful learners.

Early work by Marton and Säljö (1976) documents the different ways college-level students go about reading. The researchers explored students' approaches to reading an academic text. They told students that they would be asked to answer questions about the text after they read it. The first group attempted to understand the big picture of the text by thinking about the academic work at a broad level. The researchers believed that these students adopted a "deep approach" to learning. The second group, however, simply tried to remember basic facts from the text. They focused on what they thought they would be asked about later. The researchers deemed this a "surface approach." With respect to long-term retention of newly learned information, deep approaches lead to better learning than do surface approaches. Without some intervention to help students bridge the gaps in their ability and experience level, some students who do not have the appropriate reading skills and strategies will not be able to succeed in college-level learning environments.

Reading strategies are intentionally designed educational activities (IDEAs) intended to help students accomplish a particular goal or to complete a given task when approaching a text. Learning to use reading strategies can be essential for constructing meaning. Instructors can create reading strategies that encourage active and strategic reading, from both the skilled and less skilled reader. These are the kinds of strategies that we describe in this chapter.

Purposes of Reading Strategies

Reading strategies help readers establish goals for their reading. Doing so can help them establish specific objectives that result in deeper learning. For example, based on the expected outcome of reading, good readers may skim read to get the general idea of a text, scan (i.e., look for specific information), or do a close reading to find the meaning and the nuances within a given text. There is a place for each of these kinds of reading. Ideally, given available time, students would do all three: skim the text to get a general sense of it, scan to find the patterns in the organization, and then read closely and carefully for understanding. Reading strategies can help students learn which of these to do and when to do them by helping them set goals for their reading.

Reading strategies can provide a structure for performing appropriate tasks during reading. Such structures then present students with a pattern of strategic behavior. Explicit structures can reduce cognitive overload that can be present with dense texts and provide a clear benefit to students learning complex material (Ambrose, Bridges, DiPietro, Lovett, & Norman, 2010; Clarke, Ayres, & Sweller, 2005; Dubas & Toledo, 2015). Skilled readers often have such structures. Dowhower (2009) argues, however, that students with lower skills in reading comprehension will benefit from specific reading strategies to the extent that their efforts and outcomes compare to those of more skilled readers. Even skilled readers benefit from a wider array of tools and practice at reading with an outcome in mind.

Having a good set of tools can help students be successful not only with the reading assignment at hand, but they also learn strategies and patterns that can help them study and learn in the future. In particular, reading strategies provide students with metacognitive tools, and using these tools helps students deepen their metacognitive knowledge. For additional information about metacognition, please see chapter 8: Metacognitive Reflection. When used with reading assignments, these strategies help students better monitor their comprehension, determining what they know and do not know about the text. They can help them better keep track of their processes of examining a text. In turn, this process can help them regulate their own learning by making changes to their processes when necessary and continuing with what works well. Students who use reading strategies tend to be better equipped to learn any other material more effectively and be able to encounter and work with new information later in their lives, whether in academic or professional settings, without the direct involvement of others (Dowhower, 2009). When students can select and use a strategy on their own, they have achieved independence. Dubas and Toledo (2015) argue such strategies then can place students on the path to becoming self-directed learners.

Reading strategies can also help improve students' attitudes toward reading and the assignment in general. Many times, students, particularly those who are not efficient readers, simply do not know what to do when confronting a text. This situation can cause students discomfort and anxiety, as they realize they do not have the tools to be successful. It can create a sense of learned helplessness (Dubas & Toledo, 2015). Providing students with a specific task can provide them with clear and attainable goals, which can in turn lead to increased feelings of expectancy of being able to complete the task (Ambrose et al., 2010). Specific jobs to do can also signal that the teacher values the reading, which in turn can cause students to place higher value in it.

Types of Reading Strategies

There are many different types of reading strategies. We adapted our list below from a number of sources, including Salisbury University's seven critical reading strategies.

Prereading—Prereading involves those activities in which readers engage to learn about a text prior to reading it. This type can include answering preview questions, scanning text features or organizational patterns (e.g., subheaders), reading the introduction and conclusion for a general sense of the text, and listening carefully when an instructor describes the text to be read.

Guided reading—This type of reading strategy involves specific tasks that the reader is to complete while reading: filling in empty outlines, text annotation, taking notes, highlighting, and looking up unknown words.

Contextualizing—This reading strategy involves considering a text within its historical, biographical, and cultural contexts. This involves checking the dates of the text and any cited texts and considering what events and social trends were occurring within the approximate time frame.

Outlining and summarizing—This strategy involves identifying the main ideas of the article, restating them, and organizing them according to some logical pattern.

Postreading—In the postreading strategy, students reflect upon what they have read, whether by summarizing it, applying it to new situations, evaluating it, or connecting it to their own experiences.

We recognize that it is common to use graphic organizers while reading and also to write about reading through written responses. We address those strategies, however, in their corresponding sections in this book, which immediately follow this chapter. In Chapter 6, we present writing-to-learn information and IDEAs; in Chapter 7, we present Graphic Organizer information and IDEAs.

Sequencing of Reading Strategies

There are several different types of reading strategies, and the sequencing of the method depends upon the specific strategy selected. To provide a general sense of how the activity might unfold, we offer the following procedures.

1. **Introduce the reading strategy to the students.** Tell the students the purpose of the activity, including why you think the reading strategy is important and how it should help them with the specific assignment and as learners in the future. Provide details about the specific IDEA you have selected (see the end of this chapter for detailed information about 12 different reading IDEAs).

2. **Assign the reading.** Tell students why the reading is important and how it should help them in the course. Also provide any framework for the reading assignment, such as due dates and expected outcomes from the reading.

3. **Provide time for students to carry out the work.** Most students are more comfortable reading in their own environments, as they read at different rates and do not have the distractions of their classmates (they will have other distractions, obviously). Unless the reading is particularly short and the reading strategy IDEA may be done quickly, you should likely assign them as homework.

4. **Collect information from the students when they have completed the task.** Students will value the work more if you collect the results of their activity. You may also use class discussion for sharing results or alternately a show of hands for opinions on the assignment.

5. **Provide students with an assessment of their efforts.** Students will also better appreciate the activity if you assess it and provide them with comments on what they did well or could improve. They will likely value it more if you assign a grade, such as a low-stakes grade for homework completion or participation.

Advantages and Challenges of Reading Strategies for Instructors

The clear advantage for instructors of using reading strategies is having students who show up to class having completed the reading assignments. Many instructors know the challenge of trying to give a lecture or lead a discussion when students are unprepared. They simply cannot be good participants in the class session, and this makes instructors' jobs harder while also hampering their own learning. Reading strategies provide instructors with a direct mechanism for ensuring student preparation for the upcoming classroom. The class session in turn tends to run more smoothly and is often a more satisfying experience for instructors and students alike. These strategies are an efficient method and do not require significant class time to carry out. They tend to provide a large return on the investment of time and energy necessary to use them.

There are few disadvantages to using reading strategies. There is a risk of overdoing a specific strategy and having students tire of it and do the bare minimum just to get by. Varying the reading strategies, however, can help to address this potential challenge.

What Research Tells Us About the General Effectiveness of Reading Strategies

"Reading Strategies" is clearly a broad instructional method that includes a host of different approaches, as we described in our "types of reading strategies" section above. Thus, it is difficult to pinpoint a specific body of research that points to a definitive difference between this instructional approach and others such as lecture or discussion.

A comparison of reading texts (not with specific strategies) to other learning mechanisms, such as listening to a lecture or watching a video, yields mixed results. Brown (2011) summarized studies of reading versus listening. We share this summary in the table at the bottom of this page and in the following narrative paragraph.

The Lund (1991) study compared university students learning German with written text while the others heard the same text read as if a radio story. Students then wrote out what they remembered for five minutes. Readers recalled more overall content but fewer main ideas and more details. Park (2004) studied students at a Korean university who were learning English. Readers did better on detailed questions, but listeners did better on questions that required inference. The Absalom and Rizzi (2008) study involved comparison of online listening and text assignments. Students studied one text per week (one group studied the text, and another group studied an audio recording of the text). Listeners went into more detail on the material and sought out external sources. They were also more motivated than the readers. Lesser's (2004) study focused on acquisition of Spanish, and readers recalled more information than listeners. This body of evidence simply suggests that reading is an effective strategy for learning information, particularly the details of a large body of information.

In comparing video lectures to reading, results are also mixed. In a study comparing text to YouTube videos for computer laboratory instruction, for example, no significant differences between the two formats were found (Breimer, Cotler, & Yoder, 2012). In a study comparing text-based asynchronous learning to video-based asynchronous learning, the researcher found both methods effective for learning but that the students preferred the video-based courses (Skylar, 2009). In studies of text only versus visuals and text, the latter tended to be more effective.

TABLE 5.1 Reading vs. Listening

Readers recall more ideas overall.	Lund (1991), Lesser (2004)
Listeners remember more ideas.	Absalom and Rizzi (2008)
Listeners recall more main ideas or do better at main idea questions, while readers recall more details or do better at detail questions.	Lund (1991), Park (2004)
Listeners display deeper learning and more motivation.	Absalom and Rizzi (2008)
Listening and reading share comprehension processes but differ in decoding.	Song (2008)

In another study, researchers found that when done well, visuals and text were better for learning than text only (Fadel, 2009). This body of research suggests that reading is a good method for learning information but also that it may be supplemented with other strategies such as audio or visuals.

What Research Tells Us About How to Improve Student Learning in Classes Using Reading Strategies

Studies of the use of specific reading strategies in a course provide some insight into what kinds of activities are likely to provide the most benefit to student learning. There are several key takeaway points from the research literature.

Research Finding #1. Guided Reading Helps Learning

Using a document to guide students through readings seems to help student learning. These documents tend to have a list of questions for students to answer from a text. The questions can range in complexity from fill-in-the-blank to higher-order questions that require critical thinking. In a study examining the use of Active Reading Documents (ARD), researchers Dubas and Toledo (2015) outline a protocol they use to engage students with the readings at a higher level. They state that the documents have helped their students improve their learning and have made class time more productive.

Research Finding #2. Summarizing/Annotating Information Improves Learning

Research suggests that annotating a text by providing explanations of it, often directly on the text, whether the annotations are done online or on paper, improves student learning. For example, in a study of Taiwanese EFL students, Huang (2014) used summary writing and annotations to test 100 students' reading comprehension. The researcher found that both summary writing and annotation improved student reading performance. Similarly, Tseng et al. (2015) found that online annotations promoted student learning of 50 EFL students. They found that marking text information and adding summary notes were the most effective form of marking.

A study describing the benefits of SQ3R, which is one of the IDEAs we describe below, outlines the effects of asking students to Survey-Question-Read-Recite-Review (SQ3R) when examining course texts. Carlston (2011) asked students to document their work through completion of notes, showing the results of the activity. Results showed that when they used the approach, students retained more information as indicated by higher achievement on course exams.

Research Finding #3. Question–Answer Tasks Improve Learning

Researchers have examined several different question and answer tasks and have come to some interesting conclusions.

High-Level Questions

Cerdan et al. (2009) studied whether using high- or low-level questions has more of an influence on learning. The authors' sample included 37 undergraduates who were asked to read and answer questions displayed on a computer screen. Half of the students read the text first and then answered questions, and half only answered questions; both groups could search the text for answers. Researchers found that high-level questions improved deep comprehension, even though they did not affect immediate recall.

Student-Generated Questions

Weinstein et al. (2010) also asked the question of whether self-generated questions improve memory. The researchers undertook three experiments in which all participants were asked to read the same passage, answer a question set, and take a book test. They then read three 350–575 word passages and were divided into three groups that undertook one of three tasks: reread the passage, answered experimenter-generated question, or answered their own questions. The researchers found that questions, whether experimenter- or self-generated questions were more effective than rereading. Student generation of questions, however, took twice as long as the other methods, so it was a less time-efficient approach than experimenter-generated questions, which yielded a similar benefit.

Student-Generated Conceptual Questions

Several studies suggest that student-developed questions improve learning. Bugg and McDaniel (2012), for example, examined the effect of student self-generated questions on improved learning outcomes compared to prereading. Students were directed how to write questions. The researcher found that the self-generation and answering of conceptual questions yielded a performance boost to memory but not detailed questions. The self-generation of detailed questions yielded no benefit.

Research Question #4. Tying to the Reader Experience Improves Learning, According to Students

In a study examining what particular pedagogies online learners in a teacher education program found to be effective, Ukpokodu (2010) found that students identified writing reading response papers as among the most effective for improving their learning. That is, students felt their learning improved when they were asked to write a paper about how the readings related to their own experiences and how they experienced the text while reading.

Using IDEAs to Improve Learning with Research Strategies

In the following section of this chapter, we provide detailed descriptions of 12 intentionally designed educational activities that correlate with the research findings we presented above. We suggest that these 12 activities correlate with these key research findings as follows:

TABLE 5.2 Reading Strategies IDEAs and Research Findings

Reading IDEAs	Description	Links to Research Findings
Anticipation Guide	Students receive a set of statements about the reading prior to completing it. Students read the statements and agree or disagree with each.	Guided Reading (Research Finding #1); Question–Answer Task (Research Finding #3)
Experience-Text-Relationship	Students receive a prompt to consider the relationship between the text and their own experiences. The instructor facilitates a class discussion about students' prior experiences and how these influence their reading of a text.	Question–Answer Task (Research Finding #3); Reader Experience (Research Finding #4)
Directed Reading and Thinking	The instructor asks students to consider the title of a work and to try to determine its focus and content from that. The instructor then directs the students to read a specific section of the text and to revise their predictions based upon their reading. They repeat the process until they have discussed the entire text.	Guided Reading (Research Finding #1); Question–Answer Task (Research Finding #3)
SQ3R	The SQ3R strategy provides a set of specific steps students use for interacting with information in a text as follows: survey, question, read, recite, review.	Summarizing/Annotation (Research Finding #2); Question–Answer Tasks (Research Finding #3)

(Continued)

TABLE 5.2 Continued

Reading IDEAs	Description	Links to Research Findings
What Counts as Fact?	Students read two or more sources discussing the same topic or issue. Then, they write or discuss what each source uses as fact or proof.	Question–Answer Task (Research Finding #3)
Problematic Situation	The instructor presents an important problem. Students have to read the text in order to identify a solution for the problem. It provides students with a goal for reading.	Question–Answer Tasks (Research Finding #3)
Text Coding	This activity helps students structurally and independently work through a reading. The IDEA specifies using symbols to identify key elements of readings (confirmations, contradictions, questions, interesting point, unclear idea, etc.)	Summarizing/Annotating (Research Finding #2)
Question–Answer Relationship	Students classify question–answer relations by determining which are text explicit (coming from the same sentence in the text), which are text implicit (coming from different parts of the text), and which are script implicit (motivated by the text but coming from the reader's prior knowledge).	Question–Answer Task (Research Finding #3)
Three-Level Reading Guide	Students use a reading guide that has three parts: 1). Literal Level— Understanding the literal meaning of the words and ideas in a reading selection 2). Interpretive Level—Grasping the "message" of the selection or understanding what the author meant by the passage 3). Applied Level—Transfer information from reading to other contexts	Question–Answer Task (Research Finding #3)

Reading IDEAs	Description	Links to Research Findings
What Would You Ask?	In this IDEA, students come up with questions they would ask about the reading, thus asking them to further engage in the reading and think about it from a more critical perspective.	Question–Answer Task (Research Finding #3)
Research Paper Review	Students take on the role of reviewer of a research paper for potential publication in a journal. The student receives a research paper and a set of guidelines for the review. If possible, the student also reviews a sample of the journal for which the article is intended.	Guided Reading (Research Finding #1); Question–Answer Task (Research Finding #3)
Select a Sentence	Each student picks a sentence from the reading that contains an important idea; the instructor pulls themes and helps students think through main ideas.	Summarizing/Annotating (Research Finding #2)

The research basis behind these IDEAs means faculty can use reading strategies with confidence that they have a good and intentional design for improving student learning and putting students on the path to success. Following are detailed descriptions for how to implement these activities in the classroom.

IDEA #50: Anticipation Guide

Overview

Anticipation Guide is an activity developed by Herber (1978) whereby students are asked to respond to a series of questions and to make predictions prior to reading in order to activate prior knowledge and increase curiosity. This process helps students think about ideas and concepts prior to reading about them. The activity asks students to make predictions or respond to a set of statements about a block of material. By asking students to respond before reading, instructors are able to focus students' attention on significant concepts as well as prepare them for reading.

The activity supports reading comprehension by encouraging students to engage with prior knowledge and experiences, identify key points to look for in the reading, and use as a review after reading. Particularly useful for reading that addresses new facts and ideas, Anticipation Guides can improve comprehension, recall, and assimilation of information (Duffelmeyer, Baum, & Merkley, 1987).

Guiding Principles

Anticipation Guides build on the foundation of how effective readers approach texts by providing a scaffolded approach to reading. Good readers have clear goals for reading and constantly evaluate text in relation to their goals (Farstrup & Samuels, 2011). This IDEA helps students of all reading levels by providing a clear goal for reading (confirming or rejecting the answers to questions in the Anticipation Guide). In addition, the activity helps students with lower levels of reading comprehension learn to identify key concepts as they read by modeling effective reading approaches.

This IDEA encourages and motivates students to read closely and critically think about what they are reading. Students seek out the answers to the questions raised by the Anticipation Guide. Since the guide focuses on the most important aspects of a reading, students are prepared to consider the main points. Moreover, the guide prepares students to pay attention and critically consider the information they are reading in order to respond to the questions from the guide.

Preparation

Before beginning the Anticipation Guide IDEA, prepare the guide. First, identify the major points that you want students to gain from the reading. Next, write up 8–10 statements that will challenge students to think about the concept. The goal is to get the students to make predictions about the material they are about to read. Typically, the questions or statements are dichotomous. You may write them using a true/false, fact/opinion, or yes/no format. For example, prior to reading material about classical conditioning, you may ask students, "Do humans need to concentrate on an action in order to develop a conditioned response? Yes/No."

Process

- Share the Anticipation Guide with the class.
- Ask the students to respond to each question and be prepared to share their responses and also to be prepared to explain the logic behind their answers.

- Next, have the students read the assigned text.
- Time permitting, you can have the students reevaluate their answers in light of the information they learned from the reading.

Sample IDEA Pairings

Socratic Seminar (IDEA #7). Students complete the Anticipation Guide, and then the instructor leads a Socratic Seminar around the issues raised in the reading.

Note-Taking Pairs (IDEA #25). As they work on their guides, students work with a partner to compare answers, summarize facts, and locate misconceptions.

Select a Sentence (IDEA #61). Ask students to identify a sentence from the reading that contains an idea from the Anticipation Guide.

Pro-tips

Anticipation Guides are particularly useful for identifying the concepts and topics students do not understand through the use of questions prior to readings. You may use the answers on the questions to identify areas that may require additional explanation.

The primary goal of this IDEA is to assist students with noting key concepts and ideas and to activate prior knowledge in the areas discussed in the text. The primary purpose is not to interpret the content of the passage. The questions asked on the guide should focus specifically on content explicitly addressed in text.

This activity can be a springboard to other class activities. For example, the Anticipation Guide can be used to inform a discussion on a topic from the reading. Students are better prepared to participate in class with the improved comprehension that results from using this IDEA.

IDEA #51: Experience-Text-Relationship

Overview

Originally designed for use in teaching narrative reading to primary school students, Experience-Text-Relationship is a helpful activity to assist college students who struggle with comprehension of new and complicated material. The activity begins by asking students about their Experiences with a topic, then asking questions from the Text, and concludes by asking Relationship questions that help students bridge their own experience and the knowledge from the text.

This activity provides an easy set of questions to ask students to encourage their thinking about their own experiences with a topic and how the experience relates to the content information from a text. Experience-Text-Relationship can be used when first introducing a topic or to assist learning of a particularly difficult text. One of the values of the activity is in providing productive avenues for students to bridge their own experiences and understanding of a topic with that of a course-assigned text.

Guiding Principles

Experience-Text-Relationship proves particularly useful in activating students' background knowledge of a class topic and relating new information to this prior understanding. Specifically, culturally familiar content, as one might expect, improves reading comprehension (Carrell, 1987). Helping students think through their own experiences in relationship to a reading can assist with students developing frameworks to understand new content. This process also elaborates the connection of the text information and provides additional retrieval cues to the newly learned material.

One of the uses for Experience-Text-Relationship within primary school settings—learning complex sociocultural topics—is also effective for college students. For example, in a course that examines race and ethnicity, Experience-Text-Relationship can help students discuss their own experience with race and compare this experience with the text (Au, 1979).

Preparation

To start the activity, select a reading to apply the Experience-Text-Relationship framework. The IDEA works best with narrative texts but can be used with any reading on nearly any topic. You may also want to identify particular passages that will be read and worked through together in class. The goal of your questions should be pulling out the students' views and interpretations as part of a discussion of the text.

Process

- During the Experience phase, ask questions about the students' background and prior knowledge of the topic.
- Next, have students read a particular passage or section of the reading. Resume the discussion by asking students to identify themes in the text, important points, or confusing areas that can be clarified.
- Finally, ask questions that invite the students to draw connections between the themes and concepts from the text and their own experiences.

Sample IDEA Pairing

Snowball (IDEA #12). Rather than discussing the Experience-Text-Relationship question as an entire class, students can answer the questions through increasingly larger groups.

Journaling (IDEA #68). Ask students to connect their own experiences and the text in a thoughtful way.

Sentence Passage Springboard (IDEA #69). Students identify a particular passage from the reading that connects with their own experiences and write about the relationship between the two.

Pro-tips

This activity is most effective with texts that warrant significant attention and examination. For example, in a literature context, a book with many themes, possible interpretations, and a complex story would lend itself well to this activity.

The three parts of Experience-Text-Relationship do not need to be dealt with entirely separately. Some connections and relationships may be brought up during the text phase. As these connections naturally come up in the discussions, you can build on these and gradually move more toward a discussion of these relationships.

Depending on the sensitivity of the topic, be aware of comments related to the experience of students in class. You may want to establish ground rules that encourage respect for the experiences of others, for example. As with any discussion of sensitive topics, you need to be aware of the tenor and tone of discussions to ensure some students are not marginalized.

IDEA #52: Directed Reading and Thinking

Overview

This activity engages students in a systematic process to guide them through reading a text. Designed by Stauffer (1969), the activity provides a step-by-step approach to reading that encourages students to ask questions and to make predictions that prompts students to actively read.

Directed Reading and Thinking draws from students' prior knowledge of the reading's topic and sets a goal for reading. By asking students to confirm and revise their predictions, students actively read and improve their comprehension. Giving students a goal for their reading keeps them focused and grounds their understanding. This activity may be used with nearly all types of reading but may prove particularly useful for complex expository readings and for learning to read a foreign language.

Guiding Principles

College students read and comprehend differently when reading for study than when reading for pleasure (Linderholm & van den Broek, 2002). The Directed Reading and Thinking IDEA assists readers who are reading to learn from text by engaging them with specific tasks rather than simply asking students to read material. For this task, students skim the material, particularly titles and headings, and from that limited material make predictions about what will be presented in the text.

The most significant benefits of this activity are to provide a cognitive frame for the information and to provide a constant check for comprehension. At the end of each reading session, students revisit their predictions and, based on what they read, determine the extent of their accuracy. By thinking through the predictions and looking for proof, students approach reading with a purpose that provides a built-in check on comprehension.

Preparation

Before beginning the Directed Reading and Thinking activity, try the activity yourself. Identify stopping points in the reading where students can pause and reassess their predictions. Finally, identify important areas and themes from the text to ensure that predictions cover a range of aspects of the reading.

Process

- Ask the students to read the title and headings for a given block of material and brainstorm concepts they already know about the topic.
- Have the students quickly skim the text to look for a table of contents, graphics, pictures, topic sentences, or tables (three minutes).
- Have the students make predictions of what they think they will read about in the text. Ask them to explain the basis for their predictions.
- Next, ask the students to *read* a section of the text until your predetermined stopping point (e.g., the end of a section).
- Ask the students if their predictions were true. Ask them to *think* about their predictions and revise or create new ones. Continue this process until the class has made it through the entire reading.
- To conclude, ask questions that promote class thinking about the main concepts and ideas from the reading.

Sample IDEA Pairings

Think-Pair-Share (IDEA #15). At each stopping point, have the students think about their predictions, discuss with a pair, and then share with the class.

Gallery Walk (IDEA #28). Develop prompts that ask students to make predictions and posts these around the room. The students write their responses, read the designated section, and then return to their predictions and make changes/additions as needed.

Main Idea-Detail Chart (IDEA #80). After the conclusion of Directed Reading and Thinking, students revise their predictions to create a Main Idea-Detail Chart.

Pro-tips

Throughout the course of this activity, students may respond to a question with "I don't know." As part of helping them think through reading, do not accept this answer and push them to explore the basis for their predictions. You may need to help them process as they may not be able to fully and explicitly explain their logic.

Depending on the complexity of the reading used in this activity, students may not be able to sufficiently skim the text to identify initial predictions. If this is the case, you may prime the pump by providing a few initial areas for them to consider. The goal is to have students read with a purpose, so it is not necessary that they identify all of the important ideas at the outset.

One of the challenges of this IDEA is to avoid providing too much prior knowledge or information about the reading. The benefits of the activity come from students finding incorrect predictions and adjusting them to new ones. This activity also fosters asking questions or raising ideas in a nonthreatening environment that can prove useful throughout the educational experience. Many students constantly seek the "correct" answer and only work for that end. The nature of predictions means that some will be right and others will be wrong, which can help students learn to deal with unclear answers and evidence.

This activity may work well at the end of class as a way to discuss the upcoming material and to help frame the reading for students. Upon completion of the activity in class, the students then read the material outside of class and come to the next class period ready to discuss the content.

IDEA #53: SQ3R

Overview

The SQ3R activity provides a framework for students to better comprehend and retain information from readings assigned for class. Students often read course readings as they would any other text: start at page one and read to the end without framing the content, thinking critically about the content, and engaging the content. This IDEA offers a more systematic approach to better study the material while reading (Artis, 2008).

SQ3R is a five-step process: survey, question, read, recite, and review. The activity helps students engage with the material and improve their processing of the information through framing and reflection. Although the use of these five steps takes longer than simply reading a text, the advantages of improved understanding and recall are beneficial for students, and they improve the teaching experience.

Guiding Principles

SQ3R is built on the foundation of an information processing theory of learning (Newell & Simon, 1972; Tadlock, 1978). This theory suggests that people structure and organize information into systems of meaning. The limitations of learning are frequently attributed to limits on the ability to organize information and by encoding information in a way that facilitates recall. By providing a framework to organize new knowledge, SQ3R helps students develop understanding faster and more efficiently.

The activity also makes use of the ways the brain stores and retrieves information using short- and long-term recall. The framework of SQ3R encourages students to slow down and spend time on information, which activates the processing strengths of particularly long-term memory. By asking questions and encouraging recitation, SQ3R allows students to better store and recall information from course readings.

Preparation

Most frequently, the SQ3R activity is completed by the student outside of class as part of the assigned readings. Prior to assigning SQ3R, provide the framework for students and also explain why the activity proves useful. Students often complain that this process increases the time it takes to complete the reading; in doing so, they often fail to see the value. Providing an understanding of why it works based on the guiding principles above can help students know the value and use the activity (Tadlock, 1978).

Process

- Explain the framework of the activity in the class and assign (or suggest) students use it on the readings for homework. The following steps explain the process of the activity.
- Survey helps students gather the basic structure of the topic presented in the reading, including reading the title, headings, graphics, and any text called out such as definitions or objectives.
- Question involves turning headings and other main ideas identified in the survey stage into questions. Students should then seek answers to the questions as they read.
- In the Read stage, students read the text to capture the main ideas as identified in the survey and question stages. The goal is to write down the answers to the questions raised by filling in the main ideas without getting too bogged down by the details.
- Next, students Recite material, which assists with concentration and recall. Students look at each of the questions of a section and attempt to answer the questions (while covering up their notes).
- The Review step allows the students to consolidate learning and comprehension by reviewing each of the questions and answers.

Sample IDEA Pairings

Guided Note-Taking (IDEA #1). Along with providing a structure for taking notes during a lecture, provide a framework for reading. In addition to the five steps of SQ3R, develop specific questions that students answer as part of the activity.

Note-Taking Pairs (IDEA #25). Students complete the SQ3R activity outside of class. Pair students and ask them to compare their notes, focusing of clarifying confusing points or summarizing key ideas.

Reader Response Paper (IDEA #67). Students complete the SQ3R and then write a paper responding to the concepts from the text as well as their reactions to the reading.

Pro-tips

Many students have never been taught how to read texts or study content-rich material. This activity presents a versatile framework to use while reading. You may find it helpful to walk students through how to complete the steps in class. Taking the time to model the process in class can improve students' use of the activity and improve their reading comprehension as a result.

There are many different variations that have grown out of SQ3R such as SQ4R (survey, question, read, recite, wRite, and review) (Pauk, 1984), PQ4R (preview, question, read, reflect, recite, and review), and FAIRER (facts, ask questions, identify major/minor details, read, evaluate comprehension, and review) (Lei, Rhinehart, Howard, & Cho, 2010). Fundamentally, these all provide frameworks for self-regulation of reading. You can use any variation of this system, as the goal is to provide a way for students to work through a framework to organize and comprehend new information.

One of the more difficult, yet important, aspects of the SQ3R activity is developing good questions. Students often can easily turn headings and other readily identifiable major points into questions but struggle with developing good topic-spanning questions. As part of other class activities and in debriefing this activity, help students develop good questions. You may do this by sharing good questions raised by classmates or by providing some starter questions you identified early in the course. Helping students learn to ask questions can assist students in your class and throughout their education.

IDEA #54: What Counts as Fact?

Overview

In What Counts as Fact?, students read two or more sources discussing the same topic or issue. Then, they write or discuss what each source uses as facts or proof.

The goal is to get students to interrogate sources to understand how different authors use evidence and how well conclusions are supported. Learning this skill helps students analyze and evaluate claims made by different sources, making them more informed consumers of information.

The activity requires students to understand material, consider the arguments, and evaluate the facts provided as evidence. A wide range of source material may be used, including research publications, media reports, press releases, and white papers. Nearly any video or written material may be analyzed according to the evidence used to support assertions and conclusions.

Guiding Principles

Fundamentally, What Counts as Fact? focuses on teaching students to think critically and analyze arguments. In order to develop critical thinking in college students, research suggests focusing instruction on assisting in the practice of skills and dispositions of critical thinking (Halpern, 1999). The skills for critical thinking often transcend individual courses, but over time, college students do show an increase in critical-thinking abilities (Terenzizi, Springer, Pascarella, & Nora, 1995). What Counts as Fact? promotes the use of critical-thinking skills that, over the long term, may benefit students' skill development.

This IDEA can help foster the dispositions of a critical thinker. Simply put, this IDEA helps students understand when it is appropriate to apply critical-thinking skills or, as Sears and Parson (1991) note, develop the ethics of a critical thinker. Encouraging students to use critical-thinking skills helps them value the importance and actively use the skills to analyze the information around them.

Preparation

To prepare for the What Counts as Fact? IDEA, identify two or more sources related to a particular topic. The material may include many different types of treatments of the subject, but the goal is to find sources that use different types of arguments and facts. The differences between how authors address the subject will provide useful fodder for the class to analyze the facts presented.

Process

- Provide two or more sources of information regarding a topic. This material may be assigned as preclass assignments, or time may be given in class for students to review.
- Individually or in groups, ask the students to identify the facts in each of the treatments provided on the topic. Ask them to consider what is considered

proof, the different types of facts presented, and how well the facts provided support the conclusions of the source.

- Through discussion, ask about the different types of evidence, what is most convincing, the choices an author must make, and how to support arguments and conclusions related to the topic under examination.

Sample IDEA Pairings

In the News (IDEA #16). Students (or the instructor) identify multiple news stories around a topic and compare the articles using the What Counts as Fact? framework.

Journal Club (IDEA #23). As part of reading and analyzing research for discussion, students use the analytic approaches considering evidence as in the What Counts as Fact? IDEA.

Experience-Text-Relationship (IDEA #51). The class examines the relationships between the various material presented through What Counts as Fact? and then compares these facts and evidence to their own experiences related to the topic.

Pro-tips

What Counts as Fact? works best when students are able to both identify the facts in the material examined and how the author uses facts to support a conclusion. As a result, discussion questions toward the end of the activity that focus on the types of information identified and how this information is used by the author can help students learn to analyze conclusions.

In today's information-rich environment, a benefit of this activity is helping students consider and evaluate sources. Today's students are bombarded by many different types of sources from marketing messages to news outlets to social media. When selecting materials to use for the activity, consider where students already obtain information related to a topic. Selecting these sources in addition to more traditional ones, such as scholarly research, can help make the activity more relevant as well as make students more informed consumers of knowledge.

Students may readily acknowledge the bias of certain media outlets (Fox News vs. MSNBC), but they often do not consider the bias and framework of more scholarly sources. Through the use of this activity, you can help elucidate viewpoints and bias of researchers whether based on theoretical assumptions or the types of questions asked. Providing an opportunity to question all sources can help students develop an awareness of viewpoints across all types of information.

IDEA #55: Problematic Situation

Overview

This activity prompts students to think critically in order to determine solutions to a presented problem based on course material. At its core, students are provided a selected text or instructor-created prompt that states an important problem related to course content. Working together in small groups, students brainstorm one or more solutions to the problem using specific evidence from the text or additional readings. At the end of the exercise, groups share ideas with the entire class and decide the best answer for the Problematic Situation.

The activity is designed to help students develop the skills needed to strategically identify evidence within a reading, to create possible solutions to the issue provided, and then to evaluate alternative solutions to identify the best option. In particular, this IDEA prompts students to provide support for a solution to a situation that may be difficult in nature or have more than one valid answer to consider. Problematic Solution engages students more closely with course readings as well as challenges their initial assumptions or impressions from a text.

Guiding Principles

Problematic Situation provides an opportunity for students to develop critical-thinking skills. While understanding a key few concepts from a class is important, the real value of higher education is instructing students how to approach and think systematically about course-related topics (Gaskins et al., 1994; Halpern, 1999). This activity helps students to not only solidify course knowledge but also develop skills needed to approach complex problems in an evidence-based manner.

Solving a problem individually may certainly be possible and in many cases preferred by students, but the benefits to be gained from considering multiple perspectives is an important life skill. Problematic Situation allows for a collaborative learning environment where students interact to achieve a common goal by considering and actively sharing individual knowledge from each participant (Kirschner, Paas, & Kirschner, 2009). Collaborative learning occurs twofold in this activity, once in the small groups through creating a solution and then again among the whole-class discussion while evaluating the efficacy of multiple solutions.

Preparation

Find or create a text that presents a problem that is both relevant to the class material and has sufficiently rich content to provide students the opportunity to develop a variety of solutions. Additionally, consider whether students will pull from additional readings to develop their solutions. Try to ensure students have come to class prepared with the reading completed. A short multiple-choice quiz over the material can provide additional motivation to read the assigned material.

Process

- Give the multiple-choice test at the beginning of the class session and allow students five to seven minutes to complete the quiz.
- Divide students into groups of ideally three to five students, and share the problem with the class.
- Ask each group to identify a solution or set of solutions using evidence from the text or additional class readings. Explain to the class that it is important that each member of the team understand the problem and the solution derived by the group.
- After groups have had the opportunity to sufficiently explore the problem provided, ask students to come together as a class and discuss their solutions.
- Finally, ask students to identify the solution with the most evidence from the reading.

Sample IDEA Pairings

Formal Argument (IDEA #17). Use in the whole-class discussion portion of the activity by asking students to formally debate in favor of their proposed solutions.

Role Play (IDEA #44). Ask students to assume a specific role or perspective when approaching the presented problem.

What Counts as Fact? (IDEA #54). Provide students multiple treatments of the same problem and ask them how their solutions or evidence differs between them.

Pro-tips

This activity works best when students learn to find and use evidence from reading to support their solution to the presented problem. Students may initially struggle with how to do this work effectively. At the beginning of the activity, walk around and ask whether anyone has questions to help facilitate the group discussions.

By presenting problems with a one-sided approach or a controversial solution, you can help seed the group discussions. Asking students to find evidence in support of a historical policy position that seems counter to current-day standards can encourage students to seek out evidence. For example, in a U.S. history course, you could ask students to seek evidence of why the states should have voted against the ratification of the Constitution.

Depending on the nature of the topic, students may hold strong personal feelings about the problem or proposed solutions. As you guide the ending discussion, help students focus on the evidence from the reading to help maintain the class emphasis on ideas from the text.

IDEA #56: Text Coding

Overview

The Text Coding IDEA provides a strategy for students to more effectively read and understand course-assigned texts. Students often struggle with monitoring their own reading comprehension, and this activity helps them to focus on understanding their readings. Text Coding asks students to make notations as they read according to a predefined coding scheme. For example, a student places a star next to significant facts or ideas. By coding the text while reading, students remained focused on the meaning of what they are reading beyond simply attempting to complete an assignment for class.

Text Coding proves particularly helpful in assisting students with organizing complex and detailed readings. Rather than being overwhelmed by the amount of information in a reading, students are able to organize and reflect on the ideas presented using the coding scheme to evaluate the text.

Guiding Principles

Fundamentally, Text Coding is based on the benefits of teaching students how to use annotation skills to organize content-rich text. This approach to reading helps students engage more deeply and substantively with texts (Porter-O'Donnell, 2004). By writing as they read, students create a record of their thoughts and reactions, which facilitates comprehension and review.

Writing and writing instruction help students improve their reading comprehension (Graham & Hebert, 2011). Text Coding provides a format for students to write and make notes in a reading, bringing the advantages of writing to aid in reading comprehension. In addition, having students write as they read provides a focus on ideas and attempts to understand what is being read.

Preparation

Before using the Text Coding IDEA, identify an appropriate reading and devise a coding scheme. The codes that students use can be fairly simple at the beginning of the course and then get more complex as the semester progresses. The overall goal is to have the codes help students identify key areas in the reading, which will in turn aid in comprehension.

There are several typical codes used in this activity. Examples include a check mark for ideas that confirm prior thinking, an X for ideas that contradict, a question mark (?) for text that is confusing, an exclamation point (!) for new ideas, and a star or asterisk (*) for important ideas. In addition, you can ask students to come up with their own codes. Using or building upon student-derived codes in subsequent semesters can increase motivation for students to use this system by showing that it was developed previously by their peers.

Process

- Share the coding list and explain how students will complete the activity.
- Demonstrate how to complete the coding on a small section of the text or a separate reading to provide clarification and model how the activity works.
- Ask students to complete the reading using the coding list. You may also allow the students to add codes of their own in addition to those provided.
- After students complete the reading, have students work in small groups to review their markings and help answer questions identified.

Sample IDEA Pairings

Think-Pair-Share (IDEA #15). Students complete the Text Coding, form pairs to discuss, and then share with the class what they identified in the reading.

Note-Taking Pairs (IDEA #25). Students compare the notes from Text Coding and compare their results with a partner.

What Counts as Fact? (IDEA #54). Have students code for proofs and facts in a reading in addition to other codes from the preassigned list. After the activity, students may discuss the different kinds of evidence used along with other key areas from the reading.

Pro-tips

Briefly showing students how to Text Code written material using an overhead or document camera can quickly demonstrate how students should complete the activity.

Particularly early in learning this process, observe how students are using the codes. This approach will help identify areas of the text that require further clarification or examination during a subsequent lecture or discussion.

IDEA #57: Question–Answer Relationship

Overview

The Question–Answer Relationship activity provides a framework for examining the relationship between questions, content, and the reader's knowledge (Raphael, 1986). The primary goal of this activity is to demystify the question process by helping students to ask better questions in order to develop better reading comprehension. This activity also helps students consider the relationship between information in the reading and their own background knowledge.

Using the Question–Answer Relationship, students learn to break questions into one of four categories:

1. Right There (answer is in the text),
2. Think and Search (answer is in the text but you might have to combine it across sections),
3. Author and You (answer is not in the text but, in combination with your own knowledge, you can figure it out), and
4. On My Own (answer is not in the text, and you do not even need to read the text to answer it).

This process helps students to move from passive learners to having a more engaged approach with strategies to solve comprehension problems (Wilson & Smetana, 2011).

Guiding Principles

Teaching students to generate questions has been shown to be related to college students' reading comprehension (Rosenshine, Meister, & Chapman, 1996). As students learn to ask questions, they are able to interrogate reading and engage the content to a greater extent, allowing them to look at information differently. This engagement results in students being able to work through text and identify key information to understand.

Question–Answer Relationship builds on the concept of self-regulated learning by encouraging students to identify the types of questions in the context of their own knowledge and the text. Self-regulated learning includes not only cognitive processing but student motivation as well, which provides a richer description of student learning (Pintrich, 2004).

Preparation

In preparation for the Question–Answer Relationship activity, identify at least two readings and develop questions related to one of them. The questions should span all four of categories noted above. Ideally, the questions will challenge students to think about the core elements of the question and where they can find the answers in the text. These answers should also lead students to the main ideas and concepts from the reading.

Process

- Explain the four categories of questions to the class as an introduction to the activity: Right There, Think and Search, Author and You, and On My Own.
- Provide a set of questions about a reading related to course content.

- Divide the class into small groups and have them identify which category the questions fit inside using the Question–Answer Relationship framework.
- Provide a second reading and ask students to identify their own questions within the context of the framework.

Sample IDEA Pairings

Each One, Teach One (IDEA #30). After organizing questions according to the Question–Answer Relationship framework, each student takes a question, answers it, and then shares the answer with the class through the Each One, Teach One activity.

Author Charts (IDEA #89). After categorizing the questions from two readings, students then develop Author Charts, which help identify an author's background, biases, and motivations. This extension builds on the idea of having students study the text and the meaning of readings.

Pro-tips

This activity proves most useful in helping students understand that text comprehension is enhanced when the reader takes an active and engaged approach to conceptualizing different forms of questions one may ask about written content. That is, there is a need to analyze and comprehend a reading in order to be able to answer all of the questions that might be presented. As you work through this activity with the class, helping students recognize the role of readings will help their understanding of the content.

Depending on the students' levels and understanding, you may have to do more modeling of how to think about questions and their answers. If students struggle, you can help them work through a couple or create an additional set of questions that you work through as a class. Then, the groups can work through a second set after having walked through one set together.

Question–Answer Relationship helps students locate information in a reading, understand the structure of readings, and decide when they need to infer from a text and their own prior knowledge. The activity does not specifically center on the answers themselves, but rather how to find the answers. If the students need to identify the answers for future reference (exam review, for example), you can have them write down answers as they find them.

IDEA #58: Three-Level Reading Guide

Overview

The Three-Level Reading Guide is designed to help students identify significant information in a reading, interpret the meaning of the text, and apply this information to related material. This process is achieved by having students think about the three levels of comprehension of a text: literal, interpretive, and applied. As designed by Herber (1978), the guide helps students focus on the text, consider the information, and make generalizations from the ideas in the reading to other material.

The responses to the three levels both assists students with identifying information at the various levels and can also be used to inform class discussions. In addition, the Three-Level Reading Guide IDEA provides a way for students to make notes of their comprehension as they read through an assigned text.

Guiding Principles

Much of college instruction builds on information students derive from reading outside of class. However, students do not often understand how to learn from reading (Brown, Campione, & Day, 1981). The Three-Level Reading Guide provides a system for students to use when approaching reading. The Three-Level Reading Guide also helps them work through the levels of reading comprehension, which can help students gauge their own understanding.

In addition to being able to understand the conceptual knowledge from a reading, students benefit from text processing strategies that help them to work through a reading when their knowledge of a subject is limited (Kolic-Vehovec, Bajsanski, & Zubkovic, 2011). The benefit of the Three-Level Reading Guide is in helping students approach a reading using increasingly deep cognitive levels to broaden their understanding and skills in reading a course-assigned text.

Preparation

Prior to using Three-Level Reading Guides in class, identify a topic and appropriate reading to use for the activity. The reading can be any type of written material that allows students to think through the various levels of reading comprehension. It is most beneficial to start with text that is relatively easy for students to understand and then work into more cognitively complex or content-dense readings. In addition, it is helpful to students if you prepare notes for a discussion at the conclusion that uses the ideas raised by the students as well as other important points you identify to help the students think about the topic addressed in the activity.

Process

- Explain the levels of comprehension of a text: literal, interpretive, and applied.
- Have the students individually or in groups identify approximately eight facts or ideas that are literally in the text.
- Next, ask the students to note four to five ideas that are interpreted for what the author might mean.

- Have the students write down two to three ideas that combine with other course materials to make generalizations or hypotheses about the topic.
- Debrief with the class about what points they identified and lead a discussion of the topic based on the ideas from the text raised by the students.

Sample IDEA Pairings

Socratic Seminar (IDEA #7). Students complete the Three-Level Reading Guide, and then the instructors leads a Socratic Seminar by asking questions about the points students raised in completing the guide.

Scored Discussion (IDEA #14). After completing the guide individually or in teams, students form circles and discuss the topic of the reading while being scored on significant points raised.

Pro-tips

You can provide this activity to students to complete as they read or as a postreading activity to evaluate the information they just read. The activity works better as an in-class activity rather than as a homework assignment to be completed independently.

Three-Level Reading Guides may be used with nearly any type of written material from newspaper articles to complex, theoretical readings. The goal is to help students work through the multiple ways to evaluate any text that they read.

In addition to providing students with the skills and framework for reading, Three-Level Reading Guides provide useful fodder for class discussion. By completing the activity, students have identified parts of the text to interpret and apply to other course concepts that can be explored through discussion to clarify confusing points or draw other conclusions.

IDEA #59: What Would You Ask?

Overview

This activity is an easy way to have students critically read and analyze a text. As the name suggests, students simply write down questions they would ask the class if they were the instructor. By putting students into the role of instructor, the activity empowers students to engage with the reading differently than how they typically approach class-assigned readings.

What Would You Ask? requires students to think about the course objectives, identify key points, and draw conclusions about the most salient aspects of a reading. In addition, this IDEA proves helpful in gauging students' reading comprehension by examining the aspects of a reading that they select to ask questions to the class.

Guiding Principles

Students need training in asking questions, and teaching through the use of questions helps students learn (Graesser & Person, 1994). For a variety of reasons, students do not ask questions in class in the same ways they do in other settings. Asking questions is a skill that students can develop with practice (Hofstein, Navon, Kipnis, & Mamiok-Naaman, 2005). Moreover, students often do not know what to ask. What Would You Ask? assists students with not only developing question-asking skills but creating a supportive environment to ask questions.

This activity is supported by the notion of self-directed learning, which encourages students to take on a greater role in their own learning (Grow, 1991). Self-directed learning supports students asking questions and developing their own critical-thinking capabilities (Candy, 1991). By allowing students to practice the role of instructor through What Would You Ask?, instructors help students take responsibility, build autonomy related to their reading comprehension, and practice forming content inquiry.

Preparation

This activity requires little preparation prior to using it in class. Identify a reading or readings that the students will use to base their questions. Additionally, you may want to share a few sample questions or describe what kinds of information the students are to look for in creating their questions.

Process

- Explain the activity by asking students to play the role of instructor and to write questions based on a reading or set of readings.
- Working individually or in small groups, ask students to write down questions from the reading that they believe the instructor should ask.
- Time permitting, the students can trade and answer the questions raised by others in class.

Sample IDEA Pairings

Pause Procedure (IDEA #2). Ask students to identify questions they would ask the class about the lecture recently completed and the readings completed prior to class.

Speed Interviews (IDEA #35). Students develop a question, which they then ask each student in class to answer using the speed-dating style of Speed Interviews.

Pro-tips

One of your primary goals in this activity is to create a supportive and empowering climate for students. You can do this by walking around the classroom while students are working on questions and provide encouragement. Particularly when you first use this IDEA, you may need to provide additional assistance for students struggling with different types of questions to ask.

Related to the first tip, next encourage students to ask questions that demonstrate a range of comprehension. Students can ask fact-based questions, but they should also be encouraged to write questions that require interpretation and application of concepts discussed previously in the course.

The types of questions that students ask can give clues to what students understand as well as areas where there is confusion. Many of the questions that they develop will be about areas they understand and thus feel confident in writing questions about during this activity. Encouraging them to write about other aspects of the reading may reveal parts of the reading that should be addressed further in class.

If you are comfortable with the material and also comfortable with not being able to answer all questions asked of you, a good way to review the material is to have students ask you the questions they develop. This variation can be turned into a game whereby each team gets one point if they ask a content-related question that you do not know.

IDEA #60: Research Paper Reviewer

Overview

In this IDEA, students take on a role that many instructors have assumed at one point or another: a reviewer of a research paper for potential publication in a journal. The student receives a research paper and a set of guidelines for the review. If possible, the student also reviews a sample of the journal for which the article is intended.

This IDEA has students develop skills at reading research papers. It also helps them begin to assimilate the research process in a low-threat environment. In other words, this activity gives students exposure to the research process prior to their actually having to engage in it.

Guiding Principles

Many of us want students to develop critical-thinking skills. That is, they should not accept what they read but should weigh the claims being made. Moreover, we want them to be able to evaluate critical content in our fields, to judge the merit or value of a written work.

Evaluation is one of the core categories of Bloom's educational taxonomy of cognitive learning objectives, and it is included as a category of the revised taxonomy as well (Anderson & Krathwohl, 2000). The idea is that students should be able to make a judgment about value for a given purpose. The judgments should be based upon a clear criteria, they should be supported by data, and they should be able to be determined by standards of excellence. Evaluation is a higher-order thinking skill. Students do not always have practice with this skill, though, and practice can help them develop it.

Preparation

The first step in this activity is to select articles for student review. You may select articles that have been published previously or alternately those that appear online but have not yet been published in a peer-reviewed journal (this information is called grey literature and may include theses, online submissions, white papers, or other written documents).

The next step is to design a review form. You can base this form upon those typically used in your field. We offer the following as a sample. It is a composite of Bengtson and MacDermid (n.d.) and IEEE's (n.d.) Reviewer Guidelines.

TABLE 5.3 Research Paper Reviewer Guidelines

**Research Paper Review
Form
General Guidelines**

1) Keep in mind that reviewers serve as mentors to authors, with a goal of helping get it ready for potential publication. Both complimentary and critical comments are vital to the process. The goal is to help authors to identify the strengths of their manuscripts as well as the weaknesses.
2) You should plan to provide your overall reaction as well as a list of specific comments. What aspects of the article were strong? What needs clarification or more detail? Is the article well written?
3) You should also describe the manuscript's strengths and its weaknesses. Clearly state the objectives, contributions, and limitations of the manuscript.

Suggested Approach

Look for the "**intellectual plot-line**" of the article. You can do this from first skimming through the manuscript and then giving it a once-over read.
Next read for details.

Research Review

As you do this, ask four main questions that are central to the research review process:

• **Questions**
1. What do the researchers want to find out?
2. Is the question clearly stated?
3. Why is that important to investigate or understand?
4. Do they lay out a clear claim?

- **Methods**
1. How are the researchers investigating this? Do the authors clearly describe their research strategies? Do they present sufficient detail about the sample from which they have collected data; the operationalization of measures they have attempted to employ; and the adequacy of these measures in terms of external and internal validity?
2. Are their research methods adequate to the task?
3. Are they the most appropriate? Would other methods provide a substantial improvement; if so, would employing these methods be feasible or practical?
4. Do they provide some justification for the methods they have chosen? Does this appear to be adequate?

- **Findings**
1. What do they claim to have found out? Are the findings clearly stated?
2. How does this advance knowledge in the field?
3. How well do the researchers place their findings within the context of ongoing scholarly inquiry about this topic?
4. Does the results section tell a story—taking the reader from the research questions posed earlier to their answers in the data? Is the logic clear?
5. Are the tables and figures clear and succinct? Can they be "read" easily for major findings by themselves, or should there be additional information provided? Are the authors' tables consistent with the format of currently accepted norms regarding data presentation?
6. Do the authors present too many tables or figures in the form of undigested findings? Are all of them necessary in order to tell the story of this research inquiry; or can some be combined? Remember that tables and figures are expensive (from the standpoint of the journal) and that undigested data obscure rather than advance the cumulative development of knowledge in a field.
7. Are the results presented meaningful? Have the authors stayed within the bounds of the results their data will support?

Final recommendation

When making a final recommendation on a manuscript, please choose one of the following options:
1) *Publish As Is.* The article fulfills all of the requirements listed above and is ready for publication.
2) *Minor Revision.* The article contains a small number of easily correctable.
3) *Major Revision.* The article has significant deficiencies. The author's claims are not backed up by facts or the information included is too broad.
4) *Revise & Resubmit.* The article in its current form is not suitable for publication and requires significant rewrites. However, it does contain value and after taking into consideration the reviewer's comments would be worthy of an evaluation for future publication upon the author's resubmission of the manuscript.
5) *Not Suitable for Publication.* The article is not suitable for publication. It does not offer any value to the readers or its subject is so thoroughly incoherent that it does not merit an opportunity for a revision.

Process

- Assign the paper for students to review, and distribute the review form.
- Provide students with a time to review.
- Collect their responses, and consider having them report out, particularly if they all worked on the same paper or papers; students will want to know if they came up with the same recommendations as their peers.

Sample IDEA Pairings

Anticipation Guide (IDEA #50). Have student read the article with an Anticipation Guide and then move into a formal Research Paper Review.

Journaling (IDEA #68). Ask student to log their efforts at Research Paper Review in their journals.

Visible Classroom Opinion Poll (IDEA #93). If students are reading the same journal article, conduct the Opinion Poll to determine the class's overall recommendation.

Pro-tips

This activity can be particularly motivating for advanced students who will have to do research and who ultimately may aspire to be faculty members or researchers themselves. It provides an authentic activity that can increase student motivation and help them see the value of the activity.

Students do not typically have experience in doing formal reviews, and thus this IDEA may involve a learning curve on the part of students. Moreover, it may be a better activity for more advanced students who have developed the foundational knowledge that they need in order to be able to move to higher-order thinking skills such as analysis and evaluation.

IDEA #61: Select a Sentence

Overview

In Select a Sentence, the instructor asks each student or groups of students to identify one sentence that they believe contains a significant idea for the class topic. The instructor takes each of the sentences, pulls together themes, and helps students think through the main ideas of the class. This activity assists students in identifying key concepts from reading and analyzing ideas across readings to improve understanding of course content.

Both through the process of identifying a key sentence and by bridging themes across readings, students learn important analysis and critical reading skills. Select a Sentence can be used for dense or heavily theoretical content with which students often struggle or to compare different approaches or viewpoints across readings.

Guiding Principles

The Select a Sentence IDEA builds on the benefits of summarizing texts, which can be an effective way to demonstrate retention and comprehension of information (Brown et al., 1981). For students new to the content, summarizing can prove to be a difficult task. By taking the various sentences from the students, the instructor can model effective summarizing strategies and help students understand the core concepts related to the class.

By asking questions about the sentences students select, the instructors helps students learn to evaluate and analyze texts. Specifically, this activity can assist students with evaluating external consistency (ideas are consistent with what one already understands) and internal consistency (ideas are consistent with others in the text) (Baker, 1985). Students of different academic backgrounds and verbal abilities vary in how they comprehend, evaluate, and analyze text. Select a Sentence provides an opportunity to assist students across abilities to analyze key concepts from course readings.

Preparation

Prior to the use of the Select a Sentence activity, identify key themes along with supporting sentences. It is not necessary for the students to pick the same sentences that you do, but having a list prior to class provides two benefits. First, you will be better prepared to pull out themes from the sentences students do provide. Second, if there are areas that are important and students do not identify them, you have specific examples to bring to the discussion. Be prepared to ask clarifying or guiding questions, but be careful not to give students the impression that there are right or wrong sentences to select.

Process

- Ask students individually or in groups (depending on the size of the class) to identify a sentence that contains a significant idea or concept (three to five minutes).
- One by one, ask students to share their sentence. Write down key phrases or ideas on the board. Group the phrases by theme.
- After collecting all of the sentences, help students see the major themes from all of the sentences identified. You may use lecture, discussion, or other means. The goal is to help students see how individual sentences and readings can be analyzed to develop an understanding of larger concepts.

Sample IDEA Pairings

Gallery Walk (IDEA #28). Students write down their sentences, which are then placed around the room. Then, students move around the room and read the sentences with the goal of identifying important themes that are then discussed as a class.

Sentence Passage Springboard (IDEA #69). In this variation, students select a key sentence and then write to capture their thoughts about the sentence.

Main Idea-Detail Chart (IDEA #80). Rather than asking students to simply identify sentences with important ideas, ask them to find sentences that contain main ideas or details to fill in the Main Idea-Detail Chart.

Pro-tips

As the instructor, your goal is to take the sentences students identify and work them into useable themes. At times, students may offer a sentence that is less germane to the main course topics. In this case, you can ask additional questions to elicit information related to one of the important themes or rephrase a sentence to emphasize a part that can be included with other ideas.

For texts that are difficult for students to understand, you may want to do a variation called Select a Confusing Sentence. Rather than selecting a key sentence, students identify one that was confusing and that they did not understand. Next, you walk the students through how to understand it. This approach not only clarifies confusing content but encourages students to acknowledge when they do not understand something in class.

This activity works best when students are able to see how individual ideas and sentences form the foundation of broader concepts or viewpoints. One of the best values of this activity is showing students how to work through readings to identify these important concepts. As you develop themes while writing ideas and phrases on the board, explicitly explain your logic in grouping ideas. This type of modeling can help students see how to analyze and aggregate information in the future.

References

Absalom, M., & Rizzi, A. (2008). Comparing the outcomes of online listening versus online text-based tasks in university level Italian L2 Study. *ReCall, 20*, 55–66.

ACT. (2012). The condition of college readiness. Retrieved June 3, 2015, from http://www.act.org/research/policymakers/cccr12/readiness1.html

Ambrose, S.A., Bridges, M.W., DiPietro, M., Lovett, M.C., & Norman, M.K. (2010). *How learning works: Seven research-based principles for smart teaching.* San Francisco, CA: Jossey-Bass.

Anderson, L.W., & Krathwohl, D.R. (Eds.). (2000). *A taxonomy for learning, teaching, and assessing: A revision of Bloom's taxonomy of educational objectives.* New York: Longman.

Artis, A.B. (2008). Improving marketing students' reading comprehension with the SQ3R method. *Journal of Marketing Education, 30*(2), 130–137.

Au, K.H.P. (1979). Using the experience-text-relationship method with minority children. *Reading Teacher, 32*(6), 677–679.

Baker, L. (1985). Differences in the standards used by college students to evaluate their comprehension of expository prose. *Reading Research Quarterly, 20*(3), 297–313.

Bengtson, V.L., & MacDermid, S.M. (n.d.). How to review a journal article: Suggestions for first-time reviewers and reminders for seasoned experts. Retrieved March 5, 2015, from https://www.ncfr.org/jmf/jmf-reviewers/reviewer-guidelines

Breimer, E., Cotler, J., & Yoder, R. (2012). Video vs. text for lab instruction and concept learning. *Journal of Computing Science in Colleges, 27*(6), 42–48.

Brown, A.L., Campione, J.C., & Day, J.D. (1981). Learning to learn: On training students to learn from texts. *Educational Researcher, 10*(2), 14–21.

Brown, S. (2011). *Listening myths: Applying second language research to classroom teaching.* Ann Arbor: University of Michigan Press. http://www.press.umich.edu/pdf/9780472034598-myth1.pdf

Bugg, J.M., & McDaniel, M.A. (2012). Selective benefits of question self-generation and answering for remembering expository text. *Journal of Education Psychology, 104*(4), 922–931.

Candy, P.C. (1991). *Self-direction for lifelong learning: A comprehensive guide to theory and practice.* San Francisco, CA: Jossey-Bass.

Carlston, D.L. (2011). Benefits of student generated note packets: A preliminary investigation of SQ3R implementation. *Teaching of Psychology, 38*(3), 142–146.

Carrell, P.L. (1987). Content and formal schemata in ESL reading. *TESOL Quarterly, 21*(3), 461–481.

Cerdan, R., Vidal-Abarca, E., Martinez, T., Gilabert, R., & Gil, L. (2009). Impact of question–answering tasks on search processes and reading comprehension. *Learning and Instruction, 19*(1), 13–27.

Clarke, T.A., Ayres, P.L., & Sweller, J. (2005). The impact of sequencing and prior knowledge on learning mathematics through spreadsheet applications. *Educational Technology Research and Development, 53*(15–24).

Dowhower, S.L. (2009). Strategic stance in the classroom: A comprehension framework for helping teachers help students to be strategic. *Reading Teacher, 52,* 672–688.

Dubas, J.M., & Toledo, S.A. (2015). Active reading documents: A tool to facilitate meaning learning through reading. *College Teaching, 63*(1), 27–33.

Duffelmeyer, F.A., Baum, D.D., & Merkley, D.J. (1987). Maximizing reader-text confrontation with an extended anticipation guide. *Journal of Reading, 31*(2), 146–150.

Fadel, C. (2009). *Multimodal learning through media: What the research says.* San Jose, CA: Cisco Systems.

Farstrup, A.E., & Samuels, S.J. (Eds.). (2011). *What research has to say about reading instruction* (4th ed.). Newark, DE: International Reading Association.

Flavell, J.H. (1979). Metacognition and cognitive monitoring: A new area of cognitive-developmental inquiry. *American Psychologist, 34*(10), 906–911.

Gaskins, I.W., Guthrie, J.T., Satlow, E., Ostertag, J., Six, L., Byrne, J., & Connor, B. (1994). Integrating instruction of science, reading, and writing: Goals, teacher development, and assessment. *Journal of Research in Science Teaching, 31*(9), 1039–1056.

Graesser, A.C., & Person, N.K. (1994). Question asking during tutoring. *American Educational Research Journal, 31*(1), 104–137.

Graham, S., & Hebert, M. (2011). Writing to read: A meta-analysis of the impact of writing and writing instruction on reading. *Harvard Educational Review, 81*(4), 710–744.

Grow, G.O. (1991). Teaching learners to be self-directed. *Adult Education Quarterly, 41*(3), 125–149.

Halpern, D.F. (1999). Teaching for critical thinking: Helping college students develop the skills and dispositions of a critical thinker. *New Directions for Teaching and Learning, 80,* 69–74.

Herber, H.L. (1978). *Teaching reading in content areas.* Englewood Cliffs, NJ: Prentice-Hall.

Hofstein, A., Navon, O., Kipnis, M., & Mamiok-Naaman, R. (2005). Developing students' ability to ask more and better questions resulting from inquiry-type chemistry laboratories. *Journal of Research in Science Teaching, 42*(7), 791–806.

Houck, B.D., & Ross, K. (2012). Dismantling the myth of learning to read and reading to learn. *Reading: The Core Skill, 7*(11), 1–4.

Huang, W.C. (2014). The effects of multimedia annotation and summary writing on Taiwanese EFL students' reading comprehension matrix. *An International Online Journal, 14*(1), 136–153.

IEEE. (n.d.). Reviewer guidelines. Retrieved March 5, 2015, from http://www.ieee.org/membership_services/membership/students/reviewer_guidelines_final.pdf

Kirschner, F., Paas, F., & Kirschner, P.A. (2009). A cognitive load approach to collaborative learning: United brains for complex tasks. *Educational Psychology Review, 21*(1), 31–42.

Kolic-Vehovec, S., Bajsanski, I., & Zubkovic, B.R. (2011). The role of reading strategies in scientific text comprehension and academic achievement of university students. *Review of Psychology, 18*(2), 81–90.

Lei, S.A., Rhinehart, P.J., Howard, H.A., & Cho, J.K. (2010). Strategies for improving reading comprehension among college students. *Reading Improvement, 47*(1), 30–42.

Lesser, M.J. (2004). The effects of topic familiarity, mode and pausing on second language learners' comprehension and focus on form. *Studies in Second Language Acquisition, 26,* 587–615.

Linderholm, T., & van den Broek, P. (2002). The effects of reading purpose and working memory capacity on the processing of expository text. *Journal of Educational Psychology, 94*(4), 778–784.

Lund, R.J. (1991). A comparison of second language listening and reading. *Modern Language Journal, 75,* 196–204.

Marton, F., & Säljö, R. (1976). On qualitative differences in learning—1: Outcome and process. *British Journal of Educational Psychology, 46,* 4–11.

National Institute of Literacy. (2009). Developing national literacy: A scientific synthesis of early literacy development and implications for early intervention. Retrieved June 3, 2015, from http://lincs.ed.gov/publications/pdf/NELPReport09.pdf

Newell, A., & Simon, H.A. (1972). *Human problem solving.* New York: Prentice Hall.

Park, G. (2004). Comparison of L2 listening and reading comprehension by university students learning English in Korea. *Foreign Language Annals, 37,* 448–458.

Pauk, W. (1984). The new SQ3R. *Reading World, 23*(3), 274–275.

Pintrich, P.R. (2004). A conceptual framework for assessing motivation and self-regulated learning in college students. *Educational Psychology Review, 16*(4), 385–407.

Porter-O'Donnell, C. (2004). Beyond the yellow highlighter: Teaching annotation skills to improve reading comprehension. *English Journal, 93*(5), 82–89.

Pressley, M., Ghatala, E.S., Woloshyn, V., & Pirie, J. (1990). Sometimes adults miss the main ideas and do not realize it: Confidence in responses to short-answer and multiple choice comprehension questions. *Reading Research Quarterly, 25*(3), 232–249.

Raphael, T.E. (1986). Teaching question–answer relationships. *Reading Teacher, 39*(6), 303–311.

Rayner, K., Foorman, B., Perfetti, C., Pesetsky, D., & Seidenberg, M. (2001). How psychological science informs the teaching of reading. *Psychological Science in the Public Interest, 2*(2), 31–74.

Rosenshine, B., Meister, C., & Chapman, S. (1996). Teaching students to generate questions: A review of the intervention studies. *Review of Educational Research, 66*(2), 181–221.

Sears, A., & Parsons, J. (1991). Toward critical thinking as an ethic. *Theory and Research in Social Education, 19*(1), 45–68.

Skylar, A.A. (2009). A comparison of asynchronous online text-based lectures and synchronous interactive web conferencing lectures. *Issues in Teacher Education, 18*(2), 69–84.

Song, M.-Y. (2008). Do divisible subskills exist in second language (L2) comprehension? A structural equation modeling approach. *Language Testing, 25*, 435–464.

Stauffer, R.G. (1969). *Directing reading maturity as a cognitive process.* New York: Harper & Row.

Tadlock, D.F. (1978). SQ3R—Why it works, based on an information processing theory of learning. *Journal of Reading, 22*(2), 110–112.

Terenzizi, P.T., Springer, L., Pascarella, E.T., & Nora, A. (1995). Influences affecting the development of students' critical thinking skills. *Research in Higher Education, 36*(1), 23–29.

Thorndike, E.L. (1917). Reading as reasoning. *Journal of Educational Psychology, 8*, 323–332.

Tseng, S.-S., Yeh, H.C., & Yang, S.-h. (2015). Promoting different reading comprehension levels through online annotations. *Computer Assisted Language Learning, 28*(1), 41–57.

Ukpokodu, O.N. (2010). Teachers' reflections on pedagogies that enhance learning in an online course on teaching for equity and social justice. *Journal of Interactive Online Learning, 9*(3), 227–255.

Weinstein, Y., McDermott, K.B., & Roediger, H.L. (2010). A comparison of study strategies for passages: Rereading, answering questions, and generating questions. *Journal of Experiential Psychology, 16*(3), 308–316.

Wilson, N.S., & Smetana, L. (2011). Questioning as thinking: A metacognitive framework to improve comprehension of expository text. *Literacy, 45*(2), 84–90.

6

WRITING TO LEARN

Description

Academic writing should be an act of deep thinking and reflection. It can lead to discovery, synthesis, evaluation, creation, and communication of knowledge. As the National Commission on Writing (2003) puts it, "Writing is not simply a way for students to demonstrate what they know. It is a way to help them understand what they know. At its best, writing is learning" (p. 51). When students translate information and experience into their own words, it helps them understand, strengthen, and build their learning of content knowledge. It also helps them build and demonstrate technical as well as creative skills.

Writing became a common practice in higher education in the late 1800s. At this time, industrialization was in full force, and with it came the introduction of technologies such as the industrial printing press. There was also a shift in communication, and thus education, from a primarily oral tradition to one involving the use of printed text. Other forces were at play in higher education as well. College education, for example, shifted from being something reserved for the elite to something for serving the masses. (Trow, 1979). Moreover, the mission and types of higher education diversified (Harris, 2013), and professions became increasingly specialized, requiring more postsecondary training (Russell, 2002). For about another century after these changes, however, educators continued to use writing as a means to teach appropriate English and to test students' knowledge. However, writing was largely relegated to composition courses or final examinations and not intended to help teach student content.

Writing became a more well-recognized and arguably more central way to learn starting in the 1970s with the advent of the writing across the curriculum (WAC) movement, which is thought to have been pioneered by James

Britton (1970, 1972). This movement began with the assumption that writing is integral to learning, particularly through its demands for encoding of new information, and thus should be included in all subject areas (Marzano, 2012). WAC involves incorporating short writing assessments into courses to help students develop content knowledge (Russell, 2002). While several interesting innovations developed alongside the writing across the curriculum movement, one that holds particular promise for faculty in a range of disciplines and fields is the notion of "writing to learn" (Applebee, 1984; Beutlier, 1988; Beyer, 1980; Murray, 1997).

"Writing to learn" is a specific kind of writing assignment designed to help students think through the content of a given course. The focus of writing-to-learn activities is on improving retention of information and on deepening student understanding of it (Marzano, 2012). In brief, "writing to learn" is a means of instruction and assessment of learning that involves using short, often impromptu writing assignments. These activities often require students to engage in what resembles an advanced form of note-taking (Marzano, 2012). The activities may take only a few minutes of in-class time or be assigned as brief out-of-class activities that students bring to class the next day. Writing-to-learn activities can be used in various situations, and they are useful in most instances when students would benefit from thinking about what they are doing or why they are doing it. This form of writing differs from writing assignments designed to allow students to demonstrate achievement on final products (e.g., essay exam questions, term papers, and so forth).

Purposes of Writing to Learn

Writing requires practice, and it is commonly held that to get good at writing, it is important to write. The challenge, however, is how to grade the mountains of writing that results. One common belief in academe is that if a student produces work, it is imperative that it be graded. Nilson (2010) suggests that it is reasonable to ask students to do in-class "informal writing," such as writing to learn activities, that you do not grade. As she asserts, the reasons are plentiful because writing to learn has several important benefits for college-level teaching and learning. One reason, as Nilson rightly argues, is that writing about material can help students deepen their understanding of it, which will in turn help them retain the information longer. When planned carefully, writing assignments can help students develop content knowledge (Cavdar & Doe, 2012). The writing assignments can help students go beyond a superficial understanding of content. Writing about content, for example, can help to develop students' sensitivities to the varied interests, backgrounds, and vocabularies of different writers.

Beyond deepening foundational knowledge, writing helps students to think actively about material, which in turn can help them engage in higher-order thinking skills, such as critical thinking (Cavdar & Doe, 2012). Indeed, communication is itself a form of higher-order thinking, which is necessary for the writing process. Gottschalk and Hjortshoj (2004) suggest that writing helps students achieve deeper learning that occurs through application of language skills (pp. 14–17).

Writing-to-learn activities can also be done for the purpose of course-level assessment. That is, brief written responses to prompts can allow instructors to determine what students are and are not learning. Doing so can help diagnose confusion before the next quiz or exam or move on to other topics. Target your instruction to the best level for the students (Angelo & Cross, 1993; Cross & Angelo, 1988).

Writing-to-learn activities also can provide students with the opportunity to learn about themselves. Bolton (2010) states, "Writers can discover more about themselves, and clarify their values, professional identity and boundaries. They learn about diversity of perspective, and recognize and challenge assumptions about political, social and cultural norms." (p. xxi). Through course writing assignments, students can explore their own feelings, beliefs, values, cognitive processes, and their learning strengths and weaknesses. Self-discovery can lead to improved metacognition and self-regulation, which can help students learn better not only in the one course but also in courses that they will take in the future. In short, these activities can help students be better learners.

Types of Writing-to-Learn Activities

It's difficult to develop a strict typology of "writing-to-learn" activities because there are many forms, many of which overlap with each other and even with other categories we have in this book. Following, however, are some writing-to-learn activities that faculty from a range of disciplines and fields use in their college courses.

- **Summarizing the content.** One of the most basic forms of "writing to learn" is summarizing content from a reading, lecture, or other assignment. This form of writing to learn may include note-taking, outlining, or guided summarizing.
- **Questioning the content.** Beyond simply summarizing the content, writing-to-learn activities may be tailored to prompt students to question the content. Prompts may include responding to specific questions or crafting their own questions. Either way, students respond to the questions so that they can capture their thoughts. Their responses may be used to initiate discussions, whether full class or small group.
- **Reacting to the content.** Writing-to-learn activities can provide students with an opportunity to respond to information they have heard or read in the class. They may provide a response to a section of a text or a whole text, evaluating its quality or message. They may also provide a personal response,

which can help them tie their own experiences to the content and will help them deepen their knowledge. One option in this category is to have students write reactions to peer writing.

- **Generation of content.** Not all writing-to-learn activities are about learning received content. Some may be used to help students begin the process of creation of their own knowledge and information to share. Such activities may involve students generating and sharing ideas prior to a formal paper of their own. The audience may be peers, the course instructor, or even the general public (e.g., an opinion piece for newspaper or a wiki contribution).

- **Reflection on content.** Journals in which students summarize or reflect on course content such as reading assignments present a safe and open writing platform in which students can develop their personal views on a topic. Students keep a dedicated notebook or a journal that the students periodically turn in to the teacher, who primarily assesses it for completion of the work and for understanding of important content. Teachers may give students specific prompts or alternately allow a free-form commentary on course content. One option is to have students write a reflection to an assignment given as a part of the course.

Organizational Sequence of Writing-to-Learn Activities

Given the wide variety of approaches to writing to learn, there is no one specific sequence to follow. Some activities are a one-shot approach to responding to a prompt within a single class session, while others are ongoing activities that last throughout the term.

Marzano (2012, pp. 82-83), who researches what instructional activities work, suggests that the following five phases are particularly useful in most writing-to-learn activities, which we adapted for length.

- **Record.** In this phase, students record their understanding of the content. For example, immediately after showing students a video clip on heredity, a teacher might ask the students to record what they have learned in their notes. Students might also record their responses in graphic organizers (which we describe in Chapter 7 on Graphic Organizers). This phase of the writing-to-learn activities is geared toward summarization. Teachers typically do not emphasize punctuation, spelling, or grammar. Students produce a rough first draft of their thoughts.
- **Compare.** In this phase, students share what they have recorded with their partners, noting what is similar and different between their two recordings. During this phase, the teacher works to clear up confusion and misconceptions that students might have. If the teacher notices that a number of students are confused about specific topics, he or she addresses the issue with the whole class before moving on to the next phase.

- **Revise.** In this phase, students create a more complete and polished version of what they wrote during the recording phase. This second version is more complete because students have had the benefit of conferring with a partner and having the teacher clear up confusion and misconceptions. This version is also more polished. As students revise their initial drafts, they may be asked to pay more attention to punctuation, spelling, and grammar. The record–compare–revise cycle can occur several times during a learning unit or module.
- **Combine.** In this phase, students combine the products of the record-compare-revise cycles they have completed and then generate and defend one or more generalizations. Students support their generalizations using specific evidence.
- **Review.** This last phase occurs before an assessment. Here, students read over the generalizations they produced in the combine phase and the summaries they wrote during the record, compare, revise cycles. Students can do this independently or in groups. Although students might generate new questions that the teacher could address in a whole-class or small-group environment, the primary focus is on providing students with a comprehensive and targeted review of all the content that will be on the assessment.

These phases are useful to think about when designing writing-to-learn assignments, and which phases are used depends upon the goals of activity, the timing of the class, the number of students in the class, and so forth. Not all writing-to-learn activities necessarily demand the collaborative component that Marzano suggests, for example, but the peer work has the potential to help students deepen their learning; if time and space allow, it can be a beneficial component. Likewise, not all writing-to-learn activities require a review period, and indeed one of the advantages to writing to learn is that they are low-stress, low-threat activities, but allowing students to think and revise can produce a better product for review.

Advantages and Challenges of Writing to Learn for Instructors

Many times, we can struggle with knowing what to "do" in class. We know some of the key approaches like lecture and discussion, but when we want to mix up the class and have students actively working, it can be a challenge to determine useful activities. Writing activities are an excellent way to mix up the activities of a given class time. Although time should be dedicated to the assignment to ensure it is a good learning experience for the students, extensive preparation and resources are not needed to provide a writing assignment.

Writing-to-learn assignments can be used to break up a long lecture, which can help students improve their focus and thus learning (as we discussed in

Chapter 1). They can be used to capture the results of discussion (which can help students value discussions more, as we described in Chapter 2). They can be used to capture the learning that happened during a group activity. They simply provide a potentially meaningful use of class time.

Moreover, reading short, informal writing assignments can provide teachers with opportunities to check student progress without imposing pressure related to grades. Writing-to-learn activities that do not require grading are a time-efficient way to gauge student learning and to give students feedback that need not be formally evaluated. Not having a letter grade attached to it can be less threatening for students, which in turn can help them look for the real meaning of the comments. Finally, they can help teachers target instruction to class needs, which can be more satisfying to teachers and can help lead to better student evaluations.

Some of the same things that are advantages to writing also can be considered disadvantages. Writing does take up class time; even though a short written activity can be a good return on investment, we simply do not always have time for longer activities. If instructors collect information from students, they do need to assess at least some of it, and large classes of students can generate a great deal of written material in a short period of time. Most teachers are not experts at how to teach discipline-focused writing, and using it well involves a process of self-education about writing in the subject area and how to create well-structured writing assignments (Gottschalk & Hjortshoj, 2004).

Learning to scan to assess is something that can take practice. And giving quality feedback to students also takes practice as well as time to do well. Even with the potential disadvantages, the effort to include writing-to-learn activities is worth it.

What Research Tells Us About the General Effectiveness of Writing-to-Learn Activities

Only a few studies of writing-to-learn activities have involved a comparison to other instructional approaches. On the whole, there is some evidence that writing-to-learn activities can improve knowledge comprehension and critical thinking and even more evidence to suggest that students value writing to learn and that the activities improve their confidence. While much more research is needed on this important instructional approach, in this section, we describe several studies that involved direct comparisons between writing-to-learn activities and other instructional methods.

One study involved a comparison of general education biology students in two different treatment groups. Researchers Quitadamo and Kurtz (2007) compared the students in an experimental group, those who had a laboratory writing treatment, to students in the control group, who had traditional quiz-based laboratory assignments. The researchers compared the critical-thinking ability of the two groups of students. Their results suggest that the writing group significantly improved critical-thinking skills while the nonwriting group did not. Specifically, those who had the writing laboratory improved their analysis and inference skills significantly; those in the nonwriting group did not. Writing students also showed greater gains in evaluation skills; however, these were not statistically significant (meaning that it could not be determined that the increases were not due to chance). This study suggests that writing is an effective method to improve critical-thinking skills.

Fry and Villagomez (2012) conducted a mixed-method, quasi-experimental, repeated measures design with education majors in a required course. The researchers wanted to examine how writing-to-learn activities affected students' learning as well as their perceptions of writing to learn. Their main objectives were as follows: to identify if student scores shifted from pre- to post-test, to compare if there was a differential effect between the control and treatments groups, and to collect qualitative data about whether student perceptions changed with respect to writing to learn throughout the study period. Each week the class that received the writing to learn treatment was given a prompt to help narrow their focus when writing in their journals, whereas the control group was not. If a particular topic was relevant to a student on a given day, the student was encouraged to write about that instead; on four occasions out of the 15-week term, students could choose between two topics. Their quantitative analysis suggested that writing to learn did not affect student achievement of course goals. Their qualitative analysis, however, suggested that students valued writing to learn for making sense of course content by reasoning through their ideas and responses to class experiences. The researchers indicated that that the way they incorporated writing to learn in the classroom may have not been the best crossover to testing material, thus suggesting the importance of clear instruction, prompts, and connected test questions when wanting to generate comparable metrics in a study. Fry and Villagomez indicated their belief that writing to learn also helped instructors build rapport with students. The researchers thought this helped students improve their writing. The researchers concluded that writing-to-learn activities are worth incorporating into education classes and that thought must be given into how writing-to-learn assignments are structured in order to make them feasible and beneficial.

Similarly, Schmidt (2004) evaluated 87 undergraduate basic and RN-to-BSN nursing students who were enrolled in a Nursing Leadership and Management course. The researcher's goal was to evaluate the writing-to-learn strategy. The research method was a pretest–post-test, quasi-experimental research design. The researcher found that students participating in the course perceived significant benefits of the writing-to-learn approach. The experimental group also demonstrated a significant decrease in writing apprehension on two separate measures of writing apprehension.

Likewise, Sanchez and Lewis (2002) studied preservice teachers for a semester. The researchers found that students increased their confidence after participating in writing-to-learn activities for a semester. At the beginning of the semester in which the study was conducted, only 41% of the students rated themselves as confident writers. At the end of the semester, 89% of the students indicated high levels of confidence in writing. While researchers carefully noted that the exact cause of the results is not known, they believe that scaffolded writing assignments, structured writing in the content area, and related feedback on assignments deepened students' learning.

What Research Tells Us About How to Improve Student Learning in Courses Where Writing-to-Learn Practices Are in Place

Most of the research on writing-to-learn activities involves case studies of single courses or studies that attempt different forms of writing to determine which are the most effective. These studies provide insights into what instructors can do once they have determined to use writing-to-learn activities to make them as successful as possible.

Research Finding #1. Prework Writing Activities Improve Learning Outcomes

Some writing-to-learn activities occur before another instructional activity. For example, a brief writing-to-learn activity may be used before a more formal writing assignment. There is evidence to suggest that such prework deepens the learning for students and helps them with later demonstrations of what they have learned. Kalelioğlu and Gülbahar (2014), for example, investigated the effectiveness of six different instructional methods on student critical thinking and critical-thinking dispositions evidenced through their participation in online discussions. They used a triangulation design and found that the use of prework improved student learning and that some methods were better than others. Prior to discussion, a Socratic Seminar improved critical-thinking dispositions as evidenced through pretest and post-test comparisons. A mix of activities resulted in the best performance at improving demonstration of critical thinking in online discussion.

Research Finding #2. Teacher-Assigned Structure Improves Learning

One question to consider is whether to assign structured or unstructured writing when using writing-to-learn activities. In an older study, MacDonald and Cooper (1992) compared student-structured and teacher-structured journal writing over long periods of time in a Chinese literature course. The researchers compared these two formats based on the level of sophistication. The researchers found that students involved in the teacher-structured writing activities outperformed those using the student-structured journal activities. Those who wrote student-structured activities outperformed those who did not do any writing at all.

Research Finding #3. Writing That Connects Content to Students' Life Experiences Improves Learning

In a study conducted by Nevid (2012), the researchers compared reflective and generic writing assignments in two introductory psychology classes. In the reflective class, students wrote about how course topics related to their life. In the generic course, students wrote about what they had learned. Thus, the researchers compared writing for summary versus writing to connect content to life experiences. Researchers found that students in the reflective class outperformed those in the generic class when tested on the final exam questions about key course concepts.

Balgopal et al. (2012) compared reflective writing-to-learn methods when used with three populations of college students. These populations included the following: nonmajors at a public university, science majors at a public university, and Native American students in a two-year higher education program. The researchers were interested in documenting quantitatively that students can go from a basic appreciation about ecology toward a demonstration of how their decisions can influence ecosystems. The researchers created a writing heuristic called the Cognitive-Affective-Behavior Writing-to-Learn Model (CAB-WTL) as the format for writing-to-learn activities. In the CAB-WTL, students complete three reflective essays based on a scientific prompt. The first essay looked at students' conceptual knowledge about the prompt, the second essay gave students an opportunity to react to and reflect on the prompt, and the third essay asked students to "identify a personal dilemma and describe how they might resolve this dilemma" (Balgopal et al., 2012, p. 72). The researchers coded the essays in four categories: superficial, subjective, objective, and authentic. They then scored the essays using a rubric they devised. They found that 6% of nonmajors and 12% of majors wrote authentically by the first essay, and that 25% of nonmajors and 29% of majors were writing at the authentic level by the third essay. Ultimately, the researchers found that 33% of students across all populations showed authentic writing in ecology in at least one essay. Balgopal et al. concluded that prompted writing encourages deeper thinking and that active reading and discussion are needed in order to achieve concept learning.

Research Finding #4. Feedback Improves Student Perceptions of Learning

Wingate et al. (2011) conducted a case study that involved the implementation and evaluation of an academic writing intervention. Participants in the study were first-year undergraduate students in an applied linguistics program. The researchers asked students to complete both in-class and online writing tasks. Students received feedback on their written work. The researchers documented and evaluated the intervention based on their own notes on classroom interaction, a student questionnaire, and interviews with students, as well as a textual analysis of students' writing. They also examined the feedback students received over time. Researchers found that both students and teachers believed that the writing instruction was beneficial. Although the most work-intensive for the teachers, students valued the assessment feedback most. The researchers believed that it led to substantial improvements in some students' writing.

Using IDEAs to Improve Learning with Writing to Learn

In the following section of this chapter, we provide detailed descriptions of 15 intentionally designed educational activities that correlate with the research findings we presented above. We suggest that these 15 activities correlate with these key research findings as follows:

TABLE 6.1 Writing-to-Learn IDEAs and Research Findings

Writing-to-Learn IDEAs	Description	Links to Research Findings
Brainstorming	Brainstorming is an activity in which students list their ideas about a specific concept or topic as quickly as they can without stopping.	Prework (Research Finding #1)
Freewriting	In this prewriting activity, students write continuously for a predetermined time period, with the intent of generating a maximum amount of raw text.	Prework (Research Finding #1)
Speak-Write Pairs	This is a planning and prewriting strategy in which partners work together to support the development of ideas for writing. The writer begins the process by speaking aloud his or her ideas as the partner captures what he or she says in writing. The two partners then exchange roles.	Prework (Research Finding #1); Feedback (Research Finding #4)
Graffiti Board	In a Graffiti Board activity, the instructor offers students a broad prompt. Students respond to the question by creating "graffiti," which they make on a flip chart paper or other medium.	Prework (Research Finding #1)

TABLE 6.1 Continued

Writing-to-Learn IDEAs	Description	Links to Research Findings
Journalists' Questions	Students can use traditional Journalists' Questions to explore a course-related topic. The traditional questions associated with journalism include five "w" questions and one "h" question: *who, what, where, when, why,* and *how.* Students approach the topic by working through the six questions.	Teacher-Assigned Structure (Research Finding #2)
Reader Response Paper	At its most basic level, a Reader Response Paper requires students to interrogate their own reactions to a reading, which hopefully helps them understand that their response is part of the meaning of the text.	Personal Experience (Research Finding #3)
Journaling	Students write about content such as readings or their learning from the course.	Personal Experience (Research Finding #3)
Sentence Passage Springboard	In this writing-to-learn activity, students identify a particular sentence from a reading assignment that captured their attention, and they write to capture their thoughts about that sentence.	Teacher-Assigned Structure (Research Finding #2)
Interviews	Students conduct interviews with people in an industry, organization, or general field to gain additional context for course objectives. The data forms the basis of a writing assignment.	Personal Experience (Research Finding #3)
Wikipedia Article	The class writes a strong summary of key course concepts with the intention of submitting it to the Web-based encyclopedia Wikipedia.	Teacher-Assigned Structure (Research Finding #2)
Annotations	This IDEA requires students to move beyond a traditional summary of a reading and instead make notes on the purpose and scope of a reading or to relate the reading to a particular course project.	Teacher-Assigned Structure (Research Finding #2)
Yesterday's News	Students take time at the beginning of a class session to write a memo to a student (real or fictional) who missed the previous class. Students explain how one idea from that class (they can select which concept or point to discuss) is particularly central to understanding the course generally and the day's lecture specifically.	Teacher-Assigned Structure (Research Finding #2); Personal Experience (Research Finding #3)

Writing-to-Learn IDEAs	Description	Links to Research Findings
Field Notes	Students go on field experiences to places relevant to course concepts and then write about their experiences.	Personal Experience (Research Finding #3)
Interview Protocols	In this IDEA, students write out interview questions. They then form pairs and interview each other about a course-related topic. After all students have had a turn as interviewer and interviewee, they report to the class and write up their findings.	Teacher-Assigned Structure (Research Finding #2)
Critical Book Review	Students write up a critical review of a book related to the course.	Teacher-Assigned Structure (Research Finding #2)

The research basis behind these IDEAs means faculty can use writing-to-learn strategies with confidence that they have a good and intentional design for improving student learning and putting students on the path to success. Following are detailed descriptions for how to go about implementing these activities in the classroom.

IDEA #62: Brainstorming

Overview

Brainstorming is an activity in which students list their ideas about a specific concept or topic as quickly as they can without stopping. Brainstorming encourages people to come up with thoughts and ideas without evaluating or thinking about the items that have been generated, even those they might seem a bit off-point. Once the Brainstorming aspect has been completed, some of the ideas can be crafted into original, creative writing through further refinement. This writing can range from personal essays to formal problem-solving or briefing papers.

Brainstorming is a great activity for having students demonstrate what they already know about the topic and for use as a prewriting activity. It can help students develop ideas for solving a problem. The Brainstorming activity encourages creativity by providing a variety of topics for later consideration.

Guiding Principles

Students come to every course with some preexisting knowledge, beliefs, and attitudes. This knowledge influences how they filter and interpret what they are learning. If students' prior knowledge is robust and accurate and activated at the appropriate time, it provides a strong foundation for building new knowledge (Ambrose, Bridges, DiPietro, Lovett, & Norman, 2010). If it is inaccurate, it is important to surface that information or perspective so that it can be addressed. Brainstorming is an effective activity for activating that prior knowledge and surfacing preexisting beliefs that can be addressed prior to a more extensive activity, during which it will be more difficult to reframe existing beliefs.

Preparation

This activity typically requires little preparation. Simply determine a central topic, theme, or concept students will consider while Brainstorming. If you are asking students to brainstorm solutions to more formal problems, you will have more preparation time involved in creating the problems. Determine how much time to allocate to this activity. Typically, you will not need long, as Brainstorming activities typically last 5–10 minutes. Determine how students will record their Brainstorming, whether on a sheet of paper, a flip chart, the chalkboard, or technological device. Determine whether and how you will have students report on their Brainstorming.

Process

- Present the prompt, and tell students they will list their ideas related to it.
- Tell students they should record all of the ideas they have; they should avoid evaluating, criticizing, or thinking about the ideas but rather should simply record them.
- Announce the time limit for the activity, and ask students to begin.
- Close the activity by telling students that the time has ended.
- If desired, have student volunteers report some of their ideas, or take up their documents if you would like a record of the activity.

Sample IDEA Pairings

Circle of Voices (IDEA #18). Students simply take turns adding comments or ideas to the brainstormed list.

Role Play (IDEA #44). Ask students to assume specific identities when creating ideas. This approach can provide them with some focus. You can assign different roles so that students come at the prompt from different angles, which can produce an interesting discussion later.

Pro-tips

Individual Brainstorming is particularly effective (Miller, 2009), as students may stay more focused and generate the greatest possible numbers of ideas. Group Brainstorming can be used with group projects and can allow members to feel that they have all had input into decisions. The best approach may be to combine individual and group approaches to Brainstorming. One option is to have students brainstorm individually and then get into groups of four students to compare types of items generated. Groups may be asked to identify themes and then report out to the entire class the themes noted.

IDEA #63: Freewriting

Overview

Freewriting is a prewriting activity in which students write continuously for a predetermined time period. The intent of Freewriting is to generate a maximum amount of raw text. The idea is to focus on a specific topic but to write so quickly that students do not have time to edit the information generated; thus the focus is on quantity of content rather than form. At the end of the Freewriting session, students review the text for usable parts of it, often leading to another activity, such as a discussion or more formal writing activity.

The basic idea behind Freewriting is that everybody has something to say, but we are often hindered by the writing process or critical review of the content before it has even been expressed (Li, 2007). In some cases, excessive self-criticism or the desire to do a good job or be perfect can cause students to doubt their own abilities as writers. When such doubt occurs, the result can be "writers block," which makes the writing process extremely difficult. Freewriting is intended to help learners get past these blocks by engaging in a low-threat activity that involves thought generation. The product of a Freewrite is rarely considered a final product.

Guiding Principles

Freewriting is considered a writing-to-learn activity that involves the effort to order and represent our understandings of a given subject. It is a unique way of knowing and shaping meaning. It helps students reach understanding (Fulwiler & Young, 2000). Moreover, outlining, integrating, and synthesizing information produces better learning than simply rereading material (Bransford, Donovan, & Pellegrino, 1999).

Preparation

Determine the topic students will write about. Determine the parameters of the activity, such how long students will write. 5–10 minutes should be sufficient. Determine whether students will write on paper or use a laptop or other technology.

Process

- Announce the activity, and tell students the instructions. Inform them that they will write about the prompt for the full time allotted without stopping; they should continue writing even if nothing specific occurs to them. Inform them that the ideas are what is important, not the spelling or grammar.
- Ask students to begin the Freewrite, and monitor their progress. Prompt with the phrase "keep going" as needed.
- When the writing time has ended, ask students to look back over what they have written and highlight the best ideas.
- Consider having a second round of Freewriting to begin where they have left off, or have students move on to making use of their Freewriting by beginning the next activity.

Sample IDEA Pairings

Snowball (IDEA #12). Move from a Freewrite to a paired discussion, a discussion among four students in a group, and so forth.

Think-Pair-Share (IDEA #15). Create a Freewrite Pair Share instead.

K-W-L Chart (IDEA # 86). After the Freewrite, ask students to complete a K-W-L Chart prior to writing a final paper. They identify what they know, what they want to know, and what they learned from the Freewrite.

Pro-tips

On the surface, the Freewrite looks like an easy activity. In reality, it is challenging to do. Students will frequently get stuck and want to stop writing. It is helpful to offer them a phrase to write should they hit a block (e.g., "just keep writing").

Because this activity is challenging for students, using it over time can be effective. Some teachers use brief Freewrites in each class session. Students become used to it and get better at it over time.

An interesting closure activity for a Freewrite is to discuss how it differs from a formal writing assignment, such as the standard term paper. Going from Freewrite to draft to final product is a process, and the very act of Freewriting provides a good opportunity to discuss the importance of revision and editing of more formal writings.

IDEA #64: Speak-Write Pairs

Overview

This IDEA is a planning and prewriting strategy in which partners work together to support the development of ideas for writing. The writer begins the process by speaking aloud her ideas as the partner captures in writing what she says. The two partners then exchange roles.

The Speak-Write Pairs activity helps to develop the writer's strength and also the comfort level with spoken language. It assists with developing listening skills as the receiver of the information must listen and then capture the information in writing. It also helps the student who has trouble getting ideas onto paper write something quickly that can later be revised.

Guiding Principles

This activity provides novice writers with scaffolding to assist the writing process. That is, although the instructor selects an activity to provide intentional writing support, the peer carries out the specific support. The peer also serves as a coach, which is a critical aspect of instructional scaffolding. The activity is tailored to the needs of the individual student. The goal is to help a student reach his or her learning goals (Sawyer, 2006).

Vygotsky's (1978) zone of proximal development also is a guiding principle of this IDEA. Vygotsky believe that when a student is in the zone of proximal development (ZPD), it is much easier to learn. Peers are often closer to the learning level of the student than the instructor, thereby serving as an excellent source of assistance to the writer. Having peers provide assistance also provides students with enough support to achieve a task. Thus, peer interaction and social exchange is an effective method for developing skills and strategies.

Preparation

Develop a writing assignment. Create a series of structured prompts to help students think through the assignment. For example, if they are writing about a process, you might ask them to respond to prompts of how they will begin, what they will do next, what happens then, and so forth. If you are asking students to write an argument, you might ask for the first point, give an example, second point, give an example, and so forth. Make a handout of these prompts for students to use as a guide.

Create a list of sample constructive suggestions students might make on a writer's draft (e.g., such as "provide another supporting idea here" or "provide more detail here"). Determine how long pairs should have to work. Five to ten minutes per student writer should be sufficient.

Process

- Announce the activity, and give students directions. Ask them to begin.
- The peer uses the handout and asks the student writer the series of structured prompts related to the writing assignment.
- The writer responds to questions verbally.
- While the student responds, the partner then writes down the information exactly as the writer says it.

- The students exchange roles.
- After both students have spoken, the students take time to read their partners' "written" responses and offer the writer constructive suggestions, drawing from the list you have provided them.

Sample IDEA Pairings

Journalists' Questions (IDEA #66). Students use Journalists' Questions for the handout to respond to questions verbally.

Journaling (IDEA #68). Students follow the Speak-Write Pairs with journaling about what they learned.

Self-Assessment (IDEA #95). Students reflect upon what they did well in talking through the answers and what they can improve in the final paper.

Pro-tips

Using this strategy instills a sense of confidence in novice writers, as everything going into the piece is in their own words; they are just in someone else's handwriting at first. This IDEA also assists students who have a difficult time starting due to the "blank page" challenge.

Students should strive to transcribe their partners' words verbatim because the writer should feel confident that those are his or her words and ideas when going back to include them in the draft.

Once the students become familiar with the process, they tend to be able to do it for themselves. One way to suggest they become self-sufficient with writing is to suggest that students record themselves or talk through their ideas at home prior to an in-class writing assignment.

One additional option is to have students first work in pairs and then form a group of four with one additional pair. Once the groups of four can take turns discussing what they learned from the experience.

IDEA #65: Graffiti Board

Overview

In a Graffiti Board activity, the instructor offers students a broad prompt. Students respond to the question by writing "graffiti," which they make on flip chart paper or other medium. A Graffiti Board is a writing IDEA to improve students' thinking skills and promote their writing skills.

The activity is typically fast paced, implemented within 5–10 minutes. It provides a creative way for student to write and express their ideas. It also provides a record of their ideas and questions that may be used as a reference later in the class. Graffiti Boards can be used in a range of disciplines and fields.

They are a useful way to sum up a class experience, whether a reading, lecture, or activity.

Guiding Principles

It is widely accepted that motivation influences learning (Bandura, 1989). And students are motivated by what they find interesting. Among the things over which teachers have control that can motivate students, using a variety of active learning approaches is one of the most important.

Activities can directly engage students in material, and cooperative learning activities provide additional social support and thus motivation. Graffiti Boards are one way to vary teaching approaches. They are a change of pace, and they tend to be fun and thus engaging for students. In addition, there is a collaborative aspect to them, which enhances motivation and thus learning.

Preparation

Create a prompt, based upon a previous lesson. Select a medium for the graffiti, whether butcher paper, flip chart paper, whiteboard, or chalkboard. Gather plenty of markers or chalk depending on your medium. Determine what kind of "graffiti" you hope to elicit, whether words, phrase, pictures, or "anything goes." Identify a space in the room where several students can work on the medium at the same time. Also select a space where the Graffiti Boards may be displayed once they have been completed. Determine how many students will be in a group, and make sure you have enough paper or space and supplies for each group.

Process

- Announce the Graffiti Board activity, the teams, and the rules (for example, you may want students to remain silent while writing/drawing, and they should know that several students can and should work at once).
- Hand out paper to the groups along with the supplies that they should use.
- Announce the prompt.
- Ask students to begin their "graffiti" project, responding to the question at the top of the chart.
- Call time when the activity has been completed.
- Ask groups to swap their graffiti sheets with the next group so that each group has a new sheet.
- The new group reads what has been doodled or drawn and adds to the sheet.
- Continue the process until the original group receives their original sheet back.

- Ask students to review the boards and to prepare a brief presentation of the board to the class. Consider asking them to note areas of agreement or disagreement.
- Post boards in the classroom.

Sample IDEA Pairings

Speed Interviews (IDEA #35). After discussing a concept in a Speed Interview, students can then turn to quiet reflection in which they draw in response to the ideas generated in the discussion.

Gallery Walk (IDEA #28). While Gallery Walk and Graffiti Boards have much in common, such as collaborative groups working in large spaces, they different in content and form. Gallery Walks have formal questions and elicit formal answers. Graffiti Boards, on the other hand, provide broad prompts and ask for creative, even artistic responses. Thus, they can work well together. After answering questions in a Gallery Walk, students can respond by developing a Graffiti Board that considers the information in a new way.

Pro-tips

Groups may become bored with the activity before they receive their original sheets back. Consider having fewer groups, or call time on the activity when it seems that no new ideas are being generated.

IDEA #66: Journalists' Questions

Overview

Traditional Journalists' Questions are excellent prompts to explore a course-related topic. The traditional questions associated with journalism include five "w" questions, and one "h" question: *Who?, What?, Where?, When?, Why?, How?* For this IDEA, students approach the course-related topic by working through the six questions as if they were journalists. This IDEA is a useful strategy for helping students to develop and organize information about a topic quickly.

Guiding Principles

When students encounter knowledge, they make connections between it and other knowledge that they already hold or are developing. When these connections are meaningfully organized, students tend to learn the knowledge better and more deeply. Because of the improved associations, they are able to better retrieve and apply knowledge at a later time (Ambrose et al., 2010). Journalists' Questions provides a preexisting structure around which students may organize their thoughts and any new information. This structure ultimately helps students master content.

Preparation

Determine a writing prompt that will allow students to make good use of the six questions. Determine a time limit for the activity. Ten to fifteen minutes is a good starting place. Prepare a handout or a slide with the primary questions as well as some potential subquestions to help guide student thinking. The University of Kansas Writing Center (2011) suggests the following:

> **Who?** Who are the participants? Who is affected? Who are the primary actors? Who are the secondary actors?
>
> **What?** What is the topic? What is the significance of the topic? What is the basic problem? What are the issues?
>
> **Where?** Where does the activity take place? Where does the problem or issue have its source? At what place is the cause or effect of the problem most visible?
>
> **When?** When is the issue most apparent? (past? present? future?) When did the issue or problem develop? What historical forces helped shape the problem or issue and at what point in time will the problem or issue culminate in a crisis? When is action needed to address the issue or problem?
>
> **Why?** Why did the issue or problem arise? Why is it (your topic) an issue or problem at all? Why did the issue or problem develop in the way that it did?
>
> **How?** How is the issue or problem significant? How can it be addressed? How does it affect the participants? How can the issue or problem be resolved?

Process

- Announce the activity and the time frame.
- Present students with the writing prompt and the guiding questions you have developed.
- Ask students to begin writing, and monitor their progress while they work.
- Call time when most students have worked through the questions.

Sample IDEA Pairings

In the News (IDEA #16). Students bring in news articles as prompts for the activity.

Seeded Discussion (IDEA #20). Provide students with questions ahead of the discussion. These prompts can be particularly effective.

Jigsaw (IDEA #31). Students write about each prompt to establish baseline knowledge then divide into expert groups for the purpose of deepening knowledge prior to teaching each other.

Pro-tips

It is critical to use a prompt with sufficient depth to accommodate all six questions. Some topics lend themselves to certain questions within the Journalists' Questions better than other questions. For example, if you ask about important actors in the Civil War, students may have quite a bit to say about who but not be as clear about addressing how.

Students will work through this activity at different rates. It may be useful to assign it as homework. Alternately, if this work is done in class, it is helpful to have a "sponge activity" ready, which is an additional assignment for students who finish quickly. This sponge may be as simple as "revise your work" or an additional prompt question to work on while the other students finish the assignment.

The Journalists' Questions is not designed specifically for the typical writing-related courses. This activity can be used in a wide variety of courses, including courses in STEM or STEM-related fields (Urquhart, 2009).

IDEA #67: Reader Response Paper

Overview

Students will frequently read course content only from the point of view of a passive recipient of information. Sometimes students need to be reminded that they bring their own views and values to the subjects they study and that these attributes affect their receptivity and interpretation of the ideas under consideration. A Reader Response Paper can help to raise this awareness that readers interpret information differently based on background and experiences. At its most basic level, a Reader Response Paper requires the students to interrogate their own reactions to a reading, which hopefully helps them understand that their response is part of the meaning of the text.

Guiding Principles

As Chickering and Gamson (1987) suggest, learning is not a spectator sport. It is important for students to be actively involved in their own learning. For this to happen, it is helpful for them to discuss their learning with others, write about their reaction to readings, relate their learning to past experiences, and apply it to their daily lives. In short, to be active learners, students should make what they learn part of themselves (Chickering & Gamson, 1987). A Reader Response Paper is an excellent tool for allowing this to happen. Moreover, noting their own prejudices should help them to discover their own angle of vision, which informed their response to the material.

Preparation

Determine a reading for the class to complete. Prepare a handout that explains the assignment and presents a list of sample questions. In an open course on English composition, Lumen (n.d.) offers the following example of Reader Response questions:

TABLE 6.2 Reader Response Questions

Your paper as a whole should be sure to address these questions in some way.

- *What does the text have to do with you, personally, and with your life (past, present or future)?* It is not acceptable to write that the text has NOTHING to do with you, as just about everything humans can write has to do in some way with every other human.
- *How much does the text agree or clash with your view of the world, and what you consider right and wrong?* Use several quotes as examples of how it agrees with and supports what you think about the world, about right and wrong, and about what you think it is to be human. Use quotes and examples to discuss how the text disagrees with what you think about the world and about right and wrong.
- *What did you learn, and how much were your views and opinions challenged or changed by this text, if at all? Did the text communicate with you? Why or why not?* Give examples of how your views might have changed or been strengthened (or perhaps why the text failed to convince you the way it is). Please do not write "I agree with everything the author wrote" because everybody disagrees about something, even if it is a tiny point. Use quotes to illustrate your points of challenge, where you were persuaded, or where it left you cold.
- *How well does the text address things that you, personally, care about and consider important to the world? How does it address things that are important to your family, your community, your ethnic group, to people of your economic or social class or background, or your faith tradition? If not, who does or did the text serve? Did it pass the "Who cares?" test?* Use quotes from the text to illustrate.
- *What can you praise about the text? What problems did you have with it?* Reading and writing "critically" does not mean the same thing as "criticizing" in everyday language (complaining or griping, fault-finding, nitpicking). Your "critique" can and should be positive and praise the text if possible, as well as pointing out problems, disagreements and shortcomings.
- *How well did you enjoy the text (or not) as entertainment or as a work of art?* Use quotes or examples to illustrate the quality of the text as art or entertainment. Of course, be aware that some texts are not meant to be entertainment or art: a news report or textbook, for instance, may be neither entertaining nor artistic but may still be important and successful.

(Continued)

TABLE 6.2 Continued

For the conclusion, you might want to discuss:
- your overall reaction to the text;
- whether you would read something else like this in the future;
- whether you would read something else by this author; and
- if would you recommend read this text to someone else and why.

Process

- Announce the activity and distribute the assignment.
- Provide students with time to complete the assignment, either as homework or an in-class activity.
- Collect the assignment.
- Consider allowing students time to present their thoughts about the reading in class, either as a whole-class discussion or in small groups, and then report general findings from each group to the class.

Sample IDEA Pairings

Journal Club (IDEA #23). Students write their responses prior to discussing them with others.

Case Study (IDEA #24). Students read and respond to papers prior to completing work on a case.

Speed Interviews (IDEA #35). Students form groups quickly to discuss their responses to the readings.

Pro-tips

Students can misunderstand the level of depth that they should seek when approaching the paper. They can tend to think that it is fine to just toss off a quick opinion, without exerting much mental energy. Explain to students that while there is no right or wrong answer to a reading response, they should demonstrate their understanding by explaining the readings and supporting their reactions.

If you ask students to discuss their reactions in class, some will be greatly pleased to do so, and some will be less enthusiastic. Consider taking volunteers so that you do not put students on the spot.

With advance warning, it is also possible to have students pair up and read each other's work in class. Following the reading, each can give comments and suggestions to colleagues.

IDEA #68: Journaling

Overview

The Journaling IDEA involves having students write about their experiences as they are related to course content. They can, for example, connect course readings to their own personal or professional experiences. This activity provides students with a chance to write about what they have learned and make meaningful connections to their own lives.

Guiding Principles

One of the basic principles articulated in the theory of adult learning is that adult learners bring life experiences to their learning (Knowles, 1984). These experiences are an important resource for learning. They enjoy having the opportunity to use their experiences as a foundation for learning, and facilitative reflective learning opportunities can present them with a change to move toward a new understanding of information presented.

Moreover, adults are frequently interested in learning subjects that have an immediate relevance to their job or personal lives. Journaling provides students with an opportunity to draw on these experiences and make important connections between their experiences and course content.

Preparation

Prior to assigning Journaling, decide how often students will journal (each class, week, or for a set number of entries). In addition, decide about the prompts you will provide. For example, you might suggest that students use their Journaling to record their experiences and the relationship between themselves and course readings or lectures. You might ask them to connect their prior assumptions to what they read or heard in class (Chapnick, 2014). Finally, determine how often you will review the journal and what kind of feedback you will provide. You may choose, for example, to collect once per week, at test times, once per month, or only at the end of the course.

Process

- Announce the ongoing assignment.
- Ask students to complete journal entries at the rate you have determined ahead of time.
- Collect entries at predetermined times.
- Provide students with feedback on their entries.

Sample IDEA Pairings

Socratic Seminar (IDEA #7). Students can Journal about what they expect and hope to learn. They can follow the activity by describing what they did learn and where expectations and reality met and did not.

Journal Club (IDEA #23). As students read and discuss research, they keep a Journal of these discussions for future reference including questions, interesting points, and ideas for additional discussion.

Pro-tips

Journaling can require intense assessment time by the instructor. You may choose to ask students to highlight their entries when making connections to key content. This can help you streamline the feedback process.

Students may complete Journaling through a variety of different formats, whether written or electronic, such as through blogging. When using electronic formats and depending on the level of depth and frankness that you are requesting, allow students to decide whether or not to make their Journaling public.

There are many different types of journals, some of which may include reporting and reacting (Chapnick, 2014). Some instructors want students to reflect while they write. To ensure that students reflect, stress how the content connects with them personally. It can be useful to ask them to begin with assumptions and expectations.

IDEA #69: Sentence Passage Springboard

Overview

In this writing-to-learn activity, students first identify a particular sentence from a reading assignment that captured their attention or was difficult to understand. Once the sentence is identified, the student writes to capture any thoughts about that particular sentence. This IDEA promotes critical reading and further learning, as well as exploration of concepts and issues through writing.

The activity is applicable in a broad range of disciplines. Those in humanities courses will find it easy to use, as course assignments readily lend themselves to creative analysis. Those in more scientific disciplines, however, can also use this approach, as students may come to appreciate or critique theory and methods. This activity can be done in or out of class. It can be less formal to more formal. It is a flexible activity that allows for adaptions to suit the needs of the class.

Guiding Principles

When reading content-rich material, it is easy to assume a passive position, particularly for those who have little experience with critical reading or those who are struggling with the content. In such situations, students may read for general information and understanding rather than seeking to grapple with the complexities of a given piece of writing. Sometimes, however, students read a sentence that catches their attention, for a number of reasons. They may find a valuable bit of information, are impressed by a turn of phrase, complete disagree with an assertion, or be confused by the wording.

These sentences present opportunities for deeper exploration and learning. Asking students to read specifically for those sentences can help them engage in them. Asking students to write about these sentences takes their learning a step further. It provides them with motivation to write about something in which they are interested, which can in turn improve their learning (Ambrose et al., 2010). Moreover, having students write about a given sentence helps them to take control of their learning, which facilitates better and deeper learning.

Preparation

Identify a reading assignment for the class related to the topic. Decide whether you will conduct the activity in class or out of class. Decide how students will write and submit their responses.

Process

- Announce the activity, and ask students to identify a sentence and then write about their impressions.
- Consider having students report out about their sentences and thoughts.
- Collect the responses.

Sample IDEA Pairings

Think-Pair-Share (IDEA #15). Students simply read and write during the thinking stage and then share with their peers.

Each One, Teach One (IDEA #30). Each student can be responsible for teaching other students about the sentence they reviewed.

Speed Interviews (IDEA #35). Students in small groups exchange their sentences and responses.

Pro-tips

Sometimes an article does not contain a sentence that serves as a sufficient springboard for a good response, or at least students do not think it does. If the writing of the assigned readings is not sufficiently complex or compelling, it may be better to ask students to identify a passage instead of a single sentence. Doing so can provide them with more depth of information and can therefore allow them to create better responses in turn. The trick is to get students writing to help them better understand the critical concepts presented in a given article.

It may be helpful to provide an example of the Sentence Passage Springboard. Simply, provide the class with a few paragraphs of course-related material. Identify a specific sentence and then show how you responded to that sentence in writing. An additional step could be to identify a specific sentence in a few paragraphs and then have all students in class write a response to that paragraph. Once the writing is complete, students could get together into groups of four and compare writings. This comparison will demonstrate for students that there are many ways to respond and also indicate an appropriate level of response.

IDEA #70: Interviews

Overview

This activity provides an opportunity for students to conduct an interview with someone whose knowledge or experiences present a relevant complement to ideas discussed as part of class and to write up the experience in a formal paper. The activity helps students understand the perspective of an outside expert or other person with valuable experience beyond what they could gain from class or readings. Moreover, they have the opportunity to write about their conversations in a way that is compatible with their field. For example, students might write up the interview for a popular magazine in the field, for a newspaper, for a blog post, or for a formal social science research paper.

Interviews help students understand new perspectives and gather information largely unavailable through other sources. Students not only benefit from the information gathered but also practice active listening skills as they conduct the interview. Students can learn how to ask questions and conduct Interviews that can benefit them beyond the specific content knowledge. Finally, students have the opportunity to share what they have learned from the Interviews with others who might be interested in what the interviewee has to say.

Guiding Principles

This activity is supported by many of the well-established benefits of active learning (Bonwell & Eison, 1991). Interviews, by their nature, require students to engage in higher-order thinking skills from analysis to synthesis. Writing is another activity that often can require students to engage in higher-order thinking skills, including logical reasoning and communication. In addition, this IDEA helps students develop their own skills in addition to learning new content. Active learning through this activity has students work through the content in complex ways.

Interviews help students develop active listening skills, which can improve what students understand. Active listening focuses on the interviewee and listening to understand what is being said. Interviews ask the students as interviewers to listen to verbal and nonverbal cues to fully comprehend the information gathered. Interviews also demonstrate for students that experts in a field do not always agree on the issue at hand. Hearing a different perspective promotes critical and analytical thinking. It typically also demonstrates the importance of having sound reasoning and grounded information in advocating for one's position. Moreover, writing about the Interviews requires students to think through the nuances of the conversation and communicate what they learned with others. This skill forms the basis of Interviews and can benefit students in the course as well as later in life.

Preparation

Before assigning the Interviews activity, consider the primary purpose of the activity. You may wish to have students seek out someone in a particular career field or someone who has a particular set of life experiences. Determining the goals for the assignment will assist in developing parameters for who and how the Interviews will be conducted. Preparation should also include discussing with the students both the background work needed to conduct a successful interview and the importance of the time individuals will devote to the interview. It should also include information about how to write up Interviews, as students likely have not had prior experience in this area. The individuals being interviewed are typically busy individuals, and even 15 minutes of time is valuable. Therefore, being on time, ready to do the interview, concluding on time, and meeting writing deadlines are all important aspects of the assignment.

Process

- Share the goals and details of how the Interviews will be conducted.
- Have students schedule and conduct the Interview according to your identified parameters. An option here is to coordinate the time in which interviewees are available and assign students accordingly.
- Following the Interview, ask students to complete a writing assignment related to the Interview. You may also lead a discussion about how the Interviews went, lessons learned, and reflections by the class.

Sample IDEA Pairings

Critical Book Review (IDEA #76). Require students to select a book on a topic related to their Interview. Students read and review the book that serves to provide a useful background prior to conducting the Interview.

Shadow a Professional (IDEA #91). Students could potentially shadow the person who they will interview to learn more about what they do prior to conducting the formal interview.

Pro-tips

Students may be largely unfamiliar with how to conduct Interviews, so some training on how to structure the questions and even what types of questions to ask may prove useful. Rubin and Rubin (2005) suggest asking main, follow-up, and probe questions to gather rich details and nuanced information.

There are a variety of formats for conducting Interviews: in person, over the telephone, or via email. Consider which serve the purposes of the activity in your course. Each has advantages and disadvantages depending on the desired outcomes of the activity. Additionally, ask students to reflect on the pros and cons of the type of interview they conducted and what may have been different had they conducted the same interview with another format.

The product to be created as part of the Interview IDEA should be carefully considered. Some instructors request verbatim transcriptions while others seek a paper reporting and reflecting on the Interview.

A final option is to have students write out what questions they would ask in a follow-up interview. Incorporating what they have learned with some reflection about how a next interview would look will help them think though the interview process and what could have been done differently for the interview.

IDEA #71: Wikipedia Article

Overview

The Wikipedia Article IDEA provides an alternative to traditional student research-based writing assignments. During this activity, students are tasked with developing strong summaries of key course concepts. When working on the assignments, they hone search, reading, and communication skills. As the name indicates, students are expected to produce an article with the intention of publishing it to the Web-based encyclopedia Wikipedia.

Wikipedia provides a venue for students to produce work that is not purely for a grade but also for potential public consumption. This IDEA involves asking students to view both the research purpose as well as the final product from a perspective different than any traditional research paper assignment.

Guiding Principles

Wikipedia Article allows students to demonstrate comprehension of a course concept in both a succinct and authoritative manner. By asking students to write a short, yet holistic summary, they are developing a deeper understanding of the course material (Nilson, 2010).

This IDEA also provides a fun and different take on research. Specifically, students become aware that their work is not only going to be read by their instructor but also potentially by a broader audience (Purcell-Gates, Duke, & Martineau, 2007). The IDEA thus invites students to think like scholars and to consider who might benefit from what they produce. Moreover, because they are writing for communication to others, the assignment can have an authentic feel.

Preparation

Before using Wikipedia Article, identify a list of topics suitable for the assignment. In addition, familiarize yourself with the requirements and expectations set forth by Wikipedia or other desired location for student publication. You can find information at the following URL: http://en.wikipedia.org/wiki/Wikipedia:Student_assignments

If the goal is not to actually publish the articles online, develop a scenario or list of questions that have students consider who might search for the information they will produce. It can also help to provide them with a sample article that meets the desired level and quality of information, referencing, and writing.

Process

- Provide students with a list of research topics specific to course content.
- Ask students to think about who might benefit from the information they will present, helping them gauge their audience.
- Students use class time to begin gathering sources and researching their chosen topic.
- This assignment will most likely not be completed in one class session, thus instruct students on the final expectations of the assignment and provide them with a future due date.
- When the articles are complete, have students pair up and exchange their summaries or share their published online articles.

Sample IDEA Pairing

Microteaching (IDEA #32). Ask students to present their research and summaries to the entire class and assume the role of the instructor for a portion of class time. Students may need the chance to prepare their presentations ahead of time.

Trivia (IDEA #40). Students breakdown their articles into key topics and ideas and develop questions to be used in a Trivia game. This process helps students identify the most relevant aspects of their summary.

Journalists' Questions (IDEA #66). Students use traditional Journalists' Questions to frame their research articles. Questions include: Who?, What?, Where?, When?, Why?, and How?. These questions can also serve as the basis for student sharing at the conclusion of the activity.

Pro-tips

Depending on the level of class, the article quality or student comfort with publishing their project online may vary. The activity can still be used as an exercise exclusive of online publication.

Depending on the level of the course, students might benefit from some suggestions on how to approach their topics. Consider providing a rubric of detailed instructions on how to begin this research project inclusive of the number of references needed and possibly section headers.

As an alternative to providing students with a list of key topics to cover, ask them to brainstorm and develop a list of possible article topics. This approach allows the instructor to further gauge student understanding of course materials.

IDEA #72: Annotations

Overview

Annotations move beyond a typical summary of a reading and instead require students to note the purpose and scope of a reading or to relate the reading to a particular course project. They typically also require that students identify key ideas and briefly evaluate strengths and weaknesses in an article. They can be used for a range of article types, from descriptive to opinion to theory to research-based. Students may annotate readings assigned for the class, or they may compile Annotations that supplement the course readings of their own choosing (Writing Across the Curriculum, 2014). Thus, they are a particularly flexible writing-to-learn assignment.

Guiding Principles

When students organize, integrate, and synthesize information, they tend to remember it better than they do when simply reading it. Annotations require students to actively engage in the material, eliminating the passivity that can attend reading assignments. In short, this IDEA demands active reading and thinking about the content of what they are reading.

Preparation

Determine which reading selections students should annotate, even if that means determining that they will choose their own.

TABLE 6.3 Sample Annotation Questions

Who is/are the author(s)? Consider background, position, qualifications. If there are many, as there might be with a webpage, how would you characterize them as a group?

What was the author's stated purpose or motivation in writing the article or book, or in doing the research, or in contributing to the webpage?

Who is the intended audience? This includes scholars in a discipline, the general public, workers in an industry, professionals in a field, people with a shared passion/interest or of a certain age group or political persuasion.

Who is the publisher or sponsor? This is especially relevant if the information source is related to an organization of some sort. Find out something about them. Find their webpage, mission statement, purpose.

Are there any significant attachments, appendices, statistics, data, images, weblinks, etc. included?

What is the basis for the research or data reported? This would include things like types of information used, methodology, problem statements, or limitations.

What is the scope of the documentation? Look at the different information resources cited, their dates, formats, and quality as well as quantity.

CRITICAL COMMENT: Answering these questions will require some critical thinking on your part. Comparing the different sources of information you have found on the same topic usually helps.

What aspects of the subject are emphasized? Is the author presenting one particular point of view?

What conclusions are drawn? Issues raised? Are the conclusions drawn justified or adequately substantiated?

Can you detect any biases or fallacies in the arguments or conclusions presented?

Is anything clearly lacking? Do you feel like you have questions about what is or is NOT stated?

If information about the authors/sponsor/publisher was difficult to find or very limited, what does this lead you to believe about the validity and authority of the information provided?

How effectively is the information presented? Are you left feeling confused? Are there gaps or holes?

Are there any other qualities of the source, like style, organization, or graphics, which effect its usefulness?

Is the work functioning as a primary or secondary source in your research?

How does this particular information source compare with or relate to the others you have read on the topic? How useful was this work to you in your research? What role did it play?

Develop a handout that outlines the structure of the basic annotation. This handout will probably specify a summary of key sections and also will pose some questions that require students to think critically about that material. Santa Clara University's (n.d.) library offers the following example: Determine how students will submit their Annotations, whether in paper or electronically. Determine whether students will share their Annotations with other classmates.

Process

- Announce the activity, and present students with the handout.
- Provide them time to complete the activity.
- Take up the Annotations.

Sample IDEA Pairings

Journalists' Questions (IDEA #66). Students proceed through the six questions in order to create their annotations.

Concept Maps (IDEA #79). Students show how the different articles they have abstracted are related to each other.

Pro-tips

Students are typically slow in their first attempts at annotations. They also typically speed up with practice. Thus, they may find doing abstracts over time to be most effective, as they move faster and can thus see the benefits.

IDEA #73: Yesterday's News

Overview

For the Yesterday's News IDEA, students take time at the beginning of a class session to write a memo to a student (real or fictional) who missed the previous class. Students explain how one idea from that class (they can select which concept or point to discuss) is particularly central to understanding the course generally and that day's topic specifically. The IDEA helps students personalize learning and understand that learning has practical application and value. Yesterday's News also assists students as they move from passive listening to active transformation of information.

This activity works well across the curriculum. It can be particularly effective in the sciences where information builds in a progressive way. It can also be useful in humanities and social sciences where it is important to reinforce central concepts. The activity is intended to be brief, and, if done well, it may be done frequently. Thus, it is a flexible activity that has wide applicability.

Guiding Principles

This writing-to-learn activity is useful approach for helping students focus their attention on the subject at hand. Attention requires several different components (Mirsky, Anthony, Duncan, Ahearn, & Kellam, 1991). The first is *focus*, or the ability to select target information from an array of enhanced processing. The second is *sustain*, which means the capacity to maintain focus and alertness over time. The third component is *shift*, which means the ability to change attentive focus in a flexible and adaptive manner. Yesterday's News requires students to set aside what was going on prior to class and focus on the content. It thus requires both focus and shift.

Yesterday's News also requires that students put information that they gained from a previous session into their own words (Bransford et al., 1999), which can improve memory and retention. Moreover, if students activate prior knowledge at the appropriate time, it provides a solid foundation for new learning. Thus, they are primed and ready for new ideas and information.

Preparation

Create a template for students to use when writing their notes and to return to you, such as we illustrate in Table 6.4 which appears below. Next, determine how often students will complete this activity, whether during each class session or only at critical times for content (for example to introduce new units). Finally, decide what you will do with the information. You can use it to gauge attendance and attention or to understand what students are actually learning in class.

Process

- Announce the activity, the time they will have for writing, and the parameters.
- Provide students with a brief time at the start of class to complete.
- Collect the results.
- Analyze the information, and consider reporting key themes back to students.

Sample IDEA Pairings

This activity works particularly well in lecture courses when the instructor covers important content the day before and would like students to recall that knowledge prior to learning new material. It can also be effective with group activities, such as Discussion and Peer Tutoring, in order to reinforce the learning that has occurred.

TABLE 6.4 Sample Questions for Yesterday's News

To: The student who missed the last class session:
From:_____
Date:_____
Subject: Urgent information
Most central topic we covered in our last session:
Why this information is critical to the course:
Why this information is critical to know for today's class:

Pro-tips

Connecting ideas from previous sessions to current ones is an important way to improve learning, yet it is something of which we as teachers are not always conscious. Yesterday's News is a great way to structure that activity, and it can be done throughout the semester, particularly since it requires only a small investment of time. If done frequently, however, students may feel that the "writing a letter" aspect of it feels "hokey." It may be better applied as a Journaling (IDEA #68) activity or alternately as a quick way to call roll (students complete the handout as a way of documenting their attendance).

IDEA #74: Field Notes

Overview

Field trips have long been a staple of K–12 education, with kids piling into yellow school buses for visits to history museums, science centers, or theaters. However, the benefits of field trips extend to the college environment, particularly with an added writing component. Field Notes may be done on or off campus, and the write up of field experience typically happens out of class, whether independently or in writing teams. The major goal of Field Notes is to involve students in experiential learning outside of the typical classroom environment and deepen it with the write up of the experience.

This activity presents opportunities for students to actively engage with course ideas. The most successful Field Notes blend course content with relevant field experiences. Through combining content and experience, Field Notes support active engagement and student learning. Moreover, Field Notes can build a sense of community among the class, which can benefit learning even after the conclusion of the course; students share a common experience and then share the experience of writing about it.

Guiding Principles

Field Notes help develop a pedagogy that combines experience, critical thinking, reflection, and action (Jakubowski, 2003). While emerged in the field experience, students have the opportunity to build connections between their experiences and the classroom. Moreover, Field Notes provide opportunities to apply course information through experience in concrete, real-world settings and in writing.

Through discovery learning (Bruner, 1961), instructors present an environment to students, allowing the class to engage in their own learning within the environment. Using this more student-centered approach, Field Notes allow the opportunity to present students with learning opportunities that work in cooperation with classroom material. By presenting students with this new environment, instructors serve as a guide; students are largely responsible for their own learning experiences during the trip.

Preparation

Field Notes require more advanced planning than most of the other IDEAs. First, decide on a field experience that would augment the course content. The experience could be a simple visit on campus or more elaborate overnight trips. In addition, check with any policy regulations on your campus regarding transportation, liability, accommodations for students with disabilities, or other potential concerns. You should also determine how students will write up their experiences. Suggest, for example, that students should include descriptive information, including date and time, setting, actions, behaviors, and so forth. They should also include reflective information about what they have seen.

Process

- Share the details of the Field Note with the class early in the semester. This advanced notice is particularly important for experiences that will occur outside of normal class times.
- Prior to the trip, provide information to the students regarding logistics as well as the learning and writing expectations. Prepare students for what to expect, what they should look for, and how they should engage with the knowledge they will learn on their visit.
- Prompt students to begin writing up their notes.
- Following the experience, provide opportunities for students to apply knowledge and reflect upon their experiences. This closure may be completed through a class discussion, written assignment, or both.

Sample IDEA Pairings

Responsive Lecture (IDEA #6). Students develop a list of questions from the Field Notes. The instructor then answers the questions and provides a short lecture as follow up.

Today I Learned (IDEA #90). Ask students to complete a sentence stem reflecting on what they learned from the experience.

140-Character Memoir (IDEA #94). Students create short memoirs about their experience on the Field Note. This activity provides an opportunity for students to recall and reflect on their experiences.

Pro-tips

One of the best learning opportunities from Field Notes involves providing outlets after the experience for applying new knowledge and reflecting on experiences.

Encouraging students to engage in application and reflection helps students make connections and think critically about the Field Note.

Likely as not, one or more students will not be able to participate in the experience. You will need to consider how they will gain a comparable experience and what they will do as a substitute writing assignment.

A key consideration in Field Notes is how you will assess students. Inform students ahead of time how they will be assessed, which will help set their expectations for the experience and resulting write up.

Following the experience, ask students to evaluate their experiences. Students may have useful suggestions that can help you improve the activity in the future.

IDEA #75: Interview Protocols

Overview

Learning is facilitated by connecting material to other material and thinking about information in new and creative ways. The Interview Protocols IDEA provides an effective method for students to do exactly that. This approach works particularly well for addressing challenging, ill-defined problems with no right or wrong answers. In this activity, student develop an interview protocol, complete with questions related to the topic at hand, and a plan for analyzing their results. They next work in pairs to interview each other. After students take a turn as either the interviewer or the interviewee, they write up a short report on their findings and ideas (Kagan, 1994). This final writing can be easily completed in a journalistic style or alternately in a form that approximates a social science research paper.

The Interview Protocol IDEA encourages students to think about what they want to know and how they can find it out. They must weigh competing ideas and think critically (and swiftly) in asking follow-up questions. The activity can help students tackle difficult course concepts as well as consider a variety of different viewpoints on an idea or issue. This IDEA also develops listening and conversational skills along with the ability to write up interview data. This IDEA also has the additional benefit of helping students to learn some skills related to being interviewed and interviewing others. These are critical skills students will likely need at some point.

Guiding Principles

This activity fosters the development of active listening skills and oral and written communication skills. Interview Protocols provide a structure to ensure students are asking appropriate questions as well as actively listening to and engaging with the ideas of others. Interview Protocols provide an opportunity for students to participate in active and engaged learning in a meaningful way. A major strength of an active learning approach is that it fosters the development of critical thinking and allows students to engage directly with course content (Meyers & Jones, 1993). The interview process requires that both interviewer and interviewee consider course content, share ideas, consider alternatives, and respond to each other. The writing aspect of this activity, both in the planning stage and in the processing stage, ensures that students are writing to learn.

Preparation

Determine what will be the content, idea, or process that will serve as the foundation for the interview. Depending on the topic upon which the Interviews will be based, you may simply note what material from the class textbook needs to be read, provide additional readings to be completed prior to class, or make suggestions as to what material students will need to read to be prepared for the activity. You may also find it beneficial to develop a few sample interview questions for the groups or allow the interviewers to submit their own questions to you for review prior to the interview. All active and engaged learning activities benefit from framing the expectations and also providing a few strategies to make the experience more beneficial. As Interview Protocols are relatively rare in higher education, this may be the first time students are exposed to this activity. As a result, framing and guiding the students will be particularly beneficial.

Process

- Ensure students know the time frame for the Interview Protocols and the primary objectives that should be realized by the end of the activity.
- Ask students to develop questions, whether independently or collaboratively. They may all decide to use the same questions, or they may determine they will each use their own.
- Have the students break off into their dyads and find a place for the interview to take place.
- One student interviews another, then the students trade roles. The pair may join another pair.
- Students write up a brief summary of what was learned from the point of view of the interviewee and interviewer.

Sample IDEA Pairings

Responsive Lecture (IDEA #6). Students create interview questions from the lecture. You then cover the material students determine is important to the topic through the Interviews.

In the News (IDEA #16). Using the news article as the source for the Interviews, students assume a persona from the news story or ask questions to elicit responses to the current event to be explored.

Role Play (IDEA #44). One student assumes the role of a historical figure, a political leader, or another person relevant to the topic. The other student interviews the personality to identify key points and opinions.

Pro-tips

Some pairs may finish this interview portion of this activity much more quickly than others. It may prove beneficial to have additional or supplemental questions for groups who finish early to provide additional information or more detailed discussions. Keeping groups engaged will not only provide additional learning for speedier groups but allow slower pairs to use the time allotted without feeling rushed.

Be sure to monitor the student Interviews. Information and questions raised can be used in subsequent lectures or discussions to clarify or reinforce important points.

For the writing aspect of this activity, it is a good idea to let students work on this outside of a face-to-face classroom, as students will process and write at different rates.

IDEA #76: Critical Book Review

Overview

For a Critical Book Review, students read and evaluate a book on an important topic related to the class. This activity provides students with the opportunity to consider and communicate their own reading of a text. By sharing a general overview of the book with a reader, the student synthesizes information. By communicating his or her judgment of it, a student practices evaluation. Thus, the activity helps students to develop both foundational knowledge and to practice higher-order skills such as analysis and evaluation as well as communication.

Guiding Principles

The ability to evaluate is a widely recognized goal of higher education. Indeed, it is one of the core categories of Bloom's educational taxonomy of cognitive learning objectives, and it is included as a category of the revised taxonomy as well (Anderson & Krathwohl, 2000). The idea is that students should be able to make a judgment about value for a given purpose.

Many instructors want students to use their evaluation skills to consider readings within our content area. That is, students should not simply accept what they read on the face of it but instead should weigh the claims being made. Moreover, we often want students to be able to evaluate critical content in our fields, to judge the merit or value of a written work.

Students do not always have practice with this skill, however. Yet practice provides students with an opportunity to use and rehearse their skills As Ericsson, Krampe, and Tesch-Romer (1993) assert, an individual develops expertise through practice. In particular, it is important for students to break down the skills and work on them in smaller chunks that are paired with feedback.

A Critical Book Review is a way to help students practice their skills in this activity. They practice analysis of an author's ideas when they have to share a summary and their own critiques of the value of the text. Through examining a student's written response to a reading for the course, the teacher will be able to assess the student's general comprehension and critical analysis.

Preparation

The first step in this activity is to determine a book or to determine how students will select a book to review, whether through a predetermined list or of their own choosing.

The next step is to develop a set of guidelines for a Critical Book Review. You can base these guidelines upon those typically used in your field. Empire State College's Writing Center (n.d.) offers the following guidelines for writing a Critical Book Review, which we have adapted for length in the following table:

TABLE 6.5 Guidelines for Writing a Book Review

Critical Book Review

- **Summary of the book**
  - Identify the author, date, title, and publisher.
  - Describe the topic in a way that is consistent with the author's intentions.
- **Identification of main argument or thesis**
  - Summarize the author's primary thesis
  - Describe the author's goal
- **Evaluation of support for the argument**
  - Describe whether and how the author supported his or her thesis; consider the logic of the argument as well as the quality of the supporting evidence
  - Describe whether the author has accomplished his or her goals
- **Personal remarks**
  - Provide your thoughts, comments, reactions, critiques, or opinions
  - Include your individual observation and experience
  - Consider your own logical analysis and evaluation
  - Draw interpretations from outside sources, such as secondary writings addressing the same topic offered by the work under review.

Process

- Assign the book for students to review, provide them a list from which to choose, or provide them with parameters for selecting their own book.
- Distribute the review form.
- Provide students with time to read the book and complete the review.
- Collect their responses, and consider having them report out, particularly if they all worked on the same paper or papers.

Sample IDEA Pairings

Circle of Voices (IDEA #18). Students read the book and discuss in small groups prior to completing the Critical Book Review.

Each One, Teach One (IDEA #30). Students each read a different book and teach other students in the class about it.

Journaling (IDEA #68). Students log their Review of the book and any other readings in their journals.

Pro-tips

This activity can be motivating for students if the reading selected is an engaging one. A dull read will result in a dull review. Advanced students, in particular, will appreciate having some autonomy in their selection of books, so it can be helpful to provide them with a list of potential reading or parameters for selection; if you do the latter, you may want to ask students to submit their choices to you prior to reading the book to ensure that everyone has made an appropriate selection.

Students do not typically have experience in doing formal reviews, and thus they may need a sample of what an effective review looks like. Moreover, the activity may be better suited to a group of advanced students who have developed the foundational knowledge that they need in order to move to higher-order thinking skills such as analysis and evaluation.

References

Ambrose, S.A., Bridges, M.W., DiPietro, M., Lovett, M.C., & Norman, M.K. (2010). *How learning works: Seven research-based principles for smart teaching.* San Francisco, CA: Jossey-Bass.

Anderson, L.W., & Krathwohl, D.R. (Eds.). (2000). *A taxonomy for learning, teaching, and assessing: A revision of Bloom's taxonomy of educational objectives.* New York: Longman.

Angelo, T.A., & Cross, K.P. (1993). *Classroom assessment techniques: A handbook for college faculty.* San Francisco, CA: Jossey-Bass.

Applebee, A.N. (1984). Writing and reasoning. *Review of Educational Research, 54*(4), 577–596.

Balgopal, M.M., Wallace, A.M., & Dahlberg, S. (2012). Writing to learn ecology: A study of three populations of college students. *Environmental Education Research, 18*(1), 67–69.

Bandura, A. (1989). Self-regulation of motivation and action through internal standards and goal systems. In L.A. Pervin (Ed.), *Goal concepts in personality and social psychology* (pp. 19–85). Hillsdale, NJ: Erlbaum.

Beutlier, S.A. (1988). Using writing to learn about astronomy. *Reading Teacher, 41*(4), 412–417.

Beyer, B.K. (1980). Using writing to learn in history. *History Teacher, 13*(2), 167–178.

Bonwell, C.C., & Eison, J.A. (1991). *Active learning: Creating excitement in the classroom.* Washington, DC: George Washington University.

Bransford, J., Donovan, M., & Pellegrino, J. (1999). *How people learn: Bridging research and practice.* Washington, DC: National Academy Press.

Britton, J. (1970). *Language and learning.* New York: Penguin.

Britton, J. (1972). *Writing to learn and learning to write.* Urbana, IL: National Council of Teachers of English.

Bruner, J.S. (1961). The act of discovery. *Harvard Educational Review, 31*(1), 21–32.

Cavdar, G., & Doe, S. (2012). Learning through writing: Teaching critical thinking skills in writing assignments. *Political Science and Politics, 45*(2), 298–306.

Chapnick, A. (2014). Reporting, reacting, and reflecting: Guidelines for journal writing. *Faculty Focus.*

Chickering, A.W., & Gamson, Z.F. (1987). Seven principles for good practice in undergraduate education. *American Association of Higher Education Bulletin, 39*(7), 3–7.

Cross, K.P., & Angelo, T.A. (1988). *Classroom assessment techniques: A handbook for faculty.* Ann Arbor, MI: National Center for Research to Improve Postsecondary Teaching and Learning.

Ericsson, K.A., Krampe, R.T., & Tesch-Romer, C. (1993). The role of deliberate practice in the acquisition of expert performance. *Psychological Review, 100*(3), 363–406.

Fry, S.W., & Villagomez, A. (2012). Writing to learn: Benefits of limitations. *College Teaching, 60*(4), 170–175.

Fulwiler, Toby, & Young, Art (Eds.) (2000). Introduction. *Language connections: Writing and reading across the curriculum.* WAC Clearinghouse Landmark Publications in Writing Studies. Originally published in print in 1982 by National Council of Teachers of English, Urbana, IL. Retrieved from http://wac.colostate.edu/books/language_connections/

Gottschalk, K., & Hjortshoj, K. (2004). *The elements of teaching writing: A resource for instructors in all disciplines.* Bedford St. Martin's Professional Resources.

Harris, M.S. (2013). *Understanding institutional diversity in American higher education.* San Francisco, CA: Jossey-Bass.

Jakubowski, L.M. (2003). Beyond book learning: Cultivating the pedagogy of experience through Field Notes. *Journal of Experiential Education, 26*(1), 24–33.

Kagan, S. (1994). *Cooperative learning.* San Juan Capistrano, CA: Kagan Cooperative Learning.

Kalelioğlu, F., & Gülbahar, Y. (2014). The effect of instructional techniques on critical thinking and critical thinking dispositions in online discussion. *Educational Technology & Society, 17*(1), 248–258.

Knowles, M. (1984). *Andragogy in action.* San Francisco, CA: Jossey-Bass.

Li, L.Y. (2007). Exploring the use of focused freewriting in developing academic writing. *Journal of University Teaching & Learning Practice, 4*(1).

Lumen. (n.d.). Writing for success: Reader-response. Retrieved January 11, 2015, from https://lumen.instructure.com/courses/56913/pages/writing-for-success-reader-response

MacDonald, S.P., & Cooper, C.M. (1992). Contributions of academic and dialogic journals to writing about literature. In A. Herrington & C. Moran (Eds.), *Writing, teaching, and learning in the disciplines* (pp. 137–155). New York: MLA.

Marzano, R.J. (2012). Art and science of teaching. *Writing to Learn, 69*(5), 82–83.

Meyers, C., & Jones, T. (1993). *Promoting active learning: Strategies for the college classroom.* San Francisco, CA: Jossey-Bass.

Miller, J. (2009). Evidence-based instruction: A classroom experience comparing nominal and brainstorming groups. *Organizational Management Journal, 6*(4), 229–238.

Mirsky, A. F., Anthony, B. J., Duncan, C. C., Ahearn, M. B., & Kellam, S. G. (1991). Analysis of elements of attention: A neuropsychological appraoch. *Neuropsychology Review, 2*(2), 109–145.

Murray, H. G. (1997). Effective teaching behavior in the college classroom. In R. P. Perry & J. C. Smart (Eds.), *The scholarship of teaching and learning in higher education: An evidence-based perspective* (pp. 171–204). New York: Agathon Press.

National Commission on Writing in America's Schools and Colleges. (2003). *The neglected "R": The need for a writing revolution.* New York: College Entrance Exam Board.

Nevid, J. S. (2012). *Psychology: Concepts and application.* Boston, MA: Cengage Learning.

Nilson, L. B. (2010). *Teaching at its best: A research-based resource for college instructors.* San Francisco, CA: Jossey-Bass.

Purcell-Gates, V., Duke, N. K., & Martineau, J. A. (2007). Learning to read and write genre-specific text: Roles of authentic experience and explicit teaching. *Reading Research Quarterly, 42*(1), 8.

Quitadamo, I. J., & Kurtz, M. J. (2007). Learning to improve: Using writing to increase critical thinking performance in general education biology. *CBE-Life Sciences Education, 6,* 140–154.

Rubin, H. J., & Rubin, I. S. (2005). *Qualitative interviewing: The art of hearing data* (2nd ed.). Thousand Oaks, CA: Sage.

Russell, D. R. (2002). *Writing in the academic disciplines: A curricular history.* Carbondale: Southern Illinois University Press.

Sanchez, B., & Lewis, K. (2002). Writing to learn: A study of pre-service teachers demonstrated increased content knowledge through the use of structured writing assignments. *Delta Journal of Education, 3*(1), 42–51.

Santa Clara University. (n.d.). Writing an annotation. Retrieved January 4, 2015, from http://www.scu.edu/library/research/general/upload/writingannot.pdf

Sawyer, R. K. (2006). *The Cambridge handbook of the learning sciences.* New York: Cambridge University Press.

Schmidt, L. (2004). Evaluating the writing-to-learn strategy with undergraduate nursing students. *Journal of Nursing Education, 43*(10), 466–473.

Trow, M. (1979). Aspects of diversity in American higher education. In H. J. Gans, N. Glazer, J. R. Gusfield, & C. Jencks (Eds.), *On the making of Americans: Essays in honor of David Riesman.* Camden, NJ: University of Pennsylvania Press.

University of Kansas. (2011). Prewriting strategies. Retrieved February 23, 2015, from http://writing.ku.edu/prewriting-strategies

Urquhart, V. (2009). *Using writing in mathematics to deepend student learning.* Denver, CO: McREL International.

Vygotsky, L. S. (1978). *Mind in society: The development of higher psychological processes.* Cambridge, MA: Harvard University Press.

Wingate, U., Andon, N., & Cogo, A. (2011). Embedding academic writing instruction into subject teaching: A case study. *Active Learning in Higher Education, 12*(1), 69–81.

Writing Across the Curriculum. (2014). Annotations. Retrieved November 4, 2014, from http://wac.colostate.edu/intro/pop5c.cfm

7

GRAPHIC ORGANIZERS

Description

Graphic organizers enable students to organize new knowledge. They present a structure around which students may hang thoughts, ideas, facts, terms, or other critical course content. Graphic organizers allow students to illustrate concepts for themselves by providing a way to visually demonstrate and communicate relationships between ideas and content, often drawing from an existing pattern or template. With increased information available to students, it is becoming increasingly important to find mechanisms that allow for visual processing of information. Entirely new fields, such as visual analytics (Keim, Kohlhammer, Ellis, & Mansmann, 2010), are being developed to help think about how to process large amounts of information. These useful tools help learners to conceptualize how information interacts through defining features; cause and effect; comparison and contrast; sequences; cycles; and hierarchies, categories, and other mechanisms.

Graphic organizers have been used for decades, having been brought to the fore in education generally through the cognitive theories of American psychologist David Ausubel. Ausubel (1968) argued the human mind organizes ideas and information in a logical schemata. He further argued that people learn when they integrate new information into existing concepts in their existing schemata. Ausubel proposed that teachers can help students organize new information in a meaningful way, in particular by providing them with an organizing structure. This structure was what he termed an advance organizer. Interest in advance organizers have gained popularity recently, as they help direct students' attention to important information by reminding students of relevant prior knowledge and highlighting relationships (Woolfolk, Winne, Perry, & Shapka, 2010).

Ausubel identified two kinds of advance organizers: comparative and expository. Comparative organizers focus on activation of prior knowledge and relating it to incoming information, whereas expository organizers help students organize and clarify new information. Although discussed and developed 50 years ago, these organizers work together to augment the learning process and are a critical aspect of scaffolding, which continues to be an effective strategy for teaching and learning (Shepard, 2005). Graphic organizers are one type of advance organizer that cuts across both of Ausubel's types. Graphic organizers are typically visual or illustrative models into which text may be incorporated.

Purposes of Graphic Organizers

Graphic organizers have myriad potential uses and have been used extensively in a range of higher education disciplines and fields. They also may be used by many different populations in higher education settings. Students, for example, can use graphic organizers as a study tool to help them as they work to understand complex concepts. Faculty members can use graphic organizers prior to a lesson to help students identify their prior knowledge. That is, they can help students match new knowledge to prior knowledge and to deepen their understanding of content. Graphic organizers also can be used during instruction. For example, instructors can use graphic organizers to demonstrate key concepts as they model complex thinking for either a small group or full class. Alternately, instructors might ask students to use a graphic representation as they document and organize information from a lecture or other class activity. In addition, small groups can use graphic organizers as a way to start and foster group discussion. Graphic organizers also may be used after instruction to help students summarize what they have learned. These instructional tools also have potential as an assessment, as they offer faculty a different view of student knowledge and understanding.

Types of Graphic Organizers

There are many different types of graphic organizers, and Dexter, Park, and Hughes (2011) believe that graphic organizers can be considered to be in one of four main categories: semantic mapping, semantic feature analysis, syntactic feature analysis, and visual displays.

Semantic mapping. This category of graphic organizers, also referred to as concept mapping, provides students with a structure for identifying the most important and relevant information from a lecture or reading. Typically, the key concept is placed in the center of the diagram, and supporting details are listed around the main idea and connected by lines. The thickness of lines may be drawn to represent the strength of the connection, curved lines may be drawn to show indirect connections, and dotted lines may be drawn to show considered concepts

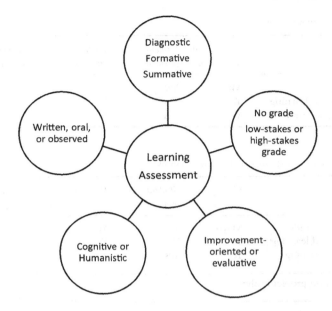

FIGURE 7.1 Semantic Map

that are related but have no direct connections to the concept being discussed. Similarly, the circles themselves and shading may be drawn to represent importance or emphasis. The point is that much information can be conveyed in a single image. See figure 7.1, above, for an example of a semantic map.

Semantic feature analysis. This category of graphic organizers typically takes the form of a table or chart that lists coordinate concepts across the x-axis and subordinate concepts along the y-axis. Organizing information into such a chart enables students to identify and represent hierarchical relationships. See an example of a semantic feature analysis in Table 7.1, which appears on the following page.

Syntactic/semantic feature analysis. This category takes semantic feature analysis one step further. It also relies on tables or charts but includes text that requires students to articulate what they see in the chart and may call attention to new vocabulary words. See Table 7.2 on the following page.

Visual displays. This category of graphic organizers highlights the different relationships between items, such as the following:

- temporal (e.g., timeline)
- spatial (e.g., decision tree)
- sequential (e.g., flowchart)
- hierarchal (e.g., taxonomy)
- comparative (e.g., Venn diagram)

TABLE 7.1 Semantic Feature Analysis

	Has a group component	Students solve problems	Problem(s) is / are unstructured	Students present solutions
Case-based learning	Maybe	Yes	Yes	Maybe
Problem-based learning	Yes	Yes	Yes	Yes
Team-based learning	Yes	Yes	No	Yes

TABLE 7.2 Syntactic/Semantic Feature Analysis

	Has a group component	Students solve problems	Problem(s) is / are unstructured	Students present solutions
Case-based learning	Maybe	Yes	Yes	Maybe
Problem-based learning	Yes	Yes	Yes	Yes
Team-based learning	Yes	Yes	No	Yes

1) _____ are the *instructional methods* focused on problem solving.

2) _____ requires *collaborative learning*.

3) _____ has the most structured form of *problem-solving learning*.

Visual displays are among the most flexible format of the different types.

Within these four broad categories, graphic organizers can take on many different formats. The literature contains a wide spectrum of examples in which graphic organizers have enhanced learning in a variety of different classrooms, including Venn Diagrams (IDEA #78), Concept Maps (IDEA #79), T-charts, cycle maps, spider charts, family trees, fishbone diagrams, and a host of others.

Sequence of Graphic Organizer Activities

As with many instructional methods, the basic sequence is planning, implementing, and concluding. These different phases are not overly structured but rather provide a general outline of the steps an instructor might undertake when deciding to use and implement graphic organizers in a college classroom.

Planning: Constructing or Choosing Graphic Organizers

The first step in being successful when using graphic organizers is to choose or create the most appropriate one for the task at hand. As we have alluded to, some organizers are better for lists, others are better for processes, others are better for relationships, and others may be best for hierarchies. Most faculty use preexisting structures when choosing graphic organizers, and there are many preformatted resources available to teachers online, such as the following:

- Education Place: http://www.eduplace.com/graphicorganizer/
- Enchanted Learning: http://www.enchantedlearning.com/graphicorganizers/
- Education Oasis: http://www.educationoasis.com/curriculum/graphic_organizers.htm

Moreover, most word processors include existing graphics that teachers can use for instructional purposes. For example, Word has several "Smart Art" structures that can form the base of a graphic organizer for instructional use. Finally, we provide several examples or structures faculty might choose in our IDEAs below.

Beyond the basic structure, however, it is important to determine whether and how much information to provide for students in the organizer. Merkley and Jefferies (2001) suggest the following steps:

- Analyze the learning task for words and concepts important for the students to understand.
- Arrange them to illustrate the interrelationships and pattern(s) of organization.
- Evaluate the clarity of relationships as well as the simplicity and effectiveness of the visual.
- Substitute empty slots for certain words in order to promote students' active reading.

In short, these authors recommend selecting a basic structure, filling in a graphic organizer, and then removing some or all of the ideas and information to create space for students to fill in. The amount of material removed is best related to the complexity of the graphic and the level of the learner. The goal is for the task to be challenging, but not so difficult as to discourage the learner. Overall, the basic idea is to know what you wish to achieve with the graphic organizer and to be sure that students can complete the task.

Implementing: Introducing and Inviting Students to Complete Graphic Organizers

After creating graphic organizers, the next step is to introduce them to students. Merkley and Jefferies (2001) offer the following suggestions:

- Verbalize relationships (links) among concepts expressed by the visual.
- Provide opportunity for student input.
- Connect new information to past learning.
- Make reference to the upcoming text.
- Seize opportunities to reinforce decoding and structural analysis.

The idea is to be detailed enough for the activity to be useful but not to supply all of the information to students; they need the structure, and they are responsible for providing the content, whether by recording what they read or hear or by generating their own information.

Concluding: Closure for the Activity

When using graphic organizers, it is a good idea to provide closure to the activity so students understand what they have done well and what they could have improved. Doing so also helps students to see the relevance of the activity and therefore value it more. Activity closure may be accomplished by sharing the organizer model, having students compare their completed graphic organizers to those created by their peers, or collecting the organizers and providing written responses.

Advantages and Challenges of Graphic Organizers for Instructors

Graphic organizers are easy to use, particularly with the large number of preformatted options available online. They demand little class time, and students may even complete the work out of class in preparation for a class session. They provide a way to help faculty to vary their instructional methods and may be used to change up a number of instructional methods, from lecture to collaborative learning. They also provide faculty with a documentation of student learning that typically may be assessed quickly to gain an understanding of what students are learning and what they are not. This teaching for learning method offers a high reward for the investment of time that it requires.

One challenge is simply to identify which graphic organizer to use for the task at hand. Each type of graphic organizer serves a specific purpose; however, one type of organizer may be more effective than another for a particular instructional activity. For example, visual displays may be most effective for maintaining and transferring concepts, while semantic mapping is best for immediate factual recall (Dexter et al., 2011). Thus, which graphic organizer to choose is dependent upon a number of factors including the level of the student, the content to be taught, the educational context, and so forth. Choosing and using graphic organizers demands deliberate consideration on the teacher's behalf (Merkley & Jefferies, 2001). Another challenge is that students may not be familiar with this instructional approach, so they may have a learning curve. A final challenge is determining a method to assess the graphic organizers produced by students. A grading rubric will certainly assist with this process, but grading graphic representations for someone not trained to do so may be challenging. As a hint, it may be helpful to consult with someone in the visual arts as to an assessment method for such assignments.

What Research Tells Us About the General Effectiveness of Graphic Organizers

Much like graphic organizers themselves, their attending research has developed over time. There now is sufficient evidence from which faculty may draw information about this approach. Research has demonstrated the effectiveness of graphic organizers in improving learning outcomes. It suggests that graphic organizers are an effective tool for improving vocabulary knowledge as well as conceptual knowledge (Moore & Readence, 1984). Moreover, there is solid evidence to support their use in higher education. When considered on a number of variables including student grade level, university students demonstrated the greatest learning effects from the use of graphic organizers (Moore & Readence, 1984).

Several recent studies provide solid support for the use of graphic organizers for improving student learning. Jiang (2012), for example, considered the relationship between graphic organizers and the development of reading comprehension of 340 college-level English as a Foreign Language students enrolled at a Chinese university. The researcher demonstrated that the graphic organizers significantly improved student comprehension. Students also maintained the improvement over time.

Similarly, in a study of 102 students from Jordan, Al-Hinnawi (2012) investigated the relationship between use of graphic organizers and vocabulary. Half of the students learned English vocabulary words using traditional methods while the other half learned using graphic organizers that helped them learn eight features: spelling, pronunciation, part of speech, meaning in the first language, meaning in the foreign language, synonym, antonym, and using it in an example sentence. Both groups participated in three separate evaluative tests. Those who used graphic organizers scored higher on the vocabulary tests than the students who used traditional learning methods. After sequential testing throughout the study, students who used graphic organizers also showed more growth from test to test than did the control group.

Several studies also point to the idea that students value using graphic organizers and believe that they improve their learning. Yin (2012), for example, implemented tree diagrams to measure 37 students' knowledge in an introductory statistics education course. The researchers found that students' performance on the tree diagrams was significantly correlated to their performance on statistics achievement tests. Students believed that the tree diagrams were helpful to their organization of statistical knowledge. Thus, this study signals that students value graphic organizers as a study aid.

Similarly, DeMeo (2007) investigated the use of a decision map to help students in an introductory chemistry course to develop general problem-solving skills. Sixty students participated in the study. The author used questionnaires to gather information about students' perceptions of their own achievement in problem solving, understanding concepts, and organizing information. The researcher found that the majority of students believed that the maps helped their learning. Moreover, 78% of students indicated that they would use the maps in the future to answer similar types of problems. This finding demonstrates that students believe that graphic organizers help them improve their learning outcomes and that they believe they can use the tool in similar settings.

In an attempt to document the students' experiences with graphic organizers, Mackinnon (2006) used a survey, focus groups, and semistructured interviews. The intent of the study was to examine student perceptions of the effect of electronic concept maps in teaching a contentious issue in biology. The researcher provided 68 students with the electronic concept maps. Students were to further develop the content maps in two key ways: hyperlinking concepts from the map to learning logs and hyperlinking their own relational phrases to electronic discussions. The research revealed that students were positive about using the hyperlinked graphic organizer. Students noted improvements to their ability to formulate arguments, lead effective discussions, and substantiate their conceptual frameworks.

What Research Tells Us About How to Improve Student Learning in Courses Using Graphic Organizers

In addition to the evidence of general effectiveness of graphic organizers in higher education settings, there are several important lessons that we can draw from research that suggest potentially beneficial ways to use graphic organizers.

Research Finding #1: The Timing of the Graphic Organizer Is Related to Student Learning

The general consensus of the research appears to be that graphic organizers are best presented after the content. That is, graphic organizers can help students bring together ideas and information they have received better than they can help students preview it. The research, then, upholds the assumption that graphic organizers indeed work better as reviews and overviews than as previews. In a study of timing of implementation of graphic organizers, Shaw et al. (2012), for example, presented 111 undergraduates with graphic organizers at different phases of the learning process. Some of the students received the organizers before reading or listening to narration of a 3,400-word text, and some received them afterward. The researchers measured knowledge retention and transfer of the two groups. They found that students who received the graphic organizers after the content transferred knowledge better than those who received them before.

Similarly, in their comprehensive review of the research on graphic organizers, Moore and Readence (1984) reported that the point of implementation is an important factor in the magnitude of improvement of the learning outcome. Graphic organizers used as a prereading activity were associated with small average effect sizes. On the other hand, graphic organizers that were used after a reading yielded larger improvements in learning outcomes, as determined by effect sizes. These authors also concluded that efforts to improve learning outcomes may be more successful when graphic organizers are introduced after the learning material.

Research Finding #2: Degree of Completion of the Organizer Is Related to Student Learning

One question faculty may have about using graphic organizers is whether to have students create their own structures or to provide students with empty structures, partially filled structures, or completed structures. Research in this area seems to uphold some of the research we described in Chapter 1 related to guided notes. That is, while some structure seems to be beneficial, a fully completed organizer may not be the best approach. In a study involving three quasi-experiments (students were not randomly assigned to groups) and one true experiment (in which students were randomly assigned to groups) by Robinson et al. (2006), some students were given a completed graphic organizer while others were given a partially completed organizer that covered course content. Those who received the partial organizer completed it during lecture. Researchers measured performance on note-taking and on tests. All students took better notes. Those who had to complete their own organizers, however, scored higher on quizzes (Robinson et al., 2006). The active learning that takes place when students complete their own organizers appears to deepen their learning.

Investigating whether to have students create their own structure, Stull and Mayer (2007) conducted three experiments in which comparisons were made between author-provided graphic organizers or margin space for constructing graphic organizers by the participant. The experiments varied the amount of complexity of the task, providing or requiring the development of 27 organizers (most complex), 18 organizers (intermediate complexity), or 10 organizers (least complex). In this series of experiments, the authors did not find significant differences across the three groups for retention but did see increasing levels of transfer of information as the task became less complex. Also, findings indicate that, overall, students showed deeper understanding and required less time to learn when they were provided with graphic organizers as compared to when they generated the organizers. These results are consistent with cognitive load theory: if the task is too complex, then learning is hindered. The results support the idea that while it is important to challenge learners for the sake of interest, having tasks that are too demanding can hinder learning.

Research Finding #3: Type of Organizer Is Related to Student Perceptions of Learning

As we indicated above, there are many different types of organizers of information. One question that arises is whether the type of organizers selected is related to the learning that occurs. It is easy to speculate that it is, and some research suggests that the type of organizer selected is related to student learning. Chen et al. (2007), for example, compared two types of advance organizers, graphics and text, to determine their relationship and the development of information literacy of students in an online undergraduate health care ethics course. The researchers did not find a statistical difference in performance between the control and experimental groups, but students did indicate a positive attitude toward the advance organizers. In particular, they valued the graphic ones for their learning.

Studies seem to support the idea of matching the kind of organizer with the intended learning goal. For instance, Mautone and Mayer (2007) examined the relationship between using graphic organizers and student comprehension of scientific graphs. In total, 209 students (121 female and 88 male students) participated in three experiments. Some students were shown different types of cognitive aids prior to viewing graphs, while other students were not provided with the aids. All students were asked to complete a written summary of the information the graphs contained. Students who received structural aids intended to improve their organization generated more relational statements but not more causal statements than students in the control group. Students who received concrete graphic organizers to facilitate integration of new knowledge with prior knowledge generated more causal statements but not more relational statements than students in the control group. Students who received both types of aid increased both types of statements.

Kiewra (2012) documents that the matrix is a useful method for organizing information. It appears that "The graphic matrix's form signals the information's structure, extracts important ideas, and localizes related information both topically and categorically" (p. 3). A matrix is a structure made of up sequences and hierarchies. Kauffman and Kiewra (2010) asked college students to study information related to types of wildcats in text, outline, or in a matrix organizer. The three displays had identical information with some discrete facts. After students studied for 15 minutes, they took three tests: one on single facts and two on relationships. The matrix group learned more facts and were able to locate more global relationships than the other two groups.

Using IDEAs to Improve Learning Graphic Organizers

In the following section of this chapter, we provide detailed descriptions of 13 intentionally designed educational activities that correlate with the research findings we presented above. We suggest that these 13 activities correlate with these key research findings, as we indicate on Table 7.3 which appears on the following page.

The research basis behind these IDEAs means faculty can use graphic organizers with confidence that they have a good and intentional design for improving student learning and putting students on the path to success. Following are detailed descriptions for how to implement these activities in the classroom.

TABLE 7.3 Graphic Organizer IDEAs and Research Findings

Graphic Organizer IDEAs	Description	Links to Research Findings
Hypothesis Proof Organizer	This IDEA offers a formal structure in which students list hypotheses, evidence, and revised hypotheses.	When (after) (Research Finding #1)
Venn Diagrams	The instructor uses a Venn Diagram consisting of three overlapping circles to demonstrate the connection or overlap of key course concepts.	Type (visual) (Research Finding #3)
Concept Maps	Students organize and represent knowledge of a subject through a series of nodes and ties between nodes.	Type (visual) (Research Finding #3)
Main Idea–Detail Chart	The instructor asks the class to identify the main ideas of a section of text. After writing down the main ideas, students go back to each and add two to three important details or aspects of the main idea. This IDEA is helpful for reviewing and summarizing important text.	When (after) (Research Finding #1)
Timeline	This IDEA is to present a graphic representation of the passage of time, with key events illustrated chronologically on a horizontal line	Type (visual) (Research Finding #3)
Visual Lists	Working individually, in groups, or as a class, students draw a "T" and label the two columns created (e.g., Pro and Con). Students then list ideas and conclusions to support each side. This IDEA works well in having students draw comparisons between two conflicting positions.	Type (visual) (Research Finding #3)

(Continued)

TABLE 7.3 Continued

Graphic Organizer IDEAs	Description	Links to Research Findings
3–2–1 Process	The 3–2–1 Process helps students analyze text and other course materials. The first task is to come up with three central issues from class materials and readings. The second is to identify two items that they do not understand. The third is to post a question they would like answered.	When (after) (Research Finding #1)
Matrix	Using at least two concepts with similarities or differences, the instructor draws a Matrix. The students are then asked to mark or describe the similarities or differences in the cells of the Matrix.	Type (matrix) (Research Finding #3)
Cause & Effect Chains	A sequence chain is used to demonstrate a series of events that are a result of one another or are caused by one another, for example, through a chain reaction.	Degree of completion (Research Finding #2)
K-W-L Chart	The instructor provides students a starting prompt. Students reflect and brainstorm what they already understand about the provided topic. Students are then asked to develop questions of additional information they want to learn or expect to learn about the topic when reading a provided text. In the final step, students review their created questions and decide whether or not the reading provided adequate answers and what additional information would be helpful.	Type (matrix) (Research Finding #3)

Graphic Organizer IDEAs	Description	Links to Research Findings
Zone of Relevance	Students consider the relevance of their ideas in relation to a question or issue, identifying each idea on a Zone of Relevance diagram as more or less relevant than the other ideas.	Type (visual) (Research Finding #3)
Force Field Analysis	Factors that foster or inhibit change act as a "force field." Students complete a chart considering the influence of these changes.	Type (matrix) (Research Finding #3)
Author Charts	This IDEA helps students organize information about major and minor characters in a text or authors. Completed Author Charts are useful tools for understanding an author's background, bias, and motivations.	Type (visual) (Research Finding #3)

The following intentionally designed educational activities are variations of graphic organizers.

IDEA #77: Hypothesis Proof Organizer

Overview

The Hypothesis Proof Organizer provides a vehicle for students to visually understand important hypotheses and the evidence necessary to determine their accuracy. The IDEA consists of a chart on which students list hypotheses in one column and evidence that supports/disproves a hypothesis in a second column. Some instructors also add a third column where students revise the original hypothesis in light of the evidence. This graphic organizer helps students visualize the scientific method and how hypotheses and evidence interact with one another.

Hypothesis Proof Organizers require that students develop an understanding of how to create and test a hypothesis. Although this IDEA has obvious applications in science classes, instructors in any discipline that uses hypotheses can use the organizer. The activity provides an especially useful way to consider the role of evidence in testing hypotheses and revising them for future tests.

Guiding Principles

Fundamentally, the Hypothesis Proof Organizer are based on the power of using the scientific method to guide students in learning new concepts. Research shows that students demonstrate better comprehension and application of theoretical content when learning through the use of hypotheses and evidence (Lawson, Baker, Didonato, Verdi, & Johnson, 2006). This IDEA provides a useful tool for instructors when helping students learn to navigate the scientific method and develop their deductive reasoning skills.

This IDEA is supported by the research on skills acquisition that suggests that instructors can improve students' skills by facilitating exploratory learning (Anderson, 1987). When learning new skills such as revising hypotheses, Hypothesis Proof Organizers assist students by providing a structure for them to explore working with hypotheses and evidence.

Preparation

Prior to beginning the Hypothesis Proof Organizer, decide if students will complete the IDEA as a class, in groups, or individually. If completing as a class, the Hypothesis Proof Organizer can be done on the board; otherwise, a brief form can be created. Identify the initial set of hypotheses with which students will be working rather than asking students to create from scratch. You should also create a template, such as we illustrate in the following figure:

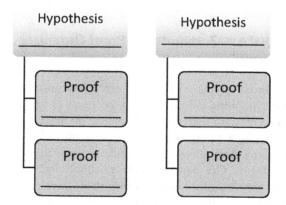

FIGURE 7.2 Hypothesis Proof Organizer

Process

- Hold a brief lecture or discussion on the value of hypotheses and how to test them.
- Have the students work on the Hypothesis Proof Organizer in groups, individually, or as an entire class.
- After completing the hypotheses and evidence columns, lecture or lead a discussion about concepts in the columns.
- If desired, have students revise their hypotheses based on the evidence and information from the lecture/discussion.

Sample IDEA Pairings

SQ3R (IDEA #53). Using the framework of SQ3R, students read about the concepts they will use in their Hypothesis Proof Organizer. This preparation gives them a solid foundation to be able to complete the organizer.

Yesterday's News (IDEA #73). After completing their Hypothesis Proof Organizer, students complete a writing assignment describing what they learned from the IDEA to a hypothetical student who missed the class session.

Visible Classroom Opinion Poll (IDEA #93). Throughout the activity, ask students to line up based on how much they believe a hypothesis is true or false.

Pro-tips

Particularly for students new to this process, you may need to provide an example or walk through one hypothesis-evidence-revision process for the class. This modeling exercise can give students a better idea of how to complete the activity.

You may prefer to have your class complete the Hypothesis Proof Organizer together and serve as a moderator/facilitator to the activity. In this approach, you can ask questions, correct inaccurate assumptions, and overall guide the IDEA.

A useful approach for using this IDEA is to have students complete the chart as they collect evidence. For example, in a laboratory setting, students can have a list of hypotheses in the first column that they test with experiments. Based on the result of the experiments, they can revise the hypothesis in the third column.

IDEA #78: Venn Diagrams

Overview

Venn Diagrams allow students to organize data and information while making comparisons. The goal is to have students compare and contrast information, typically using two or three overlapping circles. Students write course concepts inside the circles, which each represent one category. If a concept relates only to one category, it is listed inside the corresponding circle. If the concept overlaps between categories, the student lists it in the overlapping space.

This activity helps students understand the relationship and connection between various concepts. Specifically, Venn Diagrams help in student recall and application of course-specific content (Otto & Everett, 2013). In addition, they assist in understanding logic and complicated ideas by visually demonstrating the connections between ideas (Burgess-Jackson, 1998).

Guiding Principles

The advantage of graphic organizers is how they help "show the interrelationships among parts as well as the relationship of the parts to the whole" (Barkley, Major, & Cross, 2014, p. 261). Complex ideas are easier to understand graphically as they help students make sense of the information and focus on applying content.

The Venn Diagrams IDEA builds upon Ausubel's (1963) theory of meaningful verbal learning. This theory suggests students learn new material through methods that clearly assist in organizing information. The goal is to help connect new information with existing knowledge to develop meaningful learning. Venn Diagrams help students comprehend new knowledge by comparing and contrasting new ideas within the diagram with prior understanding.

Preparation

Identify at least two to three course concepts that students can compare and contrast through the use of Venn Diagrams. It is particularly helpful to overall learning to have students integrate a newly introduced topic with previously discussed content. Alternatively, students can work through several new ideas to help build understanding. Create a template, such as the one we provide in the following figure:

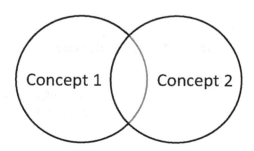

FIGURE 7.3   Venn Diagram Template

Process

- Draw the Venn Diagram on the board or pass out copies. Identify the categories for each circle but give no other information.
- As an entire class, ask students to identify elements of each of the categories, noting where they should be located on the Venn Diagram. Alternatively, have students work in groups to complete their diagram and then compare as a class.
- When students identify elements, help them consider alternatives and the relationships between the elements and broader categories.
- Once completed, have student make small groups of three to four students and compare Venn Diagrams. Although they should be similar, students will note that there are many ways to organize the information.

Sample IDEA Pairings

Pause Procedure (IDEA #2). Ask students to complete the Venn Diagram using material from the just-completed lecture.

Snowball (IDEA #12). Students work in increasingly larger groups to discuss and refine their Venn Diagrams.

What Counts as Fact? (IDEA #54). Students take the two readings and identify facts in each reading. The facts are then put into the Venn Diagram to compare and contrast ideas.

Pro-tips

Although Venn Diagrams are typically circles of similar size, this is not a requirement. You may adjust the size as necessary or use different shapes entirely. Additionally, although most Venn Diagrams include two or three circles, you can include nearly any number of shapes and sizes depending on the complexity of the subject under examination.

The note-taking structure should be specific but fairly skeletal. Fuller notes require less work on the part of the students. Completely unstructured notes leave students to their own devices, and they are often less skilled at note-taking than we might imagine.

During the activity, monitor and encourage student conversations by walking around the classroom. Listen to make sure students are engaging with the material and for key ideas emerging across multiple groups. These commons ideas can provide useful information during the debriefing after the activity.

IDEA #79: Concept Maps

Overview

Concept Maps are a useful activity for having students graphically organize, explain, and represent course-related knowledge. Typically, key course concepts are drawn in circles or boxes with lines between them representing the relationship between the concepts. In addition, students label the lines with descriptions of the relationship. The activity helps students develop a foundational understanding of significant concepts for a class as well as demonstrate their comprehension of the mapped concepts.

In order to draw a concept map, students need to identify key concepts and develop conclusions about the concepts in order to complete the map. The activity is useful for measuring comprehension, reviewing concepts for examinations, or helping students draw linkages across class sessions.

Guiding Principles

Concept Maps take advantage of spatial information to assist students in drawing comparisons across concepts (Hall, Dansereau, & Skaggs, 1992). In addition, graphically displaying information can help students better comprehend the structure of knowledge through the use of hierarchy as part of mapping. Within an engineering course, Zvacek, Restivo, and Chouzal (2012) found that the use of Concept Maps improved student performance and students reported that the maps helped improve their comprehension.

This IDEA works well in light of our understanding of human memory. Specifically, learning how to structure multiple concepts requires the multiple iterations between our working and long-term memory (Anderson, 1992). Concept Maps provide a framework that helps the brain organize and structure complex information.

Preparation

Before using Concept Maps, identify a specific question to guide student work. In addition, create your own list of concepts that can be referenced during the activity to make sure students are covering all of the relevant information. You'll want to explain the concept of nodes (the central concepts) and ties (the lines that link ideas). You can draw a simple image like the following to illustrate:

Process

- Pose a specific question that clearly specifics what the Concept Map will address. For example, "What are effects of poverty on schooling?" or "What are the major classifications of plants?"
- Have the students individually or in small groups create a list of the most significant and relevant concepts.
- Have the students draw their maps, including the concepts from their list and the relationships between concepts.

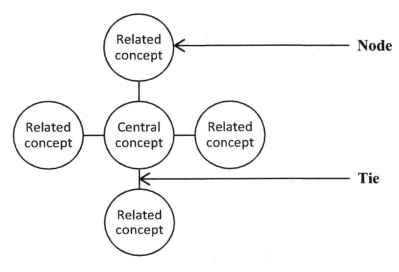

FIGURE 7.4 Nodes and Ties

• As an entire class, ask some or all of the students or groups (depending on the size of the class) to share their Concept Maps and rationales. Alternatively, ask students to submit maps for feedback or assessment.

Sample IDEA Pairings

Milling (IDEA #27). Ask students to work on their Concept Maps, leaving gaps for where they lack understanding. Students then ask questions and poll each other to fill in the remaining parts of their maps.

Crossword Puzzles (IDEA #36). Students complete their puzzles and then use the answers as concepts in a Concept Map.

Speak-Write Pairs (IDEA #64). This is a planning process that helps students create ideas for writing as well as their Concept Maps. In pairs, one student speaks aloud their ideas while their partner writes them down. This pairing helps students create material to be in a Concept Map. Students then use their map for a writing assignment.

Pro-tips

Concept Maps may be completed as a one-time exercise, but students can benefit from drawing multiple maps or revising their maps over the course of a semester. As students work on additional iterations of the maps, they demonstrate how much students are learning. Moreover, the additional levels of complexity that subsequent maps show reveals how students understand nuances of course concepts later in the class.

As an alternative to having a class draw a map, you may provide an incomplete version of a Concept Map for students to finish, which has been found to improve student recall (Katayama & Robinson, 2000). For example, relationship lines may be left blank for students to add, or some concepts may be omitted for students to add based on their understanding.

Depending on the course content, students might benefit from some suggestions on how to draw their maps. You can to encourage students to draw multiple relationships or a hierarchical map if you sense they are struggling. Also, students sometimes need help identifying what constitutes a concept for purposes of this activity, and an example may prove useful.

IDEA #80: Main Idea-Detail Chart

Overview

The Main Idea-Detail Chart IDEA helps students identify the main ideas and details of a particular topic by pulling important facts out of a reading. Identifying key information within a reading and then determining details of that key information is a valuable academic skill. This IDEA helps students think about the relevant importance of content.

The Main Idea-Detail Chart activity encourages active reading and asks students to think critically while reading. As the name of the IDEA suggests, students fill in a chart where they identify the main idea of a reading (or section of reading) along with supporting details. The activity is designed to provide a simple but useful framework for students to interact with the reading. Furthermore, instructors find Main Idea-Detail Charts useful for assessing student comprehension of reading assignments and for ensuring the reading is at the appropriate level for the students in the course.

Guiding Principles

Main Idea-Detail Charts encourage students to engage in inductive reasoning, which asks students to discover evidence supporting significant concepts. The goal in teaching through an inductive approach focuses on providing specific examples or ideas and moving to underlying notions only after first establishing the need to understand the concept (Prince & Felder, 2013). Helping students understand the main ideas and supporting details provides a foundation of knowledge before moving to more abstract or theoretical aspects of course content.

Students of all ages struggle with understanding expository reading that conveys information, ideas, and facts (Merkley & Jefferies, 2001). In fact, Main

Idea-Detail Charts are often used in early elementary education as students first learn to pull information out of readings. The value of this IDEA in the college classroom is that students read material of which they may have little prior knowledge or understanding. This activity helps students get "back to the basics" of reading to assist students with comprehending and navigating complex reading content.

Preparation

Prior to the use of the Main Idea-Detail Chart IDEA, identify a reading and a framework for the chart. In the simplest form, the chart can include boxes for students to fill in the main idea and supporting details. More elaborate versions might include relationships between concepts or multiple layers of details. Demonstrate by providing a sample or a template, such as we offer in Figure 7.5 below.

Process

• Distribute the Main Idea-Detail Chart to the class. This can be done in a prior class session if students are to complete the chart on homework readings.
• To complete in class, provide time for students to go through the reading and fill in the chart. There will be some variability based on the complexity of the chart or readings, but five minutes is typically sufficient to fill out the chart once the reading has been completed.
• Ask students to compare their charts in groups or debrief as an entire class.

Sample IDEA Pairings

Guided Note-Taking (IDEA #1). By using both IDEAs together, students compile detailed notes both on lectures and assigned readings.

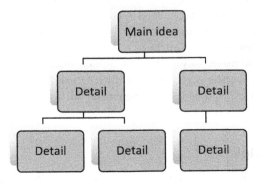

FIGURE 7.5 Main Idea-Detail Chart

Case Study (IDEA #24). In this use, the class reads through the case and identifies the main ideas (or issues) along with supporting facts to assist with understanding the case example.

Jigsaw (IDEA #31). Students complete parts of the Main Idea-Detail Chart and then work with classmates to fill in missing pieces.

Pro-tips

This activity works particularly well when students are reading dense material or new content for which they do not have prior knowledge. The chart helps provide students with a goal for their reading, which in turn can improve how students pull out ideas.

The structure of the Main Idea-Detail Chart should be consistent with your purpose for using the activity. For example, if you want students to identify details around a specific main idea, provide the idea and ask students to complete the rest. If your goal is to ask students to draw out the key concepts, provide a more skeletal structure. Overall, the chart should encourage active reading and assist students in identifying the most significant information.

Students can complete the Main Idea-Detail Chart prior to class. This saves class time to answer questions and discuss the information from the reading. This approach also encourages students to come to class prepared for engaged discussions pertaining to the course material. In addition, reviewing the charts completed prior to class provides a baseline for how the class is grasping concepts that can inform future lectures and discussions.

IDEA #81: Timeline

Overview

Timeline is an activity that helps students understand relationships and connections over time. As suggested by the name, students construct or fill in a Timeline of key events, actors, and themes related to course content. The IDEA is frequently used for historical content, but any content that can be graphically demonstrated over time can be used with a Timeline.

The activity offers an easy format for students to understand how people, places, events, and concepts change over time. Timelines can prove useful for a variety of purposes, including learning new material, organizing information, and examination preparation.

Guiding Principles

Timelines prove especially useful as a tool for conceptually organizing information. Specifically, the format of the IDEA provides a clear structure for visually depicting complex events that change over time. The easy readability of a

Timeline enables students to better understand causal relationships and learn to define these relationships (Allen, 2011).

In addition, students can struggle with connecting course concepts to larger themes, particularly historical themes. Timelines can help people make connections between isolated events and broader trends in a variety of settings, not just history courses (Curry, 2009). Without a better understanding, concepts appear in isolation and without the connection to broader class objectives. This IDEA helps students situate new concepts into a broader framework of understanding while activating prior knowledge.

Preparation

This IDEA requires little advanced preparation. You may want to identify key ideas to be included in a Timeline as a guide for students. Additionally, a skeletal Timeline could be created that students fill in during class. You may wish to offer a template, such as we illustrate in Figure 7.6, which appears below.

Process

- Asks the class to draw a Timeline or shares a worksheet of a Timeline for students to complete.
- Students can complete the Timeline during a lecture or other classroom learning or after the completion of part of class. They can work individually, in pairs, or in small groups.
- As an entire class, ask for the main ideas included and answer any remaining questions.

Sample IDEA Pairings

Who Am I? (IDEA #38). Students play Who Am I? using important historical figures or ideas. After the game, they put these concepts in chronological order using a Timeline.

Anticipation Guide (IDEA #50). In addition to the Anticipation Guide's set of statements to which students respond while reading for class, provide a partial or complete Timeline for students to complete or reference while reading.

Author Charts (IDEA #89). Students complete a Timeline with the major trends, events, and ideas that inform an author's writing.

FIGURE 7.6 Timeline

Pro-tips

The IDEA is most effective when students can contribute to their Timelines over several class sessions. Doing so allows students to continually add new information and organize it in light of material from prior classes.

If students are completing their Timelines after learning, you can move around the room, monitoring students and answering questions that arise. During a debriefing session after the activity, you can answer common questions for the entire class or bring up important points you noticed while observing the activity.

In addition to use as a classroom activity, assign Timelines as homework. While students complete readings prior to class, they create a Timeline that helps them make sense of what they are reading as well as unclear areas to be addressed in class.

IDEA #82: Visual Lists

Overview

In this activity, students create a list of opposing points or sides of an argument. Visual lists provide a simple approach to having students analyze the points and counterpoints of course content. Most frequently, the instructor draws a "T" on the board or piece of paper and labels each side of the crossbar with different positions (e.g., Pro and Con) (Faust & Paulson, 1998).

In completing Visual Lists, students are asked to consider two aspects of an issue and encouraged to analyze course information to develop the ideas for the list. The activity proves useful for a variety of purposes such as analyzing opposing positions, drawing comparisons between concepts, or brainstorming new conclusions.

Guiding Principles

Students often respond to a challenge of solving problems and demonstrate additional motivation when engaging in problem-solving activities (Svinicki & McKeachie, 2013). Visual Lists build on this idea by presenting an opportunity for students to consider two sides of an issue or concept. Looking for connections, comparisons, and differences can serve as a powerful encouragement for learning.

Similar to the benefits of debating as a form of instruction, creating Visual Lists requires students to thoroughly consider both sides of an issue or concept and thus builds on the foundation and strengths of debates and argumentation. Engaging in argumentation demonstrates course-content comprehension by noting similarities and differences among course content (von Aufschneider, Erduran, Osborne, & Simon, 2008).

Preparation

Before using Visual Lists in class, consider the topic of focus for the activity. You might select a topic with two clear sides or one with more gray area, forcing students to parse the topic more closely. You may want to provide a template for the lists, as doing so can make them easier to scan and assess. See Figure 7.7 below for an example.

Following the creation of the list, use lecture or discussion to help students draw comparisons and contrasts between the ideas generated.

Process

- Draw the structure on the board and label the two columns on either side of the figure (e.g., Core Beliefs of Federalists and Anti-Federalists in U.S. History).
- Have the students come up with ideas to populate the two columns. This can be completed individually, in groups, or as a class.
- After lists have been created, you might wish to add additional items or ask for comparisons between the two columns.

Sample IDEA Pairings

Formal Argument (IDEA #17). Students working in groups or as an entire class create the arguments using the Visual List. Then, the class divides into two groups to have a Formal Argument based on the ideas on the list.

Clustering (IDEA #34). Have students transfer information and connections in order to complete the Visual List.

Brainstorming (IDEA #62). Rather than methodically creating the Visual List, students are encouraged to list their ideas as quickly as possible.

Pro-tips

This activity is most effective when students are able to develop full lists on each side of the concept. As a result, having students work in pairs or groups often leads

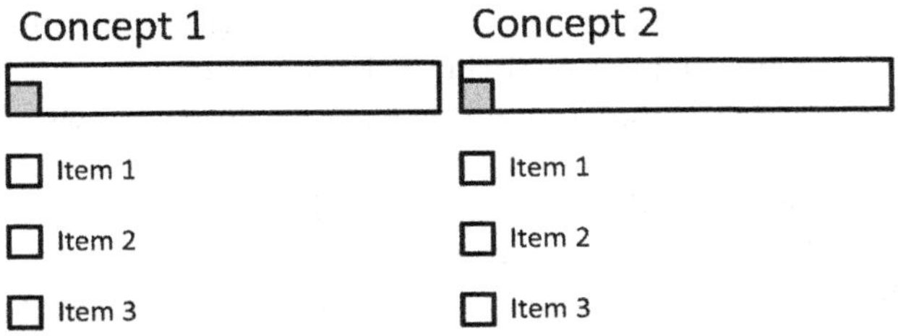

FIGURE 7.7 Visual List Template

to more fully developed lists when students are able to help each other. One additional option is to have groups first work on one side of the issue and then pass their sheets to another group, which fills in the opposing side of the issue.

During the Visual Lists activity, closely listen to the discussions each group is having while developing its list. In particular, notice the first ideas that students list (as these may be areas of greater comprehension), and notice those where students struggle with comparisons; this can provide useful areas to explore through discussion or lectures after the activity concludes.

Unless there are specific areas you want students to address, allow students to struggle some in creating their lists. Often, students will quickly identify a few items for each column, but then they may get stuck. Rather than immediately providing assistance, let students work through the challenge, as this will help them better develop their own analytic ability.

IDEA #83: 3–2–1 Process

Overview

The 3–2–1 Process helps students analyze text and other course materials. The first step for students is to identify three central issues from class materials and readings. Next, students identify two aspects of the material they did not understand well. Last, students pose a single question to the author (or course instructor). The goal of the process is to help students think critically and analyze course content in a systematic way.

The 3–2–1 Process also helps students deeply engage with material using a fairly simple analytic process (Van Gyn, 2013). By working through this process, students are better prepared to discuss the material or work with it in other ways. In fact, one of the major benefits of the 3–2–1 Process is how the format prompts students to interact with course materials, which in turn leads to improved comprehension and understanding.

Guiding Principles

The 3–2–1 Process encourages a learner-focused classroom rather than an instructor-focused one (Lipton & Wellman, 1999). By completing this activity, students engage and ask questions of material that further their own understanding. The goal of the instructor in facilitating this activity is in mediating the interaction between students and the course material. This approach helps students find meaning and understanding relevant for the class.

The 3–2–1 Process helps students scaffold information by providing a way for students to work through new information by relating it to existing material. A scaffolded approach enhances student learning (Marzano, 2007). In addition, the logical process of the steps helps students work toward larger questions and, ultimately, conclusions about the content.

Preparation

This IDEA requires relatively little advanced preparation. If you are going to use the questions identified in the overview of this section, you only need to identify what course materials students will use to complete the process. If you decide to use different questions, you will need to determine these ahead of time. You might also want to provide a handout for students to use to record their responses. See Table 7.4 below for an example.

Process

- Describe the 3–2–1 Process and what questions students will answer for each of the three steps.
- Have the students write out answers either individually or in small groups.
- As an entire class, ask some or all of the groups to share their answers. Make note of the areas that they did not understand and questions raised during the discussion. These aspects can be addressed immediately or as part of later lectures or discussions.

Sample IDEA Pairings

In the News (IDEA #16). Students identify three key issues, two parts they did not understand, and a question to the author of the news story.

Sentence Passage Springboard (IDEA #69). In addition to writing down reactions, students can work through the 3–2–1 Process to help understand the concepts from the sentence or passage.

Pro-tips

The 3–2–1 Process activity scales well with different content and classes of varying size. Students can work individually, in groups, or as an entire class to complete

TABLE 7.4 3–2–1 Process

Step	Questions
3	
2	
1	

the activity. Depending on the complexity of material, adjust the length of time allocated for the activity appropriately.

You can adjust the IDEA to be used many different ways in addition to the questions noted above. For example, in a political science course, you might ask students to identify three key differences between political systems, two effects of a political system on individual rights, and one question they would pose to the author of the resource.

During the activity, monitor and encourage student conversations by walking around the classroom. Listen to make sure students are engaging with the material and for key ideas emerging across multiple groups. These commons ideas can provide useful information during the debriefing after the activity.

Students could come to class with the 3–2–1 Process complete and pair with three other students to form groups of four. At that point, the groups might attempt to ask the single questions that individuals have posed to the author or to you.

IDEA #84: Matrix

Overview

The Matrix strategy visually displays information to students in a systematic way that easily allows them to compare and contrast key course concepts. Rather than displaying information in an outline, a Matrix organizes information across categories and common elements to enable students to quickly see similarities and differences within the material (Robinson & Kiewra, 1995).

This IDEA requires students to read and understand a large amount of material and to summarize that information in a user-friendly way. In addition, a Matrix can be used for a variety of instructional purposes, such as introducing new concepts, reviewing ideas from previous class sessions, and preparing for an exam. The visual representation of content is helpful for students in reviewing and understanding course material.

Guiding Principles

A Matrix provides students a way to quickly and succinctly comprehend information by using computational efficiency (Larkin & Simon, 1987). Reading a Matrix helps students understand concepts without requiring substantial effort to draw connections implicitly between ideas. By reducing the amount of time and effort needed to organize information, students more easily and efficiently improve their learning of course material.

This strategy can also improve the application of course content. Katayama and Robinson (2000) found that students who took notes using a Matrix demonstrated gains on application tests. In most class settings, the application of material suggests higher levels of comprehension. Thus, the use of a Matrix can help students make sense and apply important concepts.

Preparation

Before deciding to use a Matrix, consider whether to provide a completed one or have students complete it as part of class. Additionally, consider what material and categories will be included in the Matrix to best organize the material for the students. As one of the benefits of a Matrix is helping students compare and contrast, consider what elements students should examine given the content. Provide a handout, such as the one we illustrate in Figure 7.5, which appears below.

Process

- Provide a partial or complete Matrix for the class.
- Ask student to fill in the Matrix while studying material prior to class, during a lecture, or after a unit of content as a review.
- Asks questions and clarify important comparisons demonstrated on the Matrix.

Sample IDEA Pairings

Guided Note-Taking (IDEA #1). Students are provided a partial Matrix, which they fill out during the lecture. The use of the Matrix encourages active listening and engagement with the lecture.

Lecture Bingo (IDEA #9). The Matrix can be designed similar to a Bingo card, and students complete the Matrix as part of gameplay.

Gallery Walk (IDEA #28). A variety of Matrices are displayed, and students walk around the room comparing them.

Pro-tips

The Matrix IDEA is most useful when students can examine and compare ideas over a given block of material. Carefully considering what elements students

TABLE 7.5 Matrix

	Feature 1	Feature 2	Feature 3
Item 1			
Item 2			
Item 3			

should compare across various concepts will help students focus on the most important and relevant aspects of the content.

When preparing a Matrix, there is a tendency to be too brief or only use keywords in describing ideas. One of the most powerful aspects of a Matrix rests in the ability to display a larger amount of text yet remain readable. The text included in a Matrix should be comparable with what you would include in a standard outline.

Students often struggle with how to properly take notes. A skeletal Matrix helps students by requiring them to substantially complete the Matrix but provides enough of a guide to ensure students capture all of the relevant information. The goal is to provide a framework but still require students to provide the bulk of the information, thus ensuring greater comprehension.

One additional option is to have students share their completed Matrix with one another in small groups. This variation would allow students to fill in, or strengthen, any concepts that need additional attention.

IDEA #85: Cause & Effect Chains

Overview

In this activity, students work to identify and illustrate the causal relationships between events. As a graphic organizer, the Cause & Effect Chain reinforces the notion that an event or other change can serve as a catalyst for an effect, which in turn can become a cause for a future effect and so on, leading to the idea that all of the preceding causes are triggers of the final effect. A Cause & Effect Chain can be represented by way of a comparison to dominos. When dominoes are lined up in sequence, if you knock one domino over, the subsequent dominos will fall. If one domino fails to fall, the chain reaction ends. Thus, each domino that precedes it contributes to the fall of the final domino.

The Cause & Effect Chain graphic organizer consists of a box labeled "initial cause," then subsequent boxes labeled both "cause" and "effect," with a final box labeled "effect"; each box is linked with arrows moving from the initial to the final box that serve to guide the students' thinking through a series of events or reactions. We offer an illustration in Figure 7.8, which appears on the following page.

Guiding Principles

Cause & Effect Chains asks students to relate and reason information presented in class or in a reading or written assignment. In other words, the graphic organizer allows students to develop and demonstrate inductive and deductive thinking patterns (Gallavan & Kottler, 2007).

Additionally, the use of a Cause & Effect Chain helps students identify individual steps in a sequence as well as the "holistic causal interconnection" among

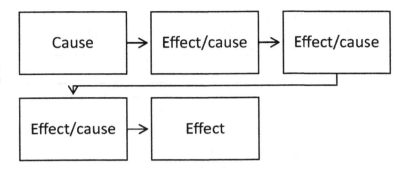

FIGURE 7.8 Cause & Effect Chain

each cause/effect (McCrudden. Schraw, Lehman, & Poliquin, 2007), thus helping students develop logical reasoning through understanding how a small change or event can initiate a scalable or broad consequence. This understanding is particularly beneficial when discussing the importance of historical events or science systems.

Preparation

Cause & Effect Chains, like many graphic organizers, are helpful in aiding students' grasp of complex concepts by breaking them down into manageable pieces. Thus, prior to implementing this activity, make sure the topic covered provides enough complexity for the Cause & Effect Chain to be useful. Create a handout to give students that includes a place to indicate initial cause, the subsequent effects/causes as a result of the initial cause, and then the final effect, leaving a space for students to fill in their responses. See Figure 7.9, which appears on the following page, for an example.

Process

- Introduce a class concept that centers on a sequential component.
- Provide students the handout of the Cause & Effect Chain.
- Ask students to work individually or in small groups to complete the provided handout.
- As a whole class, ask students to walk through the entire Cause & Effect sequence, explaining any areas that may have caused confusion.

Sample IDEA Pairings

What If (IDEA #13). Have students work through the initial cause and effect sequence, and then provide them with an alternative initial cause and ask them to work through the sequence again, discussing changes in the sequence.

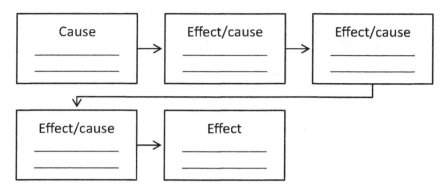

FIGURE 7.9 Cause & Effect Chain Handout

Each One, Teach One (IDEA #30). Have each student be responsible for developing knowledge about a particular cause/effect and explain that portion to students in a small group.

Pictionary (IDEA #39). Use the game structure provided to fill out and reveal each element of the Cause & Effect Chain.

Pro-tips

Some sequences may be easy for students to work through. It is a good idea to have a few questions or scenarios prepared that disrupt the chain in some fashion, thus requiring students to go back and work through the sequence again to account for the disruption. For example, if students outline the cause/effect chain as a result of the initial cause of President Lincoln being elected to office, ask them to work through what may have happened if he had never been elected.

During the activity, monitor and listen to make sure students are engaging with the material, be aware of common themes or places where students trip up in working though the handout, and plan to address issues these during the whole-class discussion.

When leading the group discussion at the end, have students only express and explain one portion of the chain at a time. This structure allows for multiple students to participate and encourages students who may not feel confident in their whole product to speak up about the portion they feel they grasp.

IDEA #86: K-W-L Chart

Overview

The K-W-L Chart IDEA guides an entire group of students through a process of how to think about a topic. The chart is comprised of three columns: K: What do you **know** about a topic; W: What do you **want to know** about a topic; L:

What information did you **learn** from class session about the topic. By using this chart, instructors are able to be more responsive to students' prior knowledge and interests during class sessions (Ogle, 1986).

This activity helps activate students' background knowledge, sets a purpose for the class, and helps students monitor their own understanding of course content. The chart may also be used for class sessions or readings assigned outside of class.

Guiding Principles

Students more frequently engage with material that they find interesting and that builds upon their prior knowledge (Tobias, 1994). Instructors can use the K-W-L Chart to tap into prior knowledge and interest in material to improve learning and student motivation.

By developing the K-W-L Chart for multiple individuals in a class, the instructor is able to create a cooperative sense among the class in achieving learning objectives. The chart does not simply list one person's individual knowledge or questions but may list items from the class as a whole. This means that students will work to achieve learning that maximizes their own learning as well as those of their classmates. The collaborative process helps promote interaction among students as well as facilitates a positive learning climate (Johnson & Johnson, 1999).

Preparation

The K-W-L Chart requires no preparation prior to class. Your goal as instructor is to facilitate a conversation that encourages the class to fully develop the list of items in each column. See our example in Table 7.6 below.

Process

- Explain the K-W-L Chart.
- First, give student approximately three minutes to create a list of knowledge they have about a topic prior to class.
- Next, give students approximately three minutes to provide a list of ideas they want to learn. You may want to ask questions to clarify what information they need to learn before beginning the day's class.
- At the end of class, give students approximately three minutes to provide a list of what they learned.

TABLE 7.6 K-W-L Chart

Know	Want to Know	Learned

Sample IDEA Pairings

Journal Club (IDEA #23). Use to allow students to research answers to their lingering questions.

Freewriting (IDEA #63). Students engage in Freewriting regarding the topic for the day's class. After a set time, students complete the K-W-L Chart based on ideas raised in their writing.

Pro-tips

One of the best benefits of K-W-L Charts is that they allow for adjusting lessons based on the information gained during the activity. Leave additional time to address questions and issues raised by the class. This IDEA will not only engage students but increase their motivation to participate in class when they get to help determine the direction of the course.

K-W-L Charts can be varied to incorporate many different aspects. For example, you can use K-W-L-S, with S standing for **still** need to learn. Others ask students to include summaries as part of the chart. Still others have S stand for what **surprised** you about the material. However, all of these variations emphasize illuminating prior knowledge and current comprehension efforts to help students chart their learning progress.

It can often help to write the K-W-L Chart on the side of the board where both you and the students can see the chart as class progresses. Doing this illustration provides a guide for the class to ensure topics and questions are addressed.

IDEA #87: Zone of Relevance

Overview

In this IDEA, students consider the relevance of their ideas in relation to a question or issue, identifying each idea on a Zone of Relevance diagram as more or less relevant than the other ideas. This activity provides students with an opportunity to reflect upon recent readings or lectures (Historical Association, 2011). It also can help them prepare for writing or testing, as they must sift through what is the most relevant information and what is related but less relevant.

This activity has relevance in a number of fields. It is particularly important for subjects in which argument is key. Students sift through the most important ideas, which can help them better frame their ideas. Thus, it may have particular use in humanities and social science. It may also be used in scientific fields in which students need to discern which evidence is most important to answering a research question. It is, in short, a useful approach to support deductive reasoning.

Guiding Principles

Organization of information is important to student learning (Ambrose, Bridges, DiPietro, Lovett, & Norman, 2010). While we typically think of organization as something that is done thematically, organizing it by its relative importance is a useful skill. Being able to complete the task of weighing the relative importance of ideas and information can not only help students be better able to retrieve knowledge but also apply it to new situations.

Preparation

Decide whether students will complete this activity individually, in pairs, or in small groups. Develop the Zone of Relevance image, which likely will resemble a bull's-eye target, with several rings showing least relevant to most relevant ideas, concepts, or words. We provide an example in Figure 7.10, which appears below.

Create the appropriate resources. For individuals, for example, consider creating handouts. For groups, consider larger diagrams on flip chart paper, with index cards upon which they might write ideas to post on the board.

Process

- Announce the activity and the time frame students will have to complete the work.
- Provide individuals or teams with supplies.
- Ask students to generate a list of ideas.
- Ask students to locate each idea on the Zone of Relevance graphic, arranging them from least important to most important.
- Ask students to discuss their terms and placement of them with their peers.

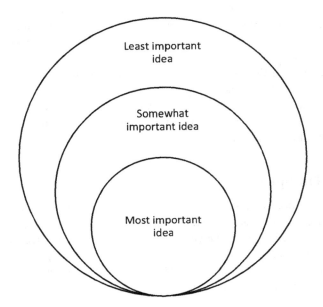

FIGURE 7.10 Zone of Relevance

Sample IDEA Pairings

Socratic Seminar (IDEA #7). Use after the Socratic Seminar, as students can process the information they heard by listing it and then posting it to the Zone of Relevance graphic. Students brainstorm a list of ideas they received in response to the questions and rate them on a Zone of Relevance.

Circle of Voices (IDEA #18). Use to demonstrate that learning did occur in the activities and allow students to rank what they learned.

Problematic Situation (IDEA #55). Ask students to rate the information available in order to solve a problem.

Pro-tips

This activity is best paired with another, as students need content in order to be able to complete this activity requiring higher-order thinking. This activity also is something that should be relatively fast paced, or students will become bored with it. It is best done within 5 or 10 minutes.

IDEA #88: Force Field Analysis

Overview

One important aspect of reflection can be to have students consider why things are the way they are and why they do not change. Factors that encourage and discourage change can act as a "force field" that have the potential to keep change from happening and instead can keep an issue at equilibrium. A Force Field Analysis requires students to examine these changes and reflect upon their influence on the status quo.

A Force Field Analysis has many potential applications. It can be used in any field that is centered on social or organizational issues, whether sociology, anthropology, business, education, nursing, or many others. Questions that could be used in a Force Field Analysis, for example, might include what forces are related to poverty, school nutrition, or same-sex marriage.

Guiding Principles

Force Field Analysis requires students to engage in higher-order thinking skills such as analysis and evaluation. It also either indirectly or directly requires students to use decision-making skills. Lewin (1943), a social psychologist, developed this concept. He believed that interaction with and understanding of the world was critical to an individual's development. He also thought it essential to break down common misconceptions of social phenomena.

TABLE 7.7 Force Field Analysis Chart

Forces suggesting change (positives)	Desired change	Forces resisting change (negatives)	Desired change
1.		1.	
2.		2.	
3.		3.	
4.		4.	

Preparation

Choose a topic in your field related to change. Create a handout in which students write on one side what forces influence change; on the other side, students write what forces resist change, as shown in Table 7.7 above.

Process

- Announce the activity and the time frame.
- Announce the topic and distribute the worksheet.
- Provide students with time to complete the answer.
- Use their responses as a basis for discussion.

Sample IDEA Pairings

Think-Pair-Share (IDEA #15). Have students think and pair before completing the analysis. Alternately, have them do the analysis and then share their results with each other.

Top 10 (IDEA #47). Ask students to develop a Top 10 list of forces suggesting change and forces resisting change.

Journaling (IDEA #68). Ask students to record their thoughts in their journals.

Pro-tips

This activity has an authentic feel to it, and it can be made even more authentic if it is presented along with a real-world scenario to set it up (e.g., students have been asked to serve as consultants to investigate a problem). In this way, it may be turned into a fairly significant project rather than a simple listing of concepts.

IDEA #89: Author Charts

Overview

This IDEA encourages students to think beyond single texts to consider a particular author's background, biases, and motivations. Modified from character charts used to organize characters in a narrative text, Author Charts provide a framework for students to think about the role of the author in a reading.

Author Charts ask students to develop an understanding of the influence of an author while reading. The activity encourages students to interrogate not simply the text itself but also the author. By understanding an author's perspective, students are better able to comprehend and interpret what they read. The activity can be useful for many class settings, from graduate students seeking to learn major researchers in a field to new students first learning to think about different authors.

Guiding Principles

Author Charts promote deeper student interaction with class text. Comprehension monitoring is a critical component of a student's reading process (Baker & Anderson, 1982). In other words, successful reading comprehension is influenced by the ability of a student to monitor mastery of a text. The format of Author Charts provides students a structure that allows them to systematically dissect a reading and check their understanding.

Students often approach texts without a solid understanding of possible biases presented. It is important for students to have a strong sense of the author or authors' motivations behind their writing (McLaughlin & DeVoogd, 2004). Author Charts encourage students to develop an understanding of an author's background and point of view that possibly influences his or her writing.

Preparation

When using the Author Charts activity, identify significant authors that warrant the completion of a chart. In addition, prepare a partial list of attributes of an author to supplement those identified by the class. As students complete the chart, be prepared to ask guiding questions to help students think about areas not raised. Figure 7.11 on the following page provides an example.

Process

- Ask students to consider the important aspects of an author, including the author's background, biases, and motivations.
- On the board, create a list for the important aspects of each author to be completed.
- As an entire class, ask questions that cause students to compare and contrast various authors and how the aspects should inform the reading of their work.

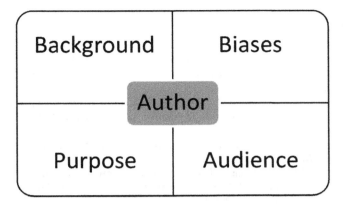

FIGURE 7.11 Author Charts

Sample IDEA Pairings

Take A Guess (IDEA #8). Ask students to take a guess about the facts and ideas related to an author. Then, lecture on the author and accompanying reasons while students circle key facts they guessed correctly.

Crossword Puzzles (IDEA #36). Students complete the Crossword Puzzle and use the answers to fill out the Author Chart.

Reader Response Paper (IDEA #67). After considering the aspects of an author, students write a response with their reactions to the author's voice and the reading.

Pro-tips

This activity proves most effective when students can evaluate the impact of an author on how they should read the work. You can help students think about this by asking them to consider ways a reading might be different if a particular aspect were different. In addition, students can start considering these issues when comparing similar authors that approach a topic differently. Fundamentally, the goal is to get students to think about the author as an active agent in writing and an aspect of a text that should be actively considered.

Although this activity may be easiest for students to complete by comparing two authors with different backgrounds and approaches to a problem (such as Lincoln-Douglas or Washington-Dubois), students can benefit most from being able to decipher more subtle differences. How might an author's methodological approach influence what the students' found? How does geography influence an author's stance on a political topic? Asking "how" questions encourages students to consider various influences the authors and their works.

References

Al-Hinnawi, A. (2012). The effect of graphic organizer strategy on university students' English vocabulary building. *English Language Teaching, 5*(12), 62.

Allen, R.B. (2011). *Visualization, causation, and history.* Paper presented at the iConference, New York, NY.

Ambrose, S.A., Bridges, M.W., DiPietro, M., Lovett, M.C., & Norman, M.K. (2010). *How learning works: Seven research-based principles for smart teaching.* San Francisco, CA: Jossey-Bass.

Anderson, J. (1987). Skill acquisition: Compilation of weak-method problem solutions. *Psychological Review, 94*(2), 192–210.

Anderson, O.R. (1992). Some interrelationships between constructivist models of learning and current neurobiological theory, with implications for science education. *Journal of Research in Science Teaching, 19*(10), 1037–1058.

Ausubel, D.P. (1963). *The psychology of meaningful verbal learning.* New York: Grune & Stratton.

Ausubel, D.P. (1968). *Educational psychology: A cognitive view.* New York: Holt, Rinehart, and Winston.

Baker, L., & Anderson, R.I. (1982). Effects of inconsistent information on text processing: Evidence for comprehension monitoring. *Reading Research Quarterly,* 281–294.

Barkley, E.F., Major, C.H., & Cross, K.P. (2014). *Collaborative learning techniques: A handbook for college faculty.* San Francisco, CA: Jossey-Bass.

Burgess-Jackson, K. (1998). Teaching legal theory with Venn diagrams. *Metaphilosophy, 29*(3), 159–177.

Chen, B., Hirumi, A., & Zhang, N.J. (2007). Investigating the use of advance organizers as an instructional strategy for web-based distance education. *Quarterly Review of Distance Education, 8*(3), 223–231.

Curry, J. (2009). Examining client spiritual history and the construction of meaning: The use of spiritual timelines in counseling. *Journal of Creativity in Mental Health, 4*(2), 113–123.

DeMeo, S. (2007). Constructing a graphic organizer in the classroom: Introductory students' perception of achievement using a decision map to solve aqueous acid-base equilibria problems. *Journal of Chemical Education, 37*(4), 540–546.

Dexter, D.D., Park, Y.J., & Hughes, C.A. (2011). A meta-analytic review of graphic organizers and science instruction for adolescents with learning disabilities: Implications for the intermediate and secondary science classroom. *Learning Disabilities Research & Practice, 26,* 204–213.

Faust, J.L., & Paulson, D.R. (1998). Active learning in the college classroom. *Journal on Excellence in College Teaching, 9*(2), 3–24.

Gallavan, N.P., & Kottler, E. (2007). Eight types of graphic organizers for empowering social studies students and teachers. *Social Studies, 98*(3), 117–128.

Hall, R.H., Dansereau, D.F., & Skaggs, L.P. (1992). Knowledge maps and the presentation of related information domains. *Journal of Experimental Education, 61*(1), 5–18.

Historical Association. (2011). Extended writing. Retrieved December 1, 2015, from http://www.history.org.uk/resources/secondary_resource_4124,4125_126.html

Jiang, X. (2012). Effects of discourse structure graphic organizers on EFL reading comprehension. *Reading in a Foreign Language, 24*(1), 84–105.

Johnson, D.W., & Johnson, R. (1999). *Learning together and alone: Cooperative, competitive, and individualistic learning* (5th ed.). Boston, MA: Allyn & Bacon.

Kauffman, D.F., & Kiewra, K. (2010). What makes a matrix so effective? An empirical test of the relative benefits of signaling, extraction, and localization. *Instructional Science, 38,* 679–705.

Katayama, A. D., & Robinson, D. H. (2000). Getting students "partially" involved in note-taking using graphic organizers. *Journal of Experimental Education, 68,* 119–133.

Keim, D., Kohlhammer, J., Ellis, G., & Mansmann, F. (2010). *Mastering the information age: Solving problems with visual analytics.* Goslar, Germany: Eurographics Association.

Kiewra, K. (2012). Using graphic organizers to improve teaching and learning. *Idea Paper #51.* The Idea Center.

Larkin, J.H., & Simon, H.A. (1987). Why a diagram is (sometimes) worth ten thousand words. *Cognitive Science, 11*(1), 65–99.

Lawson, A.E., Baker, W.P., Didonato, L., Verdi, M.P., & Johnson, M.A. (2006). The role of hypothetic-deductive reasoning and physical analogues of molecular interactions in conceptual change. *Journal of Research in Science Teaching, 30*(9), 1073–1085.

Lipton, L. & Wellman, B. (1999). *Pathways to understanding: Patterns and practices in the learning focused classroom.* Guildford, VT: Pathways.

Lewin, K. (1943). Defining the "field at a given time." *Psychological Review, 50,* 292–310.

Mackinnon, G. (2006). Contentious issues in science education: Building critical thinking patterns through two-dimenstional concept mapping. *Journal of Educational Multimedia and Hypermedia, 15*(4), 433–445.

Marzano, R.J. (2007). The art and science of teaching: A comprehensive framework for effective teaching. Alexandria, VA: ASCD.

Mautone, P., & Mayer, R.E. (2007). Cognitive aids for guiding graph comprehension. *Journal of Educational Psychology, 99*(3), 640–652.

McCrudden, M.T., Schraw, G., Lehman, S., & Poliquin, A. (2007). The effect of causal diagrams on text learning. *Contemporary Educational Psychology, 32*(3), 367–388.

McLaughlin, M., & DeVoogd, G.L. (2004). *Critical literacy: Enhancing students' comprehension of text.* New York: Scholastic.

Merkley, D.M., & Jefferies, D. (2001). Guidelines for implementing a graphic organizer. *Reading Teacher, 54*(4), 350–357.

Moore, D.W., & Readence, J.E. (1984). A quantitative and qualitative review of graphic organizer research. *Journal of Educational Research, 78*(1), 11–17.

Ogle, D.M. (1986). K-W-L: A teaching model that develops active reading of expository text. *Reading Teacher, 39*(6), 564–570.

Otto, C.A., & Everett, S.A. (2013). An instructional strategy to introduce pedagogical content knowledge using Venn diagrams. *Journal of Science Teacher Education, 24*(2), 391–403.

Prince, M.J., & Felder, R.M. (2013). Inductive teaching and learning methods: Definitions, comparisons, and research bases. *Journal of Engineering Education, 95*(2), 123–138.

Robinson, D., Beth, A., Odom, S., Hsieh, Y., Vanderveen, A., & Katayama, A. (2006). Increasing text comprehension and graphic note taking using a partial graphic organizer. *Journal of Educational Research, 100*(2), 103–111.

Robinson, D.H., & Kiewra, K.A. (1995). Visual argument: Graphic organizers are superior to outlines in improving learning from text. *Journal of Educational Psychology, 87*(3), 455–467.

Shaw, S., Priya, N., Michael, M., & Robinson, D.H. (2012). Graphic organizers or graphic overviews? Presentation order effects with computer-based text. *Educational Technology Research and Development, 60*(5), 807–820.

Shepard, L.A. (2005). Linking formative assessment to scaffolding. *Educational Leadership, 63*(3), 66–70.

Stull, A., & Mayer, R.E. (2007). Learning by doing versus learning by viewing: Three experimental comparisons of learner-generated versus author-provided graphic organizers. *Journal of Educational Psychology, 99*(4), 808–820.

Svinicki, M., & McKeachie, W.J. (2013). *McKeachie's teaching tips: Strategies, research, and theory for college and university teachers* (14th ed.). Belmont, CA: Cengage Learning.

Tobias, S. (1994). Interest, prior, knowledge, and learning. *Review of Educational Research, 64*(1), 37–54.

Van Gyn, G. (2013). The little assignment with the big impact: Reading, writing, critical reflection, and meaningful discussion. *Faculty Focus.* Retrieved from http://www.facultyfocus.com/articles/instructional-design/the-little-assignment-with-the-big-impact-reading-writing-critical-reflection-and-meaningful-discussion/

von Aufschneider, C., Erduran, S., Osborne, J., & Simon, S. (2008). Arguing to learn and learning to argue: Case studies of how students' argumentation relates to their scientific knowledge. *Journal of Research in Science Teaching, 45*(1), 101–131.

Woolfolk, A.E., Winne, P.H., Perry, N.E., & Shapka, J. (2010). *Educational psychology.* Toronto: Pearson Canada.

Yin, Y. (2012). Using tree diagrams as an assessment tool in statistis education. *Educational Assessment, 17*(1), 22–50.

Zvacek, S.M., Restivo, M.T., & Chouzal, M.F. (2012). *Visualizing understanding with concept maps.* Paper presented at the 15th International Conference on Interactive Collaborative Learning (ICL).

8

METACOGNITIVE REFLECTION

Description

As renowned sociologist Mezirow (1997) suggests, "A defining condition of being human is that we have the ability to understand the meaning of our experience" (p. 5). A primary way we gain such understanding is through active reflection upon those experiences. Metacognitive reflection is the practice of drawing from both cognitive and affective information and acting intentionally on the information through the processes of synthesis and evaluation. Dewey (1933), a famous educator who advocated for experiential learning, describes reflection as follows: "active, persistent, and careful consideration of any belief or supposed form of knowledge in the light of the grounds that support it and the further conclusions to which it tends [that] includes a conscious and voluntary effort to establish belief upon a firm basis of evidence and rationality" (p. 118).

Reflection is part and parcel of meaning making and learning. It guides learning and actions by allowing individuals to create "meaning from past or current events that serves as a guide for future behaviour" (Daudelin, 1996, p. 39). Dewey, who is often credited with bringing the concepts of learning and reflection together in education, asserted the importance of reflection to learning by stating that "We do not learn from experience . . . we learn from reflecting on experience" (Dewey, 1933, p. 78). Daudelin (1996) echoes Dewey, arguing that reflection is the "process of stepping back from an experience to ponder, carefully and persistently, its meaning to the self through the development of inferences" (p. 39). When used as an instructional approach, reflection allows students time to take in and absorb the information, process what it means to them, and consider what they think about what they learned.

Intentional reflection for learning necessarily involves a metacognitive action, in which a student thinks about thinking after being engaged in the learning process. Initially studied as a developmental process in children (Baker & Brown, 1984), researchers began to realize the importance of metacognition and reflection. As a result, they started studying how experts use these processes. The hope was that by better understanding how experts reflected on their own learning, processes could be developed to teach novices how to think about their own learning while engaged in a learning process (Hatano & Kayoko, 1986). This line of research led to a variety of conceptualizations as to what metacognition is and how it can be taught. Swartz and Perkins (1989) describe metacognition as the act of becoming aware and learning to control one's thought processes. Fusco and Fountain (1992) describe metacognition this way: "the monitoring and control of attitudes, such as students' beliefs about themselves, the value of persistence, the nature of work, and their personal responsibility in accomplishing a goal" (p. 240). Along the same lines, Barell (1992) suggests that feelings, attitudes, and dispositions all play a critical role in metacognition as "thinking involves not only cognitive operations but the dispositions to engage in them when and where appropriate" (p. 259). For example, when an instructor asks a student to complete a mathematics problem, the student engages in a cognitive process to come up with an answer to the problem. The student's awareness of the process and strategy used to solve the problem is metacognition (Flavell, 1979).

Despite being constantly engaged in learning activities, students typically do not consider the process of how they learn. Specifically, students who are new to a concept or process find it incredibly difficult to recognize gaps in their own understanding. Moreover, students tend to hold fast to their preexisting ideas, even when they are incorrect (Garner & Alexander, 1989; Land, 2000). Recently, researchers and instructors have recognized the need to intentionally and explicitly weave metacognitive strategies into teaching and learning activities. Students need practice at thinking about thinking so that they can become adept at monitoring, assessing, and improving their own performance and ability to learn.

Metacognitive reflection activities provide a vehicle for students to think about thinking. Students who participate in metacognitive reflection engage in one or more of the following:

- Make connections to prior learning experiences
- Clarify what they are to learn
- Make plans for learning
- Document the learning processes
- Actively recall what they have learned
- Identify successes and failure in learning
- Identify areas for improvement and growth.

When assigned metacognitive reflection tasks, students make meaning from their experiences overtly, whether in written or oral form. Metacognitive reflection activities guide students through the process of reflecting on what they have learned, comparing intended to actual outcomes, evaluating their cognitive strategies, analyzing and drawing connections between relationships, and synthesizing meaning of not only what they have learned but also how well they did in the learning processes. Metacognitive reflection activities encourage students to produce personal insight and learn from their learning experiences.

Purposes of Metacognitive Reflection

The main purpose of metacognitive reflection is to help students understand the thinking process and ultimately deepen their learning. Reflection helps students develop higher-order thinking and learning skills, which are increasingly considered critical for new learning to happen. Metacognitive reflection also helps students become more active and engaged in the learning process. These activities provide students with an alternative platform to understand assignments, curriculum, and their own learning journeys. As Boud et al. (1985) explains, "Perhaps if we can sharpen our consciousness of what reflection in learning can involve and how it can be influenced then we may be able to improve our own practice of learning and help those who learn with us" (p. 8).

Types of Metacognitive Reflection

There are many different ways instructors have brought metacognitive reflection into the classroom. In the following section, we offer a few of the primary activities that frequently are identified as overtly reflective, particularly when used with the appropriate prompt.

Questioning

Well-designed questions encourage students to reveal their insights, understandings, and applications of their own learning. Good questioning guides students through thinking about what they learned, what they did well in the process, and what they can do to improve in the future. Student responses can be either written or oral, but the key is to develop a good prompt that guides students in thinking about their own learning and their roles in it rather than telling students how they should think or the processes they should employ in learning.

Logs

When they write a log, students keep track of the efforts that they took during the learning activity. For example, they may log readings to document that they have completed them. Alternately, they may log hours spent studying for a class session or an examination. The process makes them more aware of the work that they have or have not done to prepare for a class-related task.

Interviews

Interviews allow for an instructor to ask questions of a student or group of students or for a group of students to question their classmates. The interview questions focus on what students learned during a class session or learning module. They may also guide students toward looking for ways that they can apply what they have learned in the future. Interviews can provide teachers and students with opportunities to listen with understanding and empathy, to think and communicate clearly, and to question and pose problems.

Evaluations

Whether conducted individually or as a group, evaluations can be particularly effective tools for students to practice metacognitive reflection. They prompt students to think about specific aspects of their planning, actions, and outcomes, rating what they did well and what they could improve upon in future learning endeavors.

Presentations

Students can participate in individual or group presentations to share experiences and insights they have about the course material and to reflect upon what they have learned (Bringle & Hatcher, 2000). They may also consider how they can apply what they have learned in other contexts. Such presentations can provide opportunities for students to organize their experiences and understanding and also to creatively display and express their knowledge of the material (Bringle & Hatcher, 1999).

Additional Activities

There are two common reflection activities that we address in other sections of this book. The first type of reflection that we cover elsewhere in this book is Discussion, which is explored in Chapter 2. When discussions about the learning process occur, students can realize that making meaning is an important goal of the discussion. Furthermore, discussions provide students with the opportunity to listen and learn about each other's metacognitive strategies, which can provide tips for them to include in their own practices.

The second type of reflection is Journaling, which we address in Chapter 6: Writing to Learn. When journals are used for reflection, students do not simply create summaries and take notes. Rather, they describe what they have learned and how they could apply that learning in the future. These types of journals are "written documents that students create as they think about various concepts, events, or interactions over a period of time for the purposes of gaining insights into self-awareness and learning" (Thorpe, 2004, p. 328). Reflective journals ask students to direct their attention toward connecting course materials to outside experiences and existing knowledge (Muncy, 2014). These journals may also be completed in online formats by using blogging or microblogging platforms.

Organization/Sequence of Metacognitive reflection

Metacognitive reflections can take several forms. The Gibbs (1988) Reflective Cycle provides a useful model for thinking through the various phases of reflection. This model allows students to challenge their assumptions, explore new ideas related to thinking about thinking, and promote self-improvement. Figure 8.1 represents the basic steps of the process, which we also describe in our narrative.

Stage 1: Description of the Event

In this stage, students provide specific and relevant details. The phase is descriptive rather than analytical. As a result, it might include information such as what

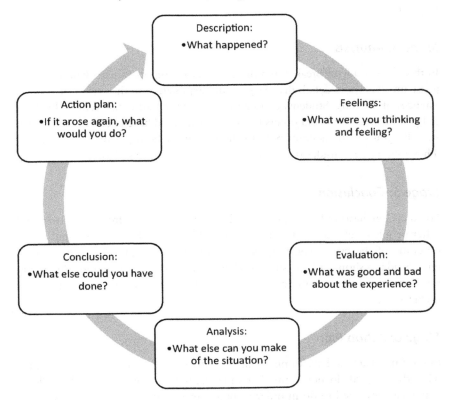

FIGURE 8.1 Gibbs Reflective Cycle

happened, the student's part in what happened, the role other actors played, and the result.

Stage 2: Feelings

Next, students recall what they were thinking. This phase is still descriptive, and the focus is on personal feelings and thoughts. It includes considerations such as: Why do you remember this event? How you were feeling prior to it? What feelings did you have when the event began? What you were thinking or feeling during the event itself? How did you feel about how the event ended? What do you think about the event now?

Stage 3: Evaluation

In this phase, students make a positive or negative judgment about what has happened. They do not spend time in analysis, but rather offer a general evaluation. They consider what was positive about the experience and what was more negative.

Stage 4: Analysis

In this phase, students break down the event into component parts (analysis). This phase involves more details than Stage 3 and exploration of the causes and consequences of learning. Students consider questions such as: What went well? What did you do well? What did others do well? What could have been better? In what way did you or others contribute to the outcomes, both positive and negative? They might also consider the question of "so what?" in this phase.

Stage 5: Conclusion

For the Conclusion phase, students seek to draw relevance from their own and other people's feelings and actions in terms of how they both contributed to the outcome of the event. The purpose of this phase is to learn from the experience. Students should ask questions such as what they could have done differently, what prevented them from doing so, and what they learned about themselves as learners.

Stage 6: Action Plan

In the final stage, students think about encountering the situation again and plan what they would do next time. For instance, they might consider the following: what they need to do in order to be better prepared, what areas they could improve, and what specific steps they need to take to make improvement.

To facilitate metacognitive reflection in the classroom, it is important to develop a classroom culture of metacognition and metacognitive strategies. Tanner (2012) suggests three recommendations to accomplish this: giving students license to identify confusion with respect to the material or processes being learned, integrating metacognitive reflection into the credited coursework, and modeling of reflection by the instructor. These three items make reflection explicit and an expected part of any course.

Advantages and Challenges of Metacognitive Reflection for Instructors

There are many advantages for instructors of using metacognitive reflection. The improved learning that can result (see the following section on research) is a significant advantage. In addition, reflections provide valuable information that can allow for assessment not only of student knowledge but also their metacognitive processes. Thus, instructors can adjust their teaching, adding in deliberate metacognitive activities as needed to develop better classroom strategies. Many of these reflections can be done outside of class, which can make them a time-efficient way to gather information about student learning.

One challenge of metacognitive reflection is that the process can take a significant amount of class time to do well. Reflection by nature is an activity that cannot and should not be rushed. Moreover, it can be a challenge to determine whether these activities should be done independently or collaboratively. Individuals foster their own growth when they control their learning, and, at times, the best path for this is reflection that is done alone. However, reflection is also enhanced when individuals explore their learning with others.

A final challenge pertains to the expectation of how instructional time should be spent. Traditionally, class time has been used to learn content and processes, all under the assumption that the student comes to the course knowing how to think and learn. As a result of this norm, instructional time spent on metacognitive reflection may been viewed as a waste of instructional time by some students and colleagues.

What Research Tells Us About the General Effectiveness of Metacognitive Reflection

Common sense suggests that thinking about what they have learned and how they have learned it would help students to deepen their learning. But does the research support that assumption? The short answer is that we have insufficient research to lay claim to the notion that it works better than not reflecting; few studies compare reflection versus no reflection. However, research studies on using reflection suggest that reflection does encourage student learning and that both students and teachers value the process.

The closest related research to date suggests that teaching practices that incorporate a metacognitive process increase students' ability to transfer learning to new settings and contexts (Bransford, Donovan, & Pellegrino, 1999). These approaches to teaching and learning include ones that intentionally encourage sense-making, self-assessment, and reflection on what went well and what could be improved.

Palincsar and Brown (1984), Scardamalia et al. (1984), and Schoenfeld (1991) are among the early researchers working on the benefits of reflection. Recent research studies have upheld findings from earlier ones. In a study by Zhao et al. (2014), for example, researchers conducted a case study of undergraduate chemistry classrooms, in which metacognitive activities were introduced. Through examination of student reflections, the researchers documented that the activities help students move beyond surface approaches of memorization to deeper learning, as suggested in early work on this subject (Marton & Säljö, 1976a, 1976b). The authors speculated that these approaches would help students beyond the confines of the chemistry course and into their future academic endeavors.

Such findings are evident not only in face-to-face courses but also online ones. Cacciamani et al. (2012) studied student learning of 67 undergraduates in an online class to understand how to foster knowledge development in online and blended courses. They found that ample opportunities for metacognitive reflection were one of three critical factors for fostering higher levels of agency for sharing ideas and working with others and knowledge building; the other two factors were high levels of participation on the part of the students and a supportive facilitator style on the part of the instructor.

What Research Tells Us About How to Improve Student Learning Through Reflection

In addition to the developing literature on effectiveness of reflection for learning, some researchers have investigated particular aspects of metacognitive reflection most likely to help students develop desired learning. From this literature, we see several key factors for effective metacognitive reflection.

Research Finding #1. Teacher-Designed Prompts Improve Capacity for Metacognitive Reflection

Kauffman et al. (2008) examined how student practice with problem solving paired with self-reflection prompts improved their capacity to solve problems. The study focused on a course that was carried out in a Web-based learning environment. The researchers considered both independent and collaborative problem solving. They found that the students who received the problem-solving prompts wrote with more clarity than those who did not. Reflection prompts also had a relationship to problem solving and writing but only when paired with the problem-solving prompts. The researchers argued that it is important for students to have a solid grasp of what they are being asked to reflect upon for the activity to be useful.

Research Finding #2. Student Self-Regulation of Their Work Improves Learning

Isaacson and Fujita (2006) studied the relationship between metacognitive knowledge monitoring and classroom performance of 84 undergraduate students enrolled in an introductory educational psychology course. Students completed 10 weekly in-class tests and had the option to choose questions to answer. They were also asked to identify the number of hours they studied for the tests, how confident they were, and what their predictions of these results were, both before and after they completed the test but prior to grading. Researchers found that students who had high scores were more accurate at predictions, more realistic in their goals, and more likely to predict accurately and revise accurately based upon actual performance. They also were more likely to choose test questions to which they knew the answers. The researchers hypothesized a relationship between self-regulation and academic success. Many students, however, do not have these skills automatically, and practice and teacher-guided activities can improve their performance.

Research Finding #3. Self and Group Assessment Improves Learning

Several studies show the benefit of student self and peer evaluation. Lynch et al. (2012), for example, examined student satisfaction with learning in a preservice course for education majors. The course included a project-based learning module in which students provided feedback on their own and each other's work. The authors found that self and peer assessments improved learning outcomes; in particular, they improved critical-thinking skills. The students, however, indicated a preference for instructor feedback.

Similarly, Mok et al. (2006) conducted a study of a metacognitive approach to student self-assessment in a teacher education course. The study involved five case studies of teacher education programs that included student self-assessment at the beginning, middle, and end of the learning module. Students represented their learning through concept maps, and their progression in self-assessment was captured through interviews. Students believed that the metacognitive aspect improved their learning. From the start of the study to the end, they became more aware of their thinking and their learning processes. The teachers believed that the feedback they received from the self-assessments improved their teaching.

Using IDEAs to Improve Learning with Metacognitive Reflection

In the following section of this chapter, we provide detailed descriptions of 11 intentionally designed educational activities (IDEAs) that correlate with the research findings we presented above. We suggest that the IDEAs correlate with these key research findings as we indicate in Table 8.1, as follows:

TABLE 8.1 Metacognitive Reflection and Research Findings

Reflection IDEAs	Description	Links to Research Findings
Today I Learned	The instructor gives students a sentence stem to start a reflection, such as "Today I Learned."	Prompts (Research Finding #1); Self-Assessment (Research Finding #3)
Shadow a Professional	Students spend a set amount of time shadowing a professional in a specific field of study related to the course. Students reflect on how well the experience and the profession would fit their own interests.	Self-Assessment (Research Finding #3)
Wrappers	"Wrapping" activities involve creating a set of questions for students to use to reflect upon an assignment or exam; the Wrapper typically has both preactivity and postactivity questions	Prompts (Research Finding #1); Self-Assessment (Research Finding #3)
Visible Classroom Opinion Poll	The Visible Classroom Opinion Poll quickly demonstrates the opinions of students on a topic. Students move to a particular spot in the classroom that demonstrates their opinion.	Prompts (Research Finding #1)
140-Character Memoir	Students write a first-person account in 140 characters or fewer. Having students create short memoirs that focus on their learning can provide a prime opportunity for reflection and learning. Moreover, this activity is a kind of writing with which students are familiar and use regularly in their own lives, by way of Facebook statuses and Twitter posts.	Prompts (Research Finding #1); Self-Tracking (Research Finding #2); Self-Assessment (Research Finding #3)

Reflection IDEAs	Description	Links to Research Findings
Self-Assessment	Students complete an assessment of their own efforts and outcomes in a learning task.	Self-Assessment (Research Finding #3)
Group Assessment	Students complete an assessment of a group's processes and products.	Self and Group Assessment (Research Finding #3)
Elevator Pitch	This IDEA prompts students to create a short oral summary that quickly communicates information of value.	Prompts (Research Finding #1)
Learning Log	Students document their time and effort in preparing for an assessment, such as an examination.	Self-Tracking (Research Finding #2)
Cultural Encounters	Students are tasked with engaging with culture outside of their typical daily routine.	Prompts (Research Finding #1)
Post Hoc Analysis	After a discipline- or field-related event has been reported, students reflect upon the event, looking for patterns that were not apparent ahead of time. They record their findings in writing, basically reporting issues, trends, and themes.	Prompts (Research Finding #1)

The research basis behind these IDEAs means faculty can use metacognitive reflection strategies with confidence that they have a sound and intentional design for improving student learning and putting students on the path to success. Following are detailed descriptions for how to implement these activities in the classroom.

IDEA #90: Today I Learned

Overview

Today I Learned (TIL) is a guided reflection activity in which students are asked to respond to a single prompt: Today I Learned (alternately: What is the most important thing you learned today?). It provides students with a chance to order their thoughts and to identify something significant and important from the lesson. It helps them understand the relevance of a given session or assignment. And it provides the instructor with feedback on what students believe they have gained from the learning activity. The activity is particularly flexible. It can be used in any discipline, and it takes only a few minutes to implement.

Guiding Principles

As Chickering and Gamson (1987) suggest, students need the opportunity to reflect on what they have learned. To reflect, students need a chance to act upon and process information they have encountered. Unfortunately, they do not always do so naturally but instead need prompting. TIL provides students with the opportunity to make meaning of their experiences. It prompts students to reflect by synthesizing and evaluating information and what it has meant to them. To this end, the process deepens and strengthens their learning. It also provides the instructor with information about what students learned and, in turn, what they did not. This invaluable information can help instructors make adjustments to their next activities to ensure that students have met the intended learning goals.

Preparation

Little preparation is needed for this activity. Simply set aside sufficient time at the end of class to either call on students or to have them respond in writing. For a small class, five minutes at the end of a session typically is sufficient time. For a larger class, having students respond to the Today I Learned prompt on an index card is a good option for the activity.

Process

- Conduct the learning activity, whether lecture, discussion, group work, or other.
- Announce the activity, and set the parameters, including time frame for responding and method of response (orally or in writing).
- Ask students to respond to the prompt "Today I Learned."
- Collect the responses by having students state what they learned or collecting the written responses.

Sample IDEA Pairings

Find the Flaw (IDEA #10). Ask students to reflect on what they learned about the misinformation to help solidify the correct information.

Formal Argument (IDEA #17). Ask students to reflect on what they learned as a result of participating in the structured activity, particularly if they had to argue for a side with which they disagreed or had to switch sides.

Microteaching (IDEA #32). Ask students to reflect on what they learned after each individual lesson.

Pro-tips

Today I Learned is what is known as a "sentence stem." Other stems can be sub-stituted for this one, including the following as indicated on the Baylor Web site in an article titled "Applying theory into the classroom":

- Today I learned . . .
- I don't understand . . .
- I would like to learn more about . . .
- I need help with . . .
- A question I have is . . .
- Please explain more about . . .
- The most important thing I learned today is . . .
- Three things I learned today are . . .
- The thing that surprised me today was . . .
- I am still confused about . . .
- I wish . . .
- The best part of class today was . . .

The term "Today I Learned" has been popularized on an Internet site (Reddit. com), but faculty for years have been asking students about what they learned in class. Some students might appreciate the reference to popular culture, while others might think it trivializes the activity. Gauge your audience to determine whether to use the TIL term when announcing this activity.

IDEA #91: Shadow a Professional

Overview

Shadow a Professional provides an opportunity for students to gain hands-on experience about a particular career field or profession. As one would assume, this activity has students learn about a job by witnessing firsthand a "day in the life" of a professional. The activity provides students with an avenue to gain exposure and knowledge about a career outside of class.

This IDEA is primarily designed to give students an understanding of a career and to provide a link between a profession and course content. Through this activity, students are able to consider the suitability of a career, gauge their ability to apply course content, and gain a more realistic view of a profession.

Guiding Principles

Through Shadow a Professional, students can apply knowledge in a real-world setting, which is a key part of Kolb's (1984) cycle of learning. Kolb suggests stu-dents benefit from concrete experience that directly engages students in situations.

By pairing students with active professionals, Shadow a Professional provides a format to support and encourage students to think through this key part of the cycle of experiential learning. Shadow a Professional also allows for students to observe the complexity of a field they may not otherwise see. This activity is useful in the health-related fields, particularly as it relates to the increasing use of interdisciplinary teams (Riva et al., 2010).

A critical component and foundation for the learning to be gained from Shadow a Professional is in debriefing. Specifically, debriefing helps students to process their experiences in order to facilitate learning (Dennehy, Sims, & Collins, 1998). Asking students to reflect and debrief about their experiences provides a vehicle for students to connect with course content, reconcile their expectations with the experience, and compare their experiences with classmates.

Preparation

Shadow a Professional may vary a great deal depending on the nature and content of the course you are teaching. Courses related to more professional fields may have specific types of careers for students to shadow. In less professional or vocational courses, students may have a great deal of flexibility in determining who they will shadow. It is necessary to decide well before the activity (and likely before the course begins) what parameters you will include on professional selection. In addition, when using this activity, determine what your role will be in setting up the experiences as the primary organizer, facilitator, or only intervening in the case of problems.

Process

- Prior to the start of the term, identify professionals who are willing to be shadowed. If the process goes well, those willing to have a student shadow them for a period of time will likely agree in the future, making it less challenging to find professionals each time this activity is used.
- Early in the term, explain the purpose, expectations, and logistics of the activity.
- Have the students contact a professional to arrange the shadowing experience. You may want to provide a template for them to use when making their initial contact. It is extremely important that the students act in a professional manner, as they represent you and your institution.
- On an agreed upon day, students will shadow their professionals and follow the daily work the professionals complete. Typically, students follow for an entire workday, although this may be modified as needed. Again, stress the importance to students that they show up dressed appropriately for the job of the professional, that they show up on time, and that they act in a professional manner throughout the experience.

- Following the shadowing experience, provide opportunities for students to debrief with other classmates about their experiences. In addition, you may want to require a written reflection.

Sample IDEA Pairings

Microteaching (IDEA #32). Students lead a short lesson about content related to their shadowing experience.

Interviews (IDEA #70). Students interview someone in an industry or organization. This interview is followed up with Shadow a Professional, either the interviewee or someone else.

Graffiti Board (IDEA #65). Students respond to a prompt about their shadowing experience by creating graffiti on flip chart paper.

Pro-tips

Although Shadow a Professional may lead to additional opportunities later, make sure that both students and the professionals understand the scope of the activity is simply to observe the professional on a given day. This experience is less involved than interning or volunteering for an organization.

Students will gain the most from the experience if they conduct research on the organization and professional they will be shadowing. You may want to require background research as part of class prior to the activity to ensure students are sufficiently prepared for the experience.

Depending on students' knowledge of the professional area, you may want to provide information for students to be successful. If there are special dress requirements or other jobsite-specific requirements, make sure students are aware of these ahead of time. If you are not familiar with all of the career fields, you may provide a list of questions for which students should obtain answers prior to their experience. In addition to job-specific needs, reminding students of general professional expectations such as promptness and respect will help prepare students to participate in this activity.

IDEA #92: Wrappers

Overview

A Wrapper is a self-monitoring activity that surrounds a preexisting learning or assessment task and that encourages "learning about learning." "Wrapping" activities involve creating a set of questions for students to use to reflect upon an assignment or exam; the Wrapper typically has both preactivity and postactivity questions.

It is possible to use Wrapper around any preexisting part of a course, whether a lecture, homework, or test. Thus, this IDEA is particularly flexible and lends itself to use in any discipline or field. It also adds only a few minutes of time to any assignment and is intended to be an integrated part of the activity, making it a good investment of time and energy given the potential benefit that it creates.

Guiding Principles

As Ambrose et al. (2010) suggest, students who learn to monitor and adjust their own learning are better learners in the long run. As the authors also suggest, students do not often engage in self-monitoring activities naturally. Instead, many of them need direction on how to go about it and practice developing and honing their skills. Wrappers provide these functions. They help students to develop skills in monitoring their own learning so that they learn to adapt as necessary. Wrappers also are intended to help students identify their own strengths and weaknesses so that they can strive to capitalize on their assets and improve in areas of deficit. Wrappers also tend to ask students to reflect on their preparation time as well as study strategies, a process that helps them to become more self-aware.

Preparation

Choose the type of wrapper you will use. The Center for Teaching and Learning at Texas University (n.d.) suggests the following kind of Wrappers:

> Exam Wrappers include questions about preparation strategies, surprises, remaining questions, study goals for the next unit, and so on. This type of Wrapper helps students reflect on their study strategies to identify the best ways to prepare for future exams.
>
> Homework Wrappers include questions about students' confidence in applying their knowledge and skills both before and after completing an assignment. This type of Wrapper gives students immediate feedback concerning the accuracy of their perceptions.
>
> Lecture Wrappers include questions at the beginning of class about what students anticipate getting out of a lesson or questions at the end of class about the key points of the lesson. Having students compare their key points to your points can help students develop skills in active listening and identifying important information.

Create a handout to provide students that presents the questions that surround the learning activity or assessment.

Process

- Present students with the handout, and ask them to respond to the preactivity questions.
- Complete the original activity or assessment.

- Ask students to complete the handout by responding to the postactivity questions.
- Take up the Wrappers.

Sample IDEA Pairings

Wrappers necessarily are paired with other activities, and thus they may be paired with any of the other IDEAs from any of the other sections in this book. As the different types of Wrappers indicate, they may be particularly useful with lecture, as they help students to think about the important points made. They also have use, however, as reflection upon some of the student-directed activities, such as Discussion and Reciprocal Teaching; in particular, Wrappers can help students see the value of those activities and to identify and solidify the learning that took place during them. Homework Wrappers are beneficial for using along with Reading, Writing, and Research IDEAs.

Pro-tips

These activities can feel contrived to students, who may feel like they are busy-work and not see the inherent value in completing them. Assigning a few points to them can encourage fuller participation.

Wrappers can be used frequently, and they can be faded over time so that students eventually take over the reflection responsibilities on their own. In this way, Wrappers are a form of scaffolded learning reflection.

IDEA #93: Visible Classroom Opinion Poll

Overview

The Visible Classroom Opinion Poll quickly demonstrates the opinions of students on a particular topic. The activity has a variety of names and forms. For example, Values Line, Stand Where You Stand, and Four Corners are all variations. In a Values Line, students line up between two points according to how strongly they agree or disagree with a statement. Similarly, in Four Corners, students move into the corner of the classroom that fits their opinion. Corners are frequently arranged by options (such as strongly agree, agree, disagree, and strongly disagree). Stand Where You Stand is a variation similar to Four Corners, in which students spend time thinking and writing prior to arranging themselves by a poster with an opinion (typically strongly agree to strongly disagree) and then justify their decisions. For an easy Visible Classroom Opinion Poll, simply have students raise their hands to respond to a question.

This IDEA encourages students to form opinions, consider contrary opinions, and provide a justification for their positions. Using this approach can encourage students to actively participate in class and is useful when the class and discussions become lethargic. The activity encourages participation and engagement with other students in class. It may be used in a wide range of disciplines and fields, and it can be a quick activity that is part of a broader class activity.

Guiding Principles

Visible Classroom Opinion Poll requires active learning, as suggested by Chickering and Gamson (1987). The activity requires students to analyze a statement, consider their own opinions as well as those of their classmates, and apply course concepts. By ensuring that students actively consider course content and their own views, this strategy can help students develop critical-thinking skills, improve oral communication, and demonstrate better comprehension.

To the extent that groups form to some degree around students' identities, the class presents an opportunity to explore multiple worldviews, personal experiences, and issues of diversity. Kardia and Sevig (2001) describe how intergroup dialogue can help students better understand their own identities and those of their classmates. Dealing with the question of group identities and conflict that may arise in class provides an opportunity to help students develop both individually and as a group.

Preparation

This activity requires a controversial statement that will elicit different student responses. If using the Four Corners or Stand Where You Stand approach, think of three to five options related to the topic (it does not have to specifically be four).

Process

- Write controversial statements or prompts on the board.
- Have students decide on their positions without discussing with classmates (one minute).
- Once students signal their vote, whether by raising their hands or moving to an identified corner of the room, have students form groups with those of similar responses to discuss the basis for their opinion.
- After a few minutes of discussion as a group, ask a spokesperson to present the group's views.
- Alternatively, have the group discuss the opposite view and make the case for that position. You can also rearrange groups so that new groups have members with a variety of opinions.
- To conclude, ask students to signal whether they have changed views, or ask for a show of hands if their opinion changed.

Sample IDEA Pairings

Snowball (IDEA #12). Use the Visible Classroom Opinion Poll as a springboard for a Snowball discussion.

Freewriting (IDEA #63). After students express their opinions, have them Freewrite about why they believe what they do.

Pro-tips

An advantage of this activity is that it gets students up and moving. When the class has low energy or you need a change of pace, this activity can energize a class by getting students up and moving for a minute.

While the activity works well with asking opinions (agree-disagree), it can also be used for other kinds of prompts. For example, in a U.S. History course, students could be asked to arrange themselves along a line of whether the founders should have kept the Articles of Confederation (on one end) or created the Constitution. Alternatively, using the Four Corners version, students could select which First Amendment right is they believe is most important (religion, speech, press, or assembly).

Students may hesitate to show their opinion or be influenced by the choices of others. To avoid this, you can have students pick a number between 1 and 10 (1 for strongly agree and 10 for strongly disagree) before they line up. Then when lining up, students simply have to arrange themselves by number.

IDEA #94: 140-Character Memoir

Overview

A memoir is a first-person account of someone's life; it is, in short, an autobiography. It can be more or less focused on a particular aspect of one's life and can be crafted to fit that purpose. Having students create short memoirs that focus on their learning can provide a prime opportunity for reflection. Moreover, this activity is a kind of writing with which students are familiar and use regularly in their own lives, by way of Facebook statuses and Twitter posts. Indeed, students are increasingly familiar and comfortable with technology and social media, and they use it regularly for both personal and class purposes (Faculty Focus, 2010; Gemmil & Peterson, 2006). Because of this, for students today, a 140-Character Memoir is a natural and authentic form of writing.

Guiding Principles

Adult learning theory (Knowles, 1984) suggest that adult learners will find the most value in learning activities that have immediate relevance for their personal or professional lives. A 140-Character Memoir asks them to make a clear connection between their personal lives and the subject matter. It also provides them with a chance to share their experiences and how these inform their learning, which will ultimately make their learning more relevant and thus meaningful.

Preparation

Determine whether you will use this as a one-time activity, or if you would like students to update their Memoirs more regularly. Choose a prompt that moves students toward the kind of reflection you hope to elicit, for example:

- Write a 140-Character Memoir that summarizes your experiences with the course content.
- Write a 140-Character Memoir that situates you in relation to our last session.
- Write a 140-Character Memoir that captures how you feel as a student right now.

Determine what medium to use to capture the Memoirs. You may, for example, ask students to turn in their Memoirs on paper or alternately to post them to Twitter.

Process

- Announce the activity and the time frame for completing it.
- Ask students to complete the memoir.
- Collect the responses.
- Consider reporting out on key themes.

Sample IDEA Pairings

Icebreakers (IDEA #46). Simply ask students to share their 140-Character Memoirs in one of the questions to be asked of students.

Journaling (IDEA #68). Students use the activity as a springboard for a Journal Entry in which they discuss how who they are intersects with their learning in the subject.

Interview Protocols (IDEA #75). Students review their 140-Character Memoirs to develop interview questions.

Pro-tips

If you decide to use Twitter, which is a great medium for this assignment, we offer some caveats for doing so. While many students may have some experience with

Twitter, allow plenty of time and offer clear directions to set up accounts and familiarize students with how to use the platform. Some students may not want to be exposed by way of social media. Twitter has privacy settings that allow users to make their tweets public or private. Students may also choose to use pseudonyms. Some students will not want to use their existing accounts for classwork. In these cases, encourage students to set up a second account that they can use during class. Establishing norms and expectations can help, as can having a teaching assistant monitor the discussion to quickly alert you of any problems.

IDEA #95: Self-Assessment

Overview

This IDEA provides students with an opportunity to serve as partners in their own assessment through an active reflection process. The activity calls for students to monitor, evaluate, and reflect on their thinking and the learning process. One of the strengths of Self-Assessment its ability to encourage students to get involved and take responsibility for their own learning.

The Self-Assessment IDEA asks students to consider their own learning process, identify their progress toward a set of criteria, and create goals for their future learning (McMillan & Hearn, 2008). It encourages them to think about their own thinking and actions. Self-Assessment not only encourages reflection, but it also can help students develop metacognitive skills that may be useful to them in many learning contexts.

Guiding Principles

This IDEA encourages students to improve their self-efficacy and, as a result, improve their motivation for learning. Research shows that student engagement is built through a strong self-efficacy, or students' perception of their ability to succeed on a given task (Pintrich & Schunk, 1996). As students engage in Self-Assessment, they are able to identify their strengths and areas for improvement, which can improve their motivation for setting future learning goals (Schunk, 1990).

Self-Assessment is based on cognitive and constructivist approaches to learning through the use of student self-monitoring (Shepard, 2001). The core concept in these theories is that students construct meaning from self-assessing allowing themselves to internalize and evaluate knowledge and the learning process. By focusing, in part, on the learning process, students are better able to make connections throughout the process to improve their comprehension of new information.

Preparation

In advance of using Self-Assessment, identify aspects of learning for students to assess. Moreover, create a form or rubric for students to use in their Self-Assessment.

TABLE 8.2 Self-Assessment Form

Self-Evaluation
Student name: _____
Date: _____
Describe your work processes:
Describe your work product:
What did you do well?
What could you improve upon?

If not completed in writing, guiding questions may be identified for use in an oral version of Self-Assessment. The questions may be specific or more general, as in our example in Table 8.2, which appears above.

Process

- Describe the purpose of Self-Assessment and provide a form or questions for students to answer.
- Ask students to spend five minutes individually thinking about and evaluating their own learning.
- If desired and appropriate, ask for volunteers to share their reflections.

Sample IDEA Pairings

Learning Logs (IDEA #98). Students use their Learning Logs as data for their Self-Assessment.

Problematic Situation (IDEA #55). The instructor presents a challenging problem for students to solve. After completing the activity, students engage in a Self-Assessment by evaluating their approaches to solving the problem.

K-W-L Chart (IDEA #86). The K-W-L Chart can provide a framework for students to self-assess their own knowledge, what they want to learn, and what they learned in class.

Pro-tips

Rubrics may be used as a tool for Self-Assessment. A rubric can not only provide criteria for students to consider, but it also provides details on the levels of student work that guide students in their assessment. In a rubric, it is helpful to identify a set of criteria upon which to make a judgment and then a scale for evaluating it. For example, you might use a rubric as in our example in Table 8.3, which appears on the following page. The spaces may be left blank, as in our example or filled in with more specific examples of what achievement in each category would look like.

TABLE 8.3 Sample Rubric

	Beginning (1)	Developing (2)	Accomplished (3)	Exemplary (4)
Listening critically to group members				
Showing commitment to the group				
Participating in the activities				

Depending on the nature of the Self-Assessment, use caution when asking for students to share their reflections with the class. Having to share with classmates can cause students to censor their ideas, which can limit the effectiveness of the activity.

Today's students are often unfamiliar with Self-Assessment thanks to the dominant role of testing throughout the educational process. In addition to the inherent benefits of Self-Assessment, students can reflect and self-evaluate their own process beyond the continual search for right answers on the exam. To do so, talk about the purpose of Self-Assessment to help students understand the value of the exercise.

IDEA #96: Group Assessment

Overview

Group Assessment is beneficial for helping students to understand group activities. When done well, Group Assessment can help students to identify what they have learned, and it can help students understand their work processes. A primary goal of the Group Assessment IDEA is to help students reflect on both the group work as a whole and their individual role and level of participation and performance within the group.

Group Assessment can be implemented formally through the use of a defined form or series of defined questions. Or it can be implemented informally by asking students to take time at the end of a group exercise to reflect on the overall group work experience. The main aim of Group Assessment is to increase student accountability and autonomy through reflection of group work, thus potentially helping to increase student participation and to eliminate "free riders" during group activities.

Guiding Principles

Group Assessment builds on the advantages of group work, including having students work together to develop knowledge and to have opportunities to practice communication skills (Rau & Heyl, 1990). Upon completing the activity, students hold a better understanding of the successes and benefits of working with a group and can identify possible areas where they as individuals can improve within the context of group activity. Moreover, Group Assessment can help to establish individual as well as group accountability that in turn can help to improve the group process (Barkley, Major, Cross, 2014). Moreover, students' experience increased awareness of themselves and others that comes with involvement (Hidi & Harackiewicz, 2000).

Preparation

Before using Group Assessments, identify a group work activity that allows for rich evaluation of both individuals' contributions and overall collaboration. Additionally, think through the questions to use during the assessment activity. If desiring a more formal approach to the activity, developing an evaluation form can help to provide additional structure to help guide student responses. We provide an example in Table 8.4, which appears below.

Process

• Announce a group work assignment related to course content for that or asks students to reflect on a recent assignment.
• Students work together to complete the assigned exercise.
• Upon completing the activity, students assess how their group worked together, the individual contributions of the each group member, and their own contribution to the activity.

TABLE 8.4 Sample Group Evaluation Form

Group Evaluation Form

Evaluator's name:_____

Date: _____

On each line below, write in a group member's name, including your own. Provide a rating of the group member's participation in the following space. Use the following scale:

0: No participation
1: Minimal participation
2: Active participation
3: Exceptional participation

1. _____ Rating: _____

2. _____ Rating: _____

3. _____ Rating: _____

4. _____ Rating: _____

5. _____ Rating: _____

Sample IDEA Pairings

Formal Argument (IDEA #17). Students evaluate how the overall argument went, their group's strongest and weakest points during the argument, and how they individually contributed to their respective teams. The students then vote after they complete the assessment on which team won the activity.

Houston, We Have a Problem (IDEA #42). Upon completing this problem-solving-based game, students evaluate how well their team worked together toward a solution. Additionally, this pairing would be an opportunity to ask students to think about what they would have done differently now that they have completed the task.

Self-Assessment (IDEA #95). At the same time students reflect on how the group work went, they reflect on their individual contribution to the exercise in a more extensive process.

Pro-tips

Group work may be more successful if students are involved in the development and execution of the assessment process. Having students to help design the evaluation form for example can improve buy-in to the activity.

Group evaluation may be completed as a one-time exercise, or it can become an integrated reflection exercise upon the completion of any group activity. The more often the activity is completed, the more comfortable students will become evaluating each other and the success of a group.

As an alternative to having students evaluate their work within a group, you can have students watch another group work together to complete an activity and ask them to assess the strengths and opportunities of what they observe. This alternative allows students to focus on evaluating group dynamics and processes without being concerned about their own contribution.

Some students may not feel comfortable expressing their opinions about their peers. If this dynamic arises, you may want to create and ensure an element of anonymity to the assessment activity.

IDEA #97: Elevator Pitch

Overview

The Elevator Pitch is a short, oral summary that is intended to quickly communicate information of value (Pincus, 2007). The speaker communicates the information to someone who is important to the speaker and who has a potential stake in the information. The intent of the communication is persuading the other person to act on the information.

The Elevator Pitch is a type of Role Play. The scenario for the play is an accidental meeting with someone in an elevator. The pitch typically lasts only as long as the average elevator ride. The idea is that if the pitch is interesting enough, the conversation will continue or result in a meeting to discuss the concept further (Pincus, 2007). That is, there is a hypothetical reward implied in a job well done.

When used as a teaching technique, the Elevator Pitch requires students to sum up valuable learning from a course to another person, such as a potential employer, a well-known academic, a group of peers, etc. While the Elevator Pitch has clear applications to students in business, the field in which the concept of the "Elevator Pitch" arose, it also could be used in a host of disciplines. Indeed, it has potential application in any field or discipline where thinking about what one has learned, synthesizing it, and communicating it to another is important.

Guiding Principles

The Elevator Pitch requires students to integrate information in a way that may be communicated to others. This is a critical skill. Fink (2013) calls this particular kind of learning "integration," which occurs when students can see and understand connections between ideas. He argues that these connections give students a different kind of intellectual power than other forms of learning.

After students integrate content or other important course information, they must then actively communicate it to others. When they take this step, it becomes an act of metacognitive reflection (Barell, 1992). That is, students are thinking about what they have learned in order to share it with others.

Preparation

There is little formal preparation required for an Elevator Pitch. Simply determine which information or ideas you would like students to focus on in their "pitch." The content of the pitch might come from an important course concept, a project on which students have been working, or their own research.

Process

- Announce the activity to students, and provide them with the parameters, such as the time they have to work on their pitches and how they will make the pitch (in class, though video, other?).
- Provide students with sufficient time to work.
- Ask students to make their pitches.
- Provide an assessment of the pitch: Was the pitch successful? Would the person likely continue to listen or not? Why or why not? (An interesting variation could be to have students vote on the results.)
- Provide comments and suggestions on the pitch. You may provide them, or you may ask students to peer evaluate.

Sample IDEA Pairings

This IDEA will pair well with many of the Reading or Writing IDEAs. For example, after being presented with a Problematic Situation and doing research on the topic, students could create an Elevator Pitch of a potential solution for someone who has authority to do something about it. After completing a Critical Book Review, students could create an Elevator Pitch convincing a peer to read it.

Pro-tips

If done well, this technique can be particularly motivating for students. It has an embedded real-world scenario that can make it an authentic learning activity for students. It can make students see the application of content to future employment. It also has echoes of the increasingly popular three-minute thesis competition being done on college campuses around the country.

If the activity is not done well, however, it can come off as hokey. Students who do not make the connection to their future endeavors may feel silly "acting out" the scenario in front of their classmates. It can be important to be sure that trust has been established prior to employing Role Play like activities in real time. If you think students may have trouble, an alternative would be to allow them to post their pitches to a blog or threaded discussion forum, which would eliminate the "acting" aspect of the activity.

IDEA #98: Learning Log

Overview

The Learning Log serves many functions. It is a writing-to-learn activity, for example, that in turn provides a springboard for reflection about learning, and it also serves as an indirect assessment of learning. The activity involves having students start and end class by writing in their logs. In these logs, students record the processes they go through while learning something new, and they list any questions they may have. This process allows students to make connections to what they have learned, set learning goals, and reflect upon their learning. It allows teachers to gauge their learning and to tailor instruction to best meet student needs.

The Learning Log is common in scientific disciplines, and it is also used in writing across the curriculum programs. It has wide applicability across fields, and it involves little time on the part of the students to complete. It is a flexible activity that can meet a number of needs.

Guiding Principles

The act of writing about thinking helps students learn. Indeed, self-explanations of material and activities facilitate deeper comprehension, learning, memory, and transfer (Ainsworth & Loizou, 2003).

As Chickering and Gamson (1987) as well as McTighe and O'Connor (2005) suggest, giving appropriate and prompt feedback is a basic principle of good teaching. By reading the Learning Logs and providing appropriate feedback on what the student is doing well and suggestions for improvement, you directly influence students' learning.

Preparation

Consider whether you will use a template for the log. If you do, the following may be used as table headers:

- Date
- What I did and why
- What I learned from it
- How I will use it
- What questions I still have about it

You could also use prompts related to the specific class session, such as the following (from the WAC Clearinghouse):

- What one idea that we talked about today most interested you and why?
- What was the clearest point we made today? What was the foggiest point?
- What do you still not understand about the concept we've been discussing?
- If you had to restate the concept in your own terms, how would you do that?
- How does today's discussion build on yesterday's?

Determine how often students should log their learning: daily, weekly, only at class sessions, or at key assignment points.

Process

- Provide students with approximately five minutes to write at the start of class, perhaps to summarize the previous session, to reflect upon the reading materials, or to describe other in-between session activities, such as independent research or lab work. They also list any questions they have.
- Conduct class.
- Provide students with approximately five minutes to write at the end of the session, perhaps providing prompts.

Sample IDEA Pairings

This IDEA, like most of the Reflection activities, will work with most of the other IDEAs in this book. It can be a useful follow up to lectures, in which students synthesize and write about what they have learning. It can be a useful summation of group activities or out-of-class experiences, with an eye toward validating the experience for students. It can also be useful to sum up independent work, such as reading or writing. In short, Learning Logs can serve a variety of purposes.

Pro-tips

While this activity takes little time on the students' part, it can take a great deal of effort to provide useful feedback. Some instructors review the completed Learning Logs every week and skim through them, others review a single response (Writing Across the Curriculum, 2014), and others fall somewhere between these reviewing extremes. More frequent responses may be better suited to novice students, while advanced students may require less frequent review.

IDEA #99: Cultural Encounters

Overview

The purpose of Cultural Encounters is to provide students with an opportunity to interact, learn, and experience a culture different from their own in a way that augments or supplements classroom learning. Specifically, students are tasked with engaging with culture outside of their typical daily routine. For example, in an introductory psychology course, students may visit the campus museum and discuss what life must have been like in the various cultures represented through the various displays. Another example would be an accounting class watching a film on corruption in an underdeveloped nation during a discussion of the economic impact of providing aid to malnourished citizens.

Cultural Encounters present students with experiences substantively divergent from what they normally experience. This IDEA may offer many course-related benefits by increasing cultural understanding related to course topics, developing an appreciation for diversity, and preparing students for difficult classroom conversations.

Guiding Principles

At a basic level, the Cultural Encounters IDEA is based on the notion of creating significant learning opportunities to improve educational outcomes (Fink, 2003). This activity brings a complexity of real life that is difficult to create inside the confines of the classroom. By creating specific situations for students to engage with different cultures, Cultural Encounters encourage students to learn about what is around them and examine their own cultural backgrounds.

In addition, this IDEA supports the purpose of higher education in preparing students to serve as active members of a global society. Exposing students to diversity, at the heart of Cultural Encounters, forms an important foundation for enhancing college teaching and student learning (Gay, 2013). By ensuring that students consider and are exposed to cultures different from their own, this activity expands and supports the well-known benefits of diversity in higher education (Milem, 2003).

Preparation

In advance of the class completing Cultural Encounters, consider the breadth and depth of the experience desired. The activity can vary from something as simple as sharing an ethnic meal to a full-day immersion. Additionally, the availability of different cultures may dictate some of your choices. If you are located in a large city, you may have more options than someone located in a small, rural area. Overall, the goal is to provide students with an opportunity to engage with a different culture in ways that complement your course. Gaining resources and support prior to conducting this activity is also helpful. Check with your campus diversity office or have a discussion with a faculty member in an area that regularly integrates cultural diversity into the course as part of the curriculum, such as African American Studies, Women's Studies, or Anthropology.

Process

- Share with the class the requirements for the experience, including whether the class will be participating individually, in groups, or as a whole class. Also share the logistics with the students so they know what to expect.
- Prior to the experience, guide the class about how to learn from different cultures, expectations for behavior, and other relevant information they may need before engaging in the activity. If a statement is made that is perceived to be insensitive, particularly when it is done innocently, explain that in learning and understanding cultures that are unfamiliar to our own, language may be used that is not appropriate but is also not meant to be derogatory.
- Following the experience, provide avenues for students to debrief about their experiences. Ideally, you will offer opportunities for students to reflect individually and with their classmates.

Sample IDEA Pairings

The Socratic Seminar (IDEA #7). Through specific questioning, promote deeper understanding of the relevant cultural context and experiences to be gained through the IDEA.

Matrix (IDEA #84). Ask students to compare and contrast their own cultural experiences and backgrounds with what they experienced through the activity. Designate at least two concepts that students use to identify similarities or differences.

Author Charts (IDEA #89). Students examine an author's cultural background as well as treatment of different cultures. Then, the charts are compared with the students' experience as part of the Cultural Encounters.

Pro-tips

Some of the most influential versions of Cultural Encounters happen in the students' backyards. They do not need to travel to a foreign country to experience different cultures. In fact, learning about the different cultures around the corner can be a powerful lesson. Providing some examples or even a list of nearby opportunities can help students learn about neighboring cultures.

Depending on the nature of the Cultural Encounter, you might participate alongside the students. Unless mitigating circumstances arise, let the students take the lead on engaging as part of the activity. The students will inherently look to you to facilitate interactions, but it is important to have the students learn through this aspect of the experience.

To help students think through the Cultural Encounter, you can provide a sheet with questions for them to answer. These questions might be ones they ask people that they meet or may be points for them to consider while participating in the activity. It is essential to have students reflect on the experience, as doing so will deepen their learning.

IDEA #100: Post Hoc Analysis

Overview

As noted earlier in this chapter, John Dewey is often quoted as having said, "We do not learn from experience . . . we learn from reflecting on experience." The Post Hoc Analysis IDEA focuses on reflecting on an experience. After a discipline- or field-related event has been reported, students reflect upon the event by looking for patterns that were not apparent ahead of time. They record their findings in writing, basically reporting issues, trends, and themes.

This IDEA has long been used in the field of history (for example, a Post Hoc Analysis of causes of the Civil War), but this IDEA is useful in a wide range of disciplines. In finance, for example, students could examine "black swan" events such as the depression or the recent financial crisis for patterns. Engineering students could examine the Pathfinder mission to Mars to consider the actual event. Education students could examine the reauthorization of the Higher Education Act.

Guiding Principles

Student motivation and engagement in an assignment plays a critical role in the effort they exert in the outcome (Barkley, 2009). When students find value in the learning activity, they are more likely to be motivated to learn (Ambrose et al., 2010). Thus, the quality of their learning improves. Post Hoc Analysis can provide an increased sense of an "authentic" task, in that it revolves around an important event that actually happened. Students often can see the relevance of the event to the discipline or field, and they often enjoy having the opportunity to weigh in on the circumstances surrounding it.

Preparation

Find an event related to your course content and of interest to the students that lends itself to analysis. Determine how students should write the analysis, whether in an informal outline format or a more formal paper. Develop a case outlining the event, and consider assigning additional readings, depending on how much time and effort you want students to exert on the activity. Create the list of writing prompts for students. For example, you might students to respond to the following:

> What happened?
> Why did it happen?
> What does this means to your field?

Process

- Announce the activity and the parameters of the assignment, such as timing and length.
- Present the case study of the event.
- Ask students to think about the prompts.
- Ask students to complete the Post Hoc Analysis writing.
- Collect responses or have a discussion immediately following the writing.

Sample IDEA Pairings

Think–Pair–Share (IDEA #15). When students think about the prompts, they can then turn to a partner and share their ideas, prior to writing up their more formal responses. This variation allows them time to rehearse their ideas and can lead to stronger responses.

Jigsaw (IDEA #31). Different groups may be formed to study different aspects of an event, particularly events that are complex in nature and cannot be easily summed up.

Concept Maps (IDEA #79). Students consider the event from multiple perspectives and then can map out connections between themes and concepts.

Pro-tips

Novice students may not feel comfortable voicing their opinions about complex events. Advanced students may feel overly confident in providing their opinions. Providing scaffolding through the prompts, such as by giving additional prompts to novice students and more specific prompts to advance students (for example, asking them to back their claims with evidence), can be a useful way to stave off potential issues in the analysis of events and in the writing.

The Post Hoc Analysis may be used as an "add on" to assignments or activities already used in your class. Asking students to write short responses to the purpose or discoveries noted during a course-related assignment will add to the reflection and increase understanding of the material.

References

Ainsworth, S., & Loizou, A.T. (2003). The effects of self explaining when learning with texts or diagrams. *Cognitive Science, 27,* 669–681.

Ambrose, S.A., Bridges, M.W., DiPietro, M., Lovett, M.C., & Norman, M.K. (2010). *How learning works: Seven research-based principles for smart teaching.* San Francisco, CA: Jossey-Bass.

Baker, L., & Brown, A.L. (1984). Metacognitive skills and reading. In P.D. Pearson, M.L. Kamil, R. Barr, & P. Mosenthal (Eds.), *Handbook of research in reading* (Vol. 3, pp. 353–395). New York: Longman.

Barell, J. (1992). Like an incredibly hard algebra problem: Teaching for metacognition. In A.L. Costa, J.A. Bellanca, & R. Fogarty (Eds.), *If minds matter: A forward to the future* (Vol. 1, pp. 257–266). Palatine, IL: IRI/Skylight.

Barkley, E.F. (2009). *Student engagement techniques: A handbook for college faculty.* San Francisco, CA: Jossey-Bass.

Barkley, E.F., Major, C.H., & Cross, K.P. (2014). *Collaborative learning techniques: A handbook for college faculty.* San Francisco, CA: Jossey-Bass.

Boud, D., Koegh, R., & Walker, D. (Eds.). (1985). *Reflection: Turning experience into learning.* London: Kogan Page.

Bransford, J., Donovan, M., & Pellegrino, J. (1999). *How people learn: Bridging research and practice.* Washington, DC: National Academy Press.

Bringle, R.G., & Hatcher, J.A. (1999). Reflection in service learning: Making meaning of experience. *Educational Horizons, 77,* 179–185.

Bringle, R.G., & Hatcher, J.A. (2000). Institutionalization of service learning in higher education. *Journal of Higher Education, 71*(3), 273–290.

Cacciamani, S., Cesareni, D., Martini, F., Ferrini, T., & Fujita, N. (2012). Influence of participation, facilitator styles, and metacognitive reflection on knowledge building in online university courses. *Computers & Education, 58*(3), 874–884.

Center for Teaching and Learning at the University of Texas. (n.d.). Methods of assessment. Retrieved December 10, 2014, from http://ctl.utexas.edu/teaching/assessment/planning/methods

Chickering, A.W., & Gamson, Z.F. (1987). Seven principles for good practice in undergraduate education. *American Association of Higher Education Bulletin, 39*(7), 3–7.

Daudelin, M.W. (1996). Learning from experience through reflection. *Organizational Dynamics, 24*(3), 36–48.

Dennehy, R.F., Sims, R.R., & Collins, H.E. (1998). Debriefing experiential learning exercises: A theoretical and practical guide for success. *Journal of Management Education, 22*(1), 9–25.

Dewey, J. (1933). *How we think: A restatement of the relation of reflective thinking to the educative process.* Boston, MA: Heath.

Faculty Focus. (2010). Twitter in higher education 2010: Usage habits and trends of today's college faculty. Retrieved January 20, 2012, from http://www.faculty focus.com/free-reports/twitter-in-higher-education-2010-usage-habits-and-trends-of-todays-college-faculty/

Fink, D. (2013). *Creating significant learning experiences: An integrated approach to designing courses.* San Francisco, CA: Jossey-Bass.

Fink, D. (2003). *Creating significant learning experiences: An integrated approach to designing college courses.* San Francisco, CA: Jossey-Bass.

Flavell, J.H. (1979). Metacognition and cognitive monitoring: A new area of cognitive-developmental inquiry. *American Psychologist, 34*(10), 906–911.

Fusco, E., & Fountain, G. (1992). Reflective teacher, reflective learner. In A.L. Costa, J.A. Bellanca, & R. Fogarty (Eds.), *If minds matter: A forward to the future* (Vol. 1). Palatine, IL: IRI/Skylight.

Garner, R., & Alexander, P.A. (1989). Metacognition: Answered and unanswered questions. *Educational Psychologist, 24*, 143–158.

Gay, G. (2013). Teaching to and through cultural diversity. *Curriculum Inquiry, 43*(1), 48–70.

Gemmil, E., & Peterson, M. (2006). Technology use among college students: Implications for student affairs professionals. *NASPA Journal, 43*(2), 280–300.

Gibbs, G. (1988). *Learning by doing: A guide to teaching and learning methods.* Oxford: Oxford Brookes University.

Hatano, G., & Kayoko, I. (1986). Two courses of expertise. In H. Stevenson, A. Horishi, & H. Kinji (Eds.), *Child development and education in Japan.* New York: W.H. Freeman.

Hidi, S., & Harackiewicz, J.M. (2000). Motivating the academically unmotivated: A critical issue for the 21st century. *Review of Educational Research, 70*(2), 151–179.

Isaacson, R.M., & Fujita, F. (2006). Metacognitive knowledge monitoring and self-regulated learning: Academic success and reflection on learning. *Journal of Scholarship of Teaching and Learning, 6*(1), 39–55.

Kardia, D., & Sevig, T. (2001). Embracing the paradox: Dialogue that incorporates both individual and group identities. In D. Schoem & S. Hurtado (Eds.), *Intergroup dialogue: Deliberative democracy in school, college, community, and workplace* (pp. 247–265). Ann Arbor: University of Michigan Press.

Kauffman, D.F., Ge, X., Xie, K., & Chen, C.-H. (2008). Prompting in Web-based environments: Supporting self-monitoring and problem solving skills in college students. *Journal of Teacher Education, 35*(2), 179–197.

Knowles, M. (1984). *Andragogy in action.* San Francisco, CA: Jossey-Bass.

Kolb, D.A. (1984). *Experiential learning.* Englewood Cliffs, NJ: Prentice Press.

Land, S.M. (2000). Cognitive requirements for learning with open-ended learning environments. *Educational Technology and Development, 48*(3), 61–78.

Lynch, R., McNamara, P. M., & Seery, N. (2012). Promoting deeper learning in a teacher education progamme through self-and peer-assessment and feedback. *European Journal of Teacher Education, 35*(2), 179–197.

Marton, F., & Säljö, R. (1976a). On qualitative differences in learning—1: Outcome and process. *British Journal of Educational Psychology, 46*, 4–11.

Marton, F., & Säljö, R. (1976b). On qualitative differences in learning—2: Outcome as a function of the learner's conception of the task. *British Journal of Educational Psychology, 46*, 115–127.

McMillan, J.H., & Hearn, J. (2008). Student self-assessment: The key to stronger student motivation and higher achievement. *Educational Horizons, 87*(1), 40–49.

McTighe, J., & O'Connor, K. (2005). Seven practices for effective learning. *Educational Leadership, 63*, 10–17.

Mezirow, J. (1997). Transformative learning: Theory to practice. In P. Cranton (Ed.), *Transformative learning in action: Insights from practice* (pp. 5–12). San Francisco, CA: Jossey-Bass.

Milem, J.F. (2003). The educational benefits of diversity: Evidence from multiple sectors. In M. Chang, D. Witt, J. Jones, & K. Hakuta (Eds.), *Compelling interest: Examining the evidence on racial dynamics in colleges and universities* (pp. 126–169). Palo Alto, CA: Stanford Education.

Mok, M.M.C., Lung, C.L., Cheng, D.P.W., Cheung, R.H.P., & Ng, M.L. (2006). Self-assessment in higher education: Experience in using a metacognitive approach in five case students. *Assessment & Evaluation in Higher Education, 31*(4), 415–433.

Muncy, J. (2014). Blogging for reflection: The use of online journals to engage students in reflective learning. *Marketing Education Review, 24*(2), 101–113.

Palincsar, A.S., & Brown, A.L. (1984). Reciprocal teaching of comprehension monitoring activities. *Congnition and Instruction, 1*, 117–175.

Pincus, A. (2007). The perfect elevator pitch. Retrieved March 6, 2015, from http://www.bloomberg.com/bw/stories/2007–06–18/the-perfect-elevator-pitchbusinessweek-business-news-stock-market-and-financial-advice

Pintrich, P.R., & Schunk, D.H. (1996). *Motivation in education: Theory, research, and applications*. Englewood Cliffs, NJ: Merrill/Prentice Hall.

Rau, W., & Heyl, B.S. (1990). Humanizing the college classroom: Collaborative learning and social organization among students. *Teaching Sociology, 18*(2), 141–155.

Riva, J.J., Lam, J.M., Stanford, E.C., Moore, A.E., Endicott, A.R., & Krawchenko, I.E. (2010). Interprofessional education through shadowing experiences in multi disciplinary clinical settings. *Chiropractic & Osteopathy, 18*(31), 1–5.

Scardamalia, M., Bereiter, C., & Steinbach, R. (1984). Teachability of reflective processes in written composition. *Cognitive Science, 8*, 173–190.

Schoenfeld, A.H. (1991). On mathematics as sense making: An information attack on the unfortunate divorce of formal and informal mathematics. In J.F. Voss, D.N. Perkins, & J.W. Segal (Eds.), *Informal reasoning and education*. Hillsdale, NJ: Erlbaum.

Schunk, D.H. (1990). Goal setting and self-efficacy during self-regulated learning. *Educational Psychologist, 25*(1), 71–86.

Swartz, R., & Perkins, D. (1989). *Teaching thinking-issues and approaches*. Pacific Grove, CA: Midwest.

Shepard, L.A. (2001). The role of classroom assessment in teaching and learning. In V. Richardson (Ed.), *Handbook of research on teaching* (4th ed.). Washington, DC: American Educational Research Association.

Tanner, K.D. (2012). Promoting student metacognition. *CBE-Life Sciences Education, 11*, 113–120.

Thorpe, K. (2004). Reflective learning journals: From concept to practice. *Reflective Practice, 5*(3), 327–343.

Writing Across the Curriculum. (2014). Event analysis. Retrieved from http://wac.colostate.edu/intro/pop5q.cfm

Zhao, N., Wardeska, J.G., McGuire, S.Y., & Cook, E. (2014). Metacognition: An effective tool to promote success in college science learning. *Journal of College Science Teaching, 43*(4), 48–54.

9
CONCLUSION

In this book, we have presented eight instructional methods that have a solid research base to support their efficacy. From lecture to reflection, these methods have proven effective over time and across research studies. For example, active lectures can help students gain knowledge, while discussion can help students to learn to appreciate each other and deepen their learning. Peer teaching is an effective method for deepening learning of both the teacher and the learner. Games are great for review and to motivate students. Active reading helps students gain content from what they have read, and writing to learn helps them not only to process what they have learned but also to learn more. Graphic organizers are useful tools for summary as well, and they can help students retain and transfer knowledge. Finally, reflecting on what they have learned helps students transfer knowledge and skills gained in one course to others. In short, tried-and-true instructional methods tend to do what they have set out to do.

When using these methods, we necessarily think through our learning goals. We can do that by asking ourselves the basic question of what we want students to know and be able to do as a result of participation in the courses we teach. Then, we can make reasonable decisions about which methods to take up. For example, if we believe students are novices who need to learn the basic facts and terms of a discipline before they can move to higher-order thinking skills like application and integration, then lecture may well be the best instructional tool. If we want students to learn to work with others and to be respectful of others, we may want to choose discussion or peer teaching approaches. If we find that students are not engaged and we want to motivate students while simultaneously helping students learn, then games may be the way to go. If we want students to go into a reading assignment with their full attention, we might use active reading strategies. If we want to help them grapple with complex information and ideas, we might try writing-to-learn or graphic-organizing strategies. If we believe we want students to transfer information to new situations, metacognitive reflection strategies can be a good approach. In short, we should work to be mindful of what we hope students will accomplish and to attempt to select instructional methods and activities that can help us help students get there.

In each of the main body chapters of this book, we have presented an instructional method, and we have described the research that supports its efficacy. In each case, we found studies documenting effectiveness as well as student perceptions that the method helped them learn. We have also described research that suggests how we might best employ the methods to improve student learning. This research has offered specific tips for what we can do when implementing these methods to improve practice. In each chapter, we also presented activities that tie directly to these research findings. We link them directly to findings in order to help faculty ensure that they are using intentionally designed educational activities (IDEAs). For example, providing students with empty outlines helps them to learn more from lectures, and many of our IDEAs include a guided-lecture-note component.

We hope that faculty will be able to use this book to learn about these eight methods, what they are and what they do, along with the specific organizational features of each. We also hope that it will help faculty to weigh the advantages and potential disadvantages of using the method. Finally, we hope that this book will serve as a reference for learning more about the research on teaching and learning to be able to draw from the syntheses that we provide to improve instructional practice.

By presenting these research-based instructional methods and intentionally designed educational activities, we do not mean to say that these are the only approaches that exist or even that they will be the best for the students. Indeed, we would not presume to be the constructors of such a box around teaching and learning. Rather, we simply mean to identify key instructional methods that researchers have investigated and to present ways to implement activities designed around these findings in the college classroom. We mean for it to be a guide that faculty may use and adapt to their own purposes and ends.

We acknowledge that there are many variations of the activities we have described. In addition, we also acknowledge that there are many useful activities that were not included on our list. And we believe that faculty are infinitely creative people who use, refunction, and invent instructional methods to fit their purposes. Indeed, we invite you to design variations of an activity we present or to create entirely new ones that will best meet the needs of your students and the educational contexts in which you operate. For this reason, we offer the following template for creating a Do-It-Yourself intentionally designed educational activity: your own DIY IDEA.

IDEA #101: DIY IDEA

Overview

Write a brief description of the activity here. _____

_____

_____

_____

_____

_____

Guiding principles

When creating classroom activities, think about what learning principles can inform the activity. Look back in this book for some ideas. Thinking about guiding principles can inform how you prepare to use the activity. Write your own guiding principles here.

_____

_____

_____

_____

_____

Preparation

Different IDEAs require various levels of advanced preparation. Make notes about what you need to do prior to class. Include those thoughts here.

_____

_____

_____

_____

_____

Process

Write down the steps of the activity that you can use as lesson plans in class in the following space.

1) _____

_____

_____

2) _____
_____
_____

3) _____
_____
_____

4) _____
_____
_____

Pairing

Most of the time when we use an activity in class, we do not do so in isolation from other activities. Consider what activities with which your DIY IDEA would pair well and list potential pairings in the following space.

_____
_____
_____
_____
_____

Pro-tips

Each time you use an activity, you learn something that can inform future uses of your DIY IDEA. After class, write brief notes to yourself that provide helpful tips for next time.

_____
_____
_____
_____
_____

INDEX